THE CLASSICS
OF WESTERN
SPIRITUALITY

THE CLASSICS OF WESTERN SPIRITUALITY
A Library of the Great Spiritual Masters

Angela *of* Foligno
COMPLETE WORKS

TRANSLATED, WITH AN INTRODUCTION BY
PAUL LACHANCE, O.F.M.

PREFACE BY
ROMANA GUARNIERI

PAULIST PRESS
NEW YORK • MAHWAH

Cover Art: Reliquary of Angela of Foligno by an anonymous Umbrian sculptor (sixteenth century). Photo courtesy of Antonio Romagnoli.

Copyright © 1993 by Paul Lachance, O.F.M.

Library of Congress Cataloging-in-Publication Data

7/93

Angela, of Foligno, 1248?–1309.
   [Works. English. 1993]
   Complete works/Angela of Foligno; translated, with an
introduction by Paul Lachance; preface by Romana Guarnieri.
      p. cm.—(The Classics of Western spirituality)
   Includes bibliographical references (p.) and index.
   ISBN 0-8091-0460-1: (cloth)—ISBN 0-8091-3366-0 (pbk.)
   1. Mysticism—History—Middle Ages, 600–1500. 2. Angela, of
Foligno, 1248?–1309. I. Lachance, Paul. II. Title. III. Series.
BX4705.A59A2   1993
248.2'2—dc20   92-38830
                                                    CIP

Published by Paulist Press
997 Macarthur Boulevard
Mahwah, New Jersey 07430

Printed and bound in the United States of America

C.1

Contents

CONTENTS

Translator of this Volume

PAUL LACHANCE, O.F.M., is a Franciscan of the Province of St. Joseph, Canada. In 1984, he obtained a doctorate in spiritual theology from the *Pontificium Athenaeum Antonianum* in Rome. He wrote his doctoral dissertation on *The Spiritual Journey of the Blessed Angela of Foligno according to the Memorial of Frater A.* In 1987–1988, he was a fellow at the Institute for the Advanced Study of Religion of the University of Chicago. He teaches a course on the Franciscan mystics at the summer institute of St. Bonaventure University. Co-translator of a dozen books, as well as author of many articles on Franciscan and Christian spirituality, he has given numerous retreats, conferences and workshops in this country, Canada, and abroad. He is presently a member of a Franciscan mixed community in inner-city Chicago.

Author of the Preface

ROMANA GUARNIERI was born in L'Aja (Netherlands) in 1913. Since 1925 she has been living in Rome, where in 1939 she obtained her doctorate in German language and literature. In 1938 she met the noted Italian historian of spirituality Don Giuseppe De Luca with whom she collaborated in the foundation of the *Edizioni di Storia e Letteratura.* She focused her research on the movement of the "Free Spirit," and published the critical edition of the "Miroir des ames simples" by the heretical Beguine, Marguerite Porete (d. 1310). After De Luca's death in 1962, she assumed the direction of the *Archivio Italiano per la Storia della Pietà,* which he had created, and subsequently published several studies on De Luca's life and work. She is presently a member of the editorial board of the semi-annual review *Bailamme. Rivista di politica e di spiritualita,* for which she directs the section on "Piety." She has participated in numerous scholarly congresses and has published essays in various scholarly journals, and several articles in the *Dizionario degli Instituti di Perfezione.*

Acknowledgments

As I look back over the long road that has led to the completion of this work, hundreds of faces, as well as places where I have pitched my tent, flash to consciousness. I have been blessed by many who appeared along the way as sources of encouragement and direction. Only a few can be named here, but my heartfelt thanks extend to all.

The *Casa di Risparmio di Foligno* funded the critical edition and, along with the *Collegium San Bonaventura* of Grottaferrata (Rome), granted permission for the use of the text. Special thanks to Romana Guarnieri for kindly agreeing to write the preface of this volume; her profound knowledge of Angela and her times have guided me toward paths I surely would have missed otherwise. I am grateful likewise to John Farina and his successor, Bernard McGinn, editors of the Classics of Western Spirituality, for their patience and helpful guidance throughout. I owe an inestimable debt of gratitude to my two main readers, Kathryn Krug and Terry Kelley. Kathryn painstakingly checked the entire manuscript many times over, including the fidelity of the translation to the Latin original, and suggested countless improvements. Terry provided further extensive grammatical and stylistic assistance. Without their professional and dedicated collaboration the text could not have reached its present form. The responsibility for the final version, and its imperfections, remains mine. I also wish to express my sincere appreciation to the staff and community of St. Francis Retreat House, in Oak Brook, Illinois, for granting me space and time to complete this volume.

Finally, my work on Angela would not have been possible without the unwavering support of my Franciscan provincials, Henri Ethier, O.F.M., and his successor, Gilles Bourdeau, O.F.M., and the brothers of

ACKNOWLEDGMENTS

my province, especially Thaddée Matura, O.F.M., who first led me to Angela, and Pierre Brunette, O.F.M., faithful companion on the way. To them, I fraternally dedicate this volume.

Foreword

From beyond came the salutation winged by a Seraph "with eyes shining like candles." Quickened by the fiery glance, I heard the summons; trembling inwardly, I began the task, the transmission of the *Book* of the Blessed Angela of Foligno, which contains some of the most excessive and volcanic passages in all of Christian mystical literature. After years of laboring close to the conflagration—licked by the flames, but not consumed—it is with reverence and fear that I pass on the text, one meant to set ablaze "the sons and daughters who are in the world, who are on this side of the sea or beyond it." Angela's *Book* is translated here in its entirety for the first time into English from the new critical edition of the Latin text.

Angela (ca. 1248–1309) was a married woman whose husband and children died shortly after the dazzling glare of a new love had caught her eye. The atmosphere where she lived in Foligno and in the Umbrian valley (*Umbria sancta*) was fresh with the memory of the Poverello, Francis of Assisi. He was the "mirror of holiness" who showed her the way, "the ineffable light of the truest poverty." Visions of the crucified Christ, the "Book of Life," expanded her capacities to love to infinite dimensions.

The marrow of Angela's inner life, her passionate love affair with the "suffering God-man," is narrated in the *Memorial*, the first part of her *Book*, which she dictated, with precision and shuddering immediacy, to her astonished and initially incredulous scribe and confessor, the Franciscan Brother Arnaldo. In the mid-nineteenth century, the French philosopher Ernest Hello was likewise awestruck by the sublimity of Angela's revelations. In the preface to his highly influential French translation of her writings, he remarks:

1

FOREWORD

The life of Angela is a drama whose theatre is the Ineffable. A lightning bolt which jolts open the clouds. Angela's language is a hand-to-hand combat with the inexpressible. In the atmosphere in which she is immersed, human vocabulary, like someone profane stupefied at the threshold of a sanctuary, silently withdraws. Prisoner of human words, Angela, daughter of Ecstasy, like Samson, takes the gates of her prison and lifts them to the heights.

It is her deep identification and fusion with the crucified Christ that transforms Angela's life and draws her, in and beyond the divine darkness, into the secret and ineffable recesses of the Trinitarian life. Having been graced with the experience of the abysmal depths of God, she experiences her own abysmal inferiority and her voice fades into speechlessness: "my words blaspheme and make hash of what they should express."

Angela emerges from her immersion in the fathomless depths of the Trinity as a very successful transmitter of the secrets of the spiritual life, "a teacher of theologians," as she has been called. The second part of her *Book*—the *Instructions*—contains her teachings in the form of exhortations and letters to her spiritual progeny, along with accounts of further visions and locutions, a testament, and an epilogue.

One of the outstanding figures among the largely untapped resources of Franciscan mystical literature, Angela has not received the attention that is her due, even in the recent reclaiming of women's medieval mystical literature, where she is often ignored or named only in passing. There have been few comprehensive studies exploring the totality of Angela's experience, her spirituality and influence—and none based on the new critical edition. The first part of the Introduction—"Panorama of the Life and Times"—provides the backdrop on which to fittingly emblazon her contribution, and to help establish her rightful place in the pantheon of Christian, and especially medieval, mystics. The remainder of the Introduction presents a synthesis of Angela's inner journey. This journey is not in itself always easy to follow, partly because of the overlapping and reworking of the redaction and partly because of the density and incompleteness of the text itself (the scribe often admits it is "a short and defective version" of what he had heard). The Introduction also studies the main themes of her spirituality, and surveys her influence, many strands of which have until now been undetected.

FOREWORD

Finally, I wish to join the chorus of previous translators of Angela's *Book*—all acutely aware that their efforts faltered before the inexpressible—who have asked their readers to pray to the God of Angela, that one day their desire might match their longing.

Preface

In 1983, Paul Lachance and I met many times to discuss Angela of Foligno, while he was working on his doctoral dissertation.[1] For me, this meant resuming a research theme abandoned a long time ago. I had first come across Angela in about 1950, when I was hunting for traces of the Free Spirit movement in Italy. At that time I was writing the introduction to my publication of the *Mirouer des ames simples* by Marguerite Porete (d. 1310), who was the most authoritative voice of that movement (or, if you prefer, that heresy). Then I encountered Angela again more recently at a congress (in Spoleto in 1981) on Clare of Montefalco. Clare was Angela's contemporary and, like her, a determined adversary of the Free Spirits. Now, I found confirmed certain intuitions of mine about the fundamental oneness of the thirteenth-century Brabantine-Rhenish-Provençale women's religious movement and a similar movement in the Tuscany-Umbrian region, some ten years later, and without a doubt the most significant figure of the later movement was the "Beguine" Angela of Foligno, representative par excellence of thirteenth-century Italian mysticism.

In the beginning I was discussing Angela mostly as a historian of women's spirituality in those extraordinary and disconcerting years. Hers was a period in which for the first time in history, throughout the whole Christian world, an incredible number of women, within a church that had imposed on them almost total silence, now came to the fore, speaking and writing with such authority that they could not be ignored. They commanded the respect of men of great learning and authority; but in others, less prepared spiritually and culturally, they triggered panic in the face of such a widespread, unheard-of, and basically uncontrollable phenomenon. What happened was irreversible, even with all the incomprehension, misunderstanding, suffering, and persecution, which we are only now beginning to understand. Today, as

5

a result of incisive and deep studies especially in the past ten years, we have discovered the immense historic importance of these events.

In the course of our work, I became hopelessly enamored of the extraordinary woman being gradually revealed. Not of her own choosing, hers was a love story with few equals in terms of intensity and daring of experience, lucidity of judgment, delightful freedom of expression, unequalled power of evocation. Both Paul and I became inflamed by the same fire of admiration for the object of our study. This was anything but a neutral subject matter. Indeed, how could one remain neutral when speaking of or discussing—even through a third person—the love of God, the love of the God-man Jesus, who was born, lived, was crucified, died, was buried, and rose for us? The object of discussion was not one of so many theoretical and speculative works by some learned theologian that you can admire for elegant subtleties of argument, but that do not take hold of you, that indeed leave you indifferent. This was, rather, the account of the tormented relationship (daring, but doctrinally correct) of a person who lived such a love with all that she was, with a stupefying concreteness, to the point of being devoured by it in the ultimate fibers of her being. How could one speak about it, discuss it, without ending up committed more than intellectually, and without opening up a portion of the soul that had always been kept secret, even from one's own confessor? This happened repeatedly during our meetings, which were begun as "studies" and which became an unforgettable and, most likely, unrepeatable adventure.

I am still asking myself how all this happened, but I suspect it had to do with the singular nature of the text at hand. It is neither a didactic-expository treatise, nor a literary text, in poetic or customary prose form, obedient to a formal and linguistic code. Nor is it a collection of letters, more or less paraenetic, intended more to teach, to persuade, and to guide, or, ultimately, to convert, rather than simply to narrate. Rather, what we have here, precisely recorded, though in a rather disorganized and often highly emotional way, is the simple, bare, oral narrative, exact to the point of scrupulosity (at least if the numerous affirmations in the text in this regard are given the credit they seem to deserve), of a mystical text in the pure state, very rich in the extraordinary variety of its visionary phenomena, some recalled, others recorded as they were taking place. A candid, authentic narrative, without any afterthoughts, without false trappings of learning on the part of either the narrator or the recorder. Angela's text, like so many others of this type, came about as a result of the intervention of an interested third party, the usual "brother scribe," secretary-counsellor, and even confessor and spiritual director. (This is Brother A, according to the codices, Arnaldo according to a certain tradition, of whom we know nothing but that he was Angela's relative and confessor and that he was a very scrupulous collector of her words, often recorded immediately after an ecstasy.) Unlike other texts, Brother A.'s redaction, notwithstanding its linguistic ingenuity, has a rare immediacy in its elementary Latin, derived from the Vulgate, and teeming with Italian dialectical expressions. It does not seem —a rare case indeed—to be marred in any way by the sometimes deceptive, perhaps often unconscious, hagiographic concerns of the usual "secretaries" in these cases. Such concerns are very noticeable in the redaction of the "writings" of Catherine of Siena, which are far less fresh and spontaneous. These too were collected by dictation, but then they were partly reconstructed by her learned Dominican "secretaries," to force the image of the saint from Siena into a preconceived mold. Thus I would be tempted to define the *Book*—at least in its initial part, the so-called *Memorial,* the only one written by Arnaldo—even if it does not come directly from Angela's hand, as a true and authentic "author's text," no more nor less than the writings of a Hadewijch or a Porete, who did not make use of any secretaries: sole authors of their own writings, and such authors! What more can I say?

It was not the doctrines Angela presented that struck me, even if they are undeniably very rich and beautiful. On the whole, with some variations, these were already more or less familiar to me. They had been proposed with more order and rigor by Marguerite Porete in her *Mirouer des ames simples,* and above all, with greater literary propriety if less power and ardor than Angela's, by the great Hadewijch of Antwerp (middle of the thirteenth century) in her poetry, letters, and visions. What struck me then and continues to move me every time I open the *Book* is the scorching intensity and the extremely daring *concreteness* and totally feminine way in which Angela narrates her experience of being madly in love with God, striving to be chaste and yet passionately and sensually fully alive. Here is the experience of a mature woman belonging to the well-to-do class of Foligno, and no stranger to past frivolous behavior: a woman who knows the effects of earthly passionate love on the body and the soul of the one who loves. Here also is the experience of a spouse and a mother who at the very outset of her penitential journey, one that holds every promise of being stormy and leading to all sorts of extravagance—is this not the case of everyone truly in love?—in the course of just a few months loses her mother, husband, and sons, and in spite of the cruel pain of such bereavement, overwhelmed by her new love, practically ends up rejoicing. Indeed, does not this very loss provide the liberation from all earthly ties that, in a moment of true madness, she had asked of God? Does this not make possible giving herself entirely and without scruples to the one who had swept her into his fiery vortex? Make it possible for her to contemplate in ecstasy the white throat of her suffering (*passionatus*) Jesus on the cross? To lay down in his tomb, next to his dead body, "cheek to cheek," to caress and be caressed by him? To converse with him without ceasing, telling of her passion for him not only with words but with very concrete gestures (sometimes disconcerting gestures, as when she communicates with him by drinking the putrid water with which she had just finished washing the sore of a leper), lost and annihilated in a fathomless ecstasy of love? Here is, moreover, the experience of a woman who has been scorched by love and, in order to conform herself in absolutely everything to her loved one and give witness to the harsh reality of his love, chooses for herself the way of tribulation and of martyrdom. As soon as she can, she sells the last of her possessions in order to give the money to the poor, and withdraws with a trustworthy companion to live in a shabby hovel as a recluse, "incarcerated" in the passion of Christ, in absolute poverty, in hunger and thirst and lack of proper clothing, in solitude and in concealment, in subjection to misunderstanding and contempt. She, whom the Holy Spirit had declared "my spouse," "my temple," is now scoffed at, is regarded almost as one demonically possessed, and is the target for harsh insults, because she has wanted to follow, crucified with every kind of physical and moral suffering, the "suffering (*passionatus*) God-man" who on her behalf endured hunger and thirst, and for her shed his own blood. Hadewijch also has expressions of daring erotic ardor and incandescence; but because these are mediated and controlled by her poetic language they seem somehow less disturbing than the sometimes incoherent stammerings of the Folignate visionary, who is tortured by the need to express with scrupulous precision what she experiences as impossible to adequately verbalize: Every word is limited and limiting, and when these refer to God they run the risk of lying, deceiving, even blaspheming. Marguerite Porete also affirms that her speech about God is deceptive. Angela, however, has an eminently critical mind, one that affirms the preeminence of knowledge over love. In her desperate need to be precise in relating the truth about the work that God is bringing about in her, and in her ever-present fear of being "deceived," she does not *say*, but *screams* the incompetence that torments her. Gradually she

8

is pushed toward the dark abyss of absolute silence, in the metaphysical nothingness of being: the nothingness of the ego, the nothingness of all created reality outside God, who is uncreated and infinite, unknowable and inexpressible, and yet the only one who is real, present in all that exists, in an evil spirit as much as in a good angel, all truth, all goodness, all joy, all love, nothing but love, all loving and all loved.

Now we have to deal with the difficult problem of Angela's amazing cultural formation. We can—and we must—ask ourselves what were the intermediate processes that brought about the particular results we see, especially the very remarkable theological formation Angela demonstrated, just as did Clare of Montefalco. Clare in many respects is very close to Angela, not only in time and in space, but in many facets of her spiritual journey. This remarkable theological development is evident not only in the *Memorial* (for which we can hypothesize to some extent the theological and cultural influence of her brother scribe) but in her entire *Book*. In the *Instructions*, especially, Angela quite often appears as a sort of oracle who, when consulted, provides the "right" answers to some of the most controversial questions of her time, to such an extent that she was, and is still today, esteemed as a "teacher of theologians" (*magistra theologorum*).

How did this woman reach such a sophisticated level of education when she lived her whole life in the world, far from theological schools? We know that other mystics of her time, even if they were cloistered, could freely make use of conventual libraries, which were prominent then. Angela did not have the support of such libraries. We can ask ourselves the question, because no self-respecting historian would be willing to accept the old theory of "infused knowledge." The temptation would be, rather, to credit any refined culture demonstrated by a seeress, declared "illiterate" according to a classical "topos," to the deceitful meddling of unscrupulous friars who could have cleverly manipulated the text and exploited the poor woman in order to use her to endorse their own doctrines in the fierce debates of the times. It would not be the first time or, unfortunately, the last, that this has happened.

We can then—and must—ask ourselves, for example, to what extent and by what chain of events Angela came to know John Climacus's *Ladder of Paradise*. It so happened that this book was popularized during the very years in which her mystical experience blossomed. A fellow Folignate, Friar Gentile, was the friend and companion of Angelo Clareno, who translated the *Ladder* into Latin. It rapidly became a bestseller in the "spiritual" environment our visionary frequented, and cer-

9

PREFACE

tainly suggested the division into the famous "thirty steps" by which she attempted to somehow organize her own mystical journey. We must ask ourselves to what extent and by what chain of events she became familiar with the Testament of Francis or was inspired by Lives written about him—for instance, the biography by Thomas of Celano or the other one by Bonaventure—and if she had known Bonaventure's other works, particularly the *Soul's Journey into God,* which Brother Arnaldo surely had in mind when he condensed into seven steps (or *passi*) the thirty suggested by Angela. We must ask ourselves, did Angela know the mystical writings of Bernard, the great Victorines, or even William of St. Thierry? If so, how? Perhaps through the liturgy—in which there were many more texts than today? Perhaps she read or heard their works in popularizations unknown to us, or directly in the original Latin, or in one of the many florilegia or anthologies intended for the "illiterate" of the times (there are still unexplored manuscript collections full of these in our libraries). These writers are incontestably the fathers of the doctrines that nourished the experience and the meditations of Jacopone da Todi (not to mention the teachings of Francis himself), of Hadewijch or of Marguerite Porete, Angela's contemporaries, whose thoughts are often in amazing harmony with hers, even in the images and the words used, thus demonstrating a common cultural background that in good part remains to be explored.

Certainly, we can and must examine very carefully to what extent Angela made her own the teachings of these and other authors, which she certainly knew and which she reelaborated into, all told, a solid and unified whole—even if not a theological "construct"—doctrinally irreproachable yet on the very razor's edge of orthodoxy (the sort of daring for which Marguerite Porete paid on the pyre and Master Eckhart with a posthumous condemnation). Among these were the writings of Dionysius the Areopagite and John Scotus Eriugena, not to mention the *Song of Songs,* the themes of which became for many women mystics of the times a kind of unavoidable and tedious cliché, but which Angela presented with sobriety since she preferred the far more delicate and riskier theme of the divine essence. We can, moreover, ask ourselves what part was played in her spiritual and cultural formation by the so-called popular piety, the lauds, sacred drama, devotional images, pious practices, preaching, pious conversations, and the current Christian language. Certainly we can affirm that like so many other "fools for Christ" (among them her countryman and contemporary Jacopone), Angela was nourished in a special way by the letters to the Corinthians, by that Paul

10

who was happy for the sake of the Chosen One to endure weakness, insults, anxieties, persecutions, and dangerous situations; who was swept up beyond the stars—whether in the body or out of the body, only God knows—and led into a wonderful garden where he heard words never uttered before, and which cannot be repeated. We can and must ask ourselves finally to what extent can we hypothesize, or perhaps even document, how Angela's familiarity with these and other similar themes or texts may have enabled her to assimilate some of the ideas that were widespread among the Franciscan "Spirituals," and that emerge here and there in her own story, concerning the "night of the soul," "the annihilation of the person," the "ineffability of God"—ideas that throughout the centuries will both torment and delight multitudes of men and women mystics.

When all is said and done, and we have reached the end of our scholarly research, we must acknowledge that the voice of Angela remains unique and unmistakable in the chorus of writings dedicated to the love of God by the great mystics of all times and places. May the beautiful, very solid, and impassioned research of my friend Paul, together with his English version of the *Book*, both fruits of a faithful lifelong love, contribute to giving the Umbrian contemplative the place she deserves in the English-speaking world. Above all, may she light with her burning love many souls thirsting for the Absolute. Now, to conclude my affectionate presentation, I will dare to direct (in the manner of some pious medieval scribe) a small prayer to Angela, that she may obtain for them, for Paul, and for me, to be able to love Jesus, if not in the same way or measure, at least with the same authenticity and truth, with which, seven centuries ago, Angela of Foligno loved him.

Note

1. Romana Guarnieri entitled her Preface "Angela or Concerning Friendship," alluding to the fourfold relationship—Angela, the crucified God-man, the editor of this volume, and herself—that was interwoven as a result of the work on Angela's *Book*. For reasons of space and in keeping with the tenor of the Classics series, the first section of the Preface, which treats more directly on how our friendship was initiated and blossomed, is here condensed into this first paragraph. The full text is available in *Bailamme* (1991), an Italian review of which she is one of the editors.

Introduction

Panorama of the Life and Times

A wooden statue of Angela of Foligno, which serves as her reliquary, shows her as a short and slightly plump woman with a full-moon face; she is dressed in a simple tunic, wimple, and veil. Her eyes are closed and her body is in a reclining position. Large hands are visible, with fingers slightly apart, and these are gently but firmly folded over her stomach as if to reiterate what she was wont to say: "My secret is mine!" The statue radiates tranquility and repose—a body that has found its final resting place, a bed to rest on. The reproduction is lifelike and the physiognomy is characteristic of medieval Umbrian women, but it is impossible to say whether it accurately portrays Angela.[1] Like much about this great Italian mystic, who she was eludes total visibility—like a mountaintop shrouded by a sea of clouds.

As with so many mystics, especially medieval ones, almost nothing is known about the details and external circumstances of Angela's life. The date of her death, January 4, 1309, is well documented, but virtually all the information we have about her must be deduced or inferred from her *Book*. If especially the first part, the *Memorial*, affords us breathtaking vistas into her inner world, and the second part, the *Instructions*, shows a view of her role as a spiritual mother, these provide us with only a bare skeleton of her outer existence and the dates that mark her life story. Her *Book* contains only occasional glimpses of the people, the events, and the actual surroundings she was exposed to. Before I proceed to locate Angela in the context of her times and trace her inner journey, spirituality, and influence, the basic facts of her life must be set forth.

INTRODUCTION

A. Biographical Profile

In 1285 Angela, then thirty-seven years old, makes her first appearance before us in the *Memorial*, which narrates the main part of her story. This date also marks a decisive point of her life, that of her conversion, the first of the thirty steps in the spiritual itinerary she described to Brother A., her confessor, who was also to serve as her scribe. Her life previous to 1285 is almost completely unknown. According to the chronology established by M. J. Ferré, in all likelihood she was born in 1248 (within twenty-five years of St. Francis's death) in Foligno, a few miles away from Assisi.[2] Local tradition has it that "Lella," as she also came to be known,[3] was born of well-to-do, possibly noble parents, and that she lost her father while she was very young. The exact location of the house in which she lived has escaped historical notice; we know only that it was located near the church of San Francesco administered by the Franciscans.[4]

Ferré conjectures that Angela married when she was twenty years old (around 1270); her husband remains anonymous. We do know from her *Book* that she had several sons and that early in her conversion process all the members of her immediate household—husband, sons, and mother—died (around 1288, again according to Ferré).[5]

Rich, proud, and beautiful, Angela possessed a spirited and quick-witted intelligence prone to irony, and a rare sensibility. She pursued no formal studies but her mind was open and, as her writings testify, she was exceptionally cultivated. That she was able to read seems reasonably certain, but whether she was also able to write is more conjectural. She clearly dictated the *Memorial* to her scribe, Brother A., but does not seem to have adopted the same procedure for some of the *Instructions*—in particular, the letters addressed to her, which she read and responded to (in Latin), without any explicit mention of a secretary.[6] One can surmise that she learned to write, perhaps with some difficulty in Latin (or/and in her Umbrian dialect), only later in her life.[7] There is, however, no documentary evidence in her *Book* that warrants this assertion.

Fiery, passionate, impetuous by temperament, Angela seems to have enjoyed the comforts and luxuries of the world before she entered the way of penance. In a model for confession that she was later to write for her disciples, she listed a number of offenses in which there can most likely be detected the sinful profile of her own life. The avowal—to be made while gazing on the sufferings endured by the crucified Jesus for each of the offenses—includes washing, combing, and perfuming one's hair in order to be admired by others; dressing in luxurious clothes; indulging in fancy foods; delighting in fine perfumes; coveting possessions; hearing empty and harmful conversations; maligning others; letting loose with fits of anger and pride; engaging in illicit caresses and seductive behavior; "offending God by each of the senses of the body, and all of oneself"—in all of which she acknowledged herself an offender.[8]

One local tradition suggests that Angela was unfaithful to her husband. No written document, however, substantiates this hypothesis, and biographers tend to agree that if her life suffered moral deviation and disorderly affections, these were not such as to constitute a public scandal.[9] On close study of her writings, from the apprehension that was hers before vowing chastity, the shame that initially prevented her from acknowledging her sins, and the preoccupation with purity after her conversion, it does seem that the sin she felt compelled to confess at the beginning of her conversion was a sexual one. At any rate, even if the precise nature of the sin is unknown, it was a mortal sin that she thought might need the absolution of the bishop.[10]

Whatever conclusion we may come to concerning her life prior to her conversion, it is clear from the above that Angela had led a superficial, pleasure-seeking, even a sinful life.

How did this vain and worldly woman do an about-face and embark on a life of mortification and penance? The motives for Angela's conversion seem manifold and will be explored more fully in our subsequent examination of her spiritual itinerary. The only explicit ones mentioned in the *Memorial* indicate that in 1285, more or less at the midpoint of her life, she "wept bitterly" and "the fear of being damned to hell" inspired her to go to confession.[11] So ashamed was she of her sins that at first she could not bring herself to confess some of them. Receiving communion with these still on her conscience, she added the sin of sacrilege to all the rest.

In her despair, Angela turned to St. Francis to find her a confessor "who knew sins well." The saint appeared to her in a dream in the form of an elderly religious and told her: "Sister, if you would have asked me sooner, I would have complied with your request sooner. Nonetheless, your request is granted."

The very next morning Angela went to the church of San Francesco near where she lived, but she did not find the confessor she was looking for. On her way back she decided, by chance, to enter the cathedral of San Feliciano not far away. A Franciscan was preaching, a

Folignate, who happened to be a relative of hers and was also chaplain of Berardo, the local bishop.[12] Angela decided that this was the man she was looking for and made a "full confession to him." The latter assured her that, contrary to what she had feared, he could grant her absolution for her sins without the intervention of the bishop. This same Franciscan, whom most of the biographical tradition refers to as Brother Arnaldo, was very likely the same friar who subsequently was to play a decisive role in Angela's story as her confessor and as writer of her revelations.[13]

Relieved and invigorated by the full confession of her sins, Angela began her new life and embarked resolutely on the way of penance. It was initially a slow and painful process. For five and a half years, from the time of her conversion until the great vision that took place in Assisi in 1291, she struggled, "making only small steps at a time," to liberate herself from her sinful past and to grow more sensitive to the demands of her new calling.

The first nineteen steps of the *Memorial* describe this season of purification through suffering. Set ablaze by the fire and intensity of Christ's love as revealed to her through increasingly vivid and focused visions of his passion and crucifixion, Angela had one desire: to grow in amorous response by aligning her life with his, applying herself to harsh penances, and, following the example of her model, St. Francis, taking steps to become truly poor.

Standing before the crucifix, Angela strips herself of all her clothing and pledges to Christ, her newfound lover, perpetual chastity. Then feeling the need to dispossess herself ever more radically, she renounces her best garments, fine foods, and toiletry. After the death of her mother, husband, and sons, whom she had experienced as impediments to her spiritual growth, she sells her country villa (her legal right as a widow), to give the proceeds to the poor. "It was the best land that I owned," she declared.

Angela encountered considerable hostility, not only from her family but also from her spiritual advisors in the new direction her life was now taking. Thinking that perhaps she was sick or possessed by the devil—even Angela suspected this of herself—her counselors warned her of the dangers on the path of poverty and advised against it. Their opposition notwithstanding, in an effort to finally resolve her own remaining doubts, on June 28, 1291, Angela decided to go to Rome to beseech the apostle Peter to obtain for her the grace of becoming truly poor. It seems that her prayer was heard, and when she returned to Foligno she got rid of almost all her remaining possessions.

INTRODUCTION

It was also very likely in the early part of the summer of 1291 that the Franciscans of San Francesco's in Foligno, finally sufficiently impressed by Angela's determination and courage, permitted her to take the habit and make her profession in the Third Order of St. Francis.[14] In the same year, in the early autumn of 1291, Angela decided to go on pilgrimage to Assisi in order to pray to St. Francis that he might obtain for her the grace to feel Christ's presence in her soul, to observe well the Franciscan Third Order Rule she had recently professed, and above all to make her become, and remain to the end, truly poor.

With a few well-chosen companions—among these were a holy man from Puglia whom Angela had persuaded to give away all his worldly possessions to the poor and together with her to make a vow of absolute poverty, and probably her constant companion Masazuola as well—she set out from Foligno to Assisi, totally absorbed in prayer. At the crossroads beyond Spello, where a narrow road branched out to Assisi, the group stopped in a small chapel dedicated to the Trinity. It was in this chapel or nearby that she received an extraordinary manifestation of the Trinity, as promised in a vision she had recently received.

Angela was so overwhelmed by the feeling of God's tenderness within her that as the group took to the road again, she drifted behind the others. When they finally reached their destination, the Basilica of St. Francis in Assisi, Angela and her companions entered the lower basilica to pray. After a while they left for a meal, and when they returned, they went inside the upper basilica, where Angela's glance fell on a stained glass window depicting St. Francis in the bosom of Christ. Once again she was suddenly and unexpectedly awestruck by a sense of divine presence.

As this vision gradually departed from her, Angela was filled with such desolation at the thought of losing it that she began to shriek with all her might, wanting to die: "Love still unknown, why? why? why?" Her words stuck in her throat and became almost unintelligible. Before the startled eyes of her entourage she lay on the pavement of the threshold of the basilica letting out inarticulate shouts. The strange spectacle attracted the attention of the friars living in the adjacent convent, and many of them came to see what was going on. Among them was her confessor, Brother Arnaldo, now a member of the Sacro Convento community attached to the basilica. He was so ashamed of the bizarre behavior of his relative that he could scarcely hold back his anger. After the shouting stopped, he told Angela that she should never dare come back to Assisi and likewise told her companions never to bring her there.[15]

INTRODUCTION

Angela returned from Assisi to Foligno transformed. She was filled with a great peace and a feeling of intimacy with God, which was strengthened by a number of special visions. Arnaldo, however, remained very disturbed over her state. When the provincial chapter of May 26, 1292, reassigned him to the San Francesco friary in Foligno, he once again saw his penitent and began to question her about the strange phenomena that had taken place in Assisi. He strongly suspected an evil spirit had overtaken her, and he pressed her in every way that he could to be open with him and not to hide from him anything that she had experienced. He promised her, furthermore, that he would reveal her secrets to no one except some spiritual men, unknown to her, who would help him decide whether it was God or the devil at work in her.

Arnaldo was stupefied by the narrative that began to flow from Angela's lips. His first reaction was to try to inspire fear and doubt as to the veracity of what Angela had experienced—which, in fact, he succeeded in doing. Angela decided nonetheless to tell him everything and even warned him that the few sheets of paper that he had brought with him to copy what she would say would never do, that a large notebook would be necessary.

Thus was born the *Memorial,* which documents the steps of Angela's inner journey and is the main source of what we know of her story. For four years or so (ca. 1292–1296), Arnaldo, as was the custom of confessors at that time, would meet with Angela, most of the time in the church of San Francesco in Foligno, and take down as best he could—writing sometimes very hurriedly, and later translating into Latin, what she dictated in her Umbrian dialect. The nature of Arnaldo's role, as well as the considerable difficulty he encountered in the redaction of the text, will be discussed later in the Introduction. Angela, for her part, acknowledged that what he wrote, even if "truncated and weakened," was basically faithful to what she had told him.

The numinous encounters that took place during the trip to Assisi were but the prelude to further and more profound manifestations of God's love to Angela, which she was to make known to her astonished —and initially suspicious—confessor. She poured out to him what she had experienced in her spiritual itinerary: first of all, the nineteen steps (of an eventual thirty) that she had observed in herself so far and that cover the period we have treated until now. Then, with Arnaldo henceforth following her more closely, she dictated the remaining eleven. Arnaldo, however, was unable to complete all of these remaining eleven steps and decided to condense what took place in them into seven supplementary steps. Since most of the experiences related in these later steps —which took place over a period of nearly six years—delineate Angela's inner journey in greater detail than the previous ones, I will consider them more closely in the commentary. It suffices for the present purpose to mention only their most salient outer manifestations.[16]

"Christ's faithful one," as Arnaldo habitually called Angela in his narrative, was indeed on fire with God's love. From 1291 onward, in the first five supplementary steps, ever more intense visions of the crucified Christ, some involving the Eucharist, a few of the universe filled with God's presence, and still other formless visions of the attributes of God, mark her ascension. In a particularly striking episode, Angela and her companion went to serve the lepers at the hospital in Foligno on Holy Thursday, April 3, 1292. After having washed one of the lepers who was in an advanced state of decomposition, they drank of the water used for washing. Angela compared the effect "to having received communion," so filled were they with "divine sweetness."

Through these powerful, and at times startling, divine revelations, always marked by a rapidly oscillating dialectic of presence and absence, Angela's own love was transformed and she grew in identity and intimacy with her beloved, "the suffering God-man." Notwithstanding the power of the visions and experiences of God's love that she was receiving, doubts and uncertainties, periods of aridity, hostility from the Franciscans and her associates in the Third Order, temptations from the devil, and periodic death wishes plagued Angela, causing intermittent periods of agony in the midst of intense joy.

By the end of the fifth supplementary step we find Angela so firmly anchored in the certitude of God's love that she can say she has attained complete knowledge of God's overwhelming kindness, as well as of her own nothingness. In the springtime of 1294, however, these five or six months of certitude, peace, and great joy were to completely collapse.

For two mysterious years, from 1294 to 1296, Angela alternately experienced moments of deepest despair and abandonment and, almost simultaneously, moments of closest union and intimacy with God. She felt in turn chosen and damned, cherished daughter of God and terrible child of the devil. The sixth supplementary step describes the agonies of soul and body, the terrible temptations from the devil, the deep abyss into which she was plunged, while the seventh relates its opposite and complement, the sublime visions of God in and beyond the divine darkness—the highest stages of her mystical ascent. With the latter, Arnaldo brought the *Memorial* to a close.

For the thirteen years that elapsed from 1296 until her death in 1309, except for a pilgrimage to Assisi in early August 1300, very little is reliably known concerning the outer facts and circumstances of Angela's life. What comes to the fore in the material assembled in the second part of her *Book*, the *Instructions*, is her role as spiritual mother. A small community gathered around her to listen to her teachings, and it is to her disciples and admirers, far and near—the most notable being Ubertino of Casale, the turbulent leader of the Spiritual Franciscans who credited his conversion to her, probably in 1298—that a series of letters, reflections, and exhortations are addressed. In the latter part of her life, Angela was extremely reluctant to reveal the secrets of her inner life. "My secrets are mine!" she told a friar who tried to extricate further revelations from her. The *Instructions* nonetheless do contain the description of mystical experiences that occurred after the redaction of the *Memorial* (to which I will return later). Most of these are undated and a few seem to be artificial constructs composed by anonymous scribes after her death on the occasion of liturgical feasts.

From 1301 onward, Angela's life is practically unknown. A chronicler from Spello, Giovanni Targarini Olorini (d. 1348), however, records that, in 1307, she visited the Poor Clares of Spello:

> The blessed Angela of Foligno, a tertiary of great sanctity and fame, passed through Spello with her companion, the blessed Pasqualina. She visited Sister Gregoria di Vanni, a very kind and spiritual woman of the monastery of Valle Gloria in Spello, then took the Renaro Road to Assisi to visit the holy places and sacred relics. On her return to Foligno she stopped at the Church of St. Mary of the Angels.[17]

Fortunately, more details are available concerning the events surrounding Angela's death. Instruction 36 assembles in one discourse the fragments of what she had told her disciples during her final sickness (lasting from a few days before Christmas, 1308, until January 4, 1309), including her announcement of her impending death, her spiritual testament, and a final blessing to her spiritual progeny, both "present and absent." This instruction records that on the feast of the octave of the Holy Innocents, January 4, 1309, after Compline, the last canonical hour of the day, Christ's faithful one went gently into sleep and entered into the peace of the final encounter with her Beloved, who had just promised her that he would entrust to neither the angels nor any other saint the task of bringing her to him, but "would come in person" to take her with him.

The body of Angela was laid to rest in the church of San Francesco in Foligno. It soon became the object of veneration and cult. According to the aforementioned chronicler, Giovanni Olorini, "many from Spello and the surrounding area came to revere her body."[18] She was first given the title of "Blessed" by public acclaim, and later recognized as such by a decree of Clement XI on July 11, 1701. Her feast was fixed on January 4, the anniversary of her death, with a proper Mass and Office. Although often referred to as a saint, especially in France, she was never canonized by the church.[19]

B. Angela's Companion

Although she appears quite frequently in Angela's *Book*, very little information is available concerning Angela's constant and intimate companion. Codices initialize her name with M., Ma., Mas. Only one, the Trivulziana (end of the fourteenth or beginning of the fifteenth century), completes her name as Masazuola, the name I have adopted for my text, as have the editors of the critical edition.[20]

Angela, in common with other noble or wealthy medieval women, could avail herself of a servant to perform sundry domestic chores. Most likely, this was the role initially assigned to Masazuola. Eventually she became Angela's spiritual companion and confidante. Even before she had revealed the secrets of her life to Arnaldo, her confessor and scribe, Angela, as the *Memorial* records in the opening lines, had told her companion the thirty steps of her mystical ascent. Masazuola was also in direct rapport with Arnaldo, to whom she disclosed some of the mystical phenomena she had observed in Angela. Among them were the aura that surrounded her as she lay bedridden after the initial Assisi vision, and, later, a sight of her "with eyes shining like candles," as both of them were walking together along a path.[21] That Masazuola was a holy woman, "a marvel of simplicity, purity and chastity," and beneficiary of special blessings and mystical graces, is apparent in numerous occasions in the *Memorial*.[22] In one of her letters, Angela even mentions that she was envious of her companion, thinking perhaps that Masazuola was more advanced than she in divine grace.[23]

INTRODUCTION

C. Historical and Cultural Context

Mystics are rooted in the time in which they live. With so much that remains shrouded in mystery about Angela's life, it is essential to situate her life, character, and the conditions in which manuscripts of her *Book* began to circulate in the historical and cultural context in which her story was nurtured and came to fruition.

In the latter half of the thirteenth century and the beginning of the fourteenth, medieval society was in a state of great tension as it experienced profound shifts and transformations.[24] Conflicts between Church and state repeatedly shook all of Christendom, affecting every level of society. Popes were often in open warfare with the kings and rulers of Europe for political supremacy. In 1302, for instance, Pope Boniface VIII issued the bull *Unam Sanctam*, the most extreme expression and the culmination of the claims of the medieval papacy. Shortly after, in 1303, he barely managed to escape assassination at the hands of the henchmen of Philip the Fair in Anagni. His successor, Benedict XI (1303–1304), had to flee Rome, which was in revolt, to take refuge in Perugia, probably passing through or near Foligno on the way. The next pope in line, the Frenchman Clement V (1305–1314), never set foot in Italy. After him, another Frenchman, John XXII (1316–1334), a skilled but inflexible administrator, was elected after a long vacancy. In the adverse conditions in which the papacy found itself, now in exile in Avignon, he was unable to halt the process of division and disintegration of the medieval synthesis. To be sure, among the sixteen popes, kings, and rulers in the period we are concerned with, there were many deeply religious men, such as Gregory X (1271–1276); the "angelic pope," Celestine V (1294); and the canonized king, St. Louis (1226–1270). Although there were numerous attempts at reform, including the convening of two Church Councils—the Second Council of Lyons (1274) and the Council of Vienne (1311)—none of these efforts completely succeeded in stemming the long decline in the prestige of the medieval papacy, beginning after the reign of Innocent IV (1243–1254) through the "Babylonian captivity" in Avignon to the Great Schism (1378).[25]

Other profound transformations were altering the social fabric of medieval society. In Italy, in particular, with the breakdown of feudalism, the birth pangs of the city and the nation state were witness to the cruel and almost constant wars taking place between towns (communes), which often became mortal enemies in the struggle for economic and political position. Dominion see-sawed between the Guelfs, supporters of the papacy, and the Ghibellines, allies to the emperor.[26] The signs of a crumbling social and political order were everywhere. Dante aptly summarized the ensuing spiritual and political crisis in the sixth canto of the Purgatorio: "Ah, servile Italy, hostel of grief, ship without pilot/in great tempest, no mistress of provinces, but brothel."[27]

With the breakdown of feudal structures during this era, cities or communes began to emerge as centers of commercial, artistic, intellectual, and religious activity.[28] Demographic expansion during the same period was accompanied, especially in Italy, by prodigious commercial expansion. A new mercantile class extended its economic tentacles toward ever more remote reaches of Europe and the Orient, with equally far-reaching cultural and social effects.[29]

As cities and communes became prime movers of the new civilization, they became sites for the establishment of numerous and powerful universities. Paris and Bologna were among the most notable of these. The great scholastic systems elaborated in these new centers of learning vied with existing thought patterns for control of the intellectual and cultural climate. In the arts, a new, more realistic style finds its expression in the masterpieces of a Giotto and a Cimabue. A shift from the representation of Christ triumphant to Christ suffering on the cross begins to affirm itself in 1250–1255.[30] In architecture, new gothic cathedrals dot the landscape; and in literature, language breaks loose from its Latin moorings with the "Canticle of Brother Sun," the "Fioretti" of St. Francis, and the fiery lauds of Jacopone da Todi. The vernacular is to triumph with the immortal lyrics of Dante's *Divine Comedy*.

D. Spiritual Currents

My concern is not to paint a complete picture of the spiritual forces and currents moving during this period but to point out those that had strong repercussions in Italy, particularly in the Umbrian valley.[31]

In the early part of the thirteenth century, Pope Innocent III, even if he did not grasp the full significance of the new religious movements that were in ferment during his reign, had the genius to open a space within the institutional church for their emergence.[32] The most outstanding—although not the only—representatives of these new forces were the mendicant orders, those of St. Dominic and St. Francis. The rise and acceptance of the mendicants provided a bridge between the hierarchy and the representatives of the profound aspirations that were animating the Christian community, and that had until then tended to be isolated in powerful heretical movements such as the Waldensians, the Catharists, the Umiliati, and the Patarines.[33]

What most characterized these emerging new forces was a concern to return to the gospel, and the desire for a spirituality focused on the humanity of Christ, especially his suffering and crucifixion. To be sure, devotion to the humanity of Christ had already been initiated by St. Bernard, among others, in the twelfth century, but St. Francis and his followers were largely responsible for its widespread expansion in the thirteenth century by making it accessible to the masses.[34]

Linked to this devotion to the humanity of Christ was the desire to live a life in conformity to his; and more specifically, to follow the Christ who was poor and "had no place to lay his head" (Mt 8:20). The mystique and exaltation of poverty was something totally new in the history of spirituality. A life of poverty was perceived as the cure for the ills of the times, a concrete response to Christ's expectations for his church. This entailed a reform of institutions and monastic structures encrusted, as many of them were, with wealth and privilege and linked with the power of the nobility and the ruling classes.

The desire to follow and love the Christ who abased himself and became poor also inspired a direct contact with the growing and thus more visible number of the poor, not only widows and orphans but also victims of injustice and all those who live on the margins of society—the sick, lepers, prostitutes, the deprived and excluded of every sort.[35] These were looked on as replicas of the suffering Christ and to a certain extent shared with him a salvific function. Numerous texts of the thirteenth century speak, as did St. Francis, of the poor as lords and even as vicars of Christ.[36] St. Francis's embrace of the leper exemplifies in a striking way the mystique of poverty prevalent during this period.[37] For the Poverello, conversion arises from an encounter with the rejected of society as icons of Christ and mediators in the ascent toward God and the creation of a more just and fraternal social order. This growing awareness of human values and the recognition of the spiritual significance of the poor—and indeed of all created reality—established, as the noted medieval historian Marie-Dominic Chenu succinctly puts it, "a new equilibrium between nature and grace."[38]

If meditation on the sufferings and passion of Christ inspired some to go to the poor, it led others to pursue an eremitical life in abandoned grottoes, caves, and solitary places. This eremitical experience, so strong among St. Francis and his followers—and they were far from the

26

only ones—participated in what Jean Sainsaulieu has called the "golden age" of Italian eremiticism, the "second wave" of Western eremiticism.[39] The hermits of this period sought to combine the ideals of both contemplation and poverty. The precariousness of their life had the advantage of facilitating an easy and simple rapport with the surrounding populace and the poor. The same desire to imitate the poor Christ spurred others to embark on long and perilous pilgrimages to holy places along the great commercial routes that, in increasing numbers, crisscrossed Europe, extending as far as the Holy Land—a further example of the interplay between spiritual, economic, and social forces.[40]

The spirituality of the time placed particular emphasis on a strong Eucharistic piety.[41] In the Middle Ages, the Eucharist and the sacrament of penance were the only sacraments accorded serious significance. One went to Mass, however, not so much to receive the body of Christ as to see it. It was commonly held that simply to look at the consecrated host had salvific effects. Recourse to the sacrament of penance to purify one's conscience and to prepare oneself for the final judgment became more frequent and was made obligatory at least once a year at Easter by a decree of the Fourth Lateran Council (1215) for everyone who had reached the age of discretion.[42] Attention to the Scriptures—especially the psalms, the gospels, St. Paul, and the Book of Revelation—also increased. The Bible was indeed the most studied book of the Middle Ages. It was not only the basic source of theological reflection, it also served as the door to religious experience, because spiritually understood, it conveyed the secrets of the mystical life.[43] Finally, devotion to the saints (and their relics) and, in particular, to the Blessed Virgin—envisioned as beautiful Virgin, Queen of Heaven and Earth, merciful and sorrowful Mother (the closest associate of Christ's sufferings)—was widespread and served as a vehicle (even if an ambiguous one) for a new image of femininity.[44]

If it is on the level of practical existence that this new spirituality focusing on the passion and poverty of Christ had its greatest impact, one must nonetheless also observe that there was theological reflection of the highest intellectual caliber being done at this time. Among the Dominicans there was, of course, St. Thomas Aquinas and his incorporation of Aristotle into a new powerful synthesis. For the Franciscans, the necessity of cultivating knowledge without forsaking the spirit of prayer and devotion brought about a fusion of speculative and affective theology. St. Bonaventure, the most powerful exponent of the Franciscan way, attempted to give it theological grounding. He based his thought mainly on the Bible. To be sure, he also drew inspiration from St. Augustine and the Pseudo-Dionysius, the Victorines, and St. Bernard, but it was in drawing from the experience of St. Francis himself that he elaborated his most profound mystical theology. His life of St. Francis, the *Legenda Major*, was one of the most widely disseminated texts of the Middle Ages. What are usually called his "mystical opuscula," and in particular three of them, the *Itinerarium mentis in Deum*, the *Triplici Via*, and the *Lignum Vitae*, were among the most beautiful and influential of the hundreds of spiritual books of the medieval period.[45]

The spirituality of the times was not the exclusive province of the mendicants, central as they were. Especially in the latter half of the thirteenth century the works of the Latin Fathers and the Greek Fathers available in Latin translations, in particular Augustine (e.g., *The Confessions*), and Pseudo-Dionysius (along with his translators and commentators), as well as the spiritual writings of the high Middle Ages, such as those of St. Bernard (e.g., *On Loving God, Sermons on the Song of Songs*), William of St. Thierry (e.g., *The Golden Epistle*), and the Victorines, were integral parts of the libraries being built. Monks and friars helped to disseminate their ideas through sermons, spiritual direction, and various other forms of oral and written transmission.

In the second part of the century, within the medieval spirituality whose traits I have sketched, new accents can be noted, a shift of emphasis. The causes are manifold. Among them is the widening credibility gap between the institutional church and the conscience of the ordinary faithful. From 1240 onward, churchmen and clerical schoolmen seemed unable to understand the profound changes taking place within medieval society and unable to deal effectively with an emerging educated laity. They often attempted, unsuccessfully, to stop them.[46] As has already been noted, the acceleration of political, social, and cultural transformations brought about a deep crisis that had profound repercussions on the spiritual climate of the time. Apocalypticism characterized this new mood. The anxiety-ridden atmosphere became permeated with what Raffaello Morgen calls a *"fin de siècle* consciousness,"[47] which believed that Christendom had reached the fullness of time.

It was not surprising, then, that the ideas of the Calabrian abbot Joachim of Fiore would come to the fore and would be applied to the contemporary history of the church.[48] Writing in the late twelfth century, at first revered as a saint but later denounced as a heretic, Joachim had taught that there were three states of the world's history, corre-

28

sponding to the three persons of the Trinity. The first state, that of the Old Testament, was under the dispensation of the Father; the second state, that of the New Testament, was characterized by Christ's redemption of the world and the first era of the life of the church; the third, that of the Holy Spirit, was to begin sometime soon. The church would become corrupt, but two new religious orders, living in apostolic poverty, would inaugurate a new era in which there would be no need for authoritative institutions, since men and women would now live according to the spirit of God. Joachim of Fiore's writings were widely read during this period.

The expectation that the world would soon come to an end, and Christ would come to judge the living and the dead, filled the air. Boniface VIII sought to placate the faithful, who were anxious to assure their salvation, by declaring the year 1300 a Year of Jubilee. He granted special indulgences to the thousands who thronged to Rome.[49] Monks, religious, and laity prepared for and sought to identify portents of the cataclysm. Extreme groups such as the Flagellants came into being in response. Significantly enough, this last group originated in Perugia, not far from Foligno.[50] Heretical movements—not as massive as those in the twelfth and the early part of the thirteenth century—exhibited quietistic and apocalyptic tendencies (e.g., the heresy of the Free Spirit).[51] In this religious climate, mysticism flourished, especially among women.

E. The Franciscans

Even if it was not their exclusive domain, the Franciscans, as I have already begun to indicate, dominated the spirituality of the period. Francis of Assisi, as Dante so eloquently put it, "had brought forth unto the world a sun."[52] He and his brothers did not stand alone, but worked in conjunction with major social and economic changes in medieval Europe. They responded to these changes, and helped to shape them by inserting within them the purifying and liberating force of a radical observance of the gospel: following the footsteps of Christ, who was poor, renouncing all forms of power, and sharing the condition of those at the bottom of society.[53] The stigmata of Francis, the most celebrated mystical experience of the Middle Ages, marked the summit of the Poverello's radical identification with Christ, and was to serve as the dominant symbol ("an incorporated mandala"), expressed in countless paintings, for subsequent medieval and Franciscan spirituality.[54]

INTRODUCTION

The early Franciscans radically renewed both the church and society, and rapidly the truth force of their fraternal message spread contagiously to all corners of Europe and the Orient. This rapid expansion, however, did not come without problems.[55] Already during Francis's lifetime, there were growing pains, as conflicts arose about what Francis really intended, especially with regard to poverty. As long as he was alive, any attempt to depart from his ideals could be resisted, for his influence was very strong. After his death, things were different. As the important historian of the Order, John Moorman, puts it: "Poverty began to give place to security, simplicity to learning, and humility to privilege."[56] The center of gravity within the Order moved to those who believed that the Order should develop in other ways and its message be adapted to growing numbers and changing times. The rising basilica at Assisi, the vast sums of money collected for it, the growth of the scholastic movement in the university towns, the clericalization of the Order,[57] the downpour of ecclesiastical privileges, and the clashes with the secular clergy—all were symptomatic of the new age.

During his generalate, St. Bonaventure (1257–1274) tried to develop an image of Francis and his message that he thought was more in keeping with the new situation: service of the church, establishment of the friars in cities, studies, teaching, and pastoral activity.[58] The moderate reform he masterminded, however, did not meet the expectations of those within the movement who sought a more literal fidelity to the primitive Franciscan ideal. Battle lines were drawn, and the gap between the "Spirituals" and the "Community," as later historians were to call these opposing factions, widened and for some, as we shall see, even went all the way to schism and condemnation for heresy.[59]

The crisis that shook the Franciscan Order in the late thirteenth to the early fourteenth century is a complex one. The battles were waged on many fronts and much of what happened is lost in the smoke of history. However, the general course of events is clear enough to provide a framework within which to understand, subsequently, Angela's role in the polemics of this period.

At no time, not even under the quasi-formal leadership of such figures as Peter John Olivi (ca. 1248–1298) of Provence in southern France, Pietro da Macerata (Fra. Liberato, d. 1307) and Angelo of Clareno (ca. 1245–1337) of the Italian Marches, and Ubertino of Casale (1259–ca. 1338) of Tuscany, was the Spiritual party a recognizable or coherent group. For example, the Spirituals in France were quite different from those in Italy, who were more eremitically inclined. Nor could

Spirituals be identified in terms of administrative organization or systematic doctrines or teachings. They are most accurately thought of, instead, in terms of certain major tendencies, which they shared to a greater or lesser degree. The most important of these included a preference for rural eremiticism over urban conventualism, an antagonism toward worldly learning, the conviction that suffering was a necessary sign of a life in conformity with Christ and that the essence of Franciscanism lay in strict, unmitigated observance of the Rule and Testament of St. Francis.[60] It was this latter point—the fidelity to the intentions of the founder, especially in regard to the renunciation of power and a radical dispossession of material goods (*usus pauper*)—that was the center of the raging controversy.

This desire to conform to St. Francis, to keep alive the memory of a life and a manner of being that was different, was inherited by the Spirituals from a considerable number of humble and poor friars who lived in hermitages and convents in Umbria, Tuscany, and the Marches. These included some of the early companions of St. Francis who were still alive, such as Giles of Assisi, Leo, Rufino, Angelo, Bernard of Quintavalle, Masseo, and other fervent friars, including Conrad of Offida, James of Fallerone, Bentivoglia of San Severino, John of Fermo, Caesar of Speyer, and Peter of Monticulo.

Furthermore, in several of the Spiritual writers there was a marked strain of the apocalypticism that was, as already noted, endemic in the late thirteenth century literature, as well as strong interest in the application of the teachings of Joachim of Fiore to the contemporary history and reform of the church.[61] From 1240 onward, the authentic and apocryphal writings of the Calabrian abbot circulated within the Franciscan Order, and his ideas conquered vast numbers of friars who saw in his prophecies the confirmation of the historical role the Order was to play, as well as a nourishment for their apocalyptic expectation. On the basis of the Joachimite schema of thought, the Spirituals believed that, after a period of decadence and tribulation, the Order would be restored by a mysterious reformer who would lead the "new" friars to an even greater state than the first. Fidelity, then, to the ideal of gospel poverty as preached by St. Francis, referred to as the *alter Christus,* or the "angel of the sixth seal,"[62] would also bring about a reform of the "carnal" church. It would initiate a new "spiritual" church, an age of contemplatives, which would be accompanied by illuminations, ecstasies, prophecies, and visions, necessary components of the end-time.

The events that led to the demise of the Spirituals are closely intertwined with the decline of the papacy and the relaxation of the discipline of poverty by the Community. Though it is difficult to date precisely when the fire of controversy was lit, there is ample evidence to show that it began shortly after the Council of Lyons in 1274. Angelo of Clareno records that at this point, at a provincial chapter, some of the friars from the Marches in Italy were imprisoned and condemned "as heretics and destroyers of the Order."[63] The central issue seems to have been whether one should obey the pope or one's vows concerning the acceptance of property. As David Burr points out, the dissidents were also at odds with "the establishment of friars in the heart of cities; heavy commitment to worldly learning; and the scramble for burial rights, legacies and privileges."[64]

In the following years the dispute escalated. But in 1289, Raymond Geoffroi, the only minister general sympathetic to the Spirituals during this period, freed the Anconian Spirituals from prison and sent them as missionaries to Armenia. Subsequently, on the return of the dissidents to Italy in 1294, Pope Celestine V, who saw nothing but good in these zealous followers of St. Francis, granted their request to form a separate Order, the Poor Hermits of Pope Celestine. After Celestine's abdication, this concession was rescinded by his successor, Boniface VIII (who was to be labeled by Ubertino of Casale in his *Arbor vitae crucifixae Jesu* of 1305 as the mystical Antichrist,[65] and by Jacopone da Todi, as "a new Lucifer on the papal throne").[66] When the validity of Boniface's election was challenged by a manifesto (1297) countersigned by the Colonna cardinals, Jacopone da Todi, and other Spirituals, Boniface retaliated by launching a crusade against "the heretics," excommunicating the cardinals, defeating them in battle, and condemning the captives to life imprisonment, Jacopone among them.

Clement V attempted to conciliate the warring factions, especially with the promulgation of the bull *Exivi de paradiso* at the Council of Vienne in May 1312, but this attempt at compromise ended in failure. Almost immediately after his election (7 August 1316), John XXII initiated an all-out campaign to suppress the Spirituals and their cause through a series of bulls and disciplinary legislations. The main salvos of his attack were spelled out in *Quorundam exigit* (7 October 1317), *Sancta Romana* (30 December 1317), and *Gloriosam ecclesiam* (23 January 1318).[67]

Less than a month after the promulgation of *Quorundam exigit*, John XXII's efforts—spurred by leaders of the Community—to put an end to the Spirituals reached a bloody climax in Provence. At the pope's urging, the recently elected Minister General Michael of Cesena handed over twenty-six dissident friars (followers of Olivi) to the inquisitor Michael le Moine. Charged with heresy (i.e., their refusal to obey the pope as having the last word on the question of poverty), twenty-one friars recanted, one was condemned to perpetual imprisonment, and, eventually, four were burned, on 7 May 1318, in the marketplace of Marseilles.

The pyre in Marseilles signaled the end of an era in the conflict between the Spirituals and the papal-Community coalition. By then, Olivi and his writings were under suspicion, and his followers, including the Beguines (of whom more will be said later), were persecuted. Already by the end of 1317, Angelo of Clareno had been forced to leave the Order and had joined the Celestinian Hermits, and Ubertino of Casale had become a Benedictine.

Finally, the coup de grâce to the grass-roots revolt was dealt, again by John XXII (this time encouraged by the Dominicans), with the publication of *Cum inter nonnullos* (12 November 1323), which condemned as heretical the doctrine of the absolute poverty of Christ and his disciples. This tenet was shared by the Spirituals and the Community, as testified by a decision made by the Franciscan General Michael of Cesena at the General Chapter held in Perugia in 1322. Michael, along with Bonagratia of Bergamo (a leading Community spokesman since 1311), William of Ockham, and others, chose to defy the pope, accepting excommunication and exile—thus making common cause with earlier dissidents and giving added impetus to the *Fraticelli* movement.[68] Simply put, the net effect of John XXII's long series of repressive measures and the revolt of a potent wing of the Franciscans was to end the alliance between poverty and ecclesiastical authority that was a feature of the thirteenth-century medieval synthesis, and to provisionally outlaw the radical observance of evangelical poverty, which Francis had stood for.[69]

F. The Penitential Movement

On the one hand, the Franciscans were in bitter conflict during a period in which the Christian medieval synthesis was crumbling. As the church of canonists, theologians, and hierarchy affirmed itself more rigidly, it gradually lost much of its contact with the praxis of the ordinary faithful. On the other hand, an increasingly educated, vocal, and emancipated laity was emerging.[70] In the religious sphere, this lay movement developed along predominantly mystical-ethical lines. It formed part of a complex penitential movement, whose evolution, and especially its Franciscan expression, was instrumental in shaping the climate for Angela's spiritual journey.[71]

From the beginning, lay people who wanted to sanctify themselves in their own homes were associated with the Franciscan movement. The role, however, that Francis and his brothers played in the establishment of the Franciscan Third Order of Penance, as it came to be known, is the subject of hot controversy among contemporary historians.[72] Suffice it to say, for our purposes, that growing spontaneously, more or less in the shadow and under the guidance of the First Order, the Third Order enjoyed enormous influence in the thirteenth century. It was only, however, with the bull *Supra Montem* (1289), the *Regula bullata* of the Franciscan penitents issued by the Franciscan Pope Nicholas IV, that it achieved more or less fixed status as a distinct organization.

Like all other "penitents" of this loosely defined movement, those who came under Franciscan influence and inspiration were distinguished from the "regular" religious and secular society by a number of characteristics. They enjoyed many, but not all, of the privileges of the ecclesiastical state. Their profession could be called a "simple profession," to distinguish it from the one necessary to enter a regular Order. They were obliged to wear a simple garb of plain colors—grey when under the Franciscan jurisdiction, black when under the Dominicans; all members were to go to Mass regularly, say the seven canonical hours—for which the "unlettered" could substitute a certain number of Pater Nosters and Ave Marias, go to confession and receive communion three times a year, and keep certain prescribed fasts; male members were not to bear arms and had to abstain from solemn oaths (except such as were demanded by the Holy See); they were to live peacefully among themselves and serve as peacemakers in society; attendance at dances and spectacles was forbidden; and above all, they were to distinguish themselves in charitable works, such as service to the poor, the sick, and lepers. Among other obligations of the penitential state was absence of conjugal relations during certain feasts of the liturgical year, or perpetual continence—thus the appellation "continent," which appears in the *Memorial*—for the unmarried and widows. Virgins were to continue living with their parents, and widows—such as Angela of Foligno after the death of her husband—often lived with other penitents in the house of the deceased husband.

Penitents were also closely linked with the rise of the medieval urban phenomena I have already mentioned: In a number of cities in central Italy, their development is associated with the rise of crafts, guilds, and the liberal professions. These *novi cives* or *borghi* were not yet integrated into the aristocratic lineage and found in these new religious groups a response to their need for a way to seek religious perfection and their desire to integrate themselves as soon as possible into city life by creating new bonds of social solidarity.[73]

In still other cases, penitents, much like the Beguines of the Low Countries, moved toward a sort of semi-monastic life: small numbers of unmarried men and women or widows lived together, often under no official rule, but according to such regulations (a *propositum*) as they chose to draw up.[74] Occasionally, to clear themselves in the eyes of the official church (which often suspected them of being mixed up with heretical currents—as they often were), they would adopt the cover of whatever officially approved rule they found most accessible and appropriate. A good example of this type of development in Italy was the foundation of St. Clare of Montefalco, who, although under Franciscan influence, adopted the Augustinian Rule.[75]

The trend toward lay autonomy was characteristic of these "new" medieval lay people. Ultimately, if the penitents enjoyed immense influence, it was precisely, as Hebert Roeggen points out, "because they possessed their own dynamism, an enthusiasm to carry out their own affairs without the interference of the clerics. Certainly, they strongly felt the need for spiritual direction from the church, and especially from the mendicants who displayed strong and more daring gospel radicality, but by and large they did not want to be submitted to the Orders."[76]

The penitential movement, moreover, appealed to a number of mystics and anchorites who needed religious affiliation but could not live and work happily in any of the existing monasteries or religious houses. Among those of the late thirteenth century, the names of three members of the Franciscan Third Order are outstanding: St. Margaret of Cortona (d. 1279), Pier Pellinagno, the comb-maker of Siena made immortal by Dante (d. 1289),[77] and Bl. Angela of Foligno.

This desire on the part of the penitents for lay autonomy and their occasional involvement in heretical currents were among the considerations that caused the Franciscans as well as the Dominicans to be reticent toward the penitents and to hesitate before taking them under their wing.[78] Living, then, in the shadow of the mendicants—frequently close to their newly established convents—the penitents in turn influenced and were influenced by the friars. Using their own homes as a base, they became an important school of gospel perfection and leaven for the life of their times.

G. The Women's Movement

The new style of Christian life exemplified by the penitents was especially successful among women.[79] In spite of the prevailing negative view of women, which saw them as inferiors and the principal agents of sin,[80] one of the most characteristic features of the religious life in the twelfth and thirteenth centuries is the active presence of women who did not limit themselves to domestic chores but operated and manifested themselves in public with great energy and vitality. Women not only had leading roles in all the important religious movements but were also present in all the major heresies of the period.[81] Even the official church was subsequently to acknowledge women's significance by increasing their number in the pantheon of saints and the beatified.[82]

Increased opportunities for education also played a part in the gradual emancipation of medieval women. The most notable examples of the high level of culture some of them achieved (in particular those in convents) were the reading and writing of devotional literature. Considerable evidence from the saints' lives during this period indicates that many of them could read prayerbooks, liturgical manuals, or other works of devotional literature. In some instances they even went to great effort later in life to learn how to do so—and if they themselves could not read they had access to those who could. Furthermore, prompted by an impulse and a call to communicate their experience, medieval women excelled in the writing of visionary literature. According to Peter Dronke, "it is to women that we owe some of the highest flights of mystical poetry in the Middle Ages."[83] The same could be said for women's achievements in prose, either in Latin or in the vernacular.[84] Of incalculable import, also—but not easily verifiable—is the role played by wives, mothers, widows, and women in religious life in the oral transmission of religious ideas during this period.

The status of women in the Middle Ages is a complex one but it was, as I have begun to indicate, in the religious sphere that they achieved the most noteworthy success. As Caroline Walker Bynum observes, "for the first time in Christian history, we can identify a

36

women's movement (the Beguines) and can speak of specifically female influences on the development of piety."[85]

The breakdown of feudalism brought about a decline of traditional monasteries and even, to some extent, of the new foundations. Between 1180 and 1230, as I have already observed, there occurred a rise of forms of religious life more adapted to the lay state, and, as Roberto Rusconi points out, "there was a veritable 'rush' on the part of women to join them."[86] In the Low Countries, for instance, great numbers of women, who became known as Beguines (and men, known as Beghards), congregated in more or less organized communal arrangements that allowed for a noncloistered combination of prayer and work—a new form of religious life that repudiated traditional ones they considered deficient and outdated.[87] Groups of this same type soon made their appearance in the Rhineland and were later to be found in France and Italy, and as far afield as Spain, Sweden, Austria, Poland, and Hungary.[88]

The spirituality of the primitive Beguines had a strong resemblance to Franciscan spirituality, which it preceded and, in many instances, blended with.[89] The Beguine program was based on the gospel and the apostolic church (*vita apostolica*) and it was characterized by the espousal of chastity and poverty, affective devotion to the humanity of Christ, extreme forms of asceticism, and an ardent love of the Eucharist. Meditating on the sufferings of Christ motivated conversion and subsequent desire to "follow naked the naked Christ," a leitmotif of the entire period.[90] Inspired by the writings of St. Augustine and St. Anselm, but above all by St. Bernard and later Cistercians, Beguine spirituality was also influenced by currents from the Greek Fathers and apocryphal literature.

Beguines, at times, developed eremitical tendencies and elaborated a strong nuptial mysticism that occasionally took on a clearly erotic bent. At other times, they found outlets for their zeal in personal service to the poor and the sick or through the founding of hospitals and leprosariums —or combined both ecstatic encounter and service to the needy.

In Italy similar associations existed, but there seemed to have been a preference on the part of the laity—including the women—to sanctify themselves in their own homes, as demonstrated by the success and the diverse manifestations of the penitential movement. In some cases, with —and occasionally without—the authority of the bishop or local clergy, they "incarcerated" themselves and lived from the work of their hands or on the alms given to them. Alone or with one or two companions, they would live in reclusion for long or brief intense periods, either at the close periphery or along the walls of a city, in hovels or towers; or if within the city, normally, in modest houses, given for such a purpose by relatives or benefactors, often near a church or convent.[91]

H. Franciscan Women

The success of the Franciscan movement among these groups need not astonish us, considering the impact that the Franciscan preaching had on the laity. Women were especially sensitive to it. However, neither St. Francis nor for that matter St. Dominic, his contemporary, had initially intended to found a women's religious order, far less spearhead a women's movement. Even if, as Jacques le Goff points out, "there is in St. Francis and in the Franciscanism of the thirteenth century a place accorded to women not encountered in the same degree and with the same perspective in any other religious milieu of the epoch outside the Beguines,"[92] the Minorites, nonetheless, were initially diffident toward women, and Francis himself admonished his brothers not to meddle in their affairs.[93] Moreover, the itinerant way of life the friars followed was hardly adaptable to the options available to women during the period.

Among the women who associated themselves with the early Franciscan movement, St. Clare (1193/4–1253), of course, holds pride of place. Far more than simply "the little plant" of Francis, as she has been usually presented, Clare is a powerful personality in her own right. Hers is an original and indispensable contribution, the feminine dimension of the Franciscan charism. The importance of Clare and the small group of women who assembled around her at San Damiano is so great that without her it is impossible to fully understand the strength of the force for the renewal of both church and society exerted by St. Francis and the Franciscan movement.[94]

The Poor Clares, however, were soon constrained, as were all the monasteries of the time, by the increasingly stringent limitations of the cloistered life. Toward the latter half of the thirteenth century, church legislation became more strict with regard to monastic enclosure in a way that perhaps had not been foreseen by monastic founders.[95] This hardening on the part of church authorities, and even more importantly, the new spiritual needs arising within a society in the throes of change, spurred devout women to seek alternative outlets for their aspirations. Thus, as I have noted, an incalculable number of devout women found that among the Beguines, the recluses, and the various spontaneous forms of the penitential movement, they could serve God and the church in a way no longer possible in monasteries of either the ancient or the more recent type.

Among those who associated themselves more or less with the Franciscan current, two tendencies can be noted. One was characterized by a gospel life lived in proximity to and at the service of the poor. St. Elisabeth of Hungary is the one who best exemplifies this ideal. Another and even more important tendency shifted the emphasis from service to the poor (even though this was usually present) to individual asceticism and contemplation. Bl. Umiliana dei Cerchi, St. Douceline of Aix en Provence, St. Clare of Montefalco, St. Rose of Viterbo, St. Margaret of Cortona (also noted for her role as a peacemaker), Bl. Angela of Foligno, and countless others are examples of this trend.[96]

I. Mystical Flowering

Even if it involved only an elite, mysticism flourished among the religious women of the period we are looking at.[97] As André Vauchez observes: "At the end of the Middle Ages mystical union was to become the royal road of feminine holiness."[98] The current boom in studies of the medieval mystics, in particular the women, has contributed greatly to our understanding not only of the magnitude of the phenomenon, but also the complexity of its distribution. I can only touch here on some of the variety of the mystical experiences, the main spiritual currents these ecstatic and visionary women drew on, made their own, and expanded as they ascended the mystical ladder. Often these currents blended into one another—as well as with heterodox ones—and flowed daringly far from their original sources.

Certainly, that for which the term *Brautmystik* (bridal mysticism) has been coined or *Minnemystik* (love mysticism)—the love affair of the soul with God expressed by bridal imagery drawn from the *Song of Songs*—was a dominant trend, particularly among the Beguines, where this erotic mysticism coalesced with the notion of courtly love. This theme had been initiated by Bernard of Clairvaux, and developed by William of St. Thierry and the Victorines, but many medieval women mystics such as Mechthild of Magdeburg, Beatrice of Nazareth, and Hadewijch experienced and articulated their espousals with the Beloved in ways far more daring and explicit than the tradition that preceded them.

Another trend closely allied to love mysticism, and even intertwined with it, was what has become known as *Wesenmystik*, essence mysticism. Basic to this kind of mysticism is the concept that the soul in its ascent toward mystical union—an ascent described in intellectual and apophatic categories—must be emptied ("be annihilated" or "made poor"), so that the divine image be restored in it. At the summit, the mystic becomes united, "one in spirit" (*sine medio*) with the divine essence, "the One who is." The sources for this particular form of mysticism are difficult to track down, but it seems to have drawn its inspiration from Neoplatonic influences found in some Greek Fathers (in particular Maximus the Confessor, the Pseudo-Dionysius), and later rethought by John Scotus Eriugena. The outstanding representatives of this type of mysticism—which anticipated many of the themes and expressions long credited to Eckhart and Ruusbroec—were Hadewijch and Marguerite Porete.[99] The most prominent representatives of both essence and bridal mysticism affirmed, too, the primacy of love over intellect as a means of access to deep union with God,[100] a union that also found its fruition in the Trinitarian life; God-Love is indissociably Being and Trinity.

In describing the highest states of mystical union, using a wide variety of images and metaphors, some Beguine mystics (e.g., Hadewijch and Marguerite Porete)—and, as we shall see, Angela of Foligno —were so innovative that they provoked the suspicion of the official church. Both because this new tendency seemed to deny any intermediary between God and self at the heights of mystical union and because some of their tenets seemed or were thought to resemble those held by the heretics of the Free Spirit—which undermined the mediation of the church, the sacraments, and the virtues—the Beguines were massively condemned at the Council of Vienne (1311–1312), and one of them, Marguerite Porete, was burned as a heretic in Paris, in 1310.[101]

Representatives of bridal mysticism, but especially of essence mysticism, produced the most sophisticated and poetic descriptions of medieval women's mystical experience. Nonetheless, the majority of women mystics (especially in Italy), including those of the Beguine current just mentioned, found their nourishment and articulated the manner of their ascent to God by drawing from the mainly Franciscan diffusion of devotion to the humanity of Christ and identification with him, focusing in particular on his cross and passion. This form of mysticism has been described by Ewert Cousins as "mysticism of the historical event": a form of consciousness in which, through meditation accompanied by harsh ascetical practice, events of Christ's life, in particular the drama of his passion, are reenacted from within, incorporated by the mystic, and find fruition in an often startling variety of ecstatic states and paranormal phenomena.[102] These bodily repercussions of mystical states represented palpable realities of God's saving presence, a virtual musical scale of spiritual gradations, the range of which has not yet been fully inventoried and interpreted.[103]

The emphasis on the pathetic elements of Christ's humanity was fostered by a veritable torrent of devotional literature (e.g., *Meditations on the Life of Christ*[104]), pictorial imagery, sermons, poems, and treatises that related and amplified the gospel passion narrations in minute detail. Many medieval women mystics, as well as many men (e.g., Bonaventure, Suso), were attracted to this form of imaginative representation—they liked their Christ bleeding—which often aroused and triggered conversion and mystical consciousness.[105] This form of what has also been termed "passion mysticism"[106] often blended with bridal mysticism, and even with essence mysticism, as was the case for instance for Hadewijch, Beatrice of Nazareth, and Angela of Foligno.

It is significant to note, finally, that much of what we know of women mystics during this period comes from the pen of male writers. It was often men, especially members of the mendicant Orders, to whom these visionary women transmitted an amplified echo of their message. If initially ambivalent toward them, monks and friars came to see in these ecstatic women the possibility of pushing forward their own conceptions of holiness centered on mysticism and contemplation. Thus, a considerable number of *Vitae* (more numerous in Italy than in any other region)—with recurrent hagiographical themes such as flight from the world, refusal of marriage, virginity, extreme asceticism, devotion to the suffering Christ, and a preoccupation with exceptional mystical states— were written by the monks and friars to preserve the memory and spread the cult of those women who came under their direction, even if sometimes only remotely.[107] For instance, among the Franciscans, Vito of Cortona wrote a life of Umiliana dei Cerchi, Guinta Bevegnati did the same for Margaret of Cortona, Béranger de Saint'Affrique for Clare of Montefalco, and Brother A. for Angela of Foligno.[108] These lives not only served to inspire and channel the devotion of the faithful by providing a model consensus, they also presented an ideological ideal with which to defend the Franciscans against the Dominicans and the secular clergy.[109] Associated with these women mystics of the late Middle Ages, then, we often find a secretary or biographer who also served as confessor or director.[110] The practice of spiritual direction and confession was central to the maturation—and also the control—of the religious and mystical experience of these devout women.

Finally, then, religious women, excluded from the ministry of the Word, became the instruments the Spirit utilized to transmit his message to the Christian community. In this way, medieval women attained a new state of emancipation, one that was both encouraged and feared and eventually met with increasing hostility (this is also the case with some male mystics, e.g., Eckhart). In the late Middle Ages, as this hostility intensified, many visionary women were subjected to charges of heresy and witchcraft. The suppression of the Beguines by the Council of Vienne, even if its decrees were not initially enforced, and the burning of Marguerite Porete, accused of the Free Spirit heresy, are cases in point.

In this larger context of women's piety and mysticism, Angela of Foligno was to make her confession to Brother Arnaldo, her astonished Franciscan confessor who was to put her revelations into writing. Before proceeding, it is important to consider Angela's roots in the late medieval culture specific to Foligno and the Umbrian valley, where her spiritual journey had its beginning and progression.

J. Foligno

Foligno—unlike most of the cities of Umbria, which for purposes of defense are perched on mountains and hills—lies on a great fertile plain, at the convergence of two small rivers, the Topino and the Menotre, tributaries of the Tiber. On one side the lower spurs of the Apennines rise up precipitously; on the other, the less imposing range of the Martano hills. In spite of its modest population (ca. 2,000 during the Middle Ages), the commune of Foligno became powerful as a booming commercial center because of its strategic location at the crossroads of the trade routes linking Ancona, Florence, and Pisa, and thus the hub of the traffic between the Adriatic and the Tyrrhenian seas.[111]

The period that followed Angela's conversion, however, was not an easy time for Foligno, though nothing of what happened is recorded in her *Book*. In April 1279, a devastating earthquake shook the commune and, three years later, a hailstorm was followed by a hurricane of such intensity that it tossed trees from one valley to the next, leaving many wounded in its wake. In the latter half of the thirteenth century, Foligno was also involved in a war with Perugia, the battles of which took place in two successive phases: 1282–1283 and 1287–1289. Foligno was pro-imperial (Ghibelline) and Perugia pro-papal (Guelf). What was at stake was the political and economic leadership of the Umbrian valley.[112]

Earthquakes and wars notwithstanding, during the thirteenth and the early part of the fourteenth century, Foligno was not only an important commercial center but, if one is to judge by the number of churches, convents, and religious groups and personalities that emerged, a thriving religious one as well, and, as such, a crossroads of the spiritual currents alive at the time.[113] The institutional church in this period seemed to participate in the economic euphoria that Foligno was enjoying, as evidenced by the results of a census (1295–1296), ordered by Bishop Berardo, to assess the wealth of ecclesiastical property in his diocese, which included the very rich monastery of San Sassovivo.[114] It is not surprising that, in reaction, the mendicants and other reform groups were present in significant numbers.

Among the mendicants, the Franciscan presence predominates. St. Francis himself had passed through Foligno, seven miles from Assisi, a number of times.[115] In his youth, he had sold a piece of fine cloth and a horse that belonged to his father in the marketplace there, in order to procure the money necessary to restore the dilapidated church of San Damiano in Assisi. By 1255, the Franciscans occupied the old communal palace and, shortly thereafter, the friary of San Matteo, later entitled San Francesco. In 1282, the Umbrian province of St. Francis, to which the Foligno friary belonged, counted fifty-five friaries. Close by, in the numerous hermitages of the Umbrian valley and in the Marches, the memory of St. Francis was kept alive by some of his early companions: Angelo (d. 1258), Giles (d. 1262), Rufino (d. 1270), and Leo (d. 1271).[116]

Also circling in Foligno's orbit were friars of the dissident wing of the Franciscan family, the Spirituals.[117] Angelo of Clareno had several groups of followers in the region. One of his most important contacts was an Augustinian hermit, Gentile of Foligno, with whom he exchanged letters.[118] Gentile translated into the vernacular Clareno's Latin translation of John Climacus's *The Ladder of Divine Ascent*, and headed a *bizzochaggio* (a Beguine-like community) in Foligno in league with other Spirituals and the Fraticelli. Ubertino of Casale, who credited his conversion to Angela—of which more will be said later—circulated in Umbria and played a leading role in the ferment dividing the Franciscan community. Likewise, not far from Foligno lived the fiery Jacopone da Todi, the poet of the Spirituals. There are many affinities in his writings to those of Angela—they were kindred spirits—but there are no records that would indicate these two ever met. The Augustinians, the Servites, and the Dominicans were the other male mendicants who were established in Foligno during Angela's lifetime.

The presence of the women's penitential movement is more difficult to trace. Recent research increasingly demonstrates, as I have previously indicated, parallels between the semi-religious life-style and observances of the Beguines of Northern Europe and similar groups (*bizzocaggi*) in central Italy; the latter, however, were less sharply definable.[119] For instance, according to the research of Maria Sensi, there were, in Foligno, three such communities or groups—St. Maria 'de charitate,' St. Caterina delle vergini, St. Maria 'de Caresta'—which began as loosely organized penitential communities, but were institutionalized during this period and became part of the Order of the Damianites, or the Poor Clares.[120] Five others were likewise institutionalized and adopted the Augustinian Rule, and three of these communities, again according to Sensi, were in rapport with the cultural ambience of the Bl. Angela. Finally, one of them, S. Maria di Valle Verde, was a *bizzochagio* founded by the Second Order of the Servites, a women's congregation born in Marseilles. Their presence was conceivably a consequence of the commercial exchange between Provence and Foligno.[121]

The thread that connects the flow of ideas between Provence and Foligno is a slender one, but documentary evidence available shows that women adherents of the Olivi circle of Spirituals established themselves in Umbria—either before or after the condemnation of the Spirituals and the Beguines—and played an important role.[122] For instance, it is recorded that a Beguine from Carcassonne was part of the community of Clare of Montefalco, a community that closely resembled the style initiated by the Beguines, a style parallel to and perhaps in close rapport with that adopted by the circle of disciples that Angela headed.[123] Clare's sympathy for the Spirituals is well documented. Even if his role is obscure, Cardinal James of Colonna, also a noted friend of the Spirituals, was to extend his protection to Clare, as well as to the Bl. Angela, whose writings he later approved.[124]

Likewise noted in the Umbrian valley was the presence of other popular reform movements such as the Flagellanti, the Fraticelli, and, most notably, the sect of the Spirit of Freedom,[125] all (including some of the Spirituals) more or less arrogating to themselves the freedom that was supposed to accompany the Third Age, the "Age of the Spirit," promised by Joachim of Fiore. Both St. Clare of Montefalco and the Bl. Angela were to condemn adherents of the Spirit of Freedom sect in no uncertain terms. Even Ubertino of Casale, in his *Arbor vitae crucifixae Jesu,* was to denounce the errors of this heresy, which was present, according to him, among the members of the Community[126]—an accusation that some members of the Community countercharged by arguing that this heresy was instead practiced by the Spirituals. As for the influence of Joachim of Fiore, his ideas were certainly in circulation but the diffusion of his writings in Umbria is not easily verifiable at the present stage of research.[127]

In this complex web of spiritual currents and religious personalities circulating in Umbria and in Foligno during Angela's lifetime, the presence of a great number of both male and female hermits or recluses living either in the cities or in the countryside (and occasionally, as did Angela, with one or two companions) is also pertinent.[128] Aside from the Franciscans, the beatification by popular acclamation of the Beghard Giovanni da Casalina, who died on March 13, 1292, in Foligno, forcefully demonstrates that this eremitical movement was not an isolated phenomenon. His tomb immediately became a pilgrimage center, and a chapel was erected in his honor and indicated on a map of 1306. More directly related to Angela was the recognition a few years later, again by popular acclamation, of the sanctity of Bl. Pietro Crisci, whom Angela mentions in the eighteenth step of the *Memorial* ("Before, I used to make fun of a certain Petruccio, but now I could not do otherwise than follow his example"). The latter had renounced his fortune and title of nobility to live in such austere poverty that it aroused the suspicion of the Inquisition. His orthodoxy was acknowledged and a biography of his life was written subsequently by a Dominican, Brother Giovanni Gorini, in 1364.[129]

Near where Angela lived was the Franciscan church she frequented and the friary of San Francesco. As Sensi observes, this friary was "from the end of the thirteenth century indisputably one of the strong centers of the Spirituals."[130] Its guardian was Brother Francesco Damiani of Montefalco, brother of St. Clare of Montefalco. Brother A., Angela's confessor, was also a member of it for a while. Likewise, Paoluccio Trinci, as well as other leaders of the reform of the Observants, were later on to spring from it. In 1390, almost totally blind, Trinci had left his severe eremitical life at Brugliano to reside in Foligno. There he often visited the tomb of the Bl. Angela, whom he greatly admired.[131]

Finally, attached to San Francesco was a fraternity of men and women of the Order of Penance, founded in 1270, and inspired by Franciscan convictions, as well as influenced by the current of the Spirituals and the Fraticelli.[132] As yet very little is known about this fraternity, which Angela was part of, as her *Memorial* declares,[133] and in which she subsequently played such a major role as spiritual mother. As Mario Sensi concludes:

> How desirable it would be to know from Angela's text, or from other sources, the names and the roles of all those who were part of our beata's circle. Unfortunately, the available documentation on this underground Franciscanism, transparently obvious in almost every line of her *Book*, is especially deficient.[134]

The Formation of Angela's *Book*

Angela's *Book,* in particular the *Memorial,* like other mystical records, narrates a mediated experience. It is an interpretation-laden account, language about the experience of God, and not the experience itself. There are three narrators: God speaks and reveals himself to Angela, and she in turn speaks to Arnaldo, who, as the prologue to the *Memorial* affirms, then narrates what he hears. At the end both claim that it is God who signed the book.[135] Even if, then, it is Angela who is the epiphany of the Other, Brother Arnaldo played such a central role in her life as her confessor, scribe, and, eventually, her disciple that he and his complex redactional procedure merit special attention.

A. Brother Arnaldo, Angela's Confessor and Scribe

Biographical data on Arnaldo, unfortunately, are even more limited than those on Angela. We do not even know his name with certainty. The approbation that accompanies the *Memorial* simply refers to "a certain trustworthy Friar Minor who wrote, with utmost care and devotion, what was dictated to him by a certain follower of Christ." A later tradition attributed the name Arnaldo to the author of the *Memorial,* a name I have reluctantly adopted for convenience.[136]

What we do know about Arnaldo from the *Memorial* is that he was a native of Foligno and Angela's relative, confessor, and principal counselor.[137] At the time of her conversion, it seems he was also the chaplain of the bishop of Foligno, most likely Berardo of Attignano, and a member of the Franciscan friary attached to the church of San Francesco in Foligno.[138] Later, when Angela made her memorable pilgrimage to Assisi, we find him then a member of the Sacro Convento friary in Assisi. Shortly after this event, he was reassigned to the friary in Foligno and was perhaps even subsequently elected guardian of the community.[139] Furthermore, the *Memorial* mentions that, at one point, he took a trip to Lombardy,[140] and the instructions record that he was present on at least one of the pilgrimages Angela made to Assisi.[141]

As I have noted, it is only after what happened in Assisi that he started to write the *Memorial*. For some unspecified reason, Angela had not previously disclosed to him what had taken place in her life during the six years that elapsed between her conversion and the beginning of the redaction of the *Memorial*—thus Arnaldo's stupefaction and suspicion when, at his insistence, she began to dictate to him, first the extraordinary Assisi event, then the first twenty steps of her journey. As an added precaution to assure himself of her sanity (he feared she was under the spell of "an evil spirit") and orthodoxy, he told Angela that he would submit everything she told him to the judgment of "some wise and spiritual men who would never have heard of her."

Arnaldo asserts, on a number of occasions, that once having set himself to the task at hand, he was very scrupulous in taking down what Angela was telling him in her Umbrian dialect, which he in turn would hastily translate into Latin. At the close of his work, he declares:

> I took the greatest care to note accurately her very own words, as well as I could grasp them, not wanting to write anything more after I had left her. I did not know how to go about writing anything afterward, for I was very careful and fearful lest I might perhaps add something, even a single word, that she had not really said. Furthermore, I always reread to her what I wrote, repeating it many times, so that I would be sure to take down only her very own words.

When he would reread his notes to Angela, she would carefully point out that there were many weaknesses in his redaction but nothing "false or superfluous." Arnaldo felt these weaknesses keenly. Some ten times he asserts that what he had written was a short and defective version of what he had heard. He compares himself to "a sieve or sifter which does not retain the precious and refined flour but only the most coarse." Of the sublime words, he was able to note only the meanest part. One time when he reread his text to Angela, she, on her part, protested that "she did not recognize it"; that what he had written was "dry and without any savor" and did not convey the meaning she intended.

Indeed, the sublimity of Angela's revelations did not lend itself to facile transcription. Arnaldo often acknowledges that her revelations exceeded his ability to understand and report them accurately. He humbly admits that he did not have the quality of soul necessary for the task at hand. Occasionally, after meeting Angela in church, he would experience a writing block. Realizing that something was troubling his conscience, he would go to confession and when he returned, the words would begin to flow again. Furthermore, while he was taking down what Angela was telling him, he did not always have the time to consistently change, as he intended, to the third person what he heard her say in the first. Also, when he could not come up with the adequate Latin equivalent, he would leave the Umbrian words exactly as he heard them fresh from Angela's mouth.[142]

Another difficulty arose when, at one point of his redaction, some friars began to murmur against him because of all the time he was spending with his woman penitent. They complained first to the guardian, then to the minister provincial (Angelo of Perugia), about the situation. The latter for a time forbade Arnaldo to continue his colloquies with Angela in the church and from that time onward (ca. 1294), he could see her only "very occasionally." During this period, as a consequence, for the fifth supplementary step, Arnaldo resorts to the expedient of sending a young boy to take down what Angela said. When later he was to show this text to Angela she begged him "to destroy it rather than transcribe it in such a state." Notwithstanding her objections, "after translating it into Latin," he inserted this section in the *Memorial* as such, "adding nothing, somewhat like a painter painting, because I did not understand it."

At the close of the *Memorial*, "after he had written almost everything which can be found in this small book," Arnaldo wanted a final assurance that he had been faithful to his task. He besought Angela to pray, asking God to make known if he "had written anything false or superfluous." To which Angela responded that she herself had for a long time and very often asked for this grace: "And God answered me that 'everything which has been written is in conformity with my will and comes from me.'" Then God also added: "I will put my seal to it."

Finally, Arnaldo took one last precaution: "The Lord saw to it that two other trustworthy friars, acquainted with Christ's faithful one, read the text and heard directly from her everything which I had written.

They examined everything and even engaged in frequent discussions with her. And what is more, God granted them the grace to be certain of its validity, and, by word and deed, they bear faithful witness to it."

After finishing his redaction, Arnaldo, in turn, submitted all or most of the *Memorial,* as the approbation at the beginning of the *Book* indicates, to Cardinal James Colonna and a number of Franciscan theologians for ecclesiastical approval. Faloci Pulignani and Doncoeur set this date in 1297, and Thier and Calufetti (editors of the critical edition) before 1298, thus anterior to Colonna's break with Boniface VIII and while Angela was still alive. Ferré establishes it between 1309 and 1310, with the hypothesis that Ubertino of Casale had a role to play in its approbation.[143] Since Arnaldo, according to these same scholars, quite likely died in 1300, the former date is the more plausible. If the hypothesis advanced by Thier and Calufetti of a second redaction of the *Memorial* is valid, Arnaldo very likely wrote it after the approbation or did not submit it as part of his original text. According to another hypothesis proposed by Thier and Calufetti, he was also responsible for the first twelve instructions according to the sequence of manuscript B (a different sequence from that followed by their edition and my translation), which preserves the chronology of the original composition.[144]

Nothing is known about where or how Arnaldo died. A passage from instruction 26 seems to say that he celebrated his last Mass in the presence of Angela during a pilgrimage to the Portiuncula in Assisi on the Feast of the Indulgence, probably during the summer of 1300, and died shortly thereafter. This date seems to be more certain than that proposed by the *Martyrologium Franciscanum,* the Franciscan chronicler Luke Wadding, as well as the historiographer of Umbrian saints, Jacobili, all of whom set his death in 1313, and refer to him as Blessed.[145]

Thanks to Arnaldo, then, and his scrupulous concern to report Angela's spiritual journey as faithfully as possible, even if his record does not contain all the richness of her experience, we have in the *Memorial* a text that, for the most part, merits great trust. Something more, however, needs to be said of Arnaldo's role as spiritual director, the influence he exercised on Angela during the eleven years or so she was his penitent, and, finally, his redactional procedures and their effects on the text at hand.

Arnaldo emerges from the pages of the *Memorial* as a man of duty committed to accomplishing his mission once it had been entrusted to him. "I was utterly compelled by God to write," he was to repeat. As chaplain to a bishop he was undoubtedly a man with a good theological education. He mentions at one point that he has been reading Augustine. His attitude toward Angela was initially one of suspicion and reserve, perhaps because he shared a commonly held, almost visceral distrust of visions and private revelations, especially when related by a woman. Only gradually did he grow in reverence and awe before the astonishing revelations to which he was privy. When he was prohibited by his superiors from further meetings with Angela in church, he exclaimed: "If only they knew what good things she was saying." Moved as he was by the spectacle of Angela's story, and respectful of it, nonetheless, throughout the *Memorial* we find him constantly questioning, pressing for clarity, and even at times using Scripture, reprimanding his penitent (rarely is the role reversed). Arnaldo's faithful and demanding masculine presence thus served as a significant catalyst in Angela's development, calling on her to discriminate and focus inner meanings, as well as to articulate and name more clearly and precisely what she was experiencing. Moreover, as a representative of church tradition, Arnaldo performed the important function of certifying the authenticity and basic soundness of Angela's spiritual journey: a bridge between institution and praxis.

It is difficult to ascertain to what extent Arnaldo, as spiritual director, influenced the practice of Angela's daily life or her thinking. The only indication we have of the former in the *Memorial* is that, at one point early in her conversion, he objects to Angela's desire to rid herself of more of her belongings. As to his immediate influence on her thinking—and surely there was some—there is little direct external evidence of it in the dialogues recorded in the *Memorial*. As Giorgio Petrocchi points out, "In the stronger moments, marked by raw narrative realism, the interventions of Arnaldo must have been none, or almost none."[146] Clearly, throughout the narrative, Angela's personality dominates and Arnaldo remains in the background.

However, Arnaldo is more than simply a scribe, dutifully reporting Angela's story and witnessing to its authenticity. Even if it is Angela's book, he is in many ways the artisan of its composition and, as such, a co-protagonist of her communications from God. Even if his intent is to report as faithfully as possible what she told him, he nonetheless is responsible for the internal organization of her account, often juxtaposing the material of his notes without a clear link among parts. He admits that he did not always record all of her experience, either because he did not understand all that she told him, or because, as a result of his haste or the opposition from his Franciscan brothers, he did not have time to put

51

it down. Furthermore, especially with regard to the seven supplementary steps, he not only reorganizes the material he has at his disposal, but also admits inserting only what he considered "most fitting and appropriate." What is certainly clear is that the text was written in stages, and reworked in the midst of numerous interruptions.

A close reading of the text of the *Memorial* gives us further clues to Arnaldo's redactional procedure, and how Angela's words were filtered by him. If, as previously indicated, the text often bears the mark of the immediacy of Angela's spoken language, it is at other times clearly quite removed from the initial transcription. What may indeed have taken place, at least for some parts of the text, is that Arnaldo first of all took down in the vernacular—in the fifth supplementary step he explicitly mentions that a section of the text was initially written in the vernacular —what Angela told him, repeated it to her in the vernacular, then translated it into Latin. Possibly later, after reviewing his transcription, he wrote the definitive and more polished Latin text. This redactional procedure seems to be especially evident in the sixth and seventh supplementary steps. Seemingly intent on crowning his effort, he deduces the doctrine, establishes synchronisms, and is generally more attentive to composition. If the hypothesis of a second redaction (to be discussed shortly), written most likely by Arnaldo at a later date, is correct, it further clouds the picture of what comes from Angela and what is due to Arnaldo's emendations.

Thus if Angela's personality and mystical experiences dominate the book, Arnaldo's role remains essential not only in facilitating Angela's story, but also in making it available to us. He was a good and faithful scribe and also, as Ferré observes, "a very great director."[147] Although there is no conclusive textual evidence, it is quite likely that, as Angela grew in stature, the roles were reversed until she became the spiritual mother and he the disciple. It is quite possible that she addressed an important letter (instruction 8), concerning the need to grow in conformity to the suffering Christ, to Arnaldo while he was sick and near death in 1300.

Instruction 26 serves as a fitting climax to what we know of Angela's scribe and confessor. It reports that after this "intimate son" had celebrated his last Mass in Angela's presence and obtained, through her intercession, a special blessing and remission of sins, accompanied by the intercession of St. Francis in his favor, Brother A. "took off his capuche, bowed his head and wept."

B. The Two-Redaction Theory

The hypothesis proposed by Thier and Calufetti, the editors of the critical edition, of a double redaction of the original Latin text of Angela's *Book* has already been alluded to in this Introduction and is mentioned in the notes. After having examined the twenty-eight manuscripts (either in Latin or in the vernacular) at their disposition and classified them into seven families, Thier and Calufetti reach the conclusion that there were basically two redactions: an initial minor one, and another major and more complete one, written later at an unspecified moment, but probably after the approbation of the text by Cardinal Colonna and a number of Franciscan theologians (tentatively dated 1298) and before the death in 1300 of Arnaldo, the presumed redactor of both versions.[148] Their reconstruction of the first redaction is based primarily on the first family of manuscripts (B), all found in the Brussels area (fifteenth century); the second is based on the second family, the oldest and most basic manuscript of which is the Assisi codex (A) (1381), accompanied by, among others, the S. Isidoro-Roma (I) (end of fourteenth century), and the more complete Subiaco (S) (1496) codices. In this second family, an Italian manuscript, the Trivulziana of Milan (M) (beginning of the fifteenth century), is of great importance for the reconstruction of the Latin second redaction because it is based on an ancient lost codex— perhaps the original Latin codex.[149] For the final critical text, both redactions were also modified by changes adopted from the third, sixth, and seventh families of manuscripts.[150]

The arguments used by Thier and Calufetti to substantiate the two-redaction theory are complex and cannot be fully discussed here.[151] Their claim is based on a close analysis of the manuscript tradition and the fact that the second redaction contains characteristics typical of a later redactional effort, including: (a) a closer coordination of the existing text with the biographical and historical circumstances of Angela's life; (b) the inclusion of valuable material from other witnesses (e.g., the role of Angela's companion is amplified); (c) a better arrangement of the text according to thematic dependencies, with occasional subdivisions (e.g., the spiritual commentary of the seven ways in which God comes into the soul in the fifth supplementary step, and the section on divine darkness in the seventh); (d) minor changes in Angela's vocabulary to improve the style.[152]

Even if the two-redaction theory remains at the level of hypothesis,

INTRODUCTION

the indubitable merit of the work of Thier and Calufetti is that it has stabilized for the first time the critical text of Angela's writings.[153] Compared to the previous editions of Ferré, Doncoeur, and Faloci Pulignani, the changes in the text introduced in the text of the *Memorial* are minor, but the ordering and disposition of the *Instructions* are clearer and considerably improved. Abundant explanatory footnotes, along with the variants from other manuscripts, also enhance the value of this new text and edition.

The *Memorial*:
The Stages of
Angela's Inner Journey

The paucity of known outer events in Angela's life is amply compensated for by accounts of her inner experiences. It is through these that the astonishing singularity of her life becomes most strikingly apparent. Indeed, what makes the *Memorial* coherent is Angela's astonishing capacity to name the changes that take place in her life at each step of the way.

The material at hand, the imprints of the eternal in Angela's life, is abundant—even superabundant. Numerous visions, locutions, ecstasies, moments of awesome presence and dreadful absence, mediate the disclosure of the divine in her itinerary. I cannot hope here to cover everything. As a consequence, I will proceed as synthetically as possible, indicating only some of the major events and channels through which God chose to manifest himself to her, transform her, and lead her to the deep abysses of his life.[154]

In instruction 2 of the second part of her *Book*, Angela (or an unknown redactor) provides a helpful general framework for our presentation. Teaching the perils of spiritual love, she enumerates three basic transformations that God operates in the soul: (1) imitation of the works of the suffering God-man in whom is manifested God's will; (2) union with God accompanied by powerful feelings and consolation that, nonetheless, can find expression in words and thoughts; and (3) a most perfect union with God in which the soul feels and tastes God's presence in such a sublime way that it is beyond words and conception.[155]

INTRODUCTION

A. Imitation of the Works of the Suffering God-Man

The first arrows of God's love that pierced Angela struck fear in her soul. When she began on the road of penance, Angela's soul was in a state of chaos and disarray—a seething cauldron of undifferentiated emotion. In this Dantean "dark wood," fearing that she was being damned to hell, Angela took cognizance of her sins and wept profusely.

The beginning of the process of her conversion, then, had to do mainly with being graced with a painful awareness of her shadowy and sinful past, an acute fear that because of it she merited damnation. This is the only motive mentioned in the first step of the *Memorial,* but perhaps others, implicit and underlying, can be advanced to shed light on what triggered her break from the past and induced a departure toward a new life.

Angela was thirty-seven years old, more or less at the midpoint of her life, when her conversion took place. Dante, her contemporary, was thirty-five years old when he began the *Divine Comedy* with the following oft-quoted lines:

> Midway in the journey of our life
> I found myself in a dark wood,
> for the straight way was lost.
>
> Ah, how hard it is to tell
> what that wood was, wild, rugged, harsh;
> the very thought of it renews the fear!
>
> It is so bitter that death is hardly more so.[156]

Due caution must be exercised in transposing contemporary psychological insights to medievals whose life rhythm was different from ours. Nonetheless, it is conceivable that part of Angela's conversion was initiated by the experience of disorientation and anguish, the "dark wood" of the midlife crisis. Her sense of the shallowness of her previous existence, the futility and confusion of the present one, and the torment arising from the religious question (which often surges to the forefront of consciousness if it has been previously repressed) could have contributed to induce her to reorient her life and bring about a religious awakening—for pious and devout in her past life she certainly was not.

Although Angela says not a word about them, the political and social agitations taking place at the time, the anxiety-ridden atmosphere, and the wars between Foligno and Perugia—which I have previously noted—could also have had an indirect bearing on her decision to reform her life. An abyss was created in which to await the salvation of a personal wound actuated by and indissociable from a social one.[157]

It is not to be ruled out, either, that the example and preaching of the Franciscans nearby or passing through could have led Angela to examine her conscience and inspire her to straighten out her life. Furthermore, a certain nobleman of Foligno, Pietro Crisci (called by everyone "Petruccio")—who at this time himself had just converted, distributed his goods to the poor, and adopted an eremitical life of strict poverty (he lived in a tower)—seems to have provided an important role model for Angela in the choices she was to make.[158] Finally, it is significant to note that at the onset of her conversion, Angela turned to St. Francis, who appeared to her in a dream (in the form of an elderly friar), and asked him to find her a good confessor to whom she could unburden herself. The Poverello was to be a central source of inspiration throughout her journey. He appears to her in a number of visions recorded in the *Memorial* and in the second part of her *Book*. He is the model who supplied Angela's life with meaning and pattern along the path of gospel perfection. Indeed, at one point he told her, "You are the only one born of me" (instruction 21). It is conceivable that the powerful archetypal force of his example, so fresh in the memory of the Umbrian populace, was the touchstone that sparked her own beginnings.

The above considerations, however, remain hypothetical, for, to repeat, all that we know from the *Memorial* is that in the first step Angela became aware of her sinfulness, feared being damned to hell, and wept bitterly.

The initial phases of Angela's development (steps one to seven) were characterized by painful struggle and effort—a season of purification through suffering—wherein she was enabled to reorient her affectivity, strip herself of all her possessions, and gradually yield her heart to Christ, who, through the mediation of his crucifixion, was manifesting God's love to her. It was indeed the crucified Christ who increasingly granted Angela, on the one hand, knowledge of her false and sinful self, and, on the other hand, the experience of God's goodness, his forgiveness, and the healing of bitter memories.

In these early stages (steps seven to seventeen), visions of the Crucified increasingly quickened Angela's journey. Her inner lens became more and more focused as the ties with her newfound lover were intensified. She "*looks* at the cross"; "*stands* at the foot of it to find refuge";

"*sees*" the wounds of Christ "while asleep and awake"; "*enters* into the sorrow over Christ's passion suffered by the mother of Christ and St. John"; *sees* Christ's heart; *places* her mouth to the wound in his side, and "*drinks* from the blood freshly flowing from it"; *fixes* her attention on the sorrow over Christ's passion suffered by the mother of Christ and St. John in order to experience it herself.

In the seventeenth step, the quality of Angela's faith took a quantum leap. She says of this step that the Blessed Virgin gave her a faith that was different from the one she had before. "In contrast to what I now experienced," she adds, "my former faith had been lifeless and my tears forced." It would seem that what occurs in this step is Angela's definitive entrance and passage into the mystical state. To be sure, her journey up to this point had been mystical in nature. The step-by-step illuminations she had received to enlighten her way, the powerful visions of the crucified Christ, the beginnings of divine consolation that she had begun to taste, were all direct and immediate experiences of the presence of God. It was, however, only at this seventeenth step that she became conscious of having acquired a foothold, as it were, in the transcendental realm.

This step produced the effect of altering the quality of Angela's contemplation. Lifted to a new level of perception by means of the symbol of the cross, which unified and recollected her powers ("I enclosed myself within the passion of Christ"), she was now inwardly still enough to receive a new, hitherto inexperienced, inflow of divine life. In fact, she confessed that through visions, "beautiful dreams," and meditations on the Scriptures, she "began to experience the sweetness of God continually," and took such delight in divine favors that "she not only forgot the world but even herself." When describing the visions that occurred in this step, Angela speaks of being "led" into them. To her request, however, to remain in this state, God replied that what she was asking "was still not possible." Further maturation was necessary before the divine presence could settle itself more definitely in her.

As a result of her momentary but very powerful absorption into God, Angela's psyche was strung to such a high point of tension that whenever she heard God being mentioned, she shrieked. ·Likewise, whenever she saw paintings of the passion of Christ, she could hardly bear it, and fell feverish and sick (step eighteen). What Angela recalls as "the first great sensation of God's sweetness" occurred in the nineteenth step. Meditating on the divinity and humanity of Christ, she experienced such "a great consolation" that it completely overwhelmed her. She fell to the ground and lost her power of speech. Her companion, Masazuola, seeing her in this state thought she was "on the verge of death or already dead."

Graced with new purpose, Angela could no longer be content with half-measures. She desired to possess Christ totally: "I want neither gold nor silver," she prays, "even if you should offer me the whole universe, I would not be satisfied. I want only you." The response to Angela's passionate desire to find Christ far exceeded her expectations. The inner voice tells her: "Hurry, for as soon as you have finished what you have set out to do [the distribution of your belongings] the whole Trinity will come into you." Although she was stunned and doubted the veracity of the promise, by the end of the nineteenth step, we find her eagerly awaiting its fulfillment.

What we see happening in Angela in these first nineteen steps of the *Memorial* is her gradual surrender, bit by bit, to another relationship, the only one that could draw from her the immensity of love of which she was becoming capable. Although illumination begins as early as the fourth step, what predominated throughout is the purification, the necessary elimination of everything that stands in the way of progress toward union with her newfound lover. Set ablaze by Christ's love for her and feeling its heat, her soul "cries out and moans" like "a stone flung in the forge to melt it into lime, which crackles when it is licked by the flames, but after it is baked makes not a sound" (instruction 2).

More or less six years had by this time elapsed since Angela began the process of her conversion. It is impossible to determine how long "Christ's faithful one" remained in each of the nineteen steps we have covered of her journey, which Arnaldo recorded very succinctly. In the sixteenth step, she avows that she "lingered for a good while before she was able to move on to the next step. In some of the steps I lingered longer, and for a shorter time in others."

Angela's crossing of the threshold into temporary mystical union with Christ, which occurred toward the end of this period, dovetails with the second section of my presentation.

B. Union with God Accompanied by Powerful Feelings and Consolations That, Nonetheless, Can Find Expression in Words and Thoughts

The twentieth, or the first supplementary, step (Arnaldo, as I have noted, was lost in his notes at this point and condensed the remaining ten steps into seven) marks a high point of Angela's itinerary: the fulfillment of the promise of the indwelling of the Trinity in her soul. The theophany occurred while she was on pilgrimage to Assisi to implore St. Francis that he obtain from God a state in which she "might feel Christ's presence," receive "the grace of observing well" the Rule of the Third Order, which she had recently promised, and above all "become, and remain to the end, truly poor."

The full meaning of what took place on this pilgrimage seemed to disclose itself in Angela's consciousness (or at least in Arnaldo's reconstruction) in successive stages. In the initial numinous experience, which occurred while she was at a junction on the road to Assisi near Spello, what predominated was an awareness of the Holy Spirit, who promised her "a consolation which she had never tasted before." What followed was an awakening of her inner senses, a moment of rapture in which she saw the created universe resplendent with God's presence and herself as one with it. Afterward, along with a sense of the presence of the Holy Spirit, an intense feeling of the crucified Christ's presence accompanied her, as spellbound, she proceeded to the Basilica of St. Francis in Assisi. It was while she knelt before a stained-glass window depicting St. Francis being held closely by Christ that the theophany came to a stunning climax. Angela heard Christ telling her:

> Thus I will hold you closely to me and much more closely than can be observed with the eyes of the body. And now the time has come, sweet daughter, my temple, my delight, to fulfill my promise to you. I am about to leave you in the form of this consolation, but I will never leave you if you love me.

It was at this point, as she later related to Arnaldo, that Angela became fully conscious that the Holy Trinity had established a dwelling place in her: first the Holy Spirit, then Christ who was crucified for her, and finally the fullness of the Triune God, Father, Son, and Holy Spirit —"at once one, and a union of many." When pressed by Arnaldo to be more explicit about what she had seen, Angela said, "I saw something full of such immense majesty that words fail me to describe it, but it seemed to me that it was the All Good."

With this extraordinary vision Angela crossed another threshold of her mystical ascent. Now was the time of betrothal, the pledge of final union. Christ had also told her:

> You are holding the ring of my love. From now on you are engaged to me
> and you will never leave me. May the blessing of the Father, the Son, and
> the Holy Spirit be upon you and your companion.

Little wonder, then, that even if this vision withdrew itself "gently," and "gradually," the awestruck widow of Foligno began to shout and shriek almost inarticulately as she rolled on the pavement at the entrance to the basilica: "Love still unknown, why? why? why?" Hers is the cry of the wounded lover, the anguish over the departure of the Beloved, the totally Other, who had deigned to stoop down to her and now seems to slip from her grasp.

When she returned to Foligno, Angela continued to experience the aftereffects of this divine disclosure. She was enthralled and in a state of languor for eight days, hardly able to speak, move around, or "even say the Our Father." Masazuola, her companion, was witness to the outward visibility of this new state. She reported to Arnaldo that she had seen Angela in a state of ecstasy during which a magnificent star with rays of outstanding beauty emanating from her side, unfolding and coiling toward heaven. Angela's body, momentarily incandescent, was emitting signals of its redemption.

In the first five supplementary steps now under consideration, one finds a heightening of Angela's perception of Christ's passion, an ever-deepening penetration into the density of the mystery of the cross. In the great Assisi vision she had also been told that henceforth she would "experience the cross and the love of God within herself." It is as if, at this stage of her spiritual journey, she had acquired sufficient selfhood and had been so transformed by God's love that she no longer experienced the events of the cross as an onlooker, but as if she were reenacting Christ's passion in the inmost parts of her being from within the events themselves. As she herself often repeated, her mystical experience blossomed and unfolded from "within," that is, more and more in identity and union with Christ.

Among the visions that she experienced in these steps, Angela reports that once, while at Vespers and gazing upon the cross, she felt Christ within her, embracing her with the very arm with which he was crucified; at times, it seems to her that she enters into Christ's side: These were "such joyful experiences" that she could not put them into words. Another time, as, one by one, the great afflictions Christ suffered during his passion are enumerated, she says she saw "more of his passion than she had ever heard spoken of"; and when, meditating on the pain endured by Christ's soul, more acute than that of his body, she, in turn, was transformed into this pain and attained so much deeper a level of union with the crucified "that she found a peace in which she was content with everything." And on still another occasion, she reports that for three days she was stretched out on her bed and speechless while caught up in a vision of Christ and the Blessed Virgin in their glorified state. Finally, in a vision that took place on Holy Saturday, 1294, Angela entered into a mysterious communion with those events that took place in Christ during the Holy Triduum, a prelude to further such experiences. Rapt in spirit, she found herself in the sepulcher with Christ:

> She said that she first of all kissed his breast—and saw that he lay dead, with his eyes closed—then she kissed his mouth, from which a delightful fragrance emanated, one impossible to describe.... Afterward, she placed her cheek on Christ's own and he, in turn, placed his hand on her other cheek, pressing her closely to him.... Her joy was immense and indescribable.

The stunning identification and fusion with Christ crucified—and gradually with him in his glorified state—which expanded Angela's capacity to love, marks, then, these five supplementary steps of Angela's journey. To be sure, this expansion of love was accompanied by periods of doubt, temptation, persecution, and despair. The alternation of God's presence and absence—"the game of love" that God plays with the soul—caused Angela moments of great suffering and further purification. During this time, however, "Christ's faithful one" (as Arnaldo consistently calls her) was given to understand that these dark moments were of value as vehicles for her growth and development. If she suffered and wanted to suffer—even to die a martyr's death—she realized that such suffering had value not for its own sake but because of her love of the suffering Christ. Suffering thus quickened Angela's desire and became a means of expression and expansion. The more deeply she shared in its reality, the more certain she became that the divine life was present within her and that suffering is a necessary companion of love. It was the thread with which her joys were woven.

In the third supplementary step, Angela provides a startling example of the reality of suffering and Christ's power to transform it into sweetness. She and her companion had gone "to find Christ" among the lepers in the hospital in Foligno. After drinking from the water she used to wash the sores of one of the lepers, she reported that it was "so extremely sweet that it was as if I had received communion." The gesture is reminiscent of Francis's embrace of the leper, recorded in his Testament, as key to his conversion. For both Francis and Angela, Christ and the leper mutually inform one another as icons of divine disclosure. Angela, however, further radicalizes Francis's gesture. Shocking as it is to contemporary sensitivity, this embrace of abjection with what horrifies is, as Julia Kristeva, the noted French psychoanalyst and literary critic, puts it, "a fount of infinite jouissance."[159]

These five supplementary steps also record a number of visions connected with the Eucharist, the great sacrament of mystical experience for Angela as for so many other medieval mystics. She saw, for instance, the host resplendent with such beauty that "it surpassed the splendor of the sun." In another moment, "two most splendid eyes" gazed at her, extending beyond the edges of the host. In still another Eucharistic vision, she beholds the Christ Child magnificently adorned and seated on a throne. One such vision, disclosing the divine presence at the heart of all reality, merits special attention. Once, after receiving communion, God spoke to Angela as follows:

> "I want to show you something of my power." And immediately the eyes of my soul were opened, and in a vision I beheld the fullness of God's presence encompassing the whole of creation, that is, what is on this side and what is beyond the sea, the abyss, the sea itself, and everything else. And in everything that I saw, I could perceive nothing except the presence of the power of God, and in a manner totally indescribable. And my soul in an excess of wonder cried out: "This world is pregnant with God [*pregnans de Deo*]!"

Impressive and central as are these visions and colloquies with Christ crucified and those surrounding the Eucharist that mark these five steps, the formless visions that occurred during this period are even more striking and indicative of the mystical heights to which Angela had been elevated. In these Angela saw God in the attributes of some of his divine perfections, namely, Beauty, Wisdom, Power, Humility, Love, Will, Justice, and the All Good. Although not as graphically depicted as were the preceding ones, these experiences far exceed them in their suggestive and enticing power. The ineffable bursts alive in her, combining the transcendental and the personal, a state both sublime and totally inexpressible.

What Angela discovered through the transformations wrought by these five steps was the increasing assurance of God's tender and special love for her: "I love you more than any woman in the valley!" More intimately and securely she knows that "God is the love of the soul." In fact, "there is nothing in him but love and he requires nothing more of the soul than that it love him in return." More deeply united and identified with the love and will of Christ—his will and hers were "made one"—Angela became so certain of God's presence, and secure in the wisdom of his judgments, that near the end of the fifth supplementary step, she speaks of having attained simultaneously ("both together in a totally undescribable way") a true and complete knowledge of self—her poverty and nothingness—and a true and complete knowledge of the overwhelming goodness of God.

A dark night, however, loomed ahead. Her spiritual edifice had to collapse before the third transformation could occur: a perfect union with God in which the soul feels and tastes him in a sublime way that is beyond words and conception.

C. A Most Perfect Union with God That No Words or Thoughts Can Express

So total was Angela's integration at the conclusion of supplementary step five that one is taken aback by the complete breakdown in the sixth step, and in the seventh, her almost simultaneous propulsion to the summit of her mystical journey—the great visions of God in, with, and beyond the divine darkness.

Even if we put aside the density of the text itself, the analysis of these two final steps of Angela's journey is no simple matter, for the redactional problem is complex. Concerning the sixth step, for instance, Arnaldo himself confesses at the onset that he was at a loss to transcribe what was taking place in Angela at this point and was able "to write only some small part of her testimony of the sufferings she endured," because he "did not understand them sufficiently to write them." Angela likewise confesses that "the bodily ailments she endured were beyond description" and "the ailments and sufferings of her soul were even more beyond any kind of comparison." In his hesitation to record what he had heard, Arnaldo further admits waiting to write something about it until toward the end of the two-year period they lasted, when the torments had almost ceased and Angela was already in the state of the seventh step.[160] He even felt the need to check his observations with another "trustworthy" friar, whose testimony confirmed that everything Angela had said "and even more about the martyrdom she endured from these horrible torments was true."

Furthermore, in Arnaldo's understanding, the sixth step dovetails with the seventh—that of the dark visions of God and beyond. "This sixth step lasted but a short while, that is, about two years; it concurs with the seventh, the most wonderful step of all, which began shortly before it and which follows in my account."[161] Finally, the "horrible darkness" of the sixth step apparently faded, at least in its bodily repercussions, for Arnaldo observes "that what took place in this step faded in a brief space of time but not totally or completely, especially in regard to her numerous bodily ailments."[162]

A further complication stems from the redaction and compilation of the manuscript itself. According to the hypothesis of the editors of the critical edition, what is in the seventh step is the result of two redactions, one possibly written, as I have previously indicated, after the initial manuscript was presented to Cardinal Colonna and his group of examiners for approval, probably in 1297. In the editors' hypothesis this second, later redaction contains the greater part of the text of this step we have on hand—in particular, the section dealing with the great visions of God in and with darkness. If this is correct, it is possible, then, that what Arnaldo transcribed contains a fair amount of theological elaboration independent of Angela's disclosures. The editors, Thier and Calufetti, maintain that "this terminology [darkness] does not come from Angela."[163] This position has in its favor the fact that, in this step, Arnaldo is more attentive to composition; the Latin is more polished and removed from the immediacy of oral transmission. Furthermore, there is never any mention of the darkness theme in the instructions; in them, the terms *abyss* and *uncreated* are used to qualify Angela's deepest visions of God. On the other hand, throughout this second redaction, Arnaldo repeatedly affirms that it is Angela speaking, and, as before, continues to press her with his questions for further clarity on what she is experiencing. He even affirms near the beginning of this step (and the beginning of the second redaction), after her initial disclosures of her experiences of the divine darkness, that he "resisted what she said about this darkness and did not understand her." Further along in the text, he notes that Angela "was drawn out of all the preceding darkness which used to delight her so."

What seems most likely, then, is that even in this second redaction Arnaldo—scrupulous reporter that he was—based his account primarily on what he had heard Angela say, at times perhaps reporting only echoes of it, and at other times possibly amplifying it with his own theological reflection. To fittingly crown his effort, he assembled in the final step a series of texts that not only treat of Angela's highest visions of God but also develop themes that Angela had spoken about previously, such as the Eucharist, the Scriptures, poverty, self-knowledge, and her intimate relationship with St. Francis—all of which belong to the summit of her experience. Some of these themes appear in the first redaction, others in the second, as indicated in my notes to these steps.

Whatever conclusion one may come to in this regard, what seems certain is the continuity and congruity between what occurs in the final step—as well as the language used to describe it—and the previous stages of Angela's journey.[164] As to the enigma, likely unsolvable, of what part was played by Angela, strictly speaking, in the elaboration and what was due to the influence and reflection of her faithful scribe and confessor, the least that can be said is that what we have here represents a bold and vertiginous articulation of the mystical summits that, at this point in time, were deemed acceptable and appropriate in the medieval Christian community.

As I have indicated, the sequence of events in these two final steps is not clear. They seem to form an immense tableau in which the most sublime visions are interlaced with experiences of the greatest suffering and despair—the latter fading after a while, but not totally.

Instruction 4 provides a possible hermeneutic for what happens in these final stages of Angela's journey. An anonymous disciple succeeds —"with great difficulty, many prayers, and powerful arguments"—in wrenching from her the revelation of a mystical experience, a sample of many such experiences, that took place while a Mass was being celebrated in Assisi (ca. four years after the final steps). After confessing both Angela's and his own inability to describe this experience properly, he goes on to report that during this "illumination" Angela had initially been drawn and absorbed into the "fathomless depths of God,"[165] and, while she was "still under the impact of this vision," the crucified God and man appeared to her and bestowed upon her soul, in a perfect manner, the "double state" of his own life: the total absorption in the experience of the sweetness of the uncreated God and the cruel death pains of his crucifixion. Commenting further on the nature of the simultaneous reproduction of this double state, the scribe says that while in this illumination, Angela was "filled with joy and sorrow, sated with myrrh and honey, quasi-deified and crucified." Similarly, Angela herself, later on in this same instruction, describes a vision concerning her spiritual sons: "My sons seem to be so transformed in God that it is as if I see nothing but God in them, in both his glorified and suffering state, as if God had totally transubstantiated and absorbed them into the unfathomable depths of his life." We can surmise, then—even if there is no reference to them—that the nature of the experience just related is akin to Angela's immersion into the fathomless abysses of God of the seventh step and her plunge into the agony and identification with Christ crucified, "the horrible darkness" of the sixth step of the *Memorial*. In this regard it is significant, as I have noted, that in Arnaldo's report, the seventh step began before the sixth one.

How these two opposite stages coincide so closely with one another in time remains an enigma.[166] It is evident that what we have before us is a somewhat artificial construct. It seems that Arnaldo decided to insert the experiences in which Angela felt most abandoned by God in one step—the sixth—and to climax his effort by placing those in which she soared to the highest peaks of mystical union in the seventh step. Since it is impossible to determine precisely how these two opposite experiences were mingled or to what extent they succeeded one another, we are led to follow Arnaldo's lead and summarize them separately.

1. The Sixth Supplementary Step ("The Most Horrible Darkness")

Nothing prepares us for the unexpected swingback and plunge into the swirling whirlpool of darkness with which the sixth supplementary step begins. Arnaldo's account provides no indication of what might have triggered it. We can only surmise that it was an inner event, the dark night so common among great mystics and of which John of the Cross was later to give the most complete and penetrating description. Gone are the visions, the complete certitude of God's presence—the hard-won vantage point on which Angela was perched at the end of the fifth supplementary step. This edifice completely collapses, and nothing is left but a sheer and harrowing plummet into the abyss of utter loneliness and despair.

The storm, "the horrible darkness," bearing down on Angela had devastating effects on both her body and her soul. The only comparison that came to her mind to describe her state of desolation was that of "a man hanged by the neck who, with his hands tied behind him and his eyes blindfolded, remains dangling from the gallows and yet lives, with no help, no support, no remedy, swinging in the empty air."

INTRODUCTION

In this encounter with total despair, one in which body and soul tremble in uncontrollable agony, from the lowest depths there rose to Angela's consciousness the cry of final abandonment, the words of Christ on the cross as the only ones fitting to articulate her groans of anguish. She wailed and cried out repeatedly: "My son, my son, do not abandon me, my son!"

By the power and the very dialectic of Christ's burning love for her, Angela was allowed to enter the horror of his final agony and abandonment on the cross. It is this deep participation in the test of the final hour that provides meaning and illustrates most powerfully Angela's experience of the profound abyss and abandonment. To be sure, it is a partial identification and participation. As Von Balthasar points out, "the mystical dark nights, at the most, are distant approximations of the inaccessible mystery of the cross; for if the Son of God is unique, likewise his abandonment by the Father is unique."[167] Angela could do no more than share something of what happened on the cross, participate in some of its inner drama and torment—even if, in transposing Christ's last words as she did, she articulated it in terms of identification unique in the history of mystical literature.

Angela is immersed in a dark fire of purification, in the flames of a blazing furnace meant to purge her of the very roots of self-love, unruly passions, and resistance to God's will. Demons afflict her horribly. They not only remove the support of her virtues and revive in her vices with which she was familiar, but also arouse others that had been unknown to her and that rise to the surface with uncontrollable fury. Her body, she reports, is on fire—the residues of sexual disorder—and she cauterizes it with the terrible antidote of material fire. She is also given a dreadful lucidity about her own sinfulness. She perceives herself as "the house of the devil, a worker for and a dupe of demons, their daughter even," and "worthy only of the lowest part in hell." Finally, it is the last vestige of pride, which must be eradicated, for it must be completely rooted out if the soul is to be seated in the truth of its relationship before God. For love to be pure, every illusion and every trace of self-satisfaction in any good accomplished must be wiped away. Little wonder that, as the last remnants of resistance and rebellion rise to the surface from their hidden and unconscious sources, Angela's soul, in a state of havoc, rages against the night and her body swells in violent upheaval. The torrent of words and comparisons matches the fury of the assault. It is a battle waged alone in the depths of the soul. There is nobody there to help nor any consolation possible from anyone, not even from God himself. The torture is excruciating—"a veritable martyrdom."

Angela needed to live through the crumbling of her most secure foundation in the transcendental life and dwell in a "horrible darkness" —a point of no return—in order to find herself, correlatively, solidly entrenched in the depths of God's life as described in the next and final step. The cross of Christ is at the center of this mysterious transformation and reconciliation of opposites. By entering into the mysterious inner world of Christ's passion, sharing even his abandonment on the cross, she experienced a darkness that paradoxically was not eliminated but was integrated and inverted ("euphemised")[168] in order to disclose the superabundant light of the Triune God. Thus, instead of a symbol of inexplicable absence, in the next step (or almost simultaneously) darkness becomes a symbol of ineffable presence.

2. The Seventh Supplementary Step ("The Most Wonderful of All")

A major part of the seventh and final supplementary step of the *Memorial* clearly belongs to the apophatic tradition of divine darkness, which medieval and later mystics had inherited from the Pseudo-Dionysius and his translators and commentators, in particular Thomas Gallus.[169] Angela had felt the power of negation in her very being, been shaken to her foundations (indeed, overturned by it), and was now experiencing its antithesis—the total and awesome ineffability of God. Her intuition (or Arnaldo's) was that her discourse must follow suit and find its terminology in the language of negative theology whose dominant symbol is that of darkness. Using characteristic apophatic language, she declares that what she sees henceforth "in and with darkness" in this step is beyond the capacities of ordinary discursive thought, "for it is far too great to be conceived or understood."

In the initial vision of this final step, "the light, the beauty and the fullness" that Angela sees in God is so dazzling that it blinds her ordinary capacities of awareness and introduces her to a totally new modality of experiencing God. This perception of God's transcendence is not only beyond conceptualization, but also beyond her ability to understand his love and to respond to it in the same terms as in previous steps. Having lost all claims to love in the purifying darkness and aware of its parody and its untruth, she can appropriately transcribe her deeper introduction into its other dimension—"the most efficacious good seen in this darkness"—only by couching the experience in negative terms: "I did not see love there. I then lost the love which was mine and was made nonlove."[170] What seems to be occurring in this experience is that Angela's love is being transformed and transferred, being invested, so to speak, with God's own ineffable mode of loving—which some of the instructions will refer to later as "uncreated love."[171]

As a result, it is in this vision of the uncreated "in and with darkness"[172] that Angela finds her most solid and secure foothold for further ascent. Totally "recollected," reborn from its deepest center, which now resides in God, her entire spiritual organism—faith, hope, and charity—is being transformed and elevated. There is a clear contrast with the previous step. Having well-nigh lost faith then, Angela now is given "a most certain" (*certissima*) faith; having lost hope, she now has a "most firm" (*firmissima*) hope; having been made nonlove, she can now love without fear, in "continual security" of possessing God's love. The accumulation of superlatives she uses to qualify this new step also distinguishes this from all previous steps.

In the second vision of the divine darkness, Christ's faithful one reports that in this state her soul "finds its delights" and "places its hope in this secret good, one most certain and hidden" that she now understands is "accompanied with such darkness." Her consciousness is being widened so that it merges into God's own being and gaze. In the mysterious darkness she attains a state of preexistence in him, a sharing in all that is in the hidden secret depths of God. Inserted in the divine life, she discovers "everything she wanted to know" and possesses "all she wanted to possess." From this vantage point—one "filled with delights" —the language of paradox is the only one fit to translate what she now sees: "nothing and everything at once." The immensity of God's inner universe is simultaneously revealed and hidden. In the darkness, nothing is discernible and yet the all is intimately present. The joy that she derives therefrom is so great that it is "totally unspeakable."

At Arnaldo's insistence, Angela proceeds to explain further what she meant concerning this darkness and its effects. All that she had perceived and related in the previous steps—the divine power and the divine will, the omnipresence of God in all of creation, all the words and signs of God's friendship—"all this is inferior to the most secret good which is seen with darkness."

Briefly synthesized, this is the main argument of negative theology as Angela incorporates it into the account of her mystical ascent. The Dionysian schema is clearly in the background. Now that Angela has passed the watershed of the *via affirmativa*—the visions of the attributes of God related in previous steps, which she refers to as now being superseded—the *via negativa*, of which the image of darkness is a vehicle, takes over. It is because the new reality transcends all that has transpired previously that it is seen "in and with darkness." The greater the darkness, the more secret it is, the more it imparts an intuition of the fathomless depths of God and the soul's inadequacy before them. In comparison to the totality of this vision, all else is inferior, only "parts of it," in fact, considered also as "darkness," a darkness understood in its initial meaning of obscurity and deprivation. The twofold meaning of darkness in this passage—one signifying a superabundance of light and the other its absence—illustrates again the ambivalence of this symbol, how one meaning is contiguous to the other. Wholly absorbed in this sublime vision, Angela is "totally recollected." Her center of gravity is no longer in herself but in God. This gravitational pull from the depths of the divine life—"God draws me with himself [*cum se*]"—also snatches her from the clutches of "the world and the devil," who continue to assail and persecute her.

Angela's further amplification of what she sees with "such great darkness" enables us to understand what, for her, the entire lexicon of divine darkness was pointing to and fumbling to express. Here is the source and goal of Angela's entire spiritual ascent. If, at the beginning of her journey, in the Assisi vision, the Trinity was finding a place to "rest" in her, here at the summit, "in and with darkness," she claims that she finds herself "standing or lying in the midst of the Trinity."

"When I am in that darkness," Angela continues, "I do not remember anything about anything human, or the God-man, or anything which has a form. Nevertheless, I see all and I see nothing." Little wonder that her body breaks: "I fell very sick when you [Arnaldo] asked those questions and I tried to answer them." Her words crumble and fall, "blaspheme" in their attempt to depict this vision of the God who is beyond words, beyond thought, beyond love, beyond the all good, and even beyond the God-man—without form or modality. The blinding darkness has drawn her out of herself and transported her into the transcendent vitality and eminent mystery of God's inner life where everything that has accompanied and upraised her journey until now is momentarily relinquished and defaults before what is totally inexpressible and incomparable to any human reality. In the most secret place and unfathomable abyss, shrouded with great darkness, is the Triune God.

Angela specifies that she was elevated to this "most exalted and altogether ineffable way of seeing God with such darkness" three times, while the lesser mode of seeing the All Good simply "with darkness" had occurred countless times. To be sure, both the greater and the lesser darkness draw her, the former "incomparably more" and more rarely. The degree of absorption corresponds to the degree of ineffability.

According to her perception, the most ineffable darkness, symbol of the mysterious depths of the Trinity, then, is one that shades off into one of lesser intensity, the vision of the God-man. In this vision, Angela—although she does not articulate it as such—seems to have been drawn into and shared the very movement of Christ's revelation of the boundless life of the Father. What she sees with such delight proceeding from Christ's "eyes and face, so gracious and attractive as he leans to embrace her" is precisely what issues from the greater darkness in the abyss of the Trinity. It comes she says, from "within" and is so awesome that "nothing can be said about it."

This irresistible power of attraction emanating from the inmost recesses of God's life also solidifies Angela's relationship with the God-man by inaugurating the moment of mystical marriage so celebrated by the mystics, the full entrance into the unitive life: "You are I and I am you." So complete is the union and identity with Christ that the distinction between object and subject seems lost—there is no intermediary (*nihil erat medium inter me et ipsum*). Angela has become as if one with the other side. She is so filled with exhilarating joy by this wedding feast in the night and the gentle embrace of so gracious a spouse that she bursts into song and celebrates it with a laud: "I praise you God my beloved; I have made your cross my bed. For a pillow or cushion, I have found poverty, and for other parts of the bed, suffering, and contempt to rest on."

Thus does Angela celebrate the triumph of the cross. Enlightened by the visions of the great darkness, she understands the height, the width, and the depth of its saving power. The innermost secret of its source within the Trinity has been disclosed. Consonant with the Franciscan thesis of the primacy of Christ, Angela points out that even before man sinned, God the Father loved this bed and its company ("poverty, suffering, and contempt") so much that he granted it to his Son. In the self-emptying of the Son, in obedience to the Father, lies the full realization of the divine plan. His entire life lived on the bed of the cross in "poverty, suffering, and contempt" was the specific aspect in which the abasement of the Son manifested itself to Angela. In her dark visions what she glimpsed was this excessive and superabundant love of the

72

Father and the Son. For Angela, deeply identified now with the Son, the cross becomes the nuptial couch, the "bed" where she celebrates the wedding feast in joyful praise and sound: "What I feel there are no words for; what I see I never want to depart from; because for me to live is to die. Oh, draw me then to yourself!"

During this period of grace and plenitude, Angela is blessed with visions that multiply in kaleidoscopic fashion, ever changing and ever new, often blending into one another. She says that she "swam" in the boundless inner universe of the Trinity. In the delight of perceiving that God grants to all "spirit and love with measure," she becomes more deeply aware than ever of the essential rightness of all that is ("I do not recognize God's goodness more in a good and holy person, or even in many good and holy people, than in one or many who are damned"), and understands the justice of God's judgments ("What depths are found there!"). She also understands, from within her experience "in the bosom of God," the meaning of the harsh and difficult sayings of the Scriptures.

In a series of Eucharistic revelations reported in this final step, Angela also comprehends, for instance, how Christ is at once in the ciborium and yet present everywhere; sees a vision of Christ crucified, then finds herself "enwrapped in his divinity"; hears St. Francis speaking to her and confirming her in her mission to be guardian of poverty; sees Christ coming in the sacrament accompanied by a mighty and countless throng.

The dark visions that transmit a heightened awareness of God's transcendence were not, however, Angela's final revelations. In another vision, an "abysmal attraction" drew her ever more deeply into the depths of the Trinity. Now her soul was enriched with greater gifts and introduced into a state "totally beyond any she had ever experienced," and "greater than the one of the vision of God in the darkness"—a state, so to speak, above or beyond the darkness.

In this fathomless abyss, all previous supports—the life and humanity of Christ, the cross as bed to rest on, the consideration of the contempt, suffering, and poverty experienced by the Son of God, the vision of God in the darkness, everything that could be named—all fade into the background. Every previous state is put to sleep so "tenderly and sweetly," she reports, "that I could not tell it was happening." The ladder is no longer necessary when one has reached the top.[173] New, hitherto unexperienced, ineffable operations are now at work and in their spiraling movement Angela is transported more deeply within the great depths of the Trinity, the origin and principle of all that is. It is her attempt to find words for this totally inexpressible divine abyss that causes Angela to stammer, for she is painfully aware that words betray more than they reveal: "My words blaspheme and make hash of what they should express."

In an attempt, nonetheless, to give some positive content to this new manifestation of God, Angela says that, "in these totally ineffable workings," God shows himself to her in two ways: He first of all makes his presence felt, then he manifests himself to her by bestowing greater gifts, accompanied by ever-greater clarity.

The first way is reminiscent of the content of the previous vision in the darkness where she was given to understand the judgments of God. Now, however, the focus is sharper and the vision more encompassing. Continually, in the most inward depths of her soul, Angela says, she is "illumined" to understand how God is present not only in her but also "in a devil and a good angel, in heaven and hell, in good deeds and in adultery or homicide, in all things, finally, which exist or have some degree of being, whether beautiful or ugly." Indeed, while she is in "this truth," she understands the divine wisdom and economy so completely that she takes "no more delight in contemplating God in what is good than in what is evil." The duality of good and evil, heaven and earth, has been overcome.

Accustomed now to the blinding light of the divine darkness, Angela perceives, from within the Trinity in which she is absorbed, the essential rightness of all that is, including the place of evil. Totally freed (in this state she cannot sin), perfectly consoled and joy-filled, seeing at a glance all that is created, she shares in the divine serenity, the deep wisdom (*gravitatem sapientiae*) hidden from the beginning of time and now revealed to God's chosen one.

Another effect of this mode of God's presence, one different from the preceding one, is to recollect Angela's soul totally in the fathomless abysses of the Trinitarian life. In this state, she says, the divine workings are so deep and ineffable that by themselves, independently of other favors that accompany them, they represent that "good that the saints enjoy in eternal life." "Of these gifts of Paradise," she goes on to say, "some saints have more, others less"; the difference lies in the varying degrees to which God "expands" the soul and thereby confers a greater or lesser capacity to receive the Trinitarian presence. Angela anticipates here a subsequent claim that she had partially attained the beatific state.

In the second way, immediately on presenting himself in the above fashion, God discloses himself to Angela's soul with gifts and consolations so great that they surpass all the previous ones in depth (she explicitly mentions, once again, that in this stage she is "drawn out of all darkness"). The clarity, the certitude, and the abysmal profundity in which she now sees and knows God is such that "there is no heart in the world that can ever in any way understand it or even conceive it." These expansions of her soul are so ineffable that Angela insists "that there is nothing that can be said about them," for, ultimately, "there is absolutely nothing that can explain God."

To illustrate, nonetheless, the total negativity of this statement, Angela compares the sublimity of her experience to the sublimity of Scriptures. Even if the Scriptures surpass full understanding, nonetheless "one can babble something about them." By contrast, "nothing at all can be said or babbled" about the ineffable workings of this said mystical experience. Both the Scriptures and mystical experience flow from the same wellspring in God's life, and mutually enlighten one another.[174] For Angela, it is the latter, the inner experience, that enlightens the former and provides the key to the full meaning, the "secrets" of the revealed Word: "how the Scriptures were written; how they are made easy and difficult; how they seem to say something and contradict it; how some derive no profit from them; how those who do not observe them are damned; and how others who observe them are saved by them."

Straining mightily, nonetheless, to express something of the inexpressible ("I blaspheme in speaking about it"), Angela attempts to give some idea of her experience of the "totally unspeakable good" (the term that seems to condense her entire experience until now), and tells Arnaldo: "I speak to you in this fashion, so as to somehow put it in your mouth and enable you to swallow it [*imbocare*]"; Angela is like a mother bird trying to feed her young—the root meaning of *imbocare*. As to the duration of this vision, which "infinitely" surpasses all those she had previously spoken about, she says, "it is mine not only for the twinkling of an eye, but often for a good while and very often in this efficacious manner; as for the other mode, it is with me almost continually."

Angela then proceeds to locate the place within herself where this manifestation of the All Good and his ineffable workings occurs: "There is in my soul a chamber in which no joy, sadness, or enjoyment from any virtue, or delight over anything that can be named enters. This is where the All Good, which is not any particular good, resides, and it is so much the All Good that there is no other good." It is in this "chamber," the deepest, most inward part of her soul, that Angela finds the full fruition of that with which she had begun her journey: the search for the knowledge of self. In this "complete truth" she discovers the profound connaturality between God and self. If in previous moments it was "within" God that the All Good manifested itself, now it is within herself—beyond self-consciousness in the deep realm where selfhood rests—that she experiences the same ineffable reality: The deepest immanence of God in herself coincides with being in the highest transcendence of God's life.

Similarly, it is from this manifestation of God in her deep center that she understands and possesses (as before in the darkness and in the first mode, but now more comprehensively), "the complete truth that is in heaven and in hell, in the entire world, in every place, in all things, and in every creature." The entire created universe has become transparent to her—a knowledge by communion of the primal harmony of all that is, as seen from within its transcendent source. No part of creation is now strange or alienated. Everything has found its rightful place, "its complete truth." Throughout all of reality Angela sees the same all-pervading divine presence: the new creation in which God is all in all.

To speak of this vision, which Angela again insists was stronger than what she had seen in the darkness, as if by a sudden intuition she resorts to classical scholastic terminology: "I saw the One who is and how he is the being of all creatures." We are at the summit of her search; distinction between subject and object in the amorous discourse fade; knowledge and understanding can go no further; only one entity remains: participation in and pure consciousness of Being.[175] In this state she says that she is "alone with God," and "totally cleansed, totally sanctified, totally upright, totally celestial in him." Angela is one of the small number of mystics who claim a vision of the divine essence as the culmination of the mystical ascent.

Furthermore, the Being in question here is not the abstract transcendental notion of metaphysics but the Trinitarian God, who in his love has introduced Angela into intimate communion with the Three Persons. What follows in the text makes this clear. In this state, Angela asserts, God has on occasion told her: "Daughter of divine wisdom, temple of the Beloved, beloved of the Beloved, daughter of peace, in you rests the entire Trinity, indeed, the total complete truth rests in you, so that you hold me and I hold you." If in the visions of the darkness, Angela was "standing or lying in the midst of the Trinity," now an even fuller vision of the Trinitarian life is revealed to her: quasi-divine, she holds and is held by the Trinity.

INTRODUCTION

This state, which she again repeats, "surpasses any previous ones," paradoxically lasts but an instant and yet is continuous. Angela asserts that she experienced "this unspeakable manifestation of God more than a hundred times, even thousands and thousands of times, and each time her soul received something fresh, and what it experienced was always novel and different." The boundaries between heaven and earth have indeed well-nigh disappeared ("It seems that I am no longer on earth but in heaven, in God"). Only the flimsiest of veils seems to separate her from God. When, however, she is away from this supreme and unfathomable state, Angela experiences her own abysmal inferiority. She sees herself "completely full of sin and obedient to it, devious, impure, totally false and erroneous." Yet she is "in a state of quiet," which is now hers "continually."

Soaring from peak to peak in the highest reaches of the human spirit, Angela gives one last example of divine manifestation, one that she again asserts was greater and fuller even than what she had before experienced. It occurs on the Marian feast of Candlemas (2 February 1296). Concomitantly with the presentation of the Son of God in the temple, which is honored on this feast, she affirms, she too experiences "her own presentation" before the heavenly majesty—she becomes known as she is known by God. This vision is so inconceivable and unimaginable that it gives her "a new and most excellent [*excellentissima*] joy," one so different from before that it seems to her to be a "miracle." It simultaneously combines the just-related experience of the "unspeakable manifestation of God" with new delights. In this immersion in the divine life, she claims to have heard "most high words which she does not want to be written." All fear has been removed, including that of death. Nothing, she is told, can now separate her from God. To sum up what this highest mode of seeing God consists of, Angela says that she had heard God speaking to her "in words too wonderful to relate"; that the unspeakable good she has experienced "is the same good and none other than that which the saints enjoy in eternal life; but there the experience of it is different." In eternal life "the least saint has more of it than can be given to any soul in this life before the death of the body."

Angela has run ahead of history and has attained a form of consciousness that other men and women will know only when earthly life is past—she has had a foretaste, a pale and fugitive anticipation of the face-to-face vision of eternity. This vision serves as a fitting climax to the seventh supplementary step of the *Memorial*. There is nothing more

77

to relate, for there is nothing more to expect or aspire to. Arnaldo ends his effort with a "Deo gratias, Amen."

D. Further Mystical Experiences (Recorded in the Instructions)

Angela lived on for thirteen years (1296–1309) beyond the compilation of the *Memorial*. During this period, which is covered by the second part of the book, the *Instructions*, Angela's role as spiritual mother comes to the fore.[176] Only on rare occasions did she agree to reveal her inner life. "My secrets are mine!" she told a friar, one of her disciples, who tried to extricate further revelations from her. It is nonetheless from this same friar that we have a report of the state of Angela's soul during the last years of her life. Instruction 4 (alluded to earlier in the commentary on the final two steps of Angela's journey) contains a lengthy account (in his own words and not Angela's) of what he succeeded in having his spiritual mother reveal to him concerning a series of visions she had experienced while she was on pilgrimage in Assisi for the celebration of the feast of the Indulgence in 1300. During these "illuminations," Angela's soul, he reports, was absorbed and transported into the uncreated light by God and experienced simultaneously the double state of the crucified Christ: both his glorified and his suffering states at once. While absorbed in this vision, she also suddenly saw her sons being embraced by the crucified Christ with varying degrees of intensity, matching the degree of intimacy he enjoyed with each one.

In his reflections on what Angela had told him about the gifts she had received from the "infinite and limitless ocean of divine riches," the same friar observed that she seemed to be in an ongoing process of transformation, at once immersed in the ineffable light of the uncreated God and in the pain of the crucified. This state was continual and yet the illuminations changed and grew more intense, with added "ardor, joy, sweetness, and savor." These experiences were so awesome that the friar admitted that he was fumbling for words in trying to express them, and Angela herself reiterated that she felt "it was a kind of blasphemy to try to express the inexpressible."

The second series of visions reported by this brother occurred on the next day, a Monday, while Angela was in procession to the church of St. Mary of the Angels. In these visions, she saw the crucified Christ once again blessing and embracing her spiritual sons in the manner just mentioned. This time, however, she also saw how each one of them was being purified and transformed in God. It is, she said, "as if I see nothing but God in them, in both his glorified and suffering state, as if God had totally transubstantiated and absorbed them into the unfathomable depths of his life." Furthermore, as she approached the church of St. Mary of the Angels, she saw the Mother of God, totally luminous, blessing and kissing her spiritual sons and daughters (some more and some less). In her love for them, "it seemed as if the Mother of God was absorbing them into the almost infinite light within her breast."

The final series of visions occurred on Tuesday while Mass was being celebrated. This time it was St. Francis who appeared to Angela. After greeting and extending his peace to her, he then proceeded to bless Angela's spiritual sons, praise them for their fidelity in observing poverty, and assure them of his constant protection.

Apparently the friar who recorded the above visions had either forgotten or had not known all of the mystical experiences that occurred during this pilgrimage to Assisi, for another friar, probably Arnaldo, adds more data in instruction 26. Here he reports that Angela had a vision of the Portiuncula in which she saw God suddenly expanding it into a great church, "one of astonishing beauty and magnitude." He also tells of a vision that had taken place on another feast, that of St. Peter in Chains, in which Angela once again saw the crucified Christ embracing her spiritual sons according to the degree with which they had shared in his passion.

These visions, found in instructions 4 and 26, are the only ones of the second part of Angela's book that the editors of the critical edition claim are historically authentic. It seems to me, however, that a few others recorded in other instructions bear the mark of Angela's experience, even if they may be slightly amplified, and are worth mentioning. These visions are usually connected with liturgical feasts. Thus on the feast of the Purification of the Blessed Virgin (instruction 19), Angela sees the Mother of God offering her son and then placing him in Angela's arms, "a benefit totally unspeakable." On the feast of the Holy Angels in September (instruction 20), she is lifted into the angelic presence and they speak with her with "indescribable graciousness." They tell her that what the Seraphim experience before the divine majesty has been given and communicated to her. Still another instruction (21) reports that once, while she lay sick in bed, Christ and St. Francis appeared to Angela to minister to her. After Christ appeared to her by her bedside, he then presented St. Francis, the one whom, after him, "she loved the most," and the latter spoke "most secret and most high words to her," and also told her: "You are the only one born of me." Finally, assembled in instruction 36 are fragments of what Angela told her disciples during her final sickness (from September 1308 to 3 January 1309, the vigil of her death). These last words of Angela, punctuated by visions, constitute a sort of spiritual testament, a brief synthesis of her spiritual teachings. At one moment of her final discourse, she utters a significant heart-rending cry: "O unknown nothingness! O unknown nothingness! Truly, a soul cannot have a better awareness in this world than to perceive its own nothingness."

Angela had found that in her own nothingness lay her most secure foundations. In it had been revealed the fathomless abysses of the Trinity: "Whatever is mine is yours, and whatever is yours is mine," she heard God tell her. "Washed, cleansed, and immersed in the blood of Christ, which was fresh and warm as if it flowed from the body of Christ on the Cross," Angela, like a spouse prepared for her wedding, was ready for the final consummation of her journey. Christ in person, the text relates, was to come to take her with him and grant her "the stole of immortality and innocence to reign with him forever." In a jubilant mood, as if already tasting the joy of eternal bliss, and surrounded by many friars who celebrated the Divine Office in her presence, Christ's faithful one, as if gently falling asleep, died peacefully on the octave of the feast of the Holy Innocents, 4 January 1309.

As a vision that occurred during a Wednesday of Holy Week (undated, but probably toward the end of her life) records, Angela had experienced the "inexpressible and visceral love" of the "suffering God-man"; throughout her life, as here at the end, his love for her had not been a "hoax."

The *Instructions*: Angela as Spiritual Mother

The second part of Angela's *Book* contains what the editors of the critical edition have assembled under the heading *Instructions,* plus an obituary notice and an epilogue. These contain accounts of further visions and locutions, letters as well as discourses of varying length and style. If Angela's personal experience accounts for the unity of the *Memorial,* the spiritual formation of her spiritual sons and daughters is responsible for the unity of the *Instructions.* In these, Angela emerges as spiritual mother, a "great teacher in the discipline that leads to God," as one of her disciples was to note.[177]

Angela had indeed developed a great capacity for discernment in the ways of the spirit and of love. The wisdom that was hers and that is distilled in her letters and exhortations was derived from the wealth of her own experience. Grounded in her own truth and that of God, with firmness and keen insight, she was able to engender and lead others in the path of radical conformity to the suffering God-man and spiritual transformation.

Angela's teachings, then, are for the most part strongly anchored in the *Memorial.* Themes initially sounded in the various steps that led her to the summits of God's life are repeated and amplified in the *Instructions.* The main themes of her doctrine as found in the *Instructions* can be summed up as follows: the following of Christ, the suffering God-man and the Book of Life (cf. instructions 3, 5, 15, 18, 23, 34); the cross of Christ (cf. 3, 14, 22); transformation into his poverty, suffering, contempt, and also (although this is treated only minimally), his obedience (cf. 3, 7, 18, 22, 27, 34); prayer (cf. 3, 18, 34); the Eucharist (cf. 30, 32, 33); knowledge of God and self (cf. 3, 10, 14, 17, 29, 34);

humility (cf. 5, 9, 10); the signs of true love (cf. 2, 26); the legitimate sons (cf. 3, 15, 22, 23, 26); St. Francis (cf. 3, 4, 21); Mary (cf. 3, 4).

There are some doctrinal elements, however, that receive new formulations. For instance, instead of the terminology of darkness to describe the highest peaks of mystical experience, the *Instructions* use the term "the uncreated" or "uncreated love" (cf. 2, 14, 18, 22, 30). Similarly, even if the reference to seeing God as the "One who is" has its antecedents in the *Memorial* (cf. the vision of the One who is in chap. 9), it is much more characteristic of the *Instructions* (cf. 2, 7, 22, 30, 32). New also is the use of the term *transformation* (the word occurs only twice in the *Memorial*) to describe the process that leads to union with God (cf. 5, 6, 7, 22, 32, 34, 36). Special also to the *Instructions* are Angela's warnings against the aberrations of the sect of the Spirit of Freedom (cf. 2, 3, 25) and her interventions in the Franciscan quarrel between the Spirituals and the Community. Angela's didactic and mediating role in this dispute is especially dominant in the letters (cf. 7, 8, 9, 12, 13, 14, 15, 17, 18, 35).

What remains a mystery in this second part of Angela's *Book* is precisely to whom the *Instructions*, in particular the letters, were addressed, from whom the questions or letters came, and, finally, who the redactors were.

Angela clearly took quite seriously the role that had become hers in the spiritual formation and growth of what for the most part she refers to as "her sons" (although sometimes "daughters" are also mentioned). They probably belonged to the Franciscan First and Third orders, priests and laity. She seemed to be quite conscious also that her message was meant to extend itself beyond her immediate group of disciples, "to those beyond the seas," as she says in her testament.

As for the letters, six are addressed to individuals (8, 10, 12, 15, 17, 18) and six to groups (7, 9, 11, 13, 14, 35). The individual recipients are never mentioned by name, but the letters testify to the close—even intimate—rapport (e.g., instruction 18) she had with her spiritual progeny. The editors of the critical edition surmise that one of the letters was addressed to Arnaldo (instruction 8). That any of them were addressed to Ubertino of Casale is extremely problematic, as I later indicate (Sec. VI, A). As for the circular letters, it is likely that some of them were sent to friars living in hermitages, possibly in the Marches where, as the *Memorial* indicates, she had contacts.[178] Those who wrote letters to Angela, and there were "many of them" as she mentions in two instructions (7, 14), are unknown.

The redactors of the instructions, likewise, remain anonymous. That there were several of them is quite clear from the fluctuations in style. The editors of the critical edition are of the opinion that the first twelve were written by Arnaldo, in part because of their strong connections with the text of the *Memorial*.[179] After his death, Angela's direct communications to her disciples become increasingly rare, as the successive instructions demonstrate. One of them even provides an explanation for her silence and reluctance to respond to the letters she has been receiving (instruction 14). Some of these, for instance, seem to have been written without her direct collaboration (e.g., 11), and, on occasion, in a highly scholastic terminology clearly not hers (e.g., 31). Thus several instructions contain some of her words that the scribe remembered and noted, and from this nucleus he expanded, often using a previous instruction as a starting point. The tendency to systematize Angela's teachings is especially in evidence in those instructions that the editors of the critical edition date after her death (1, 12, 13, 15, 16, 17, 20, 21, 23, 24, 25, 28, 29, 33, 36). Furthermore, again according to the editors of the critical edition, several of the instructions are found in the second redaction (1, 12, 13, 15, 16, 17, 19, 20, 21, 23, 24, 25, 33, and the epilogue). On occasion, this second redaction either corrects the first or adds new material to it, such as the final paragraphs of instructions 14 and 26, and the insertion of the section on the knives that wounded Christ in instruction 3. To be noted is the fact that the end of the second redaction of the *Memorial* coincides with the date of the beginning of the first instruction (ca. 1297/1298). Throughout this text, notes will indicate the interdependencies of the instructions with the *Memorial* and with one another, as well as chronological and other explanatory data.

The redactional history of these instructions is a complex one. Manuscripts containing all or part of the corpus (and even individual instructions) circulated loosely and sometimes independently of one another and the rest of Angela's *Book* (who knows how many were lost?).[180] Number, order, sequence, and arrangement vary considerably in the available families of manuscripts and, as a consequence, in previous editions of Angela's writings. The editors of the critical edition opted to follow the sequence found in the M manuscript—an Italian codex (late fourteenth or early fifteenth century) based on the most primitive (but lost) Latin text of Angela's writings and a key for the two-redaction hypothesis—because it comes closest to the order followed by the second redaction. Since instructions 13, 17, 19, and 23 are missing from the M manuscript, these have been inserted among those they are close to thematically. I have followed (grudgingly, to facilitate reference) the sequence they have adopted, but I highly recommend that readers read the instructions in the sequence given in the manuscript group B, because this group has preserved the chronology of the original composition, and because the explanatory notes (both mine and those of the critical edition) for the individual instructions have been elaborated following B.[181]

Angela's Spirituality

Angela's *Book* is not primarily a systematic exposition of the spiritual life, but rather a loosely constructed narrative meant, as the prologue indicates, "to inspire the devotion of the faithful." Nonetheless, it is possible to reconstruct from her writings the main dimensions of Angela's spirituality.

A. Passionate Love of the Crucified, the Suffering God-Man

Angela's passionate love affair with "the suffering God-man," the crucified Christ, is the central and organizing principle of her journey. To be sure, the entire life of Christ, the Book of Life, as she was wont to repeat, inspired her conversion, but it is especially the love she experienced from contemplating Christ on the cross that transformed and widened her own capacity for love to infinite and mystical dimensions. What happened to Christ on the cross, in particular his passion and death, revealed to Angela the superabundant love of the divine plan: the paradigm of self-emptying as the exemplar and the condition for being filled with the life-giving presence of God. The deeper she was enabled to share and identify with the suffering of Christ (the dominant motif of her meditations) as well as the poverty and contempt he endured, the more the excessive love hidden in the fathomless abysses of the Godhead disclosed itself to her. Her passionate fusion with the suffering Christ, her Beloved, became so complete that she even shared his agony and abandonment on the cross. Her personal and harrowing description of this experience of mystical abandonment (the sixth supplementary step) has a special place in the history of mystical literature. In the total desolation and self-emptying of this dark moment, divine power, more awesomely than before, made itself manifest in weakness, and darkness was transvalued to reveal the fathomless abysses of the Trinitarian life.

If the cross elevates Angela to mystical heights, it likewise totally integrates and unifies her. Through its transforming mystery, it becomes the point of intersection and the bed (the mystical marriage) where the human meets with the divine, the depths with the heights, the greatest absence with the greatest presence, the total dispossession with the possession of all, the experience of nothingness with that of the ineffable plenitude of God's life. The cross is the key, also, to understanding why the two final steps, so contrary in nature, seem to occur simultaneously. In these two steps Angela was totally absorbed in the double state of Christ's life: the pain of his crucifixion as man and the sweetness of his glory as God. She was at once "crucified and quasi-deified."

B. The Trinity

If the cross is at the center of Angela's spirituality, its transforming power also enables her to become inwardly aware of the indwelling of the Trinity. Already, in the crucial vision that occurred at the beginning of her journey in Assisi she had experienced the coming of the Trinity in her soul. At the summit of her ascent, concomitantly with the mystical embrace with the crucified Christ—the mystical marriage that occurs in the divine darkness—Angela is drawn into the abysses of the Trinitarian life. The cross and the mediation of the humanity of Christ having served their function, they fade into the background (there was "no intermediary" between her and God) and what Angela apprehends, then, are the depths of the Triune God, which are beyond form and representation.

As Angela fumbles to express the ineffable operations in which she is absorbed, the dominant image she uses to articulate her experience is that of seeing the All Good—God as total love. Coexisting with this experience is an awareness—held in a dialectical tension that accompanies her entire journey, but here intensified to the fullest—of, on the one hand, the pure and uncreated nature her love has attained, and, on the other hand, her own vileness and nothingness. Totally transformed into the love and the will of the Beloved, into the uncreated dimensions in the Trinitarian life, she goes so far as to claim participation in the life

86

of the divine Being, the One who is, and perceives how he is the Being of all creatures.

In the fathomless abysses of the Trinitarian life—*abyssatio* is the term that is used the most to characterize Angela's deepest participation in the absolute transcendence of God—in which she claims she is "holding and being held," what she beholds is God's being, a being totally imbued with love. In this ineffable state, one akin to the beatific vision, Angela discovers the complete truth of her life and of all created reality: the rightful place of good and evil. As she soars these heights, words increasingly fail her to describe what she is seeing—"my words blaspheme" she repeats—and she climaxes her discourse by asserting that ultimately "nothing can explain God."

C. The Eucharist

In Angela's spirituality, there is also a close association between the visions of Christ's passion and those involving the Eucharist. Both are fonts of mystical experience, and of divine power manifesting itself in weakness. In this, as the research conducted by Caroline Walker Bynum has abundantly demonstrated, she is at one with the experience of many mystics, in particular medieval women, for whom visions of the suffering Christ occurred while the Eucharist was being celebrated.[182]

Beginning with those described in the first supplementary step, many of Angela's most extraordinary visions occur during the celebration of the Eucharist. She is particularly awestruck at the moment of the elevation of the host, as is typical of the practice of her time. At one point, what she sees in the host is of such beauty and radiance that it surpasses the splendor of the sun; at another, she sees two most splendid eyes, so large that only the edges of the host remain visible; in still another Eucharistic vision—in which she complained that the priest had put the host down on the altar too quickly—it is the Christ child, "tall and lordly, as one holding dominion," who appears to her in the host. Further on in her itinerary, Arnaldo, as was his wont, pressed her to tell whether she had seen anything new in the vision she had just told him had occurred while the body of Christ was elevated by the priest, and during which the Blessed Virgin had spoken to her and blessed her. She said no, but went on to affirm that the effect of Christ's presence in her soul at that moment was like "a fire of sweet and gentle love" and the bones in her body became so disjointed that she could hear them crack.

INTRODUCTION

The power of the Eucharist to widen Angela's consciousness to cosmic dimensions is strikingly illustrated in the fourth supplementary step. While Mass was being celebrated, she suddenly saw the whole of creation filled to overflowing, "pregnant" with the presence of God. In this same step, she also reports that having immersed herself in the dying-rising dynamics of this sacrament, she was given to understand the meaning of trials and tribulations, the dialectic of Christ's presence and absence in her life—and this quickened her to desire to give herself totally to Christ, to the point of martyrdom. In the next step, she reports after receiving communion, that she had just been granted a vision of God as the All Good. Further elaborating on the most recent effects of communion in her soul, she describes the host as more savory than any other food. It produced a most pleasant sensation as it descended into her body, and at the same time made her shake violently. To be noted in juxtaposition with this experience is an earlier episode in which, after having swallowed the water she had used to wash the sores of a leper, the taste of it was so sweet that she asserted it was like receiving holy communion.

In the final steps, Angela's Eucharistic visions deepen her understanding of the mystery of this sacrament. She sees its source within the Trinity; intuits the ubiquity of Christ's presence in it—how he is present in the ciborium and yet everywhere, filling everything; perceives how communion with him is at the same time communion with all the faithful; glimpses, also, how the sins of those who receive this sacrament unfaithfully are responsible for "breaking Christ's back." In still other ecstatic moments during Eucharistic celebrations, she passes from the experience of Christ in his humanity to that of his divinity; sees Christ appearing to her surrounded by angels, and St. Francis assuring her of her mission as guardian of poverty.

Throughout the *Memorial,* the Eucharist is a source of immense joy for Angela. It so absorbs her into God that often she can find no words to describe its ineffable operation. Summing up its effects, she asserts that receiving communion "sanctifies, purifies, consoles, and preserves the soul." Even if she often proclaims her unworthiness to receive communion, she also professes wanting to do so daily. It is probably because the Eucharist was such a source of nourishment for her that she speaks at one point of her temptation not to eat or to eat only very little.[183]

In one episode, which has thus far escaped the notice of students of Angela's spirituality and Eucharistic devotion, she seems to arrogate for herself a kind of priestly role. In the second supplementary step, in a context reminiscent of the Last Supper, she is told that the blessing she performs over the food and drink she has received as alms has power to take away not only her own sins, but likewise those of her companions and whomever they share them with.[184]

A few instances of Angela's visionary experience during Eucharistic celebrations are likewise recorded in the *Instructions,* but in these it is rather her teachings, either as developed by her or, more likely, as amplified by some unknown disciples, that come to the fore.

What is probably the most noteworthy description of the transformative power of the Eucharist in Angela's life, and the one that reveals the very heart of her mystical experience during the celebration of this sacrament, is recorded in instruction 4. While in Assisi for the Feast of the Indulgence and participating in a Mass celebrated in the upper church of the Basilica of St. Francis, at the moment of the elevation, she was suddenly absorbed into the uncreated light, the fathomless abysses of God's life. While she was in this state of ecstasy, the crucified Christ appeared to her as if he had just been taken down from the cross and she saw graphically depicted the wounds his body had suffered, from which the blood seemed to flow. The effect of this vision was to transform her into the double state of his life, human and divine, and to allow her to experience simultaneously the sweetness of God and the pain of his crucifixion. While she was in this "quasi-deified and crucified state," Angela also saw a multitude of her sons appear and Christ speaking to them, embracing and coloring them with his blood, according to the intensity of their intimacy with him.

During another Mass celebrated during this same pilgrimage to Assisi, St. Francis appears in a vision to bless her and her sons and exhort them to be faithful to the way of Christ and to observe the poverty prescribed by the Rule. Further details concerning Angela's precognitive visions into the state of her spiritual sons, which occurred at Mass during this same sojourn in Assisi, are also found in instruction 26.

Angela's doctrinal developments on the Eucharist are documented mainly in instructions 30 and 32. These very likely spring from her experience, but the highly scholastic terminology is so remote from her language that one must conclude that the heavy hand of an anonymous redactor is visibly at work.

The main points of instruction 30 are as follows: (a) The God-man instituted the Eucharistic sacrifice not only as a memorial of his death, but also as a way of remaining with his faithful always; (b) this sacrament manifests his overflowing love for humanity; (c) it contains a synthesis of all his sufferings, both visible and invisible; (d) the sight of Christ's love-filled countenance and that of his pain-filled countenance summon the soul in turn to be transformed into total love and total suffering, one tempering the other.

Instruction 32 is long and complex, but its structure is clear. Angela is called on to respond to three questions concerning the Eucharist: its nature, its effects, and whether the angels and the saints in heaven experience some new joy or sweetness in this mystery. Angela concludes her discourse by exhorting everyone to dispose themselves to receive this sacrament as worthily as possible.

The Eucharist, then, is a major source for Angela's incorporation into Christ and mystical union with him. In this sacrament, she had received the "All Good," the expression that most aptly condenses her Eucharistic experience. Little wonder that in the last recorded moments of her life, Angela expressed her desire to receive communion. Since there was no priest available to provide it for her, she was greatly saddened. Remaining with this desire, she was suddenly rapt in ecstasy and saw a multitude of angels who led her to an altar and told her: "Prepare yourself to receive the one who has espoused you with the ring of his love"—a fitting prelude to her definitive union with the suffering God-man.

D. The Scriptures

In common with most medieval mystics, Angela finds the Scriptures a basic source of spiritual nourishment. Her relationship to the Scriptures, however, is a complex one. It is significant to note that unlike most devotional literature of the time, her *Book* is largely devoid of explicit scriptural references.[185] In the entire *Memorial* only five explicit biblical quotations can be detected. Of these, only one citation comes directly from Angela, the popular Lucan saying: "Behold, the handmaid of the Lord, may it be done to me according to your word" (fifth supplementary step). Two others, from Jesus' farewell discourse to his disciples (Jn 14: 21, 23), are cited by Arnaldo in the prologue. It is likewise the scribe who twice quotes Scripture (Gn 3:34 and Acts 7:55) to question Angela in the last step of her ascent. In the *Instructions*, only nineteen scriptural quotations can be detected and most of these, concentrated in instructions 3 and 5, are brief excerpts taken from Lucan or

Matthean accounts of Christ's passion (and probably inserted by the redactor).

The paucity of explicit scriptural references notwithstanding, throughout Angela's narrative one senses God's word sustaining and guiding her effort toward radical gospel living and union with God. Thematic and linguistic reminiscences drawn from the Scriptures abound in her text—many of which are noted in the translation.[186] The following are a few New Testament resonances, simply on the thematic level.

Certainly, the theme of God's love, one of Angela's central doctrines, is Johannine; the fourth Gospel's final discourse of Jesus to his disciples is the substratum for her descriptions of her deepest states of union with God (e.g., "I am you and you are I"). Her deep identification with Christ, the sharing of his crucified life, the self-emptying of Jesus according to the divine plan, the certitude that nothing can separate her from his love, the capacity of judging all things, the hearing of ineffable words at the threshold of heaven—all this suggests strong Pauline influence. Finally, the stripping away of her belongings, friends, relatives, and very self; her subjection to trials and persecutions in conformity with Christ; her reflections and meditations on Christ's legitimate sons, those who receive a special invitation to share the Lord's table and drink from his cup; as well as her association with Christ's passion and abandonment on the cross—all these are themes with clear Synoptic resonances.

It is significant to note that if one grants that Angela recited the Divine Office, it is certainly strange that there are no explicit references to the psalms in the entire *Book*, and the reminiscences of them are minor. As for the influence of the *Song of Songs*, which was so central for medieval mystics, especially women, Angela does not use its typology to express her mystical experience, but themes and terminology drawn from it are considerably present.[187]

An important example of the role the Scriptures played in Angela's spiritual evolution is suggested in step seventeen of the *Memorial* when, after meditating on a word from the gospel, even wanting to see it in writing, she was led into a vision in which she was told that the understanding of the gospel is something so "supradelightful" that if it was truly understood, "one would not only forget the world but even oneself."

The most striking illustration of Angela's relationship to the Scriptures occurs at the summit of her mystical experience. When she reaches this point it is as if the Scriptures themselves are inadequate to explain or contain the content of her visions. She claims, for instance, that she saw and felt more of the passion of Christ than the gospels or its preachers relate (fifth supplementary step); that what the Scriptures say of God does not express anything of the innermost meaning of who he is, "not even to the extent of a grain of sand compared to the whole world" (fifth supplementary step); similarly, that one can say something about the Scriptures, but her experience of God is so ineffable that to speak of it seems to her a blasphemy (seventh supplementary step); also, in response to Arnaldo's criticism that what she affirms of her experience is not found in the Scriptures, she responds that she sees no opposition between the two (seventh supplementary step). Finally, she claims that it is from within her mystical experience itself that she understands the divine source and meaning of the Scriptures, "the harsh and difficult sayings found in them, and how some are saved and others damned by them" (seventh supplementary step).

Part of the explanation for this seeming opposition between the Scriptures and mystical experience stems from Angela's dissatisfaction, oft repeated in her *Book,* with preachers and learned commentators of the revealed Word, a dissatisfaction she shared with the Franciscan Spirituals and other medieval mystics, most notably Marguerite Porete. For instance, in the *Memorial,* she judges quite severely those who know the Scriptures yet despise "the things of God"; and praises "not so much the great commentators on the Scriptures, but rather those who put them into practice." In one of the instructions (2), she reprimands in strong terms those who use the Scriptures for self-advantage and wrong purposes. Angela's exasperation with the prevailing scriptural interpretation and praxis and its dissonance with her own experience suggests, from the psychological point of view, why she kept her distance and expressed herself the way she did.

More pertinent is the fact that the illuminations Angela experienced at the vertex of her mystical ascent are perceived by her as coming directly from their source in the Godhead, thus antecedent to Scripture's composition and interpretation. What she is perhaps struggling to express is the discovery of the profound connaturality between the Scriptures and the depths of the soul, both harboring the same ineffable mystery, perceived from different vantage points.

There is, then, a profound continuity between Angela's mystical experience and the Scriptures, even if in the moments I have indicated, the former seems to come to the forefront. Finally, the key to her entire hermeneutics is the affirmation found in the seventh supplementary step: "all of Holy Scripture finds its fulfillment in the example of Christ's life." In her deep experience of the transcendence and immanence of the God-man, mystical heights and scriptural interpretation are mysteriously conjoined and identified.

E. Prayer

If, for Angela, the Eucharist and the Scriptures are touchstones for mystical experience, prayer is likewise where God is to be found. Prayer is the source of illumination and conversion. As such it is part of every stage of her growth. Her prayer life was graced, as I have noted, by an astonishing variety of visions, locutions, and raptures. The cross, the focus of her contemplation, is not a distant reality but increasingly becomes the very dynamic of her life of prayer reenacted in the inmost part of her being. She repeatedly returns to it, and is permeated and absorbed by it. In the *Instructions,* Angela insists that it is mainly through prayer that one learns how to study and meditate on the Book of Life, the suffering God-man and his teachings (see, in particular, instruction 3). Prayer, finally, is one of the main sources of knowledge of self and of God (see instructions 3, 5, 17, 29, 34).

As to the forms that Angela's prayer life took, besides the previously mentioned meditations on the Scriptures and obviously long moments of silent solitary prayer, she recited the Divine Office and valued repeating, slowly and attentively, the "Our Father of the Passion," a devotion widespread among penitents of the time. She also insists that she never abandoned what she refers to as bodily prayer: praying kneeling down, or prostrate on the ground, or with hands lifted toward heaven.

Angela's teachings on the nature, degrees, and effects of prayer are developed in the *Instructions* (see, in particular, 3 and 28). Jesus, Mary, and St. Francis are, for her, the great models of prayer. She teaches that following their example (and with the indispensable help of divine grace), fidelity in prayer and meditation on the Book of Life will "illumine, elevate, and transform the soul." As to the stages of development in prayer: One begins with corporal prayer, that is, with words and bodily movement; then one is led into mental prayer, where no thoughts except of God can occur; finally, one is led into supernatural prayer, a state of full enlightenment and beyond one's natural capacities of understanding. In these "three schools of prayer," Angela concludes, "one is transformed totally into the Beloved."

For Angela, prayer is also especially fruitful in times of temptation and tribulation. In these trials, she advocates, one should not pray with any less fervor than in times of consolation, for "forced prayers are particularly pleasing to God" (instruction 18). As to visions and consolations from God, one should not seek them nor spurn them if they come. Their purpose is to make the soul speed to God and are its food (instruction 33). They are useless, however, if they do not lead to knowledge of God and self (instruction 14).

F. Knowledge of God and Self

The theme of the knowledge of God and self is a central one in Angela's spirituality. Every step of the *Memorial* speaks about it in one form or another (see especially the protoinstruction in chap. 7). A number of instructions are devoted specifically, either in part or totally, to the development of this theme (3, 10, 14, 29, 34). From her own experience Angela had learned that it was by seeing and meditating on the crucified Christ, the Book of Life, and in living a life in conformity with his, that she had grown in the knowledge of God's goodness and, correspondingly, her own sinfulness and poverty. This twofold knowledge expanded her capacity to love. Ultimately, all the doubts of God's love that interlaced her journey are removed.[188] Totally transformed into love, she is "seated in the complete truth" of her life: the awareness of the abysses of God's love ("the most perfect and highest Good") and the abysses of her own "unknown nothingness" in adequately responding to that love.

G. The Way of the Blessed Francis

If the humanity and the passion and crucifixion of Christ played such a central role in Angela's journey, this is largely due to St. Francis, her spiritual father. She was deeply marked by the spirituality of the Poverello. His appearance to her in a dream at the beginning of her conversion; the central vision that occurs while she is looking at the stained-glass window in the basilica in Assisi in which he is depicted inserted within Christ; his appearances at the end of the *Memorial* to confirm her in her mission as guardian of poverty, a mandate that is repeated in a later vision, again in the same basilica (instruction 4); and, finally, during the last years of her life (instruction 21), his appearance to give her the stunning affirmation: "You are the only one born of me"— these visionary moments are all indicative of the archetypal role the "blessed Francis" played in her life.

What Angela understood of Francis's life and teachings is developed in the instructions, especially the one entitled the Book of Life (instruction 3), which contains her longest and most complete description of his spirituality. The path that he traced for her and others to follow consisted of his total conformity to the life and teachings of the God-man Jesus Christ by way of "the ineffable light of the truest poverty"—a path whose climax was his reception of the stigmata. Angela proceeds to name and elaborate on the two things Francis taught her in a remarkable manner: the way to be recollected in God, and the necessity of sharing in the company of Christ, namely, his poverty, suffering, contempt, and true obedience. These things, she concludes, were perfectly realized in the person of the blessed Francis, "on whom we should fix our gaze so that we might follow his example."

Another explicit reference to Francis as her teacher occurs in the second instruction in the context of the polemics concerning the heresy of the Spirit of Freedom. "Those who claim they have no desires and are not responsible for any actions," she points out, "should take a good look at the blessed Francis, who was the mirror of holiness and every perfection, yet at the end of his life proclaimed: 'Brothers, let us begin to do penance for until now we have made little progress'" (this final phrase is a quotation from Francis that can be found in Celano's first biography; it was probably widely circulated).[189]

In Angela's writings we find elements of Franciscan spirituality, as well as parallels with Francis's founding experience. These include the love of solitary prayer; the presence of joy in the midst of suffering; an encounter with lepers; the passion to live a poor life; the participation in the kenotic movement of God's salvific plan for and in Christ, his Son; the centrality of the Eucharist; the vision of created reality filled with God's grandeur; devotion to the Blessed Virgin and the Angels; and the deep identification with and affective devotion to the crucified Christ, which opens the revelation of the fullness of Trinitarian life.

In quite a few respects, however, Angela's experience differs from that of her model Francis. The theme of poverty for her is linked with that of self-knowledge, which is central to her teaching but nowhere explicit in Francis. The role of the Holy Spirit, fundamental for Francis, is scarcely mentioned in Angela's journey. The only explicit mention, in the *Memorial*, of the Spirit's role occurs in the account of her pilgrimage to Assisi when the Spirit speaks to her and inwardly prepares her for the Trinitarian vision about to take place. Similarly, God is rarely referred to as Father by Angela—only once in the *Memorial*—while that title is prominent in Francis's writings. It is, however, at the summit of the mystical ascent that Angela's experience seems to differ most markedly from that of the Poverello. Unlike Francis, Angela relies on the Pseudo-Dionysian theme of the divine darkness to articulate some of her highest experiences of God. If, at the summit, the stigmatized Francis participates in the filial relationship of God the Son with the Father, "the most High," and sings his cosmic song, the Canticle of Brother Sun, Angela speaks of being plunged into the abysses of the essence of the Trinitarian life and increasingly cries out her inability to express what she sees.

It follows, then, from the deep impact St. Francis had on her life that Angela found her spiritual home among the Franciscan penitents and enjoyed a close rapport with the followers of the Poverello who were circulating in Foligno and Umbria at that time—and who no doubt had a role to play in shaping her Franciscan orientation. For instance, of basic importance, as we have noted, was the part in her life played by Arnaldo, her Franciscan confessor and scribe, a man of considerable theological culture and one no doubt well acquainted with the Franciscan tradition and its teachings.

As I have also already mentioned, Angela belonged to the more zealous wing of the followers of the Poverello, namely, the Spirituals. Her role in the polemics of the period—except for the attacks on the sect of the Spirit of Freedom—seems to have been one of pacification and persuasion. Aside from occasional broadsides against preachers and the learned who do not practice what they preach and know, we do not find in her teachings any vituperations against "the carnal church," or its representatives, nor for that matter any Joachimite apocalyptic speculations or reference to Francis as the *alter Christus* or as the angel of the sixth seal—themes common in the writings of the Franciscan Spirituals. Rather, in the instructions she repeatedly admonishes and exhorts her spiritual sons to be of one mind and heart, to preach by example rather than contention, to remain little and humble, as necessary corollaries to embracing poverty. Nonetheless, in her burning zeal to follow Christ in "poverty, suffering, and contempt"—a triad she often repeated and one that seems to be uniquely hers—she was a natural ally of the more radical disciples (the "legitimate sons") of Francis of the first generations. It is undoubtedly not only because she was a woman but also because of her adherence to strict poverty that she was subjected to hostility, to the "contempt" of some of the friars and her fellow penitents and unnamed others.[190] It is significant to note in this regard that four of her letters to her spiritual sons treat of the role and benefits of tribulation (instructions 12, 13, 15, 17) for spiritual transformation.

It is important to stress, also, that the theme of poverty underwent considerable evolution during Angela's itinerary as recorded in the *Memorial*, and even more so in the instructions, some of which, as I have previously noted, are only an abbreviated report of her teachings, conceivably not even originating with Angela but developed and amplified by her Franciscan disciples, some, if not all of whom were of Spiritual-Fraticelli inclination. This is especially true for the instructions that treat of poverty and are dated after 1298 (e.g., instructions 4, 27, and 34). A chronological, linguistic, and source analysis (to determine the interdependency and conditioning from Franciscan and other spiritual currents) would be needed for a more balanced and thorough evaluation of the theme of poverty as found in Angela's *Book*. What follows is but a summary sketch of the main elements of this theme.[191]

For Angela, Franciscan poverty has both interior and exterior dimensions. In her interpretation of the absolute poverty of Jesus, which is mirrored in Francis, she sees both of these guides for her life as not only poor as regards all earthly possessions, friends, and relatives, but also poor in relation to their own power and self. Poverty, then, for Angela, entails the stripping away of every obstacle, material and spiritual, to perfect conformity with the life of Christ and contemplative union in love with him. It is also a means of identifying with the kenotic, self-emptying, and redemptive movement of the Crucified—the plan of salvation—for it was the poverty of Christ that recapitulated and redeemed the false poverty (one of ignorance) of the first man, Adam (instruction 3). Furthermore, holy poverty, as "the root and mother of humility and of every good," is the source of the power through which love is fully emancipated and the soul is established in its complete truth before God. Finally, then, it is a poverty not only of having but of being itself. As such, it entails the annihilation of the false self, the emptying to the point of nothingness, in order to become totally free and filled with the abundance of God's uncreated love and wisdom.[192]

H. Sect of the Spirit of Freedom

If Angela seems to have played mainly a conciliatory role in the vicissitudes between the Community and the Spirituals among the Franciscans, her position is considerably different toward the adherents of the sect of the Spirit of Freedom, whom she chastises in no uncertain terms. The second instruction, on the perils of spiritual love, seems in great part to be dedicated to warning her sons of the imminent dangers of this sect. Among the errors that she denounces is the claim made by their adherents that "they could live without desires" and were "in no way responsible for any actions," and, as a consequence, could engage with impunity in all kinds of immoral behavior, including sexual libertinage and deviations.[193] To this aberration, Angela opposes the example of St. Francis, who, even at the end of his life, preached the need for ongoing conversion, and that of the suffering God-man, who, for all of his life, demonstrated obedience to God's will "by the works of the cross and penance which were always with him." Rather than arrogantly assuming that one has reached the state of perfection and is above the law, Angela argues that the true ordering of love consists in "taking up the cross and doing penance as long as one lives." This path will lead to the humble awareness ("true annihilation") that "one is truly not the author of any good."

In instruction 3, which treats of Christ as the Book of Life, after a long exposition on the sufferings of Christ and the necessity of prayer, Angela resumes her attack on the antinomianism and false appearance of sanctity that prevailed among the disciples of the Spirit of Freedom. Again the criterion she uses to evaluate their thought and actions is whether these conform to the life of Christ, who, though "he was above the law and its author, was nonetheless, subject and a slave to it" and wanted his followers, in obedience to the Holy Spirit, to likewise "subject themselves to the law, divine precepts, and evangelical counsels."[194]

Despite, however, Angela's militancy against these sectarians of the Spirit of Freedom, "who openly oppose the life of Christ," and her desire to dissociate herself from them and their theories, her terminology and practices are on occasion not that different from theirs and other similar quietistic currents that, during this period, skirted or crossed the borders of orthodoxy. Among others: the gesture of stripping herself of her clothing before the crucifix (step eight of the *Memorial*); the blessing she receives over her alms, which has power to forgive sins in a context reminiscent of the Last Supper (second supplementary step); the drinking of the pus of a leper (third supplementary step); her impassibility toward the sufferings of Christ; but above all, the state of quiet she has attained at the highest stages of her ascent (seventh supplementary step), a state in which she claims she "cannot sin," "does not see any difference between good deeds and evil ones," sees God "without intermediary" and, subsequently, sees the divine essence and even attains a partial attainment of the beatific vision. All these episodes and the terminology used to describe them (and more can be detected in the *Instructions*) indicate, at least implicitly, that she too was nourished by these heterodox currents.[195]

I. The Blessed Virgin

Marian devotion plays an important but subservient role in Angela's spiritual itinerary. Her *Book* is interlaced with references to the Blessed Virgin, and these are often associated with visions of the crucified Christ and prayers to him. For Angela, Mary is perceived mainly as "handmaid of the Lord," "mother of the afflicted," and "queen of mercy." As "handmaid of the Lord," she is an exemplar of poverty and extraordinary humility. As "mother of the afflicted," she is the one who "suffered more from the passion than anyone else." As "queen of mercy," she intercedes for the human race (as, for instance, in a vision of Mary in her glorified state recorded in the second supplementary step of the *Memorial*); and is a fount of special blessings for Angela and her spiritual sons and daughters. This latter aspect is highlighted in a vision Angela receives during a procession toward the Portiuncula in Assisi on the vigil of the feast of the Indulgence (instruction 4). After Angela sees the crucified Christ embracing her spiritual sons, it is Mary who appears, as "the queen of mercy and of every grace," and she, in turn, leans down to Angela's sons and daughters, kisses them, and enshrouds them with her light.

In the context of considerations on the Blessed Virgin as teacher of prayer (instruction 3), Angela boldly professes her faith in the Immaculate Conception of Mary as one of the privileges bestowed upon her as a result of her intimate union with the Trinity. Finally, during a vision that occurred in the church of San Francesco in Foligno on the feast of the Purification of Mary (instruction 19), Angela sees the Blessed Virgin placing the Child Jesus in her arms. The Child was naked and as soon as Angela received him in her arms, he opened his eyes and fire emanated from them. The benefit of this vision, one filled with great tenderness and numinosity, was totally ineffable.

J. The Angels

On a number of occasions during Angela's itinerary, especially during celebrations of the Eucharist (reported in the *Memorial*),[196] the heavens open and Angela sees Christ surrounded by a multitude of angels. She perceives angels in their role of praising and contemplating the divine majesty, as well as in their task of presenting and administering to Christ, the God-man, to her, and to humanity (instructions 20 and 34). Because angels enjoy a privileged relationship with God—and probably because her own baptismal name inclined her to do so—Angela would pray to them, in particular to St. Michael (instruction 20). In joyful communication with the angels, she is even told by them that she will be granted the same experience as that of the Seraphim (ibid.), the highest order in the angelic hierarchy. Finally, on the Feast of the Holy Angels, toward the end of her life, and while she was meditating on the role that angels have in praising God, a number of angels appeared to Angela to announce her definitive espousal with Christ (instruction 36).

K. Bodily Dimension

It is significant to note that it was largely through the body that the intimate and tangible love of Christ crucified communicated itself to Angela. To be sure, it is likely that she inflicted harsh bodily punishment on herself, as was common at the time, but except for instances of fasting and the episode in the "horrible darkness" when she applies material fire to "quench" her torments, there are no explicit references to such practices either in the *Memorial* or in her *Instructions*.

Rather, if in the earlier steps the body is unable to stand the impact of the inflow of transcendental life—for example, the uncontrollable shouting after the Assisi vision, the shrieking at the sight of depictions of the passion of Christ—painfully and gradually, it is, in a sense, remade and shows signs of redemption.

After she is interiorly purified, all Angela's senses enjoy the pleasure of God's tender presence. She sees with the eyes of the spirit an incredible variety of visions of Christ and a few of the world filled to overflowing with the divine presence; hears Christ speaking to her and, in the final stages, saying "most high words" that cannot be written; smells indescribably sweet odors; feels the warmth of the divine embrace holding her tightly; and on many occasions feels her bones dislocating so that she can hear them cracking. At one point, Masazuola, her companion, reports seeing Angela's aura, like a multicolored star emanating from her body; at another point, her face radiant and her eyes shining like candles.

As we have already noted in the context of Angela's prayer life, she highly valued bodily forms of prayer, as the first school of spiritual transformation, one never to be abandoned. So many of her visionary experiences occurred while she was on pilgrimage to Assisi that it is reasonable to assume that these journeys to a sacred space, a practice widespread in the Middle Ages, were important rites of passage for her.

Furthermore, Angela had known the experience of human love. As she grows in intimacy with Christ and experiences love's divine dimension, the gestures and expressions of human love, far from being destroyed, are lifted to a new level of realization. Some of the more startling episodes and visions of the *Memorial*—the stripping off of her clothes in a gesture of self-donation before the cross; the sight of the beauty of Christ's throat and neck; the intimate moment with him in the sepulcher—are ultimately to be interpreted as expressions of the transformations of her love from the physical to the spiritual without the former being denied. Christ, indeed, had become the focus of her affective energies as well as the source of their redemption.

Finally, when as a result of her visions in the darkness Angela sings her love song and celebrates the cross as her bed, what, in part, she is extolling is the final integration of her affectivity, the transmutation of instinct into spirit. What this suggests is that at the summit of her ascent, Angela's spiritual passions are never divorced from the sexual ones. If it is with a fiery unruly body that she had begun her spiritual journey, it is with a fiery but ordered one that she receives from Christ the nuptial embrace. "Angela of Foligno, a swooning, bedded saint," exclaims Jean-Nöel Vuarnet.[197]

Like so many mystics, Angela often expresses her vehement longing to die, even to die in martyrdom. Ferré records at least twenty such instances in the text.[198] Once again it is the power of God's love, the death-life cycle of the crucified Christ, that quickens Angela's desire for the final breakthrough in her passionate pilgrimage toward the absolute:

101

"For me to live is to die," she sings to her beloved; "draw me then to yourself."

L. Iconography

Iconography played an important and often underestimated role in medieval piety, and especially popular lay piety.[199] In the visionary climate of medieval culture, spiritual understanding was often linked to the capacity to see. The goal of human sight was to see with God's eyes, or allow God to see himself through one's inner eyes of faith: the beatific vision. An importance is given to sight in Angela's *Book* that would warrant closer analysis. In instruction 3, for instance, she teaches:

> The more perfectly and purely we see, the more perfectly and purely we love. As we see, so we love. Therefore, the more we see of Jesus Christ, God and man, the more we are transformed into him by love.

For Angela and for the medieval person, imaginative visual habits broadened the range of perception of the truths of revelation. Key to this transformation of sight was the suggestive power of holy images to impress themselves on the imagination and enable the viewer to participate inwardly in the events depicted. The radiance of spiritual energy present in religious paintings had an impact on Angela's spiritual formation that was considerable, even if difficult to demonstrate precisely.

A number of explicit references in Angela's *Book* testify to the power that visual representations, in particular paintings depicting the crucifixion, exercised in her spiritual development. For instance, in the eighteenth step of the *Memorial,* Angela confesses that whenever she saw the passion of Christ depicted, she could hardly bear it, and would come down with a fever and fall sick. Her companion, as a result, hid these paintings or did her best to keep them out of her sight. Many of her meditations occurred and were intensified while her eyes were focused on an image of Christ crucified; among other examples, she mentions that once, while in prayer, the sight of the nails that had fixed Christ on the cross had such an impact on her that she could no longer stand on her feet and needed to bend over, sit down, then lie stretched out on the ground with her head inclined over her arms. Following which, she says, Christ showed her the beauty of his throat and his arms (first supplementary step). This experience, she reports, transformed her former sorrow into a joy so intense that she could say nothing about it. It is with similar emotional intensity that Angela reports what she felt when she saw a drama representing Christ's passion in a piazza in Foligno: "I entered within the side of Christ. All sadness was gone and my joy so great that I could say nothing about it" (fourth supplementary step).

In the central vision, which occurred while she was on pilgrimage in Assisi, it is again an iconographic representation that is, for Angela, a source of a powerful illumination. In the basilica of St. Francis, when she sees the stained-glass window depicting St. Francis being held closely by Christ, she is totally overwhelmed by the numinous revelations that emanate from it, and falls on the ground, screaming inarticulately.

The fifth supplementary step provides another example that demonstrates the interaction between iconography and visionary experience (and the language used to describe it) in Angela's itinerary. In attempting to describe the high level of mystical experience she has attained, Angela affirms that the state she is in is "higher than standing at the foot of the cross as Blessed Francis did" (fifth supplementary step). As Mariano D'Alatri has observed, it is highly probable that Angela was referring to either the weeping Francis at the foot of the cross depicted by Cimabue in both of his crucifixions located in the upper church of the basilica in Assisi, or the painting of the crucifixion requested by Benedetta, the Poor Clare abbess who immediately succeeded St. Clare, and which to this day is located in the Church of St. Clare in Assisi. In it St. Francis is represented kneeling and kissing Christ's feet dripping with blood.[200]

A final example, among many, of the impact of medieval iconography on Angela's visionary experience occurs in this same fifth supplementary step. On Saturday of Holy Week, she reports being in a state of ecstasy in which she found herself united with Christ in the sepulcher. After kissing his breast and his mouth, she placed her cheek on Christ's own and he, in turn, placed his hand on her other cheek, pressing her closely to him. This highly evocative and atemporal vision echoes a new theme appearing in the devotional literature of the period and represented in numerous panel paintings. In scenes depicting the deposition of Christ from the cross, the Blessed Virgin replaces Joseph of Arimathea as the person receiving the corpse from the cross, and in representations of Christ lying in the sepulcher, one finds her either bestowing a final embrace on her Son, or kneeling down and contemplating him at a distance, or drawing near to him to press her cheek against his. This latter example is what is reproduced in Angela's vision. Verses from the

Song of Songs provide further clues to the inspiration that lay behind the richness of the scenario: "Let him kiss me with kisses of his mouth!" and "His left hand is under my head and his right arm embraces me" (1:1 and 2:6). In the contemplative deepening of her appreciation of the meaning of Christ's crucifixion it was quite likely, then, that Angela's piety was stimulated by what she saw so movingly depicted in the paintings, in particular the new ways of representing the passion of Christ, which characterized this artistic moment in the Umbrian valley as elsewhere in medieval Europe (and perhaps, as with other mystics, her visions in turn stimulated artistic reproductions). In the vision just described, she duplicates Mary's role in some of these paintings, and like her, shares an intimate embrace with her Beloved in the sepulcher, a Christ dead yet, paradoxically, fully alive.[201] Similarly, in the agony of the horrible darkness of the sixth supplementary step, Angela seems to identify with Mary's state of desolation as she cries out: "My son, my son, why have you abandoned me?"

J. Angela's Spiritual Ancestry and Importance

If Angela deeply assimilated the Franciscan way, she also inherited much from other spiritual ancestors. As previously observed, her *Book*, especially the *Memorial*, is unmistakably hers, but is also the product of a particular context. Never referring to them directly in her account, Angela (and her redactors!) nonetheless adopted, and made her own, themes, ideas, and devotions that were in vogue during that time and were especially alive in the Umbrian valley. To mention a few, aside from the especially but not exclusively Franciscan ones previously mentioned: the importance of self-knowledge and the role of memory in the spiritual journey; the exchange of hearts with God; the following of the naked Christ; the measure of God's love; Christ as doctor and healer; devotion to the Sacred Heart, the Blessed Virgin, Mary Magdalene, and St. John. As these motifs as well as others helped shape her life and language, Angela would invariably bring her own originality to bear in her use of them. Thus, for instance, if, as I have noted, she drew from the Cistercian tradition of affective piety, almost completely absent in her narrative is the explicit use of the nuptial typology of the *Song of Songs,* widespread among her contemporaries, especially women. Likewise, as I have taken care to demonstrate, if her writings echo the apophatic tradition of divine darkness, she refines it to fit her own experience. In the notes that accompany my translation, I try to indicate some of these echoes, as well as those parallels with other medieval mystics that resound and abound in Angela's *Book*. To be sure, traces of other sources remain to be detected. The impact of Augustinian and Neoplatonic exemplarism, for instance, merits further attention, as well as what was probably gleaned from medieval sermons and other forms of oral transmission. Ultimately, whatever influences may have been present, the text on hand (and the experience that it describes) is so original and creative that any attempt to conclusively pin down whose impulses are being borrowed falters in the face of the powerful and independent religious genius of which this text is a witness.

The spirituality found in the *Memorial* and synthesized in the *Instructions* suggests, then, that Angela was one of the most outstanding exponents of a new wave of medieval piety that, although receptive to tradition, transcended it to forge new paths. In the wake of the energy generated by the Francis event, this piety, which was crowned by an outpouring of mystical graces, flourished among Italian women but also had its male representatives, such as Jacopone da Todi, whose affinity with Angela I also note in my text. Likewise, the peculiar brand of spirituality that blossomed in the Umbrian valley, and out of which Angela emerged as mother and teacher, had striking parallels with the Beguine spirituality of Northern Europe and in particular with its most eminent representatives, Mechthild of Magdeburg (d. 1297), Beatrice of Nazareth (d. 1268) (Cistercian abbess, but educated by the Beguines and sharing their spirituality), Hadewijch (mid-thirteenth century), and Marguerite Porete (d. 1310) (parallel passages are indicated in the footnotes to the text). Further research and closer analysis than is possible here is needed before Angela's place in the pantheon of these outstanding exponents of medieval women's mysticism, and for that matter the entire Christian mystical tradition, can be more firmly established, but the following brief considerations, I trust, will help lay the groundwork for such an effort.

What Angela perhaps has most in common with the four holy Beguines just mentioned is a fundamental impulse in which the aim of the mystical journey is to be so totally transformed by God's love that at the summits the soul is stripped of all its creatural capacities and participates in a union with God that is "without any difference" or "without intermediary." What she also shares with them is the complex and innovative interweaving of the terminology of essence and of love—union with God as the One who is, and total love—with which these mystics, in a wide variety of ways, describe their deepest experiences of God, and their plunge into the abysses of the Trinitarian life. Another characteristic of these mystics as well as of Angela is the understanding of the reciprocity between the divine depths and the depths of the soul: an awareness at once of one's nothingness or poverty and of the ineffable plenitude of the Godhead, a plenitude at times described apophatically (e.g., "nothingness," "desert," "abyss," "uncreated"). What notably differentiates Angela from her northern counterparts (and even from her spiritual father, Francis, the troubadour of Lady Poverty) is the absence in her writings of the courtly love motif that prevailed among the Beguines, including the four mentioned here.

In the free and new ways in which Angela and these four Beguines spun together these various themes, combining speculation of the highest order and experiential awareness, they came, as I have noted, increasingly under suspicion of the official church. Notable in this regard is the burning at the stake of one of them, Marguerite Porete. Of the four, she is the one to whose spirituality Angela's bears the closest resemblance. Marguerite's *Mirouer* is certainly more abstract (reference to personal experience is scant) than Angela's *Book*, but nonetheless, besides the themes shared with the other Beguines just mentioned, there are a number of significant parallels between the two works. Central among these was their description of the total passivity or state of nothingness that the transformed or annihilated soul attains when it is united with the divine essence. Marguerite's articulation of this experience and the ascent to it was seen as minimizing, if not eliminating, the role of the virtues and the mediation of sacramental and ecclesial life, and as a result was associated with the tenets of the Free Spirit heretics, especially with regard to the freedom they arrogated to themselves. Much like Marguerite, Angela also affirms that when love is totally transformed, "it is without works," but with this added caution, "it is the Uncreated that does all the work and produces the works of love." In her instructions, then, Angela more markedly distances herself than does Marguerite from the Free Spirits who, she disdainfully points out, claim that they "can live without being subject to any law and do as they please."[202] In the daring and innovative ways with which Angela and these four Beguines articulated their soarings into the abysses of the divine life, they anticipated many of the themes that were to be picked up and developed by the male Rhineland mystics, in particular Eckhart and Ruusbroec.

Angela belongs, then, to the forefront of this wave of mostly women mystics and visionaries who, in the latter half of the thirteenth century and in the fourteenth, broke new ground. Pushed to a radical situation by her personal wounds, her marginal status as a lay woman, her entanglement with the Franciscan Spirituals, and the pressure of an anxiety-ridden society (even if this factor is only implicit in her *Book*), she found new meanings from intense and affective identification with the crucified "suffering God-man" and became a source of spiritual vitality for her age and ages to come. Tradition gave Angela the title of *Magistra Theologorum*. Pertinent in this regard is the observation of an unknown disciple of hers in the epilogue of her *Book:* "It is not counter to the order of providence that God established a woman as doctor (to men's shame); to my knowledge she has no match on earth."

There are a number of other reasons for Angela's greatness. As I have pointed out, she is above all not a theoretician of mysticism; her main concern is to transmit her experience. In the often faulty, hesitating, and yet very expressive Latin of Arnaldo, the ardent and raw realism of her experience flows from almost every page like molten lava and makes her *Book* one of the finest monuments of Christian mysticism.

Certainly, the inexhaustible variety of her visions of Christ and his passion, so concrete and vivid, and her sharing in the horror of his abandonment on the cross establish Angela as an important mystic. Intimately associated with the kenotic or self-emptying movement of the divine plan realized in Christ (his "poverty, suffering, and contempt") she was filled simultaneously with the joy and glory of his divine nature and the pain and the agony of his human nature. In this coincidence of opposites, Angela perceived how the polarity of good and evil was subsumed in its total synthesis in the depths of divine wisdom. Outstanding also is her double apprehension of the divine nature under its personal and impersonal form, as both utterly transcendent to, yet completely immanent in, the human soul. In the articulation of the twofold abyss (one of the more striking characteristics of her spirituality) in which she perceives her own nothingness and the total ineffability of God, Angela is here also a soulmate of Jacopone da Todi and the Rhenish-Flemish mystics, both men and women, of the thirteenth and fourteenth centuries. It is, however, her vertiginous experiences at the summits of her ascent—the visions of God in and with darkness, her spiralings in the fathomless abysses of the Trinitarian life and the divine essence so that only the flimsiest veil separates her from the beatific state—that place Angela among the greatest mystics of the Middle Ages and of the entire

Christian tradition. Comparing her with Teresa of Avila, Ferré points out that both are queens: "Teresa in the complete and detailed teaching of the ways of prayer; Angela in the exploration of the beyond.[203]

Angela, to use the terms of the Prologue of the *Memorial*, had indeed "probed, perceived, and touched the Incarnate Word of life," and what was progressively revealed to her was the boundless love and fathomless abysses of the Trinity. To describe the total ineffability of this experience, her language had increasingly to acknowledge its limits, "that it lies, even blasphemes."

Angela's Influence

"I will do great things in you in the sight of the nations. Through you, I shall be known and my name will be praised by many nations." This annunciation at the beginning of the second supplementary step was to prove prophetic. Angela's startling story and her spirituality were to merit the esteem of and serve as inspiration to an impressive number of saints, spiritual writers, and theologians down through the ages. The stream of her influence, however, is not an easy one to follow. Very early it goes underground, only to well up in terrain often far from its source and often in very unexpected places. Many tributaries remain to be discovered. I can only indicate here some of the moments in which her direct influence on subsequent spiritual literature springs up and waters souls thirsty for the absolute.

Angela's most direct influence, of course, was on the small group of disciples, "her crown and joy in the Lord," for whom she served as spiritual mother and to whom most of her teachings were addressed. Unfortunately, as I have noted previously, very little is known about them. It does seem that some of them were friars who shared the aspirations of the Spiritual party of the Franciscans, and from the theologically elaborate tone of some of the instructions they wrote in her name (e.g., instructions 4, 32), it seems that some of them were quite learned. Most of the time they are referred to as "sons," but on occasion "daughters" are also mentioned as part of her entourage (e.g., the pilgrimage to the Portiuncula). Furthermore, Angela (or her disciples) seems to have been quite conscious of the universality of her message, one meant to extend itself beyond the confines of Umbria. In her final blessing, as elsewhere in the text, she mentions that she had been entrusted with "the care of the sons and daughters on this side of the sea and beyond it."

INTRODUCTION

A. Ubertino of Casale

Many penitents, whose number is impossible to calculate, must have heard of her and passed through Foligno to draw from the experience of the holy mother. The most notable of these was the turbulent leader of the Spirituals, Ubertino of Casale. Born in 1259, he entered the Franciscans of the province of Genoa at the age of fourteen. He taught in Florence, where he fell under the spell of Peter Olivi, and later studied in Paris for nine years. His encounter with Angela probably took place in 1298, and it was to have a decisive influence on his life.[204] In the prologue of his book *Arbor vitae crucifixae Jesu,* he sings the praises of the one to whom he attributed his conversion to a more radical ascetic life:

> In the twenty-fifth year of my religious life, it came about—I will not go into detail—that I encountered the reverend and most holy mother, Angela of Foligno, a veritable angel, to whom Jesus revealed my heart's defects and his secret kindness in such a manner that I was convinced he spoke through her. She restored a thousandfold all those spiritual gifts I had lost through my sins; so that from that moment I have not been the same man I was before. The splendor of her radiant virtue changed the whole tenor of my life. It drove out the weakness and languor from my soul and body and healed my mind torn with distractions. No one who knew me before could doubt that the spirit of Christ was newly begotten in me through her.[205]

According to Ferré, it was to Ubertino that Angela addressed at least one of her letters (instruction 18).[206] There is, however, no documentary evidence to substantiate this claim. The editors of the critical edition dismiss this hypothesis and leave open the question whether any of Angela's letters were meant for Ubertino.[207]

Yet it is significant to note that in February 1308, Ubertino, in the service of Cardinal Napoleon Orsini, a protector of the Spirituals, was in Cortona, along with four provincial ministers, to verify and approve a recent biography of St. Margaret of Cortona by Brother Giunta Bevegnati.[208] He may also have been involved in the canonization process of St. Clare of Montefalco, through whose intercession, according to one account, he was miraculously cured of a painful hernia. Furthermore, the hypothesis has been advanced that he may have been one of the unnamed signers of the approbation that appears at the beginning of Angela's *Book.*[209]

As to the direct influence of Angela's thinking on the content of Ubertino's *Arbor vitae,* in his recent study of Ubertino, Marino Damiata notes that if there are many convergences—for example, the shared insistence on the crucified humanity of Christ, his suffering and poverty, and even similar terminology—for example, "the Book of Life, namely the life of the God and man, Jesus Christ"—there are also profound differences in outlook between the two. Angela's gaze is fixed on the sufferings of Christ, while Ubertino systematically shifts his regard to those suffering with Christ within the Franciscan Order and the church—a societal interest largely missing in Angela's writings. Analogously, if both manifest a great love for St. Francis, for Angela he remains but a guide and exemplar, while for Ubertino he is so exalted, it is as if there is no one else. Both, for instance, distinguish between legitimate and illegitimate sons, but for Angela the criterion for fidelity is not to Francis, as it is for Ubertino, but to Christ. In the dispute over the issue of poverty among the Franciscans, Angela is concerned with maintaining concord and unity among the factions, a concern absent in Ubertino.[210]

B. Problems in Early Dissemination

Aside from the association with Ubertino (for which there is no documentary proof other than the cited prologue), a number of other factors that helped to create suspicion about Angela's writings may partly explain why the original and most of the early manuscripts were lost and why her name does not appear in any of the early chronicles of the Order.[211]

For instance, an important handicap to the early distribution of Angela's text may well have been the fact that it bears the sign of approval of Cardinal James Colonna, noted friend of the Spirituals. Only a few months after having signed the approbation of Angela's *Memorial* (10 May 1297), the first part of her *Book,* he (along with his nephew Cardinal Peter Colonna) was deposed and excommunicated by Boniface VIII (10 May 1297).[212] Significantly, most of the surviving manuscripts do not contain this approbation. Indeed, in one of the most important manuscripts, the Assisi codex, it seems to have been quite early scraped off, and in one of the rare early mentions of Angela, the *De Conformitate vitae B. Francisci ad vitam Domini Iesu* of Bartolomeo da Pisa (d. 1401), she is presented as having written a book approved by a cardinal, whose name goes unmentioned. Furthermore, all the other theologians who signed the said approbation remain anonymous (perhaps because they were Spirituals?).

Still another clue to the suspicion surrounding Angela's writings is the fact that in the Assisi codex, one finds written in the margin by an anonymous Franciscan that "this book was given to me by an unknown donor and I have not been able to find out who." This codex, dated as early as the first half of the fourteenth century, is entitled *Liber sororis Lellae de Fulgineo de tertio ordine sancti Francisci*. The use of the diminutive *"sororis Lellae,"* indicative of a certain proximity and familiarity, differs from all the successive manuscripts, which speak of "blessed Angela," "St. Angela," and the like. Furthermore, this codex, found in the Sacro Convento library in Assisi, was kept not in the public library, but under reserve in the "secret" one, where it was accessible to only a few—yet another indication that it was considered a dangerous book.

Even if my thesis must remain at the level of conjecture, this indirect evidence points to the strong possibility that Angela's text played a role in the quarrel shaking the Franciscan Order at that time. So as not to be guilty by association, many probably sought to keep their distance from it or used it for their own purposes in ways that effectively limited its diffusion.[213] Who knows if in some way Angela herself was not considered a partisan of the Colonna-Spirituals alliance and, much like her contemporaries Marguerite Porete and the Beguines, subject to the growing glare of the Inquisition, hot in pursuit of heretics among the mystics, especially the women?

There are still further indications that Angela's writings were viewed with suspicion. In three fourteenth-century codices containing summaries of or extracts from Angela's writings, these are presented as selections from *The Revelations of St. Elisabeth of Schönau*. Three German codices confuse Angela with Clare of Montefalco, recording the insignia of the passion found in her heart. In an Oxford codex (ca. 1384–1385), Angela's writings are found together with the *Mirouer* of Marguerite Porete.

In the late medieval period, it is perhaps not too surprising that Angela's writings found early recognition in Belgium. Three valuable codices—two in Brussels and one in Liège (1409, 1413, 1424), to which were later added one from Enghien (1485) and another from Brussels (end of fifteenth century)—all belong to the first family of manuscripts, which served as basis for the reconstruction of the first redaction in the critical edition. This is an indication perhaps that the text circulated among Beguine or, later, the Devotio Moderna circles. Toward the end of his life, Ubertino of Casale found asylum with the Benedictines of Gembloux, Belgium, where he may even have ended his days. Could he not have brought with him the text of the one who had inspired his conversion?[214]

In the fifteenth century, Angela's *Book* makes its appearance in Spain and France, and in the latter half of the sixteenth century its presence is documented in Germany.

In Italy, during this same period (fourteenth to sixteenth century), strangely enough, the circulation of Angela's text is slower than elsewhere and limited to a quite restricted area. Vernacular translations were made available that provide a clue to its geographical and chronological trajectory. These Italian versions appear in Florence, Parma, and Verona in the fourteenth century; Treviso, Milan, Perugia, and Liguria in the fifteenth and sixteenth centuries. What is hard to explain is the total absence of any mention of the first redaction.

It is interesting to note the original owners of the text. For the period between the first half of the fourteenth and the late sixteenth century, seven or eight codices come from Italian Franciscan friaries; three of the five from Belgium belonged to the Canons Regular of St. Augustine; at least six come from various Benedictine congregations; one from the Gerolamini of Barcelona; and another from the Celestines of Avignon. From this evidence, even if it is incomplete, one can deduce that the diffusion of the text outside of Italy during this period is not due to the Franciscans.

Indeed, among the Franciscans recognition of Angela's importance seems to have been slow in coming. It is only after nearly a century of absolute silence concerning Angela (since Bartolomeo da Pisa's chronicles) that her name reappears, especially in the circles of the Observance, a reform wing of the Franciscans, who regarded her as one of their heroines. In a poem dated 1465, Marino di Gionata of Agnone, a tertiary likely of Observance tendencies, mentions her among the saints and blessed dear to the reform. Three codices from the fifteenth century were found in friaries linked to the Observants (Fontecolombo, St. Bernardino dell'Aquila, and St. Fortunato of Montefalco). In this same century, Angela is also depicted, among other famous Franciscan tertiaries, in the cloisters of the Observants. The blessed Lorenzo of Villamagna, an Observant, mentions her among other holy tertiaries in a collection of his sermons (ca. 1502). A Poor Clare from the monastery of Monteluce, chaplained by the Observants of Monteripido, copied Angela's

Book in the vernacular (ca. 1507–1509). Still another codex found in Venice and dated in the fifteenth century, but certainly older, can also be traced to the Observant Franciscans. Finally, the interest in Angela's writings among these reform-minded Franciscans climaxes with the first securely known printing of Angela's *Book*, promoted by the Spanish Franciscan cardinal Francesco Ximenes, an Observant: a Latin version in 1505, and a Spanish one in 1510.[215]

It is no easy matter, then, to follow the stream of Angela's influence during the two centuries or so that followed her death. I have indicated some of the major documented paths of the dissemination of her text. Others have been traced, but questions about who and how many read her *Book* and commented on it, or how it meandered from country to country, monastery to monastery, and was passed on from hand to hand, remain in large part unanswered.[216]

C. Sixteenth to Twentieth Century

Without any claims that my list is complete, I will indicate, in what follows, some of the major wellsprings of Angela's influence from the sixteenth to the twentieth centuries. Noteworthy is the fact that by very early in the seventeenth century, Angela's writings or selections from them were available in Latin and in translation in all the major European languages (except English).[217]

The above-mentioned Spanish version of Angela's *Book*, ordered by Cardinal Ximenes, was probably the one that St. Teresa of Avila (d. 1582) came into contact with in the sixteenth century. It has been noted that Angela was among the saints known by her. There are at least two quotations in Angela's text that seemed to have directly inspired Teresa.[218] In all likelihood, this same Spanish version was also read by Bernadino de Laredo (1482–1540), who influenced Teresa.[219] St. Ignatius of Loyola (1491–1556) may likewise have known Angela from the same source.[220]

In the seventeenth century, St. Francis de Sales (1567–1627) frequently refers to Angela in his writings. In the *Introduction à la vie dévote*, he draws many of his examples from the life of St. Angela. In his preface to his *Traité de l'amour de Dieu*, he classifies her along with St. Catherine of Siena, St. Catherine of Genoa, and St. Mathilde (or Mechthilde of Magdeburg?) among those "superior women" who have best expressed "the celestial passions of sacred love." He also places her, along with Mary the Egyptian, Simeon the Stylite, and again St. Catherine of Siena and St. Catherine of Genoa, as personalities "easier to admire than to imitate."[221]

The first to attempt to write a biography of Angela was that of Ludovico Iacobili, an Italian from Foligno. He initially wrote only a few pages (1628), then composed a more ample version in his *Vite dei santi e beati di Foligno* (1628), pp. 16–28, and rewrote it, in an even more complete form, in his *Vite dei santi e beati dell'Umbria* (1647), pp. 17–28. Even if he is not always a reliable source, we can learn from him many of the local traditions that grew up around Angela's life.[222]

In 1643, the noted Jesuit hagiographer Johannes Bollandus published a Latin edition of Angela's writings that had considerable influence, since many subsequent translations were based on it. Unfortunately this edition, which was based on incomplete earlier manuscripts, confuses the order and content of Angela's story and teachings (e.g., eighteen steps instead of thirty).[223] Pope Benedict XIV (1675–1758) saw Angela as the equal of St. Teresa of Avila, St. Peter of Alcantara, St. John of the Cross, St. Bridget of Sweden, and St. Catherine of Siena.[224] St. Alphonsus Liguori (1696–1787) quotes Angela quite frequently in his writings.[225] Both Fénelon (1651–1715)[226] and Bossuet (1627–1704),[227] in their controversy on the "impossible assumptions" of the saints, agree to call on the authority of Angela to buttress their arguments. Jean-Jacques Olier (d. 1657), the founder of the Society of St. Sulpice and a leader of the French School of Spirituality, refers to her as the saint "who penetrated the double abyss, the depths of the passion [of Christ] and the heights of his divinity."[228]

Angela's writings also surfaced toward the later part of the sixteenth century in the German Pietism movement. Johann Arndt (1555–1621), whom Albert Schweitzer called "a prophet of interior Protestantism," made extensive use of her writings, especially in Book Two of his major work, *True Christianity* (1606).[229]

It is in French circles, as I have already begun to indicate, that Angela's influence is most notable, and perhaps no one has given greater impetus to the reading of her writings than the French philosopher Ernest Hello (1828–1885). In 1868, he published his translation of Angela's writings, *Le livre des visions et instructions de la bienheureuse Angèle de Foligno*. It had enormous success, enjoying as many as ten editions, the most recent one from a Swiss press in 1976. What Hello tried to do, as he indicates in his preface, is to translate, not according to the letter of the text, but according to its spirit: "I have tried to bring to life in French what was alive in Latin. I have tried to make the French cry out what the soul cried out in Latin. I have tried to translate tears."[230] In spite of its many imperfections, some due in part to the fact that he worked from an unreliable manuscript, Hello's brilliant translation catapulted Angela into the consciousness of modern French culture. Countless thousands, both in and outside the Franciscan world, came to know her through it.

St. Elizabeth of the Trinity (1880–1906) was among those acquainted with Hello's version, and she quotes it in her writings.[231] The novelist George Bernanos quotes a passage from it in his *Dialogues des Carmélites*.[232] George Bataille, perhaps the most important contemporary philosopher to explore the nexus between mysticism and eroticism, refers to Angela in his writings and, in a series of poems under the general heading "L'archangélique," composes one, "Le tombeau," in which he alludes to passages in Angela's seventh supplementary step.[233] Still another example of the influence of Hello's version is a play adapted from it by Philipe Clévenot, starring Bérangère Bonvoisin as Angela. *Celle qui ment* is the title of the play, performed in Paris and Rouen in 1984.

It was likewise in France that the first major attempt was made to produce a critical edition of Angela's writings. In 1925, Paul Doncoeur, basing his work on the Assisi codex, but with additions and corrections from the more complete version in the Subiaco codex and from other secondary codices, published first the Latin text in 1925, then a French translation a year later.[234] M. J. Ferré, after initially collaborating with Doncoeur, thought that the latter had "proceeded too hastily," broke off from him, and came up with his own Latin version, based more exclusively on the Assisi codex, and an accompanying French translation, in 1927. Ferré's version is the more reliable of the two.[235]

Shortly thereafter (1932) in Italy, M. Faloci Pulignani, an important compiler of Angela data, published a Latin edition based on the Subiaco codex. His is the least reliable of the three early twentieth-century Latin editions.[236] Shortly thereafter, also in Italy, Antonio Blasucci, O.F.M. Conv., in a number of publications, made a significant contribution to the diffusion of Angela's spirituality.[237] A Folignate, Sergio Andreoli, is a faithful contemporary compiler of Angela data, as well as translator of the first Italian translation of Angela's writings based on the new critical edition.[238] Finally, an important congress honoring the seventh centenary of Angela's conversion was held in Foligno in 1985.[239]

116

INTRODUCTION

In English literature, the first documented evidence of Angela's influence that I have been able to uncover dates back to Augustine Baker's *Holy Wisdom*, written in 1657.[240] The two earliest known English translations of Angela's writings appeared in two separate editions. One, by an anonymous English priest, appeared in 1871 and was re-edited in 1888. The other was published by Mary Steegmann in 1909. Both are based on unreliable manuscripts.[241] In the twentieth century, Evelyn Underhill quoted Angela profusely in her influential studies on mysticism.[242] More recently, medieval scholars such as Rudolf Bell, Caroline Walker Bynum, and Elizabeth Petroff refer to Angela frequently.[243]

In the contemporary arena as well, Angela's influence turns up in unexpected places. Prominent French feminists, Simone de Beauvoir,[244] Julia Kristeva,[245] and Luce Irigaray[246] are intrigued by her and quote her in their writings. Umberto Eco, in his best-selling novel, *The Name of the Rose*, puts some of the warnings of Angela about the perils of spiritual love (cf. instruction 2) in the mouth of her disciple Ubertino of Casale.[247] Robert Bly, a contemporary poet, referring to the moment of Angela's (whom he mistakenly calls "Anna of Foligno") loss of her husband and children uses this as an example of "energy transfer" from the "mammal brain" (locus of human love) to the "new brain" (locus of mystical experience).[248] Finally, Thomas Merton, who explored the mystical tradition extensively, devoted a conference to Angela for his novices at the monastery of Gethsemani. He speaks of her ("one of the wild mystics"), quite pertinently, as follows: "This is the great truth about her life: In her, passion, instead of being sort of locked up behind doors and left in a closet, becomes completely devoted to God. Passion gets completely caught up in her love for God and in the giving of herself to God.[249]

Note on the Translation

Translation of Angela's *Book* is no simple matter. The Latin is faulty, at times redundant, at other times obscure. Several layers of redaction often veil the incandescent vitality and the flow of Angela's initial dictation. What characterizes the style of the *Memorial* is its experiential quality, one close to oral thought and transmission, and the Latin is often admixed with Umbrian expressions. The *Instructions* are for the most part written in a clear and direct style, but some, especially the more doctrinal ones, are expressed in an abstract and tangled theological discourse quite removed from the immediacy and emotion-charged depths of Angela's own language. Throughout, I have tried to adhere as closely as possible to the text, leaving the obscurities, and only occasionally polishing off some additives (e.g., repetition of conjunctions) so that the luster of the original—the glow of an encrusted diamond—may better shine forth. Many imperfections remain.

It should also be pointed out that practically all the various headings (e.g., *Memorial, Instructions*) and subheadings found throughout Angela's *Book* in the present volume do not come from Angela or even from the scribe. Except for some silent borrowings from previous editions and manuscripts, they are the inventions of Thier and Calufetti, editors of the critical edition, and are meant to facilitate the understanding of the development of Angela's story and the interpretation of the ideas in the *Book*. The text of the critical edition also distinguishes what comes from the first redaction (printed in Roman typeface) and what comes from the second (printed in italic). This procedure is simply too ungainly for our purposes. Whenever appropriate, however, I have indicated in the notes the important modifications of the second redaction.

For the few biblical quotations in Angela's *Book*, I have translated directly from the text of the Latin vulgate in use at the time. In the notes

INTRODUCTION

I have followed the *New American Bible*. Unless indicated otherwise, all other translations from foreign languages are my own.

The Book of
the Blessed Angela
of Foligno

PART ONE

The *Memorial*

Approbation

Anyone who reads or sees this book, which was written with utmost care and devotion by a certain trustworthy Friar Minor to whom it was dictated by a certain follower of Christ, should be fully aware of the fact that it was seen and read by the Cardinal-deacon James of Colonna before he suffered disgrace at the hands of the sovereign pontiff, as well as by eight well-known lectors of the Order of Friars Minor, of whom one was a lector for many years in the convent in Milan, where the house of studies is located; four held the post of minister in the administration of the Province of St. Francis; two others were inquisitors for many years in this said Province and another was custodian in various custodies.[1] Moreover, three other friars, capable and intelligent enough to be lectors, examined it, as well as many other trustworthy friars, men known for their modesty and spiritual life. None of these saw any sign of false teachings in this book—on the contrary, they treat it with a humble reverence, and cherish it most dearly, like a holy book.[2]

Prologue

Those who are truly faithful know what it is to probe, perceive, and touch the Incarnate Word of Life as he himself affirms in the gospel: "If anyone loves me, he will keep my word, and my Father will love him, and we shall come to him and make our dwelling place with him." And, "He who loves me, I will reveal myself to him."[3]

God himself enables his faithful ones to fully verify this experience and the teaching about such an experience. Recently, he has once again revealed something of this experience and this teaching, through one of his faithful, to increase the devotion of his people. In the pages that follow, there is an incomplete, very weak and abridged, but nonetheless true description of it.

Why and how I, unworthy scribe, was compelled to write—as I sincerely believe—by God, and how the said faithful servant of Christ was likewise altogether compelled to speak about her experience will be explained later in its proper place, that is, at the moment when I first learned of it and began to write about it.[4]

CHAPTER I
THE FIRST TWENTY STEPS OF THE BLESSED ANGELA
IN THE WAY OF PENANCE
AND SPIRITUAL PERFECTION

A certain faithful follower of Christ related that in conversations about God with her companion,[5] she had designated (drawing from her own experience) thirty steps or transformations which the soul makes as it advances on the way of penance.[6]

The first step is the awareness of one's sinfulness, in which the soul greatly fears being damned to hell. In it the soul weeps bitterly.

The second step is the confession of sins. The soul still experiences shame and bitterness. There is not yet the feeling of love, only grief. She also told me how she had often received communion in a state of sin because she had been too ashamed to make a full confession. Day and night her conscience reproached her. And, when she prayed to the blessed Francis to find her a confessor who knew sins well, someone she could fully confess herself to, that very same night an elderly friar appeared to her and told her: "Sister, if you had asked me sooner, I would have complied with your request sooner. Nonetheless, your request is granted."

The very next morning, I went to the church of St. Francis but left it quickly. On my return home I entered the cathedral of St. Felician, where I saw a friar preaching, the chaplain of the bishop.[7] Prompted by the Lord, I decided on the spot to confess myself to him upon the condition that he also had the power of jurisdiction from the bishop to absolve me or, if not, that he could obtain it from him. I did make a full confession. After having heard it, the friar told me that if I wasn't satisfied he would repeat all my sins to the bishop and subsequently communicate his penance to me. He assured me, however, that he could absolve me without the bishop. In this step, then, the soul still feels only shame and bitterness. It does not feel love, only grief.

The third step is the penance the soul performs in satisfaction to God for its sins, and it is still grief-stricken.

The fourth step is the growing awareness of divine mercy, which granted the soul the aforesaid forgiveness and snatched it from hell. The soul begins to be enlightened, and then it weeps and grieves even more than before, and undertakes even sharper penance.

I, brother scribe, declare that in all these steps I have not written about the remarkable penances which the faithful follower of Christ performed, for I learned about them only after I had written the aforesaid steps. She had only been telling me, at this point, what was necessary to distinguish one step from another. For my part, I did not want to write down one single word which was not exactly as she had said it. I even omitted many things which were simply impossible for me to write down properly.

The fifth step is the knowledge of self.[8] Partially enlightened, the soul sees nothing but defects in itself, and condemns itself before God as most certainly worthy of hell. This is a source of much bitter weeping.

You need to be aware also that each of these steps takes time. It is indeed very pitiful and truly heartbreaking that the soul is so sluggish and moves so painfully and ponderously toward God. It takes such tiny steps at a time. As for myself, I lingered and wept at each step. My only consolation was being able to weep, but it was a bitter consolation.

The sixth step consists of a certain illumination through which my soul was graced with a deeper awareness of all my sins. In this illumination, I saw that I had offended all the creatures that had been made for me. In a very profound way, all my sins surged back into my memory, even as I confessed them before God. I asked all the creatures whom I felt I had offended not to accuse me. And then, I was given to pray with a great fire of love. I invoked all the saints, and the Blessed Virgin, to intercede for me and to pray to that Love who previously had granted me such great favors, to make what was dead in me come to life. As a result, it did seem to me that all creatures had mercy on me, and all the saints.

In the seventh step I was given the grace of beginning to look at the cross on which I saw Christ who had died for us. What I saw was still without savor, but it did cause me much grief.

In the eighth step, while looking at the cross, I was given an even greater perception of the way the Son of God had died for our sins. This perception made me aware of all my sins, and this was extremely painful. I felt that I myself had crucified Christ. But I still did not know which was the greatest gift he had bestowed—whether it was the fact that he had withdrawn me from sin and hell and converted me to the way of penance or that he had been crucified for me. Nonetheless, this perception of the meaning of the cross set me so afire that, standing near the cross, I stripped myself of all my clothing and offered my whole self to him. Although very fearful, I promised him then to maintain perpetual chastity and not to offend him again with any of my bodily members, accusing each of these one by one. I prayed that he himself keep me faithful to this promise, namely, to observe chastity with all the members of my body and all my senses. On the one hand, I feared to make this promise, but on the other hand, the fire of which I spoke drew it out of me, and I could not do otherwise.[9]

In the ninth step, it was given to me to seek the way of the cross, that I too might stand at the foot of the cross where all sinners find refuge. I was instructed, illumined, and shown the way of the cross in the following manner: I was inspired with the thought that if I wanted to go to the cross, I would need to strip myself in order to be lighter and go naked to it.[10] This would entail forgiving all who had offended me, stripping myself of everything worldly, of all attachments to men and women, of my friends and relatives, and everyone else, and, likewise, of my possessions and even my very self. Then I would be free to give my heart to Christ from whom I had received so many graces, and to walk along the thorny path, that is, the path of tribulations.

I then decided to put aside my best garments, fine food, and fancy headdress. But this was still a very shameful and burdensome thing for me to do, for at this point I was not feeling any love. During this period I was still living with my husband, and it was bitter for me to put up with all the slanders and injustices leveled against me. Nonetheless, I bore these as patiently as I could. Moreover, it came to pass, God so willing, that at that time my mother, who had been a great obstacle to me, died. In like manner my husband died, as did all my sons in a short space of time. Because I had already entered the aforesaid way, and had prayed to God for their death, I felt a great consolation when it happened.[11] I thought that since God had conceded me this aforesaid favor, my heart would always be within God's heart, and God's heart always within mine.

In the tenth step, while I was asking God what I could do to please him more, in his mercy, he appeared to me many times, both while I was asleep and awake, crucified on the cross. He told me that I should look at his wounds. In a wonderful manner, he showed me how he had endured all these wounds for me; and he did this many times. As he was showing me the sufferings he had endured for me from each of these wounds, one after the other, he told me: "What then can you do that would seem to you to be enough?" Likewise, he appeared many times to me while I was awake, and these appearances were more pleasant than those which occurred while I was asleep, although he always seemed to be suffering greatly. He spoke to me just as he had while I was sleeping, showing me his afflictions from head to toe. He even showed me how his beard, eyebrows, and hair had been plucked out and enumerated each and every one of the blows of the whip that he had received. And he said: "I have endured all these things for you."

After this, I was given an astonishing remembrance of all my sins and became aware that I was the one who had wounded him afresh with my sins and because of this, great should be my sorrow. And I did grieve more for my sins than ever before. He continued to show me the sufferings of his passion and repeated: "What indeed can you do for me that would satisfy you?" I wept much, shedding such hot tears that they burned my flesh. I had to apply water to cool it.

In the eleventh step, for the aforesaid reasons, I was moved to perform even harsher penance.[12] This step which I, brother writer, now write about is long, difficult, and yet wonderful, for her penances exceeded ordinary human capacities. I say this from what I learned afterward about them.

In the twelfth step, as it did not seem to me that there was any penance harsh enough to meet my need to break away from the world, I resolved then and there to give up absolutely everything and really do the kind of penance I felt called to do and come to the cross as God had inspired me. The grace to make this resolution was given to me by God in the following wonderful manner. I ardently desired to become poor, and I was often greatly disturbed by the thought that death could very well surprise me before I could do so. But I was also assailed by numerous contrary temptations. I imagined, for instance, that because of my youth, begging could be dangerous and shameful for me; that I might die of hunger, cold, and nakedness. Moreover, everyone tried to dissuade me from my resolution to become poor. At that moment, however, through the mercy of God, a great light came into my heart and with it a firm resolve which I believed then, and still believe, will last for eternity. In that light I made up my mind and decided that even if I had to die of hunger, shame, or nakedness, as long as this pleased God or could please God, I would in no way give up my resolve on account of those things. Even if I were certain all those evils would befall me, I know I would die happy in God. From then on my mind was made up.

In the thirteenth step, I entered into the sorrow over the passion suffered by the mother of Christ and St. John.[13] I prayed that they would obtain for me a sure sign by which I might always keep the passion of Christ continually in my memory. Thereupon, the heart of Christ was shown to me during my sleep and I was told: "In this heart, there is no falsehood, but only truth."[14] It seemed to me that this happened because I had made fun of a certain preacher.

In the fourteenth step, while I was standing in prayer, Christ on the cross appeared more clearly to me while I was awake, that is to say, he gave me an even greater awareness of himself than before. He then called me to place my mouth to the wound in his side.[15] It seemed to me that I saw and drank the blood, which was freshly flowing from his side. His intention was to make me understand that by this blood he would cleanse me. And at this I began to experience a great joy, although when I thought about the passion I was still filled with sadness.

I then prayed to God to enable me to shed all my blood for love of him just as he had done for me. I was even disposed, because of his love, to wish that all the parts of my body suffer a death not like his, that is, one much more vile. I imagined and desired that if I could find someone who was willing to kill me—provided of course that it was licit to be killed on account of one's faith and love of God—then I would beg him to grant me this grace, namely, that since Christ had been crucified on the wood of the cross, that I be crucified in a gully, or in some very vile place, and by a very vile instrument. Moreover, since I did not desire to die as the saints had died, that he make me die a slower and even more vile death than theirs. I could not imagine a death vile enough to match my desire. I even grieved deeply that I could not discover a death which would have nothing in common with those of any of the saints. I felt totally unworthy of dying as they did.

In the fifteenth step, I fixed my attention on St. John and on the mother of God, meditating on their sorrow and praying them to obtain for me the grace of always feeling something of the sorrow of Christ's passion or at least something of their own sorrow. They obtained and still obtain that favor for me. Thus, one time, St. John made me feel this sorrow to such a degree that it surpassed any I had ever experienced. From the insight I received from this experience I understood that St.

John had endured such great sorrow over the passion and death of Christ and over the sorrows of the mother of Christ that I was convinced, and still am, that he is more than a martyr.

As a result, from then on, I was filled with such a desire and determination to divest myself of all my possessions that, even though I was greatly harassed by demons not to do so, and frequently tempted by them, and even though I was forbidden by the friars and by you, as well as by all those from whom it was fitting to receive counsel, in no way could I stray from my determination, no matter what good or evil could happen to me. And if I had not been able to distribute all my belongings to the poor I would simply have left everything right then and there, for it did not seem to me that I could hold anything back for myself without seriously offending God. Nonetheless, my soul was still in a state of bitterness because of my sins. I did not know if anything I was doing was pleasing God. So, with much bitter wailing, I cried out: "Lord, even if I am damned, I still intend to do penance, dispossess myself of everything and put myself at your service." Up to this point, I was still feeling bitter sorrow for my sins and did not yet feel divine sweetness. I was transformed from this state in the following manner.

In the sixteenth step, one time I had gone to church and prayed God to grant me a grace of some kind. While I was praying the Our Father I received deep in my heart a very clear awareness of the divine goodness and my own unworthiness. I understood the meaning of each of the words I was saying deep in my heart. I recited the Our Father so slowly and consciously that even though, on the one hand, I wept bitterly because I was so aware of my sins and my unworthiness, still, on the other hand, I felt a great consolation and I began to taste something of the divine sweetness. I perceived the divine goodness in this prayer better than anywhere else, and I still perceive it better there even today. But since reciting the Our Father made me so aware of my own unworthiness and my sins, I was overcome by great shame and I hardly dared to raise my eyes. I pictured in my mind the Blessed Virgin so that she would beg forgiveness of my sins for me. For I was still feeling bitter sorrow for my sins.

At each of these previous steps, I lingered for a good while before I was able to move on to the next step. In some of the steps I lingered longer, and for a shorter time in others. At which point, Christ's faithful one also expressed her amazement: "Oh! Nothing is written here about how sluggish the soul's progress is! How bound it is, how shackled are its feet, and how ill served it is by the world and the devil."

Afterward, in the seventeenth step, it was shown to me that the Blessed Virgin had obtained for me the grace of a faith different from the one I had before. For it seemed to me as if, in contrast to what I now experienced, my former faith had been lifeless and my tears forced.[16] Henceforth, I grieved more genuinely over the passion of Christ and that of his mother. And whatever I was doing, no matter how much, it all seemed so little to me. What I wanted was to perform even greater penance. So I enclosed myself within the passion of Christ and I was given hope that therein I might find deliverance.

Then I began to receive consolation through dreams, which were numerous and gave me great comfort. My soul also began to experience the sweetness of God continually, both while I was awake and asleep; but since I still did not feel sure about these experiences they were mixed with bitterness, and I wanted something more from God.

Among her many dreams and visions, she related the following. Once I was in the cell where I had enclosed myself for the Great Lent.[17] I was enjoying and meditating on a certain saying in the gospel, a saying which I found of great value and extremely delightful. I had by my side a book, a missal, and I thirsted to see that saying again in writing. With great difficulty I contained myself and resisted opening this book in my hands, for I feared I might do so out of pride or out of too great a thirst and love. I became drowsy and fell asleep still in the throes of this desire. Immediately, I was led into a vision, and I was told that the understanding of the Epistle is something so delightful that if one grasped it properly one would completely forget everything belonging to this world. And he who was leading me asked me: "Do you want to have this experience?" As I agreed and ardently desired it, he immediately led me into this experience. From it I understood how sweet it is to experience the riches of God and I immediately and completely forgot the world. He who was leading me added that the understanding of the gospel is even more delightful, so much more so that if one understood it one would not only forget the world but even oneself, totally. He led me still further and enabled me to directly experience this. Immediately I understood what it is to experience the riches of God and derived such delight from it that I not only forgot the world but even myself. This state was so delightful and holy that I begged the one who was leading me not to let me ever leave it. He replied that what I was asking was still not possible; and he immediately led me back to myself. I opened my eyes and felt an immense joy from what I had seen, but also great sorrow at having lost it. Recalling this experience still gives me great pleasure.

From then on, I was filled with such certitude, such light, and such ardent love of God that I went on to affirm, with the utmost certainty, that nothing of these delights of God is being preached. Preachers cannot preach it; they do not understand what they preach. He who was leading me into this vision told me so.

After this, in the eighteenth step, I felt God so vividly and found such delight in prayer that I even forgot to eat. I wished that I did not need to eat, so I could remain standing in prayer. Thus the temptation—namely, not to eat or to eat only very little—slipped in, but I recognized it as a temptation. My heart was so on fire with the love of God that I never got tired of genuflections or other penitential practices.

Afterward, this fire of the love of God in my heart became so intense that if I heard anyone speak about God I would scream. Even if someone had stood over me with an axe ready to kill me, this would not have stopped my screaming. This happened to me for the first time when I sold my country villa to give to the poor.[18] It was the best property that I owned. Before I used to make fun of a certain Pietruccio, but now I could not do otherwise than follow his example.[19] Moreover, when people said that I was possessed by the devil because I had no control over my inordinate behavior—for which I was greatly ashamed—I would concur with their judgment and likewise think of myself as very sick and possessed. I could not answer those who spoke ill of me.

Also, whenever I saw the passion of Christ depicted, I could hardly bear it, and I would come down with a fever and fall sick. My companion, as a result, hid paintings of the passion or did her best to keep them out of my sight.

In the nineteenth step, during the period when I was letting out these screams, and after the wonderful illumination and consolation which I had received while reciting the Our Father, I was consoled by the first great sensation of God's sweetness. It occurred in the following manner. One time, I was inspired and drawn to meditate on the delights one experiences in contemplating the divinity and humanity of Christ. From it I received the greatest consolation I had yet experienced. It was so great that for most of that day I remained standing in my cell where I was praying, strictly confined and alone. My heart was so overwhelmed with delight that I fell to the ground and lost my power of speech. My companion then came to me and thought that I was on the verge of death or already dead. I was annoyed because she had disturbed me in that very great consolation.

On another occasion, before she had completely finished distributing all her belongings, although she had very few left, she told me that one evening, while she was at prayer, it seemed to her that she felt nothing of God and so she prayed and lamented in these terms: "Lord, whatever I am doing, I do only to find you. Will I find you after I've finished what I have undertaken?" And she asked for many other things in that prayer. The response was: "What do you want?" To this she replied: "I want neither gold nor silver; even if you should offer me the whole universe, I would not be satisfied. I want only you." And then he answered: "Hurry, for as soon as you have finished what you have set out to do the whole Trinity will come into you."[20]

At that moment, God promised me much more. He also drew me out of all tribulation and departed from me very tenderly. From then on I eagerly awaited for the fulfillment of what he had promised. I told all this to my companion, though I was still full of doubts because I felt that what I had been told and promised was much too great. Still, the savor of his departure remained and it was divine.

Following this, in the twentieth step, I went to the church of St. Francis in Assisi and it was on the way there that the preceding promise was fulfilled, just as I told you. I do not recall if I had yet managed to give away everything—no, I still had not finished giving everything to the poor. I still had a little left because a certain man had told me to wait for him while he went quickly to Apulia to divide his share of possessions with his brother who lived in that area. He told me that he would return very soon in order to give his entire share of his possessions to the poor and dispossess himself at the same time I did. He wished to dispossess himself of absolutely everything, at the same time I did, and because it was as a result of my exhortations that, through the grace of God, he had been converted and persuaded to do so, I waited for him. But afterward, I heard from a reliable source that he died on this journey and that God performed miracles through him, and that his grave was held in reverence.[21]

The step presented here as the twentieth is the first which I, the unworthy friar writing it, received and heard from the mouth of the faithful servant of Christ who related it to me. I have decided not to finish or continue it at this point except to say that this step is simply wonderful, very long, and filled with great divine revelations and the delights of divine intimacy, although the twenty-first step is even more wonderful. Having hardly begun this twentieth step, I abandon it for now and will return to it after I have briefly related how, by the wonderful workings of Christ, I came to know of these things and was compelled to write all about them.

CHAPTER II
EXPLANATIONS OF THE BROTHER SCRIBE
CONCERNING THE DIVISIONS, THE RATIONALE,
AND THE TRUTH OF THE *MEMORIAL*

The brother scribe relates how he organized the text of the *Memorial*

It should be noted at this point that I, brother scribe, with the help of God, took every care to carry out the redaction of my text from the first step to the twenty-first step, or toward the end of the second revelation, where one finds God's wonderful revelation to Christ's faithful one that what we had written was completely true and without any falsehood. I must add, however, that her account was much fuller than mine. What I wrote is but a short and defective version.[22]

From then on, however, I did not know how to continue, because thereafter, it was only on rare occasions that I could speak with her to write down what she told me. Moreover, from the nineteenth step on, I was not sure how to distinguish and enumerate the remaining steps. I have done my best to try to assemble this remaining material into seven steps or revelations. My guiding principle was to divide the subject matter according to the state of divine grace I perceived Christ's faithful one to be in, or according to what I perceived and learned of her spiritual progress; and also according to what seemed to me most fitting and appropriate.

Summary or schema of the *Memorial* for all the steps following the nineteenth

The first step which follows the preceding narrative contains the wonderful revelation of divine intimacy, locutions, and teachings. The end of the step contains the answer given to her concerning the Trinity and how she sees Christ in the sacrament of the altar.

The second step contains the revelation of the divine unctions and signs, and the vision of God as he is in paradise. It says also that God requires the soul to love him without malice, and in a lengthy discourse, briefly abridged here, shows how God himself is the love of the soul; also, that he wants the soul to have or desire to have something analogous to the true love with which he himself loved us. It is then shown through examples that every soul wanting to discover and receive divine mercy can do so just as Mary Magdalene did. Divine mercy comes from the love and goodness of the Father, and from the recognition of it by the sinner. For these two reasons, the more one is a sinner, the more one can obtain mercy and grace; for God is the love of the soul. It was also revealed to her in this step that she was pleasing to God, and that he was present in what we were writing; also that everything we had been writing was without any falsehood. Next, how her alms were blessed by God and afterward by the Blessed Virgin. Finally, the step contains the ecstasy that she experienced when she saw the body of Christ.

The third step contains the revelation of divine teachings, some understood through the ears of the body and others intelligible only to the mind's taste. It also teaches that the legitimate sons of God are those who seek to know who is this God, their Father, who gave them the gift of sonship. They do this because they truly wish to know him and please him. This step also contains what God tells them. Likewise, how they take in God's grace when they do approach him; what they are taught of how to approach him, and how to become legitimate sons of God; then, which ones among the sons of God are reproved by him. Finally, this step describes how Christ's faithful one saw and received divine wisdom whence she was able to pass true judgments.

The fourth step contains the revelation of how she was made aware of her humble state, was restored, and received divine approval. In it she also saw the whole world and all things in it as if they were almost nothing, and yet filled with the overflowing presence of God. Then, in a state of rapture or of ecstasy, she saw the power of God and the will of God and this brought satisfaction to all her questions—namely, about the predestined, the saved, the damned, the demons, and everything else. These visions contented her and satisfied all her questions. But while in them, she did not know if she was in her body or out of it.[23]

The fifth step contains the revelation of divine union and love. It begins with a wonderful revelation of the Lord's passion; there follows an ecstasy of love. It tells how she saw the Blessed Virgin interceding for the human race; how grace manifests itself in the sacrament of the altar. There is, likewise, a long teaching on how the soul is granted the certitude of God's presence, on the many ways this certitude is granted, and also on how the soul knows when it is a host of God, which is something very different. Next, there is a conversation and a lamentation which the soul makes with the body or with sensuality after returning from contemplation. Finally, this step shows how spiritual persons can be deceived, and what things are common to both the faithful and the unfaithful.

The sixth step contains the state of agony and veritable martyrdom she was in, caused by many and intolerable sufferings both from infirmities of the body and the countless torments of body and soul which demons horribly afflicted upon her. This step occurs simultaneously with the following seventh step, which is more wonderful than all the others.

The seventh step contains a revelation of which one can only say that it surpasses anything conceivable or imaginable. Neither the steps on divine intimacy, divine unctions, teachings, certitude, union, and love, nor any of the preceding, can compare with it. For when I, brother scribe, asked Christ's faithful one if what I had put in the seventh step drew her soul to God more than all the preceding, she answered that without comparison it did indeed draw her soul to God more than all of the other steps. And she added: "So much more that whatever I say about it, I seem to say nothing or to say it badly." And, afterward, she further added, "Whatever I say seems blasphemous to me. I even became completely weak when you asked me just now if it drew me more than any of the other steps thus far, and I answered that it did." This most excellent step, however, coincides for a while with what occurred in the sixth one. Nonetheless, the sixth gradually fades away and the seventh remains.

The brother scribe briefly makes known how and from whose help the *Memorial* began and was brought to completion

After the narrative which begins here comes another, which more properly belongs in the step previously noted as the twentieth, for it was the first and starting point of everything that I, brother scribe, wrote of these divine words. I began by briefly and carelessly jotting down notes on a small sheet of paper as a sort of "memorial"[24] for myself, because I thought I would have little to write. Later, after I had compelled her to talk, it was revealed to Christ's faithful one that I should use a large copy book, not a small sheet of paper. Because I only half believed her, I wrote on two or three blank pages I found in my book. Later, of necessity, I made a copy book of quality paper. However, before proceeding any further, I thought I should relate, as I have in what follows, how I came to learn of these things and how God compelled me to write.

**The brother scribe explains why he wrote the *Memorial*,
affirms that everything he wrote was trustworthy,
and indicates the difficulties of his task**

The true reason why I wrote is as follows. One day the aforementioned person, Christ's faithful one, came to the church of St. Francis in Assisi, where I was residing in a friary. She screamed greatly while she was sitting at the entrance to the portals of the church. Because of this I, who was her confessor, her blood-relative, and even her principal and special counselor, was greatly ashamed, especially because many brothers, who knew both of us, had also come to see her screaming and shouting. A holy man, who was her traveling companion on this journey, was sitting on the pavement inside the church, not very far from her, looking at her and watching over her with great reverence and a certain sadness (he is now deceased; he is the one mentioned above in the twentieth step as wanting to divest himself of his belongings at the same time she did hers).[25] Many other very good men and women, companions of hers, were waiting for her and watching over her also with reverence. Nonetheless, my pride and shame were so great that out of embarrassment and indignation I did not approach her; instead, I waited for her to finish screaming, and I kept myself at a distance. After she had ceased her screaming and shouting and had risen from the entrance and come over to me, I could hardly speak to her calmly. I told her that, henceforth, she should never again dare come to Assisi, since this was the place where this evil had seized her. I also told her companions never to bring her there again.

After a short while, I left Assisi to return to Foligno, her home town and mine. Wanting to know the cause of her shouts, I began to press her in every way that I could to tell me why she had screamed and shouted so much in Assisi. Having first received the firm promise from me that I would not say a word to anyone who might know her, she began to tell me a small part of her story, which is written following this present narrative. Amazed as I was and suspicious that it might come from some evil spirit, I made a strong effort to arouse her suspicions because I myself had so many. I advised her and compelled her to tell me everything. I wished to write absolutely everything so that I could consult with some wise and spiritual man who would have never heard of her. I told her that I wished to do this so that she could in no way be deceived by an evil spirit. I strove to inspire fear in her by showing her by examples how many persons had been deceived, and consequently how she could be similarly deceived. Because she did not yet have the degree of clarity and perfect certitude which she had later—as will be found in the writings which follow—she began to reveal the divine secrets to me and I wrote these down.

In truth, I wrote them, but I had so little grasp of their meaning that I thought of myself as a sieve or sifter which does not retain the precious and refined flour but only the most coarse. Having experienced myself a special grace from God which I had never experienced before, I wrote filled with great reverence and fear. I would add nothing of my own, not even a single word, unless it was exactly as I could grasp it just out of her mouth as she related it. I did not want to write anything after I had left her. But even when I wrote, while sitting near her, I made her repeat the words I should write many times. I wrote in the third person, although she always spoke to me concerning herself in the first person. But, in order to go faster, I sometimes left my text in the third person, and I have not yet corrected it.

And this will give an idea of how very rough was my understanding of the divine words I was hearing from her: One day after I had written as best I could what I had been able to grasp of her discourse, I read to her what I had written in order to have her dictate more to me, and she told me with amazement that she did not recognize it. On another occasion when I was rereading to her what I had written so that she could see if I had correctly recorded what she had said, she answered that my words were dry and without any savor, and this also amazed her. And another time she remarked to me: "Your words recall to me what I told you, but they are very obscure. The words you read to me do not convey the meaning I intended to convey, and as a result your writing is obscure." And another time she said: "You have written what is bland, inferior, and amounts to nothing; but concerning what is precious in what my soul feels you have written nothing."

Without doubt, this difficulty in writing was because I was inadequate to the task. I certainly did not add anything for, in truth, I could not understand everything she said. She herself did tell me that I wrote truly but in a simplified and abbreviated form. I only know how to write slowly, but out of fear of the brothers who murmured about my sitting with her in church, I had to write as fast as I could. I consider it a miracle that I could put what I wrote in order. The proof of the veracity of my text will become evident in the twenty-first step or in the second revelation of divine unctions where God revealed and told her that everything I had written was true and without any falsehood, but had been written very imperfectly.

Furthermore, if, by chance, I went to write when my conscience was bothering me, everything went so badly for both of us that I could hardly write anything in an orderly way. Therefore, I tried with all my power to have a clear conscience when I wished to talk with her and to write. Sometimes, I took the trouble beforehand to confess my sins, convinced that it was a gift of grace if, on whatever subject God inspired me to question her, the answer came in an orderly way—thanks to divine grace, working in marvelous ways beyond what I could hope for.

Nonetheless, what caused me no little pain and concern was that many of her words which seemed to me worthy of being written I had to omit in my haste, because of my inadequacy as a scribe, and out of my fear of my brothers who opposed my work. They murmured so strongly against me that as a result the guardian and the provincial strictly forbade me to write, and the latter even reprimanded me. It is true that they did not know what I was writing and how good it was.

CHAPTER III
FIRST SUPPLEMENTARY STEP
(CONTINUATION OF THE TWENTIETH)
THE REVELATION OF DIVINE INTIMACY,
LOCUTIONS, AND TEACHINGS

Here then is the starting point of my redaction, the very first step which I began to write after the screaming and shouting episode by Christ's faithful one in the church of St. Francis, as mentioned in the preceding narrative.

The wonderful and decisive events of Angela's pilgrimages to Rome (1290/1291) and to Assisi (1291)

Having returned from Assisi to Foligno, where both Christ's faithful one and I were from, I, brother scribe, began to question her and to urge her as strongly as I could, and in every way I knew, to oblige her to tell me why she had shrieked and screamed in St. Francis's church. And thus constrained by me and having first received my promise that I would reveal nothing to anyone who might know her, she began her story. She started by saying that during her trip to Assisi (about which I was questioning her), she was in a state of prayer all along the way. And among other things, she had asked blessed Francis to ask God on her behalf that she might feel Christ's presence; and likewise to obtain from him the grace of observing well the rule of blessed Francis which she had recently promised; and above all for this: that he would make her become, and remain to the end, truly poor.

She so desired to attain a state of perfect poverty that for this purpose she had gone to Rome to ask the blessed Peter to obtain this grace for her from Christ.[26] When I, brother scribe, who had been listening, read this part of my redaction to Christ's faithful one, she affirmed that the aforesaid things were true, even though she said the writing was very defective. She then added: "When I was near Rome, I felt that God had granted me the grace of the poverty I had asked for."

It was, then, when she was on her way to the church of St. Francis that she asked him—that is, blessed Francis—that he obtain for her the aforesaid graces from the Lord Jesus Christ. She related many other things which she had asked for in the prayer she was making on her way to Assisi. And when she had reached the crossroads[27] that lies between Spello and Assisi, at this junction of three roads, on a narrow path that leads to Assisi, it was said to her: "You prayed to my servant Francis but I did not want to send you any other messenger than myself. I am the Holy Spirit who comes to you to give you a consolation which you have never tasted before. I will accompany you and be within you until you reach Saint Francis's church; and no one will notice it. I wish to speak with you on this path and there will be no end to my speaking. You will not be able to do otherwise than listen because I have bound you fast. And I will not leave you until the second time you enter the church of St. Francis. Then this particular consolation will leave you, but I will never leave you if you love me."

Then he began to say: "My daughter, my dear and sweet daughter, my delight, my temple, my beloved daughter, love me, because you are very much loved by me; much more than you could love me." Very often he also said: "My daughter and my sweet spouse." And he further added: "I love you so much more than any other woman in the valley of Spoleto. I have found a place to rest in you; now you in turn place yourself and find your own rest in me. You prayed to my servant Francis and because my servant Francis loved me very much, I, therefore, did much for him. And if there was any other person who loved me still more, I would do even more for him. And I will do for you what I did for my servant Francis, and more if you love me."

These words stirred up great doubts in me and my soul said to him: "If indeed you were the Holy Spirit, you would not say such things to me for it is not fitting. I am frail and these words could be a source of pride and vanity for me." To this he responded: "Think for a moment and see for yourself if all these words can become a source of vanity and pride for you; try even to get away from these words if you can." I then did what I could to produce vanity in myself in order to test whether what he had said was true, and if he was indeed the Holy Spirit. I even also began to look at the vineyards around me in an effort to get away from these words. But wherever I looked, I could hear him saying: "This is my creature." At that I felt a sweetness, an ineffable divine sweetness.

After which I was given a vivid remembrance of all my sins and vices and saw how there was nothing in me but sins and defects. As a result I felt more humble than ever before and yet remained with the conviction that the Son of God and the Blessed Virgin Mary had stooped down to speak to me. And he also added: "If everyone in the world somehow came along with you, you would not be able to speak to them as distinct from you because everyone in the world is already with you." To free me from my doubt, he added: "I am the one who was crucified for you. I have known hunger and thirst for you; and I shed my blood for you, I have loved you so much." He then related his entire passion to me.[28]

Afterward he added: "Ask whatever grace you wish for yourself, for your companions, and for whomever you wish. Prepare yourself to receive it, for I am much more prepared to give than you are to receive." Upon hearing these words my soul cried out: "I don't want to ask for anything for I am not worthy." Once again all my sins surged back into my memory. Then my soul added: "If you were the Holy Spirit, you would not say such lofty things to me. For if you were indeed the one speaking, my joy would be so great that my soul ought not be able to sustain it." To this he replied: "Nothing can exist or be made to exist unless I will it. For now I have decided not to grant you a greater joy than this one. In the past, I have said less to others, yet one to whom I spoke upon hearing my words fell to the ground, lost his senses, and became blind.[29] I do not bestow on you a greater feeling of my presence for now, because I do not want your companions to know about it. And here is another sign of my presence. Try now to speak with your companions, and try to think of something else, either good or bad; and you will immediately become aware that you will not be able to think of anything else but God. Furthermore, I do all this for you through no merit of yours." At these words I became powerfully aware of all my sins and defects as these surged back into my memory and I felt more worthy of hell than ever. He then added: "I have done all this for you out of my kindness, but I would not have done it if you had come with other companions, who were not of such quality as these." As for the latter, they had noticed and were perplexed over my state of languor. But as for myself, every word was so very sweet to me that I was hoping we would never reach our destination or that the path we were on would never come to an end.

There is no way that I could possibly render a just account of how great was the joy and sweetness I was feeling, especially when I heard God tell me: "I am the Holy Spirit who enters into your deepest self." Likewise, all the other words he told me were so very sweet. In my eagerness, I then said: "I will be able to discern if you are the Holy Spirit if you indeed accompany me on this pilgrimage just as you have promised." To this, he replied: "I will not leave you as far as this consolation is concerned until the second time you enter St. Francis's church; but from now on I will never leave you if you love me." And he did accompany me as far as St. Francis's church, just as he said he would, and stayed with me while I was in the church and until after the meal, that is, until the second time I had entered the church.

Then, on this second time, as soon as I had genuflected at the entrance of the church and when I saw a stained-glass window depicting St. Francis being closely held by Christ,[30] I heard him telling me: "Thus I will hold you closely to me and much more closely than can be observed with the eyes of the body. And now the time has come, sweet daughter, my temple, my delight, to fulfill my promise to you. I am about to leave you in the form of this consolation, but I will never leave you if you love me."

Bitter in some ways as these words were for me to hear, I nonetheless experienced them above all as sweet, the sweetest I have ever heard. Then I turned my gaze on the one speaking to me so that I might also see him not only with the eyes of the body but also with those of the spirit. I, brother scribe, interrupted at this point to ask her: "What did you see?" She replied: "I saw something full of such immense majesty that I do not know how to describe it, but it seemed to me that it was the All Good. Moreover, he spoke many words of endearment as he withdrew from me. And he withdrew, so very gently and so very gradually.

After he had withdrawn, I began to shout and to cry out without any shame: "Love still unknown, why do you leave me?" I could not nor did I scream out any other words than these: "Love still unknown, why? why? why?" Furthermore, these screams were so choked up in my throat that the words were unintelligible. Nonetheless what remained with me was a certitude that God, without any doubt, had been speaking to me. As I shouted I wanted to die. It was very painful for me not to die and to go on living. After this experience I felt my joints become dislocated.[31]

Afterward, I left Assisi still in the thrall of those sweet words and took the road home. All along the way, I spoke about God and it was very difficult for me to be silent, but I made an effort to keep from talking, as much as I could, because of my companions.

During my return by way of this St. Francis road, he told me among other things: "I give you this sign that I am the one who is speaking and who has spoken to you. You will experience the cross and the love of God within you. This sign will be with you for eternity." And immediately I felt that cross and that love in the depths of my soul, and even the bodily repercussions of the presence of the cross; and feeling all this, my soul melted in the love of God.

I remember now that he had also said to me on the road going to Assisi: "Your whole life, your eating, drinking, sleeping, and all that you do are pleasing to me."

Once back in her home in Foligno, after the Assisi pilgrimage, Angela experienced eight days of great intimacy with God, one similar to mystical betrothal

Once I was back home, I felt so peaceful and was so filled with divine sweetness that I find no words to express my experience; and there was also in me a desire to die. The thought that I had to go on living was a great burden because of that inexpressible sweetness, quiet, peace, and delight which I felt; and because I wanted to attain the source of this experience and not lose it—that is why I wanted to leave this world. The thought of continuing to live was a greater burden for me to bear than the pain and sorrow I had felt over the death of my mother and my sons, and beyond any pain that I could imagine.[32] I lay at home enthralled by this great consolation and in a state of languor for eight days. And my soul cried out: "Lord, take pity on me and do not allow me to remain any longer in this world." On the road going to Assisi, he had predicted that I would experience this delectable and indescribable consolation in these terms: "Once back in your home, you will feel a sweetness different from any you have ever experienced. And I will not speak to you then as I have until now; but you will feel me." True enough I did feel this sweet and ineffable consolation in which I felt so peaceful and quiet that I cannot find words to describe it. I lay in bed for eight days hardly able to speak, say the Our Father, or get up to move around. He had also told me on the road to Assisi: "I was with the apostles many times, and they saw me with their bodily eyes but they did not feel what you feel. You do not see me but you feel me."

I realized at this point that this experience was coming to an end, for he began to withdraw from me and he did so very gently while telling me: "My daughter, you are sweeter to me than I am to you." And he repeated what he had already said: "My temple, my delight." At these words I realized that he did not want me to be lying down while he was leaving so I stood up. He then said to me: "You are holding the ring of my love. From now on you are engaged to me and you will never leave me. May the blessing of the Father, the Son, and the Holy Spirit be upon you and your companion." He said this at the moment of departure because I had asked him for a special grace for my companion. In response to this request he simply said: "The grace I will give to your companion will be a different one from yours." I must add that when he said: "You shall never leave me again," my soul cried out: "Oh, that I may never sin mortally." To this he replied: "These are your words, not mine."

Thereafter, I often smelled scents of extraordinary fragrances. But these experiences and others were so powerful that I cannot find words to describe them. I can say something about them, but my words are inadequate to transmit the sweetness and the delight I experienced. Many more times did I hear God speak to me with words such as the above but never at such length, nor with the same depth or with such sweetness.

Two marvelous events narrated by her companion establish the veracity of Angela's narrative

While she was lying in bed after her return from Assisi—as it was related above—her companion, a marvel of simplicity, purity, and chastity, heard a voice telling her three times: "The Holy Spirit is within Lella." Upon hearing these words she immediately went to her and began to question her: "Tell me what is going on, for this is what I've just been told three times." To this Christ's faithful one answered: "If this was told to you, it pleases me"; and she gave her approval to what she had said. From then on Christ's faithful one communicated many divine secrets to her companion.

Later, this same companion told me, brother scribe, that on one occasion when Christ's faithful one was lying on her side in a state of ecstasy, she saw something like a splendid, magnificent star shining with a wonderful and countless variety of colors. Rays of astonishing beauty, some thick, others slender, radiated from Christ's faithful one. Emanating from her breast while she was lying on her side, the rays unfolded or coiled as they ascended upward toward heaven. She saw this with her bodily eyes while she was wide awake, near the third hour. The star was not very big.

The doubts of the brother scribe are resolved as Angela expounds on the Holy Trinity[33]

One day I, brother scribe, and the unworthy writer of these divine words, was asking her how it was possible that she had been told, as related in the preceding revelation, "I am the Holy Spirit," and a little later, "I am the one who was crucified for you." After I had asked her this, she went back home. Later, she met me again and answered in these terms: Once back home, I began to ponder, for I was having some doubts about what you had asked me—and when doubts are raised about my experiences, I too am seized by doubts, because I see myself as completely unworthy of them. And while I was in that moment of doubt I was given the following suggestion: "Ask him, namely Brother A.,[34] to explain why you were told: 'The Trinity has already come into you.' Repeat to him that it has indeed already come and ask him to explain how this is possible." For my part, I was given to understand that although the Trinity had entered into me, it was no less in heaven and had not left it.

Since there was so much that I still did not understand, nor did it seem to me that I had yet received a full and intelligible answer to my questions, the voice added: "Tell Brother A. that when these words were said to you, 'I am the Holy Spirit,' and later, 'I am the one who was crucified for you,' at that moment the Father, the Son, and the Holy Spirit had entered into you." Since I still doubted that the Father, Son, and Holy Spirit had entered into me, unworthy as I am, and imagined that perhaps this had been said to deceive me, it was then repeated to me several times: "It is indeed the Trinity that has entered into you. Ask Brother A. again how this could be possible." Then I was also told that in this exchange the Father, Son, and Holy Spirit were speaking to me; and that, or so it seemed to me, I was being told that the Trinity was at once one, and a union of many. Then, as a further explanation, the example of the sun as well as other examples were presented to me, but I rejected these, for when I hear such great things I push them aside fearfully because I feel unworthy of them. What I wanted was that God would make me actually feel that on this point, the presence of the Holy Trinity in me, I could not be deceived.

This point, "the whole Trinity will come into you," is noted in the preceding step, that is, toward the end of the nineteenth, and it was fulfilled in the twentieth.[35]

A vision of the divinity and humanity of the Crucified grants Angela an explanation of the sign of the cross and the love of God which she had experienced within herself on the road back from Assisi

This is what she said to me: Once when I was meditating on the great suffering which Christ endured on the cross, I was considering the nails, which, I had heard it said, had driven a little bit of the flesh of his hands and feet into the wood. And I desired to see at least that small amount of Christ's flesh which the nails had driven into the wood. And then such was my sorrow over the pain that Christ had endured that I could no longer stand on my feet. I bent over and sat down; I stretched out my arms on the ground and inclined my head on them. Then Christ showed me his throat and his arms.

And then my former sorrow was transformed into a joy so intense that I can say nothing about it. This was a new joy, different from the others. I was so totally absorbed by this vision that I was not able to see, hear, or feel anything else. My soul saw this vision so clearly that I have no doubts about it, nor will I ever question it. I was so certain of the joy which remained in my soul that henceforth I do not believe I will ever lose this sign of God's presence. Such also was the beauty of Christ's throat or neck that I concluded that it must be divine.[36] Through this beauty it seemed to me that I was seeing Christ's divinity, and that I was standing in the presence of God; but of that moment that is all I remember seeing. I do not know how to compare the clarity and brightness of that vision with anything or any color in the world except, perhaps, the clarity and brightness of Christ's body, which I sometimes see at the elevation of the host.

As this vision receded I began to think of what had happened and entertained slight fears and afterthoughts about it; but by the time these arose I am quite certain that the vision had already receded.

The splendor and the beauty of the humanity and the divinity of Christ also shine forth from the vision of the host

When I, the brother who is writing this, heard what I believe God had wanted her to say concerning the vision of the body of Christ, I immediately noted it in my heart. Then I questioned and compelled her to tell me everything she had ever seen in this vision of the body of Christ. Under pressure from me, she began to talk: Sometimes I see the host itself just as I saw that neck or throat, and it shines with such splendor and beauty that it seems to me that it must come from God; it surpasses the splendor of the sun. This beauty which I see makes me conclude with the utmost certainty and without a shadow of a doubt that I am seeing God. When I was at home, however, the vision of Christ's neck or throat which I saw was even more beautiful, so beautiful that I believe I will never lose the joy of it. I have no way to compare it except with the vision of the host containing the body of Christ, for in the host

146

I see a beauty which far surpasses the beauty of the sun. My soul is in great distress because I am truly unable to describe this vision.

She also told me that sometimes she sees the host in a different way, that is, she sees in it two most splendid eyes, and these are so large that it seems only the edges of the host remain visible. Once even, not in the host but in my cell, I saw the eyes and these were of such beauty and so delightful to look at that, as with the vision of the neck, I do not believe I will ever lose the joy of that vision. Though I do not know if I was asleep or awake I found myself once again in a state of great and ineffable joy, one so great that I do not believe I could ever lose it.

On another occasion she said she had seen the Christ Child in the host. He appeared to her as someone tall and very lordly, as one holding dominion. He also seemed to hold something in his hand as a sign of his dominion, and he sat on a throne. But I cannot say what he was holding in his hands. I saw this with my bodily eyes, as I did everything I ever saw of the host. When this vision occurred I did not kneel down like the others and I cannot recall whether I ran right up to the altar or whether I was unable to move because I was in such a delightful contemplative state. I know that I was also very upset because the priest put down the host on the altar too quickly. Christ was so beautiful and so magnificently adorned. He looked like a child of twelve. This vision was a source of such joy for me that I do not believe I will ever lose the joy of it. I was also so sure of it that I do not doubt a single detail of it. Hence it is not necessary for you to write it. I was even so delighted by that vision that I did not ask him to help me nor did I have anything good or bad to say. I simply delighted in seeing that inestimable beauty.

CHAPTER IV
SECOND SUPPLEMENTARY OR TWENTY-FIRST STEP

The second step is the revelation of divine unction and sign, and the vision of God as he is in paradise

God gradually manifests his presence to Angela through words and revelations and defines himself as the love of the soul

a. The first great manifestation of the loving presence of God

Christ's faithful one spoke to me as follows: Some time after the year in which I had heard God speaking to me on my way to Assisi,[37] one day while I was in prayer and wanted to say the Our Father, suddenly my soul heard a voice which said: "You are full of God." I truly felt all the members of my body filled with the delights of God. And I wanted to die, just as before, when I went to Assisi, and again, when I had returned and was lying down in my cell. This present experience occurred, then, while I was once again lying down in my cell. My companion, who saw the state I was in, said that tears were streaming from my eyes, which were wide open. The voice then told me, and I felt it, that God was embracing my soul. I truly did feel that this is what was happening. But now it seems to me that everything we are trying to say about this experience reduces it to a mere trifle, because what took place is so different from what can be said about it. I myself am very ashamed that I cannot find better words to describe it.

Again, on that road to Assisi, he had also told me: "I will do great things in you in the sight of the nations. Through you, I shall be known and my name will be praised by many nations."

b. Another great experience of the loving presence of God

During this same period, while I was once again in prayer, I suddenly heard him speaking to me very graciously in these words: "My daughter, sweeter to me than I am to you, my temple, my delight, the heart of God almighty is now upon your heart." And these words were accompanied with a feeling of God's presence far greater than I had ever experienced. All the members of my body thrilled with delight as I lay in this experience.

c. The Blessed Angela receives the revelation that the love which is bestowed upon her is that of the Almighty who holds dominion over all creation

He said: "God almighty has deposited much love in you, more than in any woman of this city. He takes delight in you and is fully satisfied with you and your companion. Try to see to it that your lives are a light for all those who wish to look upon them. A harsh judgment awaits those who look at your lives but do not act accordingly." My soul understood that this harsh judgment concerned the lettered more than lay people because the former despise these works of God though they know about them through the Scriptures. And he went on to say: "So great is the love that almighty God has deposited in the two of you that he stands continually over you even if you do not always feel his presence in the same way as you do now. At this moment, his eyes are turned toward you." And it did seem to me that with the eyes of the spirit I did see his eyes and these delighted me more than I can say. I suffer now because we speak about these things as if they were mere trifles.

Great as was my joy, I had, nonetheless, a vivid remembrance of all my sins and saw nothing good in myself. I even thought that I had never done anything pleasing to God and I remembered how much I had displeased him. As a result, I once again began to doubt that such extraordinary words had been said to me. I then went on to say: "Even if I do feel you within myself, unworthy as I am, still, if you are the Son of the almighty God would not my soul experience an even greater joy, one greater than I could bear?" To this he replied: "I do not wish to deposit a greater joy in you than one you can presently bear. This is why it is tempered."

He had also replied: "It is true that the whole world is full of me." And then I saw that every creature was indeed full of his presence. He further added: "All things are possible for me. I can enable you to see me as I was when conversing with my disciples and yet not feel me, and I can also enable you to feel me as you feel me now and yet not see me." Even if these were not his exact words, my soul understood, nonetheless, what he was saying and even much more. I felt it was so. When I, brother scribe, interrupted to ask her: "How do you know that this is truly so?" She replied, "Because I have experienced how the soul feels it to be so."

d. Angela has a powerful experience of the unction of God's presence when he imprints in her a permanent sign of his love

To what I had heard above, my soul responded and cried out: "Since all that you have said is true, and as extraordinary as you say it is, and since you are God almighty, give me a sign that I may really be sure that it is you. Take away my doubt about it." I was amazed, nonetheless, that after all this I still doubted, even if my doubt was a very small one.

So I asked him then to give me a tangible sign, one that I could see, namely, that he place into my hand either a candle or a precious stone, or whatever other sign he wanted. I also added: "I will not show this sign to anyone if such is your desire." To this he responded: "This sign which you are asking for is one which would always give you joy whenever you see it or touch it, but it would not take away your doubt. Furthermore, in such a sign you could be deceived." When he told me these things, I understood that he meant much more than what we could say about it now. In fact everything he said was so much more delightful, affectionate, and full of meaning that what we are saying about it now seems like absolutely nothing at all. May God be willing that it is not a sin for me to speak about these things so badly and defectively.

Then he said to me: I am about to give you a much better sign than the one you asked for. This sign will be continuously in the depths of your soul and from it you will always feel something of God's presence and be burning with love for him. And you will recognize in your deep self that no one but I can do such a thing. Here then is the sign which I deposit in the depths of your soul, one better than the one you asked for: I deposit in you a love of me so great that your soul will be continually burning for me. So ardent will be this love that if anyone should speak to you offensively, you will take it as a grace and cry out that you are unworthy of such a grace. Know that I myself suffered from such offenses and my love for you was so great that I bore it all patiently. Through such experiences, then, you will know that I am with you. And if perchance there is no one to speak offensively to you, you will nonetheless have a great desire to be so offended. When this happens it is a sure sign of the grace of God, for I myself bore such offenses with great humility and patience.

Behold I now anoint you with a fragrant ointment, one with which a saint called St. Syricus[38] was often anointed, as well as many other saints.

I felt this unction immediately upon receiving it, and it had such a sweet effect on me that I desired to die and desired my death to be accompanied by all manner of bodily torment. And yet these torments I imagined as nothing in comparison to those of the saints who had endured martyrdom. Then I wanted and desired to be vilified by the whole world, and wanted my death to be accompanied with every manner of torment. I would have been simply delighted to pray to God for those who might make these awful things happen to me. And I marveled over those saints who had prayed to God for those who persecuted and killed them; for they should have not merely prayed for them but ought to have beseeched a special grace from God for them. For this is how I myself would have wanted to pray to God for those who did such things to me; and I would have loved them with a great love.

In this unction, then, I felt within and without a delight such as I have never experienced at any other time nor in any other circumstance, but I cannot say much—or even little—about it. It was a consolation different from what the others had been because in those other delight-filled moments I desired to immediately leave this world, but in this one I desired a lingering death accompanied with every kind of torment, and with all the torments that the world could imagine in every member of my body—even though these torments seemed to me as absolutely nothing at all. For the soul understood that this consolation was but a small fire in comparison to those benefits which it had been promised; my soul was absolutely sure of this.

And if all the wise of the world were to tell me otherwise, I would not believe them. Furthermore, if I were to swear that all who walk by this aforesaid way are saved, I do not believe that I would be lying. For he left me this sign in my soul so firmly and so clearly and with such great light, that I believe I would rather endure martyrdom than to be able to believe that it could be otherwise. The sign which he left me with and which I feel continually is that the right way to salvation consists in loving [Christ] and to want to suffer torments for the sake of his love.

At this point, I, the scribe, said to her: "Would it be your wish now to have others revile you?" And she replied: "Yes, I do have some desire for that even if on occasion it has been a source of pride for me." And the voice I had been hearing also said to me: "If you have doubts concerning this sign, namely, the ointment you have just received, ask a certain brother to whom I gave this ointment.[39] He had some understanding of it. Furthermore, the aforesaid words which you heard from me are so sublime that it does not displease me that you entertain some doubts about them, for if not, your joy would be too great for you to bear. I am pleased also that you have such enthusiasm for these words, for they are indeed very sublime. And if I wanted you not to have this enthusiasm, you would not have it."

Along with this sign of perpetual love, Angela sees the heavens open and is spiritually associated with the saints before the divine majesty

Christ's faithful one then told me that she saw God, and when I, brother scribe, asked her how or what she saw, and if she saw something with a bodily form, she responded as follows: I saw a fullness, a brightness with which I felt myself so filled that words fail me, nor can I find anything to compare it with. I cannot tell you that I saw something with a bodily form, but he was as he is in heaven, namely, of such an indescribable beauty that I do not know how to describe it to you except as the Beauty and the All Good.[40] And all the saints were standing before the divine majesty and praising him. But as for myself, it seemed to me that I stood in that presence only a little while.

Before the preceding vision he had also told me: "My beloved daughter, you are much more loved by me than I am by you." And very often he also said: "You are sweet to me, and all the saints in paradise and likewise my mother bear a special love for you, and through me you will be associated to them." But all this seemed far too little to me, namely to be associated with the saints and his mother, for such was the sweetness he made me feel that I delighted only in him. He then said to me: "I hide some of the great love I have for you on account of your weakness, for if it were otherwise you could not bear it."

And to me, brother scribe, further questioning her, she answered as follows: This will make you understand that he was the All Good. In the above experience I was called to contemplate the saints who were standing before the divine majesty and I was told that I should also look at the angels who seemed to be standing above the saints. I concluded that what I was seeing was the supreme Good as I became aware that all that was good in the saints and in the angels was from him and in him, and because I did not and could not care to look at either the saints or the angels, for I delighted only in him. Furthermore, he also told me: "I hide some of the great love I have for you." And my soul understood that he was showing me very little of this love he had for me, virtually nothing in comparison to what his love really was. Then my soul addressed him and said: "Why do you have such love for me who am such a sinner, and why do you take such delight in me when I am so ugly and despicable, and throughout my life I have offended you?" I became aware, then, that I had never done anything good that was not also filled with many defects. To this he replied: "Such is the love that I have deposited in you that I am totally unable to remember your faults; my eyes do not see them. In you I have deposited a great treasure."

My soul then felt that all this was certainly true, and I no longer doubted anything about it. I felt and I saw that the eyes of God were looking at me and in that look my soul experienced such delight that no one, not even if one of those saints from above came down to earth, could say something about it or express it adequately. Also when he told me that he was keeping hidden much of his love for me because I could not bear it, my soul replied: "If you are God almighty, you can enable me to bear it." To this he said: "But if here on earth you were granted everything you desired, you would no longer hunger for me; for precisely this reason, I do not want to grant your wish; for in this life, I want you to hunger for me, desire me, and languish for me."

Angela recalls a previous divine exhortation in which she was taught that all can and must love God

I now also recall that on that St. Francis road, during the first time he had spoken to me,[41] he said: "My sweet daughter, I love you much more than you can love me," which I countered by enumerating all my sins and defects and acknowledging my unworthiness of this great love. He had also said to me: "Great indeed is the love which I have for the soul which loves me without malice." Whence it seemed to me that he wanted the soul to be ablaze, according to its own capacities, with some of the love which he himself has for us. And, if the soul would desire to have this love, he would grant this love to it.

He further said in that conversation: "Because there are now so few good persons, faith is weak," and it seemed to me that he lamented over this. Then he added: "So great is the love which I have for the soul which loves me without malice that I would now grant even greater graces to anyone truly having this said love than I formerly granted to the saints in times past for whom it is said that God did great things for them."

There is no one who can be excused, for everyone can love him. God does not require anything of the soul save love in return, for he himself loves it and he is the love of the soul. And she further told me, brother scribe: "How vast, that is to say, how profound are these words, namely, that God does not require anything from the soul save that it love him in return!" And by way of explanation she said: "Who could hold anything back for oneself if one loves?"

Afterward, as a further explanation of these other words, namely, that God is the love of the soul, she said: God himself showed me living proof that he loves the soul and he himself is the love of the soul, by his coming into the world and his suffering on the cross, notwithstanding his greatness. Then, he explained all this to me, namely about his coming into the world and his passion on the cross even though he was so great. He showed me living proof, and he said afterward: "See then if in me there be anything but love" and he explained to me, first of all, by whom he was sent, then, why he had come and how he himself was so great, followed by an explicit demonstration of his passion, the cross, and everything previously mentioned. I saw, finally, and my soul understood with the utmost certainty, that he was nothing but love.

At this point, I, brother scribe, because I had to hurry, omitted much and summarized what she was saying. Concerning her beautiful explanations about the world I only snatched some of her words, abbreviating what she was saying, that is, writing only some and not all of what she told me.

"And it seemed to me," she also said, "that he lamented over the fact that in these times he could find so few persons in whom he could place his grace. That is why he had added that he would grant a far greater grace to those whom he found now loving him than he had granted to any saint of times past until the present."

The divine voice resolves the doubt concerning the veracity of what is written: "God is present in all that you are writing and stands there with you."

While I was writing, she also told me: "I would have scruples about divulging what I am telling you, were it not for words in which I was told that the more I speak and continue to speak about what is happening to me, the more it will remain with me."

And she further told me, brother scribe: Yesterday and today, much of what I have been hearing I did not want to retain. But today, when my conscience troubled me about something I had said to you, namely about the sign which was given to me[42] and which, when you asked, I responded that I had received, and also about my saying that I valued tribulations (which you also wrote down), and, finally, about everything that I had said about myself to you and that you wrote was really true, I was immediately given the following response: "All the things which are written here are true and there is nothing whatsoever which is said falsely; but what was said was much more complete or had much more meaning. What I said is defective, and the scribe's version of it is also weak and defective."[43] And he then showed me how I had this certainty of God's love.

He also added: "God is present in all those things which you are writing and stands there with you." My soul understood and felt that God indeed delighted over all that had been written. I was told all the above because my conscience had been disturbed concerning those things which I had said, and because I had said many things, which it would not be necessary to seek advice on, because they were so clear.

In another divine colloquy it is affirmed that there is no excuse for rejecting the Divine Doctor

When I, brother scribe, had finished writing the things said above, Christ's faithful one spoke to me as follows: I have just recently been told the following, and it has been so impressed on my heart that I can scarcely hold myself back from crying it out and proclaiming it to all, so clearly has he manifested this truth to me: No one can find an excuse for not being saved, for nothing more is required than to do what a sick person does with his doctor, that is, to show one's infirmity to him and dispose oneself to do what he says. Thus one should do nothing more, nor rely on any other medicine for oneself, but just show oneself to the doctor and dispose oneself to do everything the doctor orders, and take care not to mix in anything contrary to what he prescribes. My soul then understood that the medicine was his blood and he himself was the one who administers this medicine to the sick. And this entails nothing more for the one who is sick than to have the proper disposition so that the doctor can restore one's health and heal one's infirmity.[44]

To all this my soul felt the need to respond, for it was aware that each member of my body suffered from a particular infirmity, and it proceeded to identify the sins of each member. My soul then began to enumerate all the members and the sins proper to each one; it was aware of these sins and identified them with astonishing facility. He listened to everything patiently, and afterward he responded that it was a great delight for him to heal each infirmity immediately and in an orderly manner. And he added: "Mary Magdalene suffered as you did from her infirmities and grieved over them, and she too wanted to be freed from them. And whoever would entertain a similar desire could recover health just as she did."[45]

He offered still another example (even though for each example there would have been enough to do and meditate on for an entire day): "Those of my little children who withdraw from my kingdom by their sinning and make themselves sons of the devil, when they return to the Father, because he rejoices over their return, he demonstrates to them how especially joyful he is. Such indeed is his joy that he grants them a special grace that he does not grant to others who were virgins and had never gone away from him. And this is because of the Father's love and also because, after their return, they grieve for having offended such a majesty and realize they are only worthy of hell. It is because they reach such an awareness of the love of the Father that they receive a special joy."

Such are the things which Christ's faithful one was telling me, brother scribe, but in other words, more numerous, more expressive and full of clarity. When I read back to her what I had written, she pointed out that I had not expanded on anything, but on the contrary, what I had written was dry and condensed; nonetheless, she confirmed that what I had written was true. Then she added that today she had also been told: "Have these words inserted at the end of what you say, namely, that thanks should be given to God for all the things which you have written. And whoever wishes to stay in a state of grace should never turn the eyes of their souls away from the cross, whether it be joy or sadness which I bestow upon them or allow to happen to them."[46]

Back in her home Angela obtains God's blessing over her alms

She also told me while I was writing: Once while I was in prayer before a meal and was asking Our Lady to obtain for me a grace from her Son, namely, that through the merits of his most holy passion, he take away all my sins, absolve them and grant me his blessing; and that he do likewise for my companion; and just as he had stood up to bless the meal of the apostles before eating with them, he would likewise bless the food and drink of which we were about to partake. An immediate response was given to my request as follows: "My daughter, so sweet to me, I grant you what you ask for. I now take away all your sins, absolve both of you and bless you." And it seemed to me that what he said was meant for both myself and my companion, for his words were "both of you." He further added: "Almighty God always blesses whatever you eat and drink for as long as you live in this world."

And I was wondering if those alms which are given to us already receive this same blessing when they are given to us or if only those which we eat receive it. To this he immediately responded and said: "All the alms which we receive do contain this blessing so that whomever we share them with—such is the power already contained in this blessing—will benefit from them according to the measure of their disposition. And even if anyone received them in a state of mortal sin they would still benefit from them for they would have the effect of making them desire the sooner to convert themselves to do penance." My soul then felt that God was in me and I knew this to be true because of the spiritual joy and holy delight which I experienced as truly coming from God.

She further added that even now whenever she makes this prayer before eating she always receives the assurance that all the things said above are granted to her, and also feels that God is delighted over it, and is even delighted that she is still full of zeal to repeat this blessing always. And it seems that it pleases him that she does not desist from making the said blessing whether it is out of zeal or even out of the doubt that arises because she is not sure that the blessing has already been granted, even if she is told each time that it has been; and she feels that God looks on it approvingly and it does not displease him. Of this she receives a very clear assurance.[47]

She likewise said that she was told many times: "Ask, and ask for the right things, and what you ask for will be granted to you."

God blesses Angela at the moment of the elevation of the body of Christ during the celebration of the Holy Mass

She likewise told me, brother: Once when I was standing in the church and at the moment when people kneel down at the elevation of the body of Christ, words such as these were addressed to me by the Blessed Virgin: "My daughter, so sweet to my son." She spoke very humbly and in such a way that I experienced a new feeling in my soul, one of utmost sweetness. And she said: "My daughter, sweet to my Son and to me. My Son has already come unto you and you have received his blessing." By this she was making me understand that her Son was at that moment already on the altar, and it was as if she was telling me something new and it filled my soul with such great joy that I cannot find words for it nor do I believe that there is anyone who could express it properly. This joy was so great that I was even amazed afterward that I could in any way stand on my feet while I was experiencing it.

And the Blessed Virgin also told me: "Now that you have received the blessing of my Son, it is fitting that I too come to you and give you my blessing so that just as you received the blessing of the Son you also receive the blessing of his mother. Receive then my blessing. May it be yours from both my Son and myself. Work with all your might at loving for you are much loved, and you are called upon to attain something infinite." And then my soul experienced a joy such as never before. When these words were coming to an end, at the moment when the body of Christ was elevated by the priest, I genuflected and adored him and the same joy increased. I also want to point out that when I heard these words I was not able to kneel when the other people knelt but remained standing.

I, brother scribe, interrupted at this point to ask her if in this experience she saw something else in the body of Christ, something similar to what she was accustomed to seeing on other occasions. Her response was no, but she said that she truly felt Christ in her soul. To this, I, brother scribe, pressed her further: "How do you know that this is truly so?" And she responded as follows: Because there is nothing that sets the soul ablaze as when Christ is in the soul and delights it with his love. For then it was not like the fire with which the soul is sometimes ablaze, but was the fire of sweet and gentle love. For my part I do not doubt when such a fire is in the soul because the soul then knows that God is truly present, for no other could produce this effect. When this happens all the members feel a disjointing, and I wish it to be so. Indeed such is the extreme delight that I feel that I would want to always remain in this state. Furthermore, I hear the bones cracking when they are thus disjointed. I hear this disjointing more when the body of Christ is elevated. It is especially then that my hands suffer this disjointing and are opened.

CHAPTER V
THIRD SUPPLEMENTARY STEP

The third step is the revelation of divine knowledge through teachings, some perceptible through the ears of the body, and others understandable only through the taste of the spirit

In a parable God shows Angela how those who "descend" to follow the cross in tribulations can "ascend" to a place at his banquet as sons according to three categories: ordinary, special, and intimate

While I was writing, Christ's faithful one told me that once she had pleaded with God to give her something of himself; she then had made the sign of the cross over herself. She had also asked him to show her who were his true sons, and God had given her, among others, the following example.[48]

Imagine a man who has many friends and invites all of them to a banquet. And he sets a place aside for those who accept his invitation—for not all do—at his banquet table. This man is grief-stricken over those who do not come, for the banquet he had prepared was very lavish. All those who do come he places at his banquet table. But even though he loves all his guests and treats them all to his banquet, there are some he loves more, and these are placed at a special table near him. And those whom he loves even more intimately get to eat from the same plate and drink from the same cup as he does.

Then, with my soul very pleased by what it was hearing, I asked him: "Tell me, Lord, when do you send out this invitation to everyone?" And he answered: "I have called and invited everyone to eternal life. Those who wish to come, let them come, for no one can give the excuse of not being called. And if you want to understand how much I loved and wanted them at my table, simply look at the cross. Afterward he added: "Behold, those called are coming, and being placed at the table." And he also made it understood that he himself was the table and the food which he was offering.

I then asked: "By which way did those who were called come?" To this he replied: "By way of tribulation, such as happens to the virgins, the chaste, the poor, the long-suffering, and the sick."[49] And he proceeded to name the many categories of those who are to be saved. I understood both his reasoning and his explanations, and every word I heard was a source of great delight. I even strove to keep my eyes perfectly still so as to stay with this consolation. The above-mentioned, therefore, are those who are commonly called "sons." What he was trying to get me to understand in telling me this was that virginity, poverty, fever, the loss of sons, tribulations, and the loss of possessions are all sent by God. He named all these and gave the motive and explanation for their occurrence, which I fully understood. And he said all these are sent by God to those who are called "sons" for their own good. But when these things happen, the sons do not understand why, nor do they ponder over their meaning, and they are even troubled by them at first. It is only afterward when they come to the realization that these things are sent by God that they are able to endure them peacefully.

The ones, however, who are invited to a special table, and those whom the Lord leads to eat from his own plate and drink from his own cup, are those who wish to know who this good man is who invited them, so that they may learn how to please him. Once they become aware that they received this invitation without any merit or worth on their part, they then actively set out to please him. For they know then that they are much loved by God and are truly unworthy of this love. And because of this awareness, they go to the cross to fix their attention and regard upon it, and therein discover what love is.

By means of two parables, God reveals and explains the great mystery of the "descent" and "ascent" of his Son, who was motivated by love for us so that we may follow his path

My soul was then told how God the Father out of his love for us sent his Son; and how the Son concurred in this love, and so he came; and how he first created and then redeemed the soul. To act in an orderly fashion, he first sent the angels; and then he withdrew, so to speak, from his Father from heaven and from the dignity that was his. After this he recounted the details of his passion and related the sufferings of all his bodily members, his hardships, and the harsh and injurious words he was subjected to. And in this world, he left his mother, which was extremely painful for him; he had left the apostles as well. When I asked him what his mother's greatest pain was, he replied that it was in her heart. In short, for those who are sons in the strict sense, he recounted all the things having to do with his love, which would take a very long time indeed to write. Furthermore, since my soul not only heard, but also felt, all that he said, merely to repeat it, or hear it, as we do now, is just like nothing at all.

My soul was further told: "You are amazed that the body of Christ was tormented and suffered in this way; how much more should you be amazed over his divinity that suffered these things in his humanity, which was like a cloak for his divinity." In order to help me understand this, he gave me the example of a very noble man whose person cannot be offended, but whose house is damaged and destroyed; that is to say, his house is destroyed in place of his person. This example demonstrated to me that although God is impassible, out of his great love for us he allowed that great shame be brought to bear upon his divinity in the sight of everyone for all to see.—But I, brother scribe, did not pay much attention to this example. Out of haste, and because it was very long, I cut short this beautiful instruction and divine doctrine.[50]—This example set my soul ablaze with love and it considered the suffering of the body of Christ to be of little significance as compared to the love which came from his divinity.

My soul was further told that God having done all these things for her, and having been born for her—which also meant "having descended to such a great level of indignity and vileness" for her—it is fitting that in return the soul be thus reborn into God and die to itself, that is, to its vices and sins, and in this way "ascend to a high level of dignity." Because as soon as the soul thus dies to itself and becomes aware of how much it is loved, the life of grace is given to it and it lives in Christ.

And to those who are, strictly speaking, his sons, God permits great tribulations which he grants to them as a special grace so that they might eat with him from the same plate. "For to this table, I was also called," said Christ, "and the chalice that I drank tasted bitter; but because I was motivated by love it was sweet to me."[51] Thus for these sons who are aware of the aforesaid benefits and have received the special grace for it, even though they experience at times bitter tribulations, these, nonetheless, become sweet to them on account of the love and grace with which they are motivated. And they are even more in distress when they are not afflicted, for they know that the more they endure tribulations and persecutions, the more they will feel delight in and know God.

I was likewise given another example drawn from the cross, and it is the following: A father had sons who committed sins. And it was then explained to me how they had sinned. It so happened that the father, totally innocent, was put to death because of the offenses of his sons. And my soul was shown the place on the road where he died—at a sort of intersection of three roads—and blood could still be seen there. It stands to reason, and is to be expected, that these sons grieve over their father's painful death by the sword; and that they grieve even more for their responsibility in so cruel and ignominious a death. These sons, as a consequence, would always carry this grief in their hearts. And so grief-laden would they be that they would hence avoid and be wary of passing again on that road; and if, perchance, they should happen to pass by it again, they could not do so without suffering the greatest distress, the memory of their father's death being so fresh in their minds. How much greater then, O soul, should be your grief over the death of Christ who is so much more than an earthly father, and who died because of your sins. And he concluded: Grieve and lament, O soul, which must pass by the cross on which Christ died. What you must do is to place yourself before it to find your rest, for the cross is your salvation and your bed. You must find your delight in it because therein is indeed your salvation. It is amazing how anyone can pass by the cross quickly and without stopping. And he added that if the soul fixed its attention on the cross, it would always find fresh blood flowing from it. From this example, I understood who are the legitimate sons of God.[52]

Afterward, whenever I passed near a painting of the cross or the passion, it seemed to me that the representation was nothing in comparison with the extraordinary suffering which really took place and which had been shown to me and impressed in my heart. This is why I no longer wanted to look at these paintings, because they seemed to me to signify almost nothing by comparison to what really happened.

By two examples drawn from her own experience,
Angela teaches that the "descent" into the trials of life
and the works of charity is an "ascent" into divine joy

Since I, brother scribe, questioned her about the above, Christ's faithful one, in reply, sought to reaffirm how true it was that the sons of God feel divine sweetness in the midst of the persecutions and tribulations they suffer, as it was demonstrated to her in such a wonderful manner in the instruction from God just written. So she began to relate an example drawn from her own life, pointing out that when she had been persecuted by the friars and the "continents,"[53] she could find no words to express the quality of the sweetness she felt or the abundant tears of joy she experienced like an anointing.

I likewise challenged what she had said to me concerning the aforesaid teachings she had received from God on the theme of the sons of God; how the special sons eat from the same plate and drink from the same cup as Christ; and how, even if they initially experience this eating and drinking as bitter, it nonetheless becomes sweet for them, and indeed most delectable—I insisted that their experience was a bitter one. In response, Christ's faithful one related a story to me through which she tried to show me that it was not bitter but sweet.

This is what she told me: On Maundy Thursday,[54] I suggested to my companion that we go out to find Christ: "Let's go," I told her, "to the hospital[55] and perhaps we will be able to find Christ there among the poor, the suffering, and the afflicted." We brought with us all the head veils that we could carry, for we had nothing else. We told Giliola, the servant at that hospital, to sell them and from the sale to buy some food for those in the hospital to eat.[56] And, although initially she strongly resisted our request, and said we were trying to shame her, nonetheless, because of our repeated insistence, she went ahead and sold our small head veils and from the sale bought some fish. We had also brought with us all the bread which had been given to us to live on.

And after we had distributed all that we had, we washed the feet of the women and the hands of the men, and especially those of one of the lepers which were festering and in an advanced stage of decomposition. Then we drank the very water with which we had washed him. And the drink was so sweet that, all the way home, we tasted its sweetness and it was as if we had received Holy Communion. As a small scale of the leper's sores was stuck in my throat, I tried to swallow it. My conscience would not let me spit it out, just as if I had received Holy Communion. I really did not want to spit it out but simply to detach it from my throat.[57]

**By means of two parables and other teachings,
Angela demonstrates how those who are called to follow
the singular "descent" of the Divine Master, and reject
this invitation, do so at their great peril**

On the same day in which part of the above was written, Christ's faithful one returned to her cell and began to recite the "Our Father of the Passion,"[58] which she was in the habit of saying. As soon as she had finished she immediately heard the following: "All those whom God teaches and enlightens so that they understand his way, and who close their souls to this light and to this special teaching from God and harden their hearts—all those who know this teaching comes from God and follow a different one—all those who choose to follow the common way in spite of their conscience: all of them bear the curse of almighty God." This was repeated to her several times. She resisted hearing it since it seemed to her extremely harsh, and she was afraid it might be a lie that those to whom God gives light and grace, he later curses.

She was then presented with the example of a woman who begins to learn how to do some delicate work and puts her heart into it to such an extent that she later has to change teachers.[59]

After this example, still another was given to her, and she was told that she should relate this one to me, brother scribe, because I, being a friar, would understand it better than the previous one concerning the woman. She was told repeatedly to relate these words and example to me. God had indeed insisted: "Tell him!"

The example she presented is the following: A young boy was sent to school by his father, who took care of his expenses, dressed him up handsomely, and encouraged him to pursue his schooling. He also arranged it so that at the appropriate time he would move on to a more advanced teacher. It happens that the schoolboy neglected his studies and had to leave school to return to work in the fields. He ends up by forgetting everything he had learned. Something similar happens to the one who is first given instructions through preaching and the Scriptures and is then enlightened by God with special insights and is given to understand how to follow the way of Christ—for which purpose, the Father had him instructed first of all by others and then by himself with special teachings which he alone can give. If such a person becomes negligent in his work and intentionally hardens himself (as has been said), then, because God had destined him to be a light for others and he on his part despised this doctrine and light, God the Father takes away the light and he is accursed.

Christ's faithful one also told me that she doubted that it was possible to incur a curse in that way, and she thought it so doubtful that she was grief-stricken to hear about it. She then told her companion that she did not want to tell me about it for fear of having been deceived. "Nonetheless," she said, "I was told to tell you about this example because some of the words in it referred to you. But in my understanding these words were meant positively and not negatively, and I understood them definitely for the good."

Christ's faithful one likewise told me, brother scribe, that God at another time had preached to her at great length along the lines of what has just been written.

Through divine revelation Angela discovers herself as a vile creature and God as the supreme good who humbly abases himself

She also told me, brother scribe, that once God had spoken to her and demonstrated to her, very effectively and with many details, how she herself was nothing and was created from vile substance; how he found nothing good in her, and yet he loved her and she herself could love him; and his love is so great and perfect that when it is recalled, there is no place left for pride and in no way can any obstacles be placed in its path. After the power of God and her own vileness had been demonstrated to her, she was then told: "See what you are—you, for whom I have come." And when I became aware and felt who I was and what I had become by offending him, I felt that no creature was as vile as I.

She likewise told me, brother scribe, that once while she was in prayer and asked God to teach her, he showed her, first of all, how she had offended him in every way possible; and he said to her: "Let's begin with what you do with your hair." This was a beautiful, useful, and long instruction but I, brother scribe, could not write it because it was time for us to leave the church, and later I did not take time to do so because other things needed to be written.

Angela, enlightened by God, responds to four questions from friars

*a. By means of an example, Angela is instructed in two ways
in which God can be known in his creatures*

I, brother scribe, also wanted to know and learn from her how God can be known in his creatures. I began by referring to a holy friar of whom it was said that he possessed great knowledge of God in his creatures. At that time I was greatly disturbed by a certain scandal that was causing me pain. As a response to my question, Christ's faithful one began her explanation as follows: Once, someone came to me and told me that he knew of a man who knew God in his creatures. Afterward I began to meditate on this, namely, whether it is greater to know God in his creatures or in oneself, that is, in the soul.

After Matins, I began to ask God to reveal to me what I wanted to know. I do not recall fully the example he gave in response. It seemed to me that it concerned a powerful and very noble man who had extensive and countless possessions under his control, and men under him who had a share in these possessions. From the benefits derived from their share in these possessions, these men knew the kindness of this noble lord, for they received and shared in nothing but his kindness. But there is another type of men under this same lord who, although they know him as do the others through the possessions they have a share in, nonetheless know him far better through the way they experience him and his kindness in themselves.

When I, brother scribe, questioned her further concerning this aforementioned knowledge, she answered that it seemed to her that not only was her response to the above incomplete, but she could not now answer to those other things which I had asked. As a result, at that point I stopped writing.

Angela learns that in this life it is not possible for anyone to penetrate the mystery of the presence of Christ in the Eucharist

On another occasion, I, brother scribe, asked her how the body of Christ could be simultaneously on every altar at once.[60] She responded that she had received an answer concerning this point from God, who had told her: "It is through the divine power, which the Scriptures speak about, but which cannot be understood in this life. Those who read about it in the Scriptures have some understanding of it, and those who have personal experience of me understand it even more. But neither the former nor the latter fully understand it in this life. The time will come, however, when you will understand it."

By means of an example, God indicates to Angela how one must clearly distinguish what is one's own and what belongs to others

Once I, brother scribe, asked her to pray to God for brother Dominic of the Marches that he might not fall into error. Praying fervently, she immediately received the following answer: Everything which belongs to others must be granted to them; but as long as one is alive one must always retain what belongs to oneself. Thus with great care one must retain what is one's own and similarly give back what belongs to others, and not mix up one's own possessions with someone else's.

To illustrate the above, she was given the example of the Blessed Virgin. This is what Christ told her: "Look at how my mother retained what was her own and granted to others what belonged to them." Similarly, he presented himself as an example of one who had retained what was his own even if he had not need of it, because he was always in God the Father and God was in him.[61]

Through a wonderful vision Angela understands that divine providence is a great mystery of divine wisdom, one hidden to humans; and also receives the grace of exercising true judgments over spiritual matters and persons

She also told me, brother scribe, the following: Once I was asked to pray to God for something Brother E. of the Marches wanted to know from God and about which he had questioned me. But I did not dare pray to God for what he was asking. I simply could not pray for such a request. For even though I, myself, would have liked to know those things, it seemed to me to be an act of pride and stupidity to pray to God about them.

While I was in such thoughts, my soul was suddenly taken out of itself and in this state of ecstasy I was first placed before a table which had neither beginning nor end. I was positioned so as not to see the table itself but what was on it. And what I saw on it was of such indescribable fullness that I cannot relate nor even say a word about it, save that it was the All Good. What I perceived on that table was divine wisdom in all its fullness, and from it I realized that it was not permissible and was indeed presumptuous to seek or want to inquire into the plans of divine wisdom, because that would be anticipating what it intends to do. In that fullness of divine wisdom I really became aware of how one cannot inquire or want to know the plans of divine wisdom, for it would be presumptuous to do so.

From then on, when I come across anyone with similar questions, it seems to me that I have to tell them that they are in error. Henceforth, from what I saw on that table, namely the divine wisdom, I can judge with intelligence all spiritual persons and other spiritual matters when I hear about them or when someone tells me about them. And I no longer judge with the same sin-laden judgment which used to be mine, but with a different true judgment. This is why I do not nor can I have the awareness of sinning with this type of judgment.

There is nothing more I can say about what I saw on that table, but I do remember the word "table" and likewise that in the initial moment of the state of ecstasy I was in, I saw a table. But I cannot say more of what was on that table than what I have already said.

CHAPTER VI
FOURTH SUPPLEMENTARY STEP

The fourth step concerns how Angela was made aware of her unworthiness, was restored, and received the divine approval[62]

Angela receives a special grace in which God manifests his power in her life and that of others, thus removing all her doubts

Once she heard God speaking to her as follows: "I who speak with you am the divine power who wishes to bestow a grace upon you. And this grace, a special one, is the following: I want you to be useful to all who will see you; and not only to them; I also want you to be of service and help to all those who will think of you or hear your name mentioned. The more someone will have possession of me, the more useful shall you be to them." To this, even though my soul felt extremely joyful, I nonetheless retorted: "I do not want this grace, for I fear that it might harm me and I might become proud because of it." He immediately responded: "You can do nothing about it, because you are not the cause of it, only its guardian. Be faithful to it and render it to the One to whom it belongs." My soul then understood that in this way, this grace could do me no harm. Moreover, he had added: "I am pleased to see that you have such fears—or so it seems to me."

He also said: "Do the three things which you were told.[63] Put them to the test, for if you do so, what you asked my mother will be granted to you in a way that you have not yet experienced." I had asked the Blessed Virgin that at the coming feast[64] she obtain a grace from her Son through which I would know that I had not been deceived by the words which had been spoken to me. I was still in the joy of that discourse and in great hope that the Blessed Virgin would grant me what I had asked for in conformity with what had then been promised to me. I had even been told in that discourse that I would be given the grace that I would never do anything without God's permission.[65]

Afterward I set out to do those three things just mentioned. These had been indicated to me as follows: "God has manifested himself to you; he has spoken to you, and made it possible for you to feel his presence. He has done this to deter you from seeing, saying, or hearing anything except what comes from him." I understood that these words were said to me with great discretion.

As soon as I began to do these three said things, my heart was drawn out of all worldly concerns and placed in God in such a manner that I could neither think of nor see anything except God. Whether I spoke or ate, or whatever I did, it did not prevent my heart from always being in God. Whenever I wanted to depart from prayer in order to eat, I would first ask his permission. And he would grant it to me, saying: "Go and eat with the blessing of God the Father, the Son, and the Holy Spirit." Sometimes he would grant me this permission immediately, and at other times much later. This lasted three days and three nights.

Angela becomes aware that she has been tempted by the devil, is wonderfully liberated from the temptation, freed from her doubts, and elevated to a new state, upon reception of the sacraments of Penance and the Eucharist[66]

After this said state came to an end, one day while I was sitting at home, feeling sluggish and dejected, I heard the following: "I who speak to you am St. Bartholomew, who was skinned alive." He showered himself with praise, and myself as well, and then went on to claim that this was his feast day. This last statement filled my soul with sadness and perplexity. As a result I could no longer pray nor recollect myself. It was only later that I discovered that he had lied to me, when I realized that the feast that was celebrated on that day was not St. Bartholomew's but St. Clare's. This state of sadness and perplexity lasted ten days, through the octave of the feast of Our Lady in August, the day I went to Assisi.

[While in Assisi], she confessed herself as best she could so as to put her soul in order, and she prepared herself to receive communion. While the Mass was being sung, she placed herself near the cross and between the iron grills. In this place she heard God speaking to her with words that were so sweet that her soul was immediately and totally restored. What he told her was: "My daughter, you are sweet to me"— and words that were even more endearing. But even before this, it seemed to her that God had already restored her soul when he had spoken to her as follows: "My sweet daughter, no creature can give you this consolation, only I alone."

Afterward he added: "I want to show you something of my power." And immediately the eyes of my soul were opened, and in a vision I beheld the fullness of God in which I beheld and comprehended the whole of creation, that is, what is on this side and what is beyond the sea, the abyss, the sea itself, and everything else. And in everything that I saw, I could perceive nothing except the presence of the power of God, and in a manner totally indescribable. And my soul in an excess of wonder cried out: "This world is pregnant with God!" Wherefore I understood how small is the whole of creation—that is, what is on this side and what is beyond the sea, the abyss, the sea itself, and everything else—but the power of God fills it all to overflowing. He then said to me: "I have just manifested to you something of my power." From this I comprehended that henceforth I would be able to better understand other things.

Then he added: "Behold now my humility." I saw then the great depths of God's humility toward men. And because I had understood the power of God and perceived now his deep humility, my soul was filled with wonder and esteemed itself to be nothing at all—indeed, saw in itself nothing except pride. Also, as a result, I started to say that I did not want to receive communion, because it seemed to me that I was totally unworthy, and at that moment, I was, in fact, totally unworthy. He had also told me after he had shown me his power and humility: "My daughter, no creature can come to the point of seeing what you have seen, except by divine grace. And you have come to that point."

And close to the moment of the elevation of the body of Christ, he said: "Behold, the divine power is now present on the altar. I am within you. You can now receive me because you have already done so. Receive communion therefore with the blessing of God the Father, the Son, and the Holy Spirit. I who am worthy make you worthy."

The great joy and the indescribable sweetness that was mine as a result of that communion were such that I think they will remain with me for the rest of my life. On this point I have no doubts whatever, for I believe I was then granted what I had asked from the mother of God, and which she obtained for me from her Son. I was satisfied that what had been promised me in those words I had heard from God had been realized.

Angela, assailed by fresh doubts, sickness, and trials, is freed from them, reassured, and elevated to a sublime state by almighty God

Once, while sick and bedridden, she was told: "Brother So-and-so was named guardian. His reappointment has been confirmed and is certain." And she also heard: "Report, likewise, to your companion that his reappointment has been confirmed." And I understood right away that if he had not been confirmed as guardian of his fellow friars, the message was to be understood spiritually, that is, that he was confirmed as guardian of spiritual affairs. And as I thought afterward that the meaning of what I had heard was still hidden from me, the voice reasserted: "Tell that brother that his reappointment as guardian is certain." These words were said because I had hesitated to tell him.

While still sick and bedridden, I was also told: "Get up and kneel down, with your hands joined together." Because of my sickness I did not feel that I had the strength to get up but nonetheless managed to do so near the bed. Instead of doing exactly as I was told, I only sat down near my bed. This command was addressed to me and repeated many times while I was lying down and when I had got up in that manner near the bed. As a consequence, he reprimanded me as follows: "Get up, beat your breast, and confess your sin of disobedience in front of your companion." I then got up very joyfully. It was indeed easy and a joy for me to do so, as if I had not previously suffered any pain or sickness; and I no longer felt any pain or weakness. I then confessed myself to God in front of my companion.

He then added: "Say these words: 'Praise and blessing to the holy Trinity, and holy Mary, virgin and mother.'" And I repeated these words many times with great joy and delight.

During this period[67] I was in a state of great stress, for it seemed to me that I felt nothing of God, and I also had the impression that I was abandoned by him; nor was I able to confess my sins. On the one hand, I thought that perhaps this had happened to me because of my pride, and on the other hand, I perceived so clearly the depths of my many sins that it did not seem to me that I could confess them with adequate contrition or even so much as say them. It seemed to me that there was no way in which I could bring them out in the open. Nor could I even praise God or remain in prayer. It seemed to me that all that was left of God in me was the conviction that I had not suffered as many trials as I deserved and, similarly, that I did not want to fall away from his grace by sinning for all the good or evil or sufferings that the world has to offer, nor did I want to assent to any evil. I was in this intense and terrible state of torment for more than four weeks.

After this period I heard God speaking to me with such words as the following: "My daughter, you are beloved by almighty God and by all the saints in paradise. God has placed his love in you and he has more

171

love for you than for any woman in the valley of Spoleto." My soul had its doubts about this and cried out: "How can I believe this when I am assailed by so many trials, and it seems to me as if I am abandoned by God?" To this he responded: "It is when it seems to you that you are most abandoned by God that you are most loved by him, and he is the closest to you."

Since I still sought greater certitude and security concerning the above, I was then told: "The sign which I will grant you to indicate how much you are loved is the following: If that brother spoken of is named guardian, you will know it to be true."

When it came time to eat, I prayed God to take away all my sins and grant me his absolution through the merits of his most holy passion; and also to bestow his blessing both on myself and my companion, and likewise on you. In response he told her: "Your sins are taken away. I bestow upon all of you a blessing with the flesh of the hand that was crucified on the cross." And it seemed to me that I saw this hand blessing us, and I understood that this blessing was upon the heads of the three of us.[68] The sight of that hand filled me with delight. Then he added: "The blessing of the Father, the Son, and the Holy Spirit will be yours for eternity." I understood once again that this blessing was meant for the three of us. He further added: "Tell that brother that he should strive to become little." And also: "Tell him that he is much loved by almighty God and that he should do all that he can to love him in return."[69]

Angela is liberated from a temptation of the devil, is wonderfully restored and elevated to a mystical state through the divine power active in the celebration of the sacraments of penance and the Eucharist—and even understands something of the game God plays with the soul

After the preceding exchange, on the very same day, while I was washing lettuce, I heard these words meant to trick me: "How can you consider yourself worthy to wash lettuce?" Clearly aware of the deception, I retorted not only with indignation but also with sadness, because these words made me doubt what I had previously heard, and I said: "I am only worthy that God send me immediately to hell, and I am likewise only worthy to collect manure."

Shortly after this period of sadness and trial—only a little while after—I heard the following, and it was a source of great joy for me: "It is good that the wine be tempered with water." These words immediately dissipated my sadness and drove it away. All this was told to me on a Friday, beginning before None and continuing until after the meal. Until that day I had been in the state of the aforesaid sadness for more than four weeks. Then, that very day, I experienced the joy of which I have already spoken, but it was not strong enough to lift my sadness away completely; it only tempered it.

Until then I did not have a full desire to confess myself, but at this point the desire and the wish to confess myself and receive communion began to dawn on me, and I was told: "It pleases me very much that you receive communion because if you receive me, you have already received me; and if you do not receive me, you have already received me. If you wish, you can receive communion tomorrow with the blessing of the Father, the Son, and the Holy Spirit. Do so out of reverence for almighty God, the Blessed Virgin Mary, and the saint, namely St. Anthony, whose feast falls on Saturday, that is, tomorrow morning."[70] To this he added: "You will receive a new grace, one which you have not yet had."

On the following morning, I waited for the said friar to come hear my confession, in order to be disposed to receive communion as I had been told to do in the preceding conversation. But when I saw that the hour of Tierce was passing and that the friar whom I was expecting did not arrive, both my companion and myself were filled with sadness, and my companion began to weep. However, I suddenly heard God telling me: "Do not be sad, for the trial you have endured, like the other one, was only for your own good and in your interest. You will not lose the grace promised to you; rather than having less, you will have more of it." I did not believe him; I doubted his words. To this he retorted: "Believe what I am telling you, because my promise that you will not lose this grace is as valid as the one concerning the grace that you were to receive upon receiving communion." These words gave me a great and lasting peace, and, knowing that I had been told I would not lose the grace promised to me, I was able to exhort my companion not to weep or feel afflicted.

After this, on the following Thursday I went to church, and a certain friar spoke to me in such a way that I was moved to confess myself and receive communion. I went ahead and confessed myself to this friar, for the grace had been granted me to do it. After this, while Mass was being celebrated, I was given the grace of a certain illumination in which I saw myself so full of sins and defects that I lost my power of speech and I could not say a word, for I thought that the communion I was about to receive would be for my condemnation.

Afterward, however, I found myself admirably disposed, and I was able to immerse myself totally within Christ. And I threw myself into him with a faith and a certainty far greater than I ever had or experienced, as far as I can recall. I immersed myself within him as if dead but with a wonderful certainty that he was making me come alive. And when I received communion I experienced an indescribable feeling of God's presence. He granted me a peace through which I was given to understand, or rather to feel, that all the trials and tribulations I had been afflicted with until now—or could be afflicted with in the future—were all for my own good. I was content with the fact that I seemed to have lost God's presence. I was granted a new grace which I had not received before. That communion led my soul to this perception and desire, namely, to want to give itself totally to Christ because it saw that Christ gave himself totally to us. The desire for martyrdom delighted me anew. I awaited and desired it. And I even delighted more than usual in all the pain that could be in it for me; I longed for it.

After the above things were said I, brother scribe, asked her to pray to God that he enlighten both of us on the doubt she had expressed. In response, she was told: "Tell this brother: 'Why is it that throughout this period of trial she did not love less but more when it seemed to her that she was abandoned?' Tell him also: 'I am the one who sustains her, because if I did not sustain her she would be overwhelmed.' And add: 'The meaning of what took place had been hidden from you.'" To illustrate what he was saying he also told her the following: "I want to give you an example drawn from ordinary life. It concerns a father who had a son who was very dear to him. This father, who loved his son dearly, gave him food, but in due measure. He himself apportioned it in such a way that it would be of most benefit to him. He did not allow him to drink wine and to eat more than necessary lest it harm him. He apportioned it in such a way as to favor his growth."

Christ's faithful one also told me, brother scribe: After I had heard the above, God often and repeatedly accomplished wonders for my soul which I understood no one could make possible save God alone. For example, once my soul was lifted up in God and my joy was so great that if it lasted I believe that my body would immediately lose the use of all its senses and all its members. God often plays like this with and in the soul. When the soul tries to seize him, he immediately withdraws.[71] The soul nonetheless remains in a state of great joy, and this joy is accompanied by a certitude that it is God who is at work, and in no way can it doubt this in the least. I can provide no comparison nor give a name to what I see or feel in this experience. In the past this experience was usually different from what it is now, but at all times it is totally indescribable.

As I have just pointed out, the present experience, which is now more frequent, is different because the joy that accompanies it is of another nature and with a different effect. My soul cannot fix itself in this state, for when this happens the soul immediately returns to itself, although the great joy from the experience abides. And Christ's faithful one also told me, brother, while I was writing: "I am waiting for a still greater joy to be given to me."

Angela is embraced by the arm of the Crucified and goes into his wound, experiences the savor of God's power, and is filled with the joy of spiritual certainty

Then, shortly after I had written the above, that is, a little while afterward, Christ's faithful one told me, the brother who was diligently questioning her, the following: Once I was at Vespers and was gazing at the cross. And while I was thus gazing at the cross with the eyes of the body, suddenly my soul was set ablaze with love; and every member of my body felt it with the greatest joy. I saw and felt that Christ was within me, embracing my soul with the very arm with which he was crucified. This took place right at the moment when I was gazing at the cross or shortly afterward. The joy that I experienced to be with him in this way and the sense of security that he gave me were far greater than I had ever been accustomed to.

Henceforth my soul remained in a state of joy in which it understood what this man, namely Christ, is like in heaven, that is to say, how we will see that through him our flesh is made one with God. This was a source of delight for my soul beyond words and description, and it was a joy that was abiding. From it I was left with such security that even if all that we have written were not true, there would not remain any doubt whatever in me that it was God at work in me and that, most certainly, he is responsible for this state. I was so completely certain that God was at work in me that even if everyone in the world were to say that I ought to doubt this, I would not believe them. This is why I am amazed now when I recall how I sought reassurance in the past and relief from my

175

doubts, for now there can be no doubt whatever within me concerning the certainty that it was God at work.

My delight at the present is to see that hand which he shows me with the marks of the nails on it, and to hear him say: "Behold what I have suffered for you and for others." The joy which seizes my soul in this moment can in no way be spoken of. And in no way whatever can I be sad concerning the passion; on the contrary, my joy is in seeing this man, and to come to him. All my joy now is in this suffering God-man.[72]

At times it seems to my soul that it enters into Christ's side, and this is a source of great joy and delight; it is indeed such a joyful experience to move into Christ's side that in no way can I express it and put words to it. Hence when the passion of Christ was presented on the Piazza Santa Maria,[73] the moment when it seemed to me one should weep was transformed for me into a very joyful one, and I was miraculously drawn into a state of such delight that when I began to feel the impact of this indescribable experience of God, I lost the power of speech and fell flat on the ground. I tried to move a little way away from the persons around me, and I considered it a miracle that I was able to withdraw a little. I lay there on the ground; my power of speech and use of my members was gone. It seemed to me that I had indeed entered at that moment within the side of Christ. All sadness was gone and my joy was so great that nothing can be said about it.

Prior to this experience just related, my companion and I had wept very often, and we were in a state of longing. My longing was that I be not deceived, and that I would know for certain that I had not been deceived. And I thought: "If only I could know that I was not deceived, that is all that counts!" And now I am so filled with certitude about what happened that I no longer have any doubt, nor is it possible for me to doubt.

Questioned on the controversy over "the absolute but measured power of God," Angela relates how in a mystical vision she came to know the mystery of the will, power, goodness, wisdom, and justice of God, and this finally took away all her doubts

One day, after I had written the above and I had returned from Lombardy, I, brother scribe, questioned Christ's faithful one about something my companion and I had discussed on our way back to Foligno. I had told my companion that I would ask her what she thought about the question we had discussed. Christ's faithful one answered as follows: Once while I was in prayer I had questions which I hoped God would resolve, not that I had any doubts, but I wanted to know more from him. This is what I asked him: "Lord, why did you create man, and after you did, why did you allow us to sin? And why did you allow so much suffering to be inflicted upon you for our sins, when you could have just as well made it possible that without any of it we could be just the same as we are, be able to please you, and be endowed with as many virtues?"[74]

My soul understood without the shadow of a doubt what I have just said, namely, that God without any of the aforesaid suffering could have enabled us to share in virtue and salvation. It seemed to me that I was coerced and compelled into asking and thinking about such questions when I was in prayer, for what I really wanted to do was to pray and remain in a state of prayer. But I was thrust into those questions by God, or so it seemed to me. These questions, which I have just mentioned, remained with me for many days, not that I had any doubts in my mind about their resolution, but it was just as I said.

I was given to understand in response to my questions that God had allowed things to happen as they did to better demonstrate his goodness to us and because it was more suited to our condition. But I was still not satisfied with this response, for my understanding of it was still not complete. What I certainly understood was that God could have saved us in another way if he had wanted to. At a certain moment, immersed in these thoughts, my soul was drawn out of itself to perceive that the mystery of what I was asking had neither beginning nor end. And the soul when it was in that state of darkness[75] wanted to return to its normal state but could not; it could not move forward or go back to itself. After that my soul was suddenly lifted up and illumined to see the indescribable power of God, as well as his will. From these visions I received a most complete and certain understanding of everything I had asked about. All former darkness immediately withdrew. So when I was plunged into that previous darkness, I lay flat on the ground, but when I was in the state of greatest illumination, I stood straight up on my feet, on the very tips of my big toes. I was so joy-filled, and my body felt so agile, healthy, invigorated, that I had never experienced anything like it.

And I was in such a fullness of divine light that in the joy-filled vision of the power of God and the will of God, I not only understood the things I had been asking about, but I also understood, to my complete satisfaction, about all God's creatures. What I was fully satisfied about was the destiny of all those who had been saved and all who were going to be saved, the damned, the devils, and all the saints. But I can in no way find words to express any of this, for it is totally beyond our human capacities to do so. Although I fully understood that God could have done things otherwise, if he had so desired, nonetheless, knowing his power and goodness, I could not imagine any better way he could have made his power and goodness known to us, or a better way he could have made us assimilate them. Thereafter, I was so content and secure that were I to know for certain that I would be damned, I could find no reason in it for grief, and I would keep right on working and do what I could to pray and honor him. And as a result, my soul was in a state of peace, quiet, and stability, the like of which I cannot recall ever having experienced so fully and so continuously. So great was this state that it seemed to me that nothing I had experienced before had been such a great state. The effect in me was that my vices were put to death and my virtues strengthened, virtues through which I was enabled to love whatever happened to me, whether it was beneficial or harmful, that is to say I found no displeasure in it. At this point, she also told me, brother scribe, that now I could and should understand that in that vision of the power and will of God which she had seen, she had been given full satisfaction concerning all her questions, and concerning the destiny of the saved and the damned, and the role of the devils and the saints. And although aware that she should have more care for herself than for any other creature, nonetheless, even if she knew herself to be damned, she would not grieve over it, so complete was her present understanding of the justice of God.

Afterward, that is, after I had seen the power and the will of God, my soul was suddenly drawn and uplifted to an even higher state, or so it seemed to me. Then I did not see either the power or the will of God in the same way as before, but saw something stable, firm, and so indescribable that I can say nothing about it save that it was the All Good. My soul found itself in a state of joy altogether beyond description. In this vision I did not see love, but something indescribable. I had been drawn out of the former state I was in and placed into this extremely lofty and indescribable one.[76] I cannot tell whether while I was in that extremely lofty state I was standing or whether I was in the body or out of it.[77]

The preceding question, whose answer God so miraculously revealed to Christ's faithful one, was close to the same question which my companion and I were treating on the road back from Lombardy. I, brother scribe, had then proposed that I would question Christ's faithful one on it.

CHAPTER VII
FIFTH SUPPLEMENTARY STEP
THE FIFTH STEP IS THE REVELATION
OF DIVINE UNION AND LOVE

Visions of the passion of Christ transform Angela's soul and her share in them prepare her for union with God

a. Angela's heart becomes humble and is in deep pain
as she sees the great poverty of Christ

At my request, the revelation of the passion of the Lord related here at the beginning of the fifth step (which deals with divine union and love) was written down first in the vernacular by a young boy.[78] I had to proceed in this fashion because during this period I had been forbidden by my brothers to speak with Christ's faithful one to take down what she said. As a consequence, it was so badly written that when Christ's faithful one heard it reread to her, she told me that I should destroy it rather than transcribe it in such a state. But since I did not have the time to go over it with her and to correct it, I translated it just as it was into Latin, adding nothing, somewhat like a painter painting, because I did not understand it. What follows, therefore, was initially written in the vernacular.[79]

Christ's faithful one related it as follows: Once I was meditating on the poverty of the Son of God incarnate. I saw his poverty—its greatness was demonstrated to my heart, to the extent that he wished me to see it—and I saw those for whom he had made himself poor. I then experienced such sorrow and remorse that I almost fainted.

God wanted to demonstrate to me even more of his poverty. And I saw him poor of friends and relatives. I even saw him poor of himself and so poor that he seemed powerless to help himself. It is sometimes said that the divine power was then hidden out of humility.[80] But even if this has been said, I say that God's power was not hidden then, because he himself has taught me otherwise. From this vision of the poverty of the Son of God, I experienced and felt an even greater sorrow than before, for in it I recognized so much of my own pride that joy was no longer possible.

b. Angela is plunged into a state of extreme sorrow as a result of a vision of the unheard-of sufferings of the body of Christ, which exceed all human comprehension

Another time, I was once again standing in prayer and meditating sorrowfully on the passion of the Son of God incarnate. Then, through God's will, the passion was shown to me, that is, he himself granted me to see more of his passion than I have ever been told, and he saw that I perceived more of his passion than I have ever heard spoken of. For Christ had foreseen all the hearts impiously hardened against him, everyone contriving to destroy his name, and how they constantly kept in mind their purpose to destroy him. He had also foreseen all the subtle cunning they employed against him, the Son of God; their manifold designs and plans, and the extent of their rage against him; all their preparations and everything they thought about how they could even more cruelly afflict him—for the cruel sufferings of his passion were indeed acute and manifold. And he had also seen all the sufferings, the injuries, and the shame he would be submitted to. All this my soul was aware of, and it saw more of his passion than I want to tell; I don't want at this point to say anything more about it.[81]

Then my soul cried out loudly: "O holy Mary, mother of the afflicted one, tell me something of your Son's pain which no one else but you can possibly recall. For you saw more of his passion than any other saint; and as I perceive it, you not only saw it with your bodily eyes, but also pictured it with your imagination, and out of the continual ardent devotion that was yours toward the one you loved." At this point, my soul cried out in extreme pain: "Is there any saint who can tell me something of this passion which I have not yet heard spoken of or related, but which my soul has seen, which is so great that I find no words to express it?" My soul saw such suffering!

At this point, Christ's faithful one, in an explanation of the above, told me, brother scribe, that her soul had seen so much of the passion that it understood that even though the Blessed Virgin had seen more of it and mentioned more of its details than any other saint, still she herself could not—and neither could any other saint—find words to express it. Christ's faithful one said she understood this so well that if any saint were to try to express it, she would tell him: "Are you the one who sustained it?"

Christ's faithful one also added: My pain, then, exceeded by far any that I had ever experienced. That my body could not sustain me then should not be cause for wonder, for at that point I could feel no joy. I indeed lost my usual capacity for joy, and during this period it was impossible for me to recover it.

c. A vision of the immense suffering of the soul of Christ transforms Angela's soul into a sharer of the pain of Christ, and, as a result, she is admitted to an exceptional union with God

On still another occasion, I was shown the acute pain which was in Christ's soul. I was not surprised that it was a great pain, for that soul was most noble, and did not deserve any punishment; but Christ suffered what he did out of his immense love for humanity. Since in this instance it is the human soul and not the body which offends God, I now understood why the soul of the Son of God had to be in such pain. Because the sins were great and those committing them so numerous, the pain, as a consequence, had to be great. Christ, you suffered out of the great compassion that was yours for your elect,[82] and because their entire purpose was to destroy you and because they did not know you, I perceive that you were submitted to the rudest possible treatment. All this is at once cause for great praise of the goodness of God but also for even greater distress for humanity. But if I were really to speak my mind about this, it would be said I was in error. Let whoever does not understand, believe; for I cannot say more.

The soul of Christ suffered still other pains from all the torments and afflictions his body endured—all of these converged in his soul. This acute pain, so intense that the tongue cannot express it nor is the heart great enough to imagine it, was all part of the divine plan.[83] I saw such deep pain in the soul of the Son of the Blessed Virgin Mary that my own soul was deeply afflicted and transformed in such pain as I had never known before; and all my joy was gone.

Likewise, divine goodness granted me, afterward, the grace that from two there was made one, because I could not will anything except as he himself willed. How great is the mercy of the one who realized this union!—it almost completely stabilized my soul. I possessed God so fully that I was no longer in my previous customary state but was led to find a peace in which I was united with God and was content with everything.—I found everything up to this point written in the vernacular.

On Holy Saturday, Angela, in ecstasy, has a vision of herself united with Christ in the sepulcher

On Holy Saturday,[84] after what has just been related, Christ's faithful one told me the wonderful and joy-filled experiences of God which were now hers. Among other things, she related to me, brother scribe, that on that very day, in a state of ecstasy, she found herself in the sepulcher with Christ. She said she had first of all kissed Christ's breast —and saw that he lay dead, with his eyes closed—then she kissed his mouth, from which, she added, a delightful fragrance emanated, one impossible to describe. This moment lasted only a short while. Afterward, she placed her cheek on Christ's own and he, in turn, placed his hand on her other cheek, pressing her closely to him. At that moment, Christ's faithful one heard him telling her: "Before I was laid in the sepulcher, I held you this tightly to me." Even though she understood that it was Christ telling her this, nonetheless she saw him lying there with eyes closed, lips motionless, exactly as he was when he lay dead in the sepulcher. Her joy was immense and indescribable.[85]

Angela describes the workings of love which prepare her soul for mystical union with God, and, subsequently, a state of ineffable and stable inner peace

Once, during this same Lent, as Christ's faithful one further told me, it seemed to her that she was in a state of great spiritual aridity. She prayed to God that he give her something of himself for she felt very dry and deprived of every good. And then the eyes of her soul were opened and she had a vision of love gently advancing toward her. She saw the beginning of it but not the end, only its continuation; and for the color of this love, she could find no comparison. And suddenly she saw it coming toward her with the eyes of her soul, more clearly than can be seen with the eyes of the body, and as it approached her it moved like a sickle. But this should not be understood to mean that it could be compared to anything spatial or measurable; rather, it moved like a sickle because, as it approached her, love at first drew back not bestowing itself as much as it had led her to understand it would, and as much as she did understand it would at that time; and this made her languish for more. (Again, the movement of the sickle was not something that could be compared to anything spatial or material because it was a reality perceptible only to her mind through the ineffable workings of divine grace.) Afterward, Christ's faithful one was immediately filled with love and inexpressible contentment which, satisfactory as it was, nonetheless generated in her a hunger so unspeakably great that all her members dislocated.[86]

As a result of this vision, her soul was in a state of languor. What she wanted to see and feel was God, and not any creature. She did not speak nor could she make any words come out, but her soul spoke inwardly and cried out to God not to leave her languishing in such a death, for she regarded life as death. She also first called upon the Blessed Virgin, and then invoked and beseeched all the apostles to accompany her in kneeling before the Most High and implore him not to make her suffer this death, namely, the present life, but to enable her to attain the One she was feeling. She similarly invoked and cried out to blessed Francis and the Evangelists. Christ's faithful one also told me many other things which occurred while she was in this state.

One of the things she told me was the following: I, who thought myself at that moment to be in a state of total love because of the love I was feeling, heard God speaking to me, and he said: "There are many believed to be in a state of total love who are actually in a state of hatred; and, on the other hand, there are many who think they are in a state of hatred but are in one of love."[87] To this my soul responded: "Am I, who think myself to be in a state of total love actually in one of hatred?" He did not respond directly to this with words, but he made me see clearly and to feel with utmost certitude the answer to my question. I was then entirely satisfied and I do not believe I could henceforth cease being so. No creature could convince me otherwise. Even if an angel told me otherwise I would not believe him but would retort: "You are the one that fell from heaven."

And I saw in myself two sides and it was as if these had been separated by a furrow. On one side I saw fullness of love and every good, which was from God and not from me. On the other side I saw myself as arid and saw that nothing good originated in me. By this I discovered that it was not I who loved—even though I saw myself as total love—but that which loved in me came from God alone. Afterward God's love and mine converged, which brought about an even greater and more burning love than before. As a result my desire was to hasten toward that love.

Between this love, which was so great that at that time I could hardly imagine a greater one save when that other deathly love came over me—between this first love, then, and that other deathly one, which is the most ardent of all, there is one in between, about which I can say nothing, for it is of such great depth and a source of such joy and gladness that, I repeat, it cannot be put into words. In this state, I did not want to hear anything at all about the passion, nor did I want to hear God's name mentioned in my presence, for my experience of him was so delightful that anything else would be an impediment, for it would be less than that experience. And whatever is said about the gospel or about any other divine revelation seems to me as nothing, for what I saw of God was incomparably greater.[88]

When that love leaves me I nonetheless remain so totally contented, so angelic, that I can love reptiles, toads, serpents, and even devils. Whatever I see happening, even mortal sin, does not disturb me; that is, it causes me no displeasure, for I believe that God in his justice permits it. And even if a dog were to devour me, I would not care, and it seems to me that I would not feel the pain or suffer from it. This state is higher than standing at the foot of the cross as blessed Francis did. My soul moves from one state to the other. Seeing the flesh of the one who died for us increases my soul's desire to see more of it, and come closer to it. These states are sources for me of supreme and joy-filled love, without any sorrow over the passion.

I, brother scribe, asked her if there were any tears in this state.[89] She answered that there were no tears at all, but on one occasion along with the love she experienced she also remembered the priceless value of the precious blood of Christ, through which she was granted firm assurance that her sins had been forgiven. She marveled how these two expressions of love could co-exist. Christ's faithful one also added that at this point she rarely experienced pain over the passion. Rather, meditating on the passion showed her the way and was an example to her of what she must do.

A vision of the Virgin Mary and of Christ in their glorified state increases Angela's desire for death in order to be united with them

On another occasion Christ's faithful one said: My soul was elevated. I was not in prayer at that time, but had lain down to rest, for it was after a meal. So, not expecting it, my soul was suddenly elevated, and I saw the Blessed Virgin in glory. I had great delight in seeing a woman placed in such a position of nobility, glory, and dignity as was the Blessed Virgin, and in seeing her placed in the position of interceding for the human race. It likewise was an inexpressible delight for me to see her displaying such human concern and adorned with such indescribable virtues. While I was contemplating this spectacle, suddenly Christ in his glorified humanity appeared seated next to her. I perceived then how he had been crucified in his flesh, tormented and covered with opprobrium. And while I had an extraordinary perception of all the torments, injuries, humiliations, and defamations which he suffered, nonetheless for my part I was in no way grieved over these; rather, they were a source of such delight that I cannot speak about it. I lost the power of speech and I thought I would die. The mere thought of not dying was a source of extreme pain for me, as well as the thought of not yet being able to attain this totally indescribable good which I had seen. This vision lasted without interruption for three days. It did not prevent me from eating or anything else, but I ate little and was continually lying down. I was stretched out on my bed and could not speak. And when God's name was mentioned in my presence I could not bear it because of the state of immense delight I was in.

While at prayer, and especially upon receiving the Eucharist, Angela often experiences the All Good in God and Christ

Once Christ's faithful one confessed herself to me, brother scribe, as was her wont, with such a perfect awareness of her sins and with such contrition and abundant tears from the beginning of her confession until almost the end, and with such honesty, that I wept from it, and my heart was firmly persuaded that even if the entire world were deceived, God would not permit that one so true and upright could be. I deliberated over this persuasion in my heart because, having heard such exceedingly great things from her, I marvelled at them, for they had stirred some doubts in me and tested my credulity.

The following night she was sick almost to the point of death, and it was a great struggle for her to come to the church of the friars the next morning. I celebrated Mass and gave her communion. After I had given her communion, before her departure, I pressed her to tell me if God had granted her a special grace. She responded as follows: Before receiving communion, just as I was about to do so, I was told: "Beloved, the All Good is within you, and you come to receive the All Good." And then it seemed to me that I saw almighty God. I, brother scribe, asked her if she had seen something with any form. She said she had not. But I pressed her further, and she responded: I saw a plenitude, a beauty wherein I saw the All Good. This vision came suddenly—it was the furthest thing from my mind—while I was praying, meditating, and confessing my sins before God. My prayer was that the communion I was about to receive be not for judgment over me but for mercy. Immediately and abruptly I heard the words which I have just related. Then I began to think: "If the All Good is already in me, why am I to receive him again?" An answer was immediately provided: "One does not exclude the other." And before entering the choir to receive communion, I had also been told the following: "The Son of God is on the altar according to his humanity and his divinity, and he is accompanied by a multitude of angels." Since I had a great desire to see him with the angels, as I had been told I would, I was then shown that beauty and plenitude of God I have already mentioned. Afterward when I approached the altar, in a similar fashion, I saw God, and I heard it said: "Thus you will stand before him in eternal life." She also said that he had called her "my beloved," and he often called her by this name.[90]

She then added that recently when she receives communion, the host lingers in her mouth. She said that it does not have the taste of any known bread or meat. It has most certainly a meat taste, but one very different and most savory. I cannot find anything to compare it to. The host goes down very smoothly and pleasantly not crumbling into little pieces as it used to do. It disintegrates very quickly, she said, and does not stay hard as formerly. It goes down so smoothly that if I had not been told that one must swallow it right away, I would willingly hold it in my mouth for a great while. But at that moment, I also suddenly remember that I must swallow it right away. And as I do so, the body of Christ goes down with this unknown taste of meat. It goes down so smoothly that afterward I do not need to drink any water.[91] This is not the way it usually happens for me, for I usually have to make an effort to make sure that nothing of the host remains between my teeth. In this present experience, it goes down immediately, and when it descends into my body it produces in me a most pleasant sensation, and this can be detected outwardly because it makes me shake so violently that I must make a great effort to take the chalice.

While I, brother scribe, was writing the preceding as well as I could grasp it from her as she was saying it, suddenly she interrupted me and said: "Listen to what I have just been told. God said to me: 'You have told him much but if I did not wish it, you would not be able to tell him anything.' I tried not to tell you this, but in no way could I restrain myself from telling you what has just now been told to me."

While I was writing this, I asked her: "Does something happen to you when you make the sign of the cross?" She responded: "Something new does happen now when I make the sign of the cross. When I make it quickly and do not place my hand on my heart, I feel nothing. But when I first of all place my hand on my forehead saying, 'In the name of the Father,' then on my heart saying, 'And of the Son,' I immediately experience love and consolation, and it seems to me that in doing so I find there in my heart the one whom I name." She further added: "I would not have told you this if I had not been advised to do so."[92]

The seven ways in which God comes into the soul to reveal his presence

Christ's faithful one, responding to a question put to her concerning the Pilgrim, and another question which I, brother scribe, asked her, namely, whether the soul can be assured of possessing God in this life, replied that she knew that the Pilgrim had come into her soul, but did not know if she had granted him hospitality.[93]

a. The first way: God comes into the soul as an unexpected gift of grace, but the soul is still unaware that it is God himself who is present

I, brother scribe, asked how she knew that God had come into her soul, and she responded to my question with one of her own: "Does God come into the soul without being summoned by it to do so?" To this I replied: "I do believe that he does come in this fashion." Christ's faithful one in turn responded to this as follows: Sometimes God comes into the soul without being summoned, and when he does, he instills in the soul both fire and love, and sometimes a sweet feeling of his presence. The soul believes that this experience comes from God and delights in it. But it is still unaware that he himself is in the soul, that is, it does not perceive that he is in the soul, but is aware of the presence of his grace from which it takes delight.[94]

b. The second way: The soul experiences God's coming into it
when it mysteriously hears divine words which make it secure
in the knowledge that God is present

The soul also experiences God's coming into it when it hears him speaking very sweetly to it, which greatly delights the soul, for it then feels his presence. But a doubt remains, even if it is a very small one, because the soul is not really certain that God is in it. It seems to me that this happens because of the ill-will or defect of the creature; or because it is God's will that the soul will not as yet be secure and certain of his presence.

The soul nonetheless is assured that God is within it because it feels him in a way that is different from usual, with doubled intensity and with such divine fire and love that all the fears of soul and body are taken away. The soul speaks about these things, though it never heard them spoken by any mortal, and understands them with such great clarity that to be silent about them is painful. If it keeps silent, it does so out of deep concern not to displease love, and because it believes with the utmost certitude that these exceedingly lofty matters would not be understood —for when it does say something about them, it sees and experiences that it is not understood—and also because it does not want to say: "I myself experienced such lofty revelations" out of its deep concern not to displease love.

She added that when sometimes, because of the great zeal that was hers for the salvation of her neighbor, she did say something about these revelations, she was reprimanded and told: "Sister, go back to Holy Scripture, for they say nothing about these revelations, and we do not understand you." Thus once when I was lying down, languishing from the experience of this excessive love, and I began to ask you if the soul could be assured of possessing God in this life, and I spoke to you about what I was feeling, you reprimanded me and referred me to the Scriptures.[95]

c. The third way: The soul experiences God's coming into it
when it receives the grace to want God perfectly
and God becomes the soul's companion

In this felt experience wherein the soul finds the certitude that God is within it, the soul is given the grace of wanting God so perfectly that everything in it is in true and not false harmony. False harmony exists when the soul says that it wants God but does not really mean it, because its desire for God is not true in everything, in every way, or in every respect. Its desire for God is true when all the members of the body are in harmony with the soul, and the soul in turn is in such harmony with the heart and with the entire body that it becomes one with them and responds as one for all of them. Then the soul truly wants God, and this desire is granted to it through grace.

Hence when the soul is told: "What do you want?" it can respond: "I want God." God then tells it, "I am the one making you feel that desire." Until it reaches this point, the soul's desire is not true or integral. This form of desire is granted to the soul by a grace by which it knows that God is within it, and that it is in companionship with God. This gift is to have a desire, now a unified one, in which it feels that it loves God in a way analogous to the true love with which God has loved us. The soul feels God merging with it and becoming its companion.[96]

*d. The fourth way: The soul experiences God coming into it
   when it sees itself informed with his great fullness*

In the fourth way, the soul is granted the gift to see God in the following fashion. It is first told by God: "Look at me." And then the soul sees him taking shape within itself and it sees him more clearly than a person can see another person, for the eyes of the soul, in this experience, see a fullness of God of which I am not able to speak. What they see is a spiritual and not a material reality which is inexpressible. The soul delights in this vision, and this is an evident sign for it that God is within it. The soul then cannot look at anything else except that vision, and it fills the soul with God's incomparable presence. This beholding, in which the soul cannot look at anything else, is so deep and so profound that it grieves me not to be able to say anything about it. This vision is not tangible or imaginable, but something ineffable.[97]

*e. The fifth way: The soul experiences God coming into it when it is
   renewed by divine unctions and thus understands that God is within
   it. In the sixth way, God's love embraces the soul so tenderly that
   it produces bodily effects which are related by Angela's companion*

In still many other ways does the soul know that God comes into it, ways which cannot be doubted. I will now speak of two of these.

One way consists of an unction which suddenly so revitalizes the soul and renders every member of the body so docile and in harmony with it that nothing can touch it or offend it, and no event great or small can disturb it. In this experience the soul feels and hears God speaking to it. Furthermore, in this great and totally ineffable unction, the soul knows with the utmost certitude and clarity that God is within it, and that no saint in paradise nor any angel could cause this experience. But this experience is so ineffable that it grieves me not to be able to come up with anything to compare it to. God forgive me, for I would so much like to say all I know about it, but I would desire to do so only to manifest his goodness, if it so pleased him.[98]

Still another way in which the soul knows that God is within it is by an embrace which God bestows upon the soul. Never has a mother embraced her son with such love, nor can anyone else on this earth be imagined who embraces with a love that nears the indescribable love with which God embraces the soul. He presses it to himself with such tenderness and such love that I think that no one on earth who has not had this experience can believe it. Since I, brother scribe, resisted her on this point—for I found it hard to believe—Christ's faithful one responded: "One could perhaps believe something of it but not its full expression."

This embrace of God sets ablaze a fire within the soul with which the whole soul burns for Christ. It also produces a light so great that the soul understands the fullness of God's goodness, which it experiences in itself, and which is, moreover, much greater than the soul's experience of it. The effect then of this fire within the soul is to render it certain and secure that Christ is within it. And yet, what we have said is nothing in comparison to what this experience really is.[99]

I, brother scribe, asked her, at this point, if the soul shed any tears in this state. Christ's faithful one responded that the soul did not then shed any tears, either of joy or of any other kind; for this is another state, far superior to the one where the soul sheds tears of joy.

In this state, God, likewise, produces in the soul such a superabundance of joy that it does not know what more to ask for; more, if this state lasted, I would consider myself to be in paradise. This joy has an effect that can be observed in every part of the body. Everything bitter or injurious or whatever else one could be afflicted with becomes sweet. Moreover, I could not conceal the effects from my companion.

Then I, brother scribe, questioned Angela's companion concerning this point. She told me that once while she and Angela were walking together along a road, the countenance of Christ's faithful one became white and radiant, then ruddy and joyful, and her eyes grew large and shone so brilliantly that she no longer seemed herself. This same companion also told me: "When I saw Angela in this state I was filled with sadness and feared that someone, a man or a woman, would meet us and notice her in this state. I told Angela, 'Why don't you at least try to cover your face? Your eyes seem to shine like candles.'" This companion, because she was shy and very simple, and still did not know all the gifts of grace Angela had been granted, then began to lament and beat her breasts with her fists, and said to Christ's faithful one: "Tell me why this is happening to you? Try to get out of sight or hide yourself somewhere, for we cannot walk around if you are in such a state." Out of her simplicity and ignorance, she then cried out: "Woe is me, what are we going to do?" Christ's faithful one, for her part, trying to console and reassure her, told her: "Do not fear, for even if we meet someone, God will help us." This happened not only once but so many times that her companion said she could not count them.

Christ's faithful one herself also told me: This joy lasted for many days, and certain joys I believe will never go away but will grow greater and find their total fulfillment in heaven. For now I am not without them in my life; hence when something sad happens to me I immediately recall the joys of that state and I am not troubled.[100]

She added that there are many other ways in which the soul knows without any doubt that God is within it, but it would be impossible to tell them all.

f. The seventh way: The soul experiences God coming into it when it grants hospitality in itself to him as the Pilgrim, and this is the greatest and most indescribable experience of the goodness of God

Christ's faithful one also told me, brother scribe, that in all the cases above, the soul knows that God has come into it. But, she added, we have not said anything yet about how the soul grants hospitality to him. Everything we have said thus far comes nowhere near to expressing what the soul knows when it grants hospitality to the Pilgrim.

Christ's faithful one went on: When my soul knows that it has given hospitality to the Pilgrim, it reaches such a level of understanding of the goodness of God, indeed of his infinite goodness, that when I return to myself, I know with the utmost certainty that the more one feels God, the less is one able to say anything about him, for the very fact of feeling something of this infinite and unutterable Good renders one incapable of speaking about it.

Since I resisted her on this point, Christ's faithful one elaborated:

Would that when you go to preach you could understand, as I understood when I knew I had given hospitality to the Pilgrim. For then you would be absolutely unable to say anything about God, and neither could anyone else. Then I would like to come to you and tell you: "Brother, say something to me, now, about God." And you would not be able to say anything at all or come up with any thought about God, his infinite goodness being so far beyond anything you could possibly say or think. In this state, I must add, the soul does not lose its self-awareness or the body the use of any of its senses; rather, one is in complete possession of oneself. And thus if you had attained this state, you would then say to the people with total self-assurance: "Go with God, because about God I can say nothing."

In this experience, she further added, nothing with a bodily form can be seen. But this happened to me only once. From this, I likewise understood that all those things which have been said in the Scriptures, or for that matter by everyone from the beginning of the world until now, do not seem to me to express anything of its innermost meaning, not even to the extent of a grain of sand compared to the whole world.[101]

g. In the aforementioned ways of God's coming into the soul,
   even the body is involved and made to obey the soul

After what has just been related, Christ's faithful one told me, brother scribe, that when the soul is made secure of God's presence, the body is likewise made secure, and is ennobled, and restored along with it, although to a much lesser degree. The body, then, also shares in the benefits which the soul feels. The soul speaks to the body, bestows gifts on it, and very gently tells it: "You see now what are the benefits that you experience through me, and how these are infinitely greater than you could receive if you were on your own. You feel also how much greater will be the good things that are promised to you if you cooperate with me; and you know what benefits we have lost when you did not cooperate but opposed me." Then the body, ashamed of itself, submits to the soul, and says that it will henceforth obey it in every way, and admits how obligated it is to the soul for the great benefits it has received through it, benefits which the body feels and which are superior to anything it could know, desire, or even imagine on its own. Thus the body, ashamed of itself, decides to submit to the soul and henceforth obey it. The body also makes its complaint known to the soul: "My delights were bodily and vile, but you who were of such nobility and favored with such divine delights should not have cooperated with me or allowed me to lose your immense benefits." The body complains to the soul, and its laments are long and sweet as it feels the sweetness that is in the soul which is far beyond what it could ever aspire to on its own.[102]

There is a triple deception in love when it is impure or intemperate, or when God permits it to undergo trials

Christ's faithful one said that there are diverse ways in which spiritual persons can be deceived.[103]

One of the ways occurs when love is not pure, that is, when it is mixed with self-interest or self-will. For when love is mixed with self-interest, it becomes worldly, and the world entices it and praises it. And all worldly enticement is illusory, for the world is full of illusion. The more the world praises the soul and commends it, the more will there be an increase of those tears, sweetnesses, tremors, and clamors which are signs that spiritual love is impure. Even though in this state of impure spiritual love there are tears and sweetnesses, these do not take place in the soul, but in the body, for impure love does not enter into the soul. The sweetness of this experience quickly disappears, and the person, likewise, quickly forgets it; even, at times, when the person is aware of these effects, bitterness sets in. I have experienced all these things myself.

And I would not know how to discern these things well if my soul had not reached complete truth about itself. For when love is pure, you consider yourself as worthless, see yourself as dead and as nothing, and present yourself to God as dead and putrid. You lose all remembrance of praise or any good in yourself. You even see yourself as so evil that you do not believe that any saint could fully free you, only God. However, you do at times have recourse to the prayers of the saints for assistance before God, because you consider yourself so unworthy that you do not dare pray to God on your own. Thus you entrust yourself to Mary and to other saints so that they may come to your aid. Furthermore, when you receive praise from someone, you consider such praise as totally laughable. It is God who places true and pure love into the soul, and this enables the soul to see its defects and the goodness of God. The tears and sweetness which occur then are never an occasion for bitterness but rather for certitude. This said love leads the soul within Christ, and in such a state it knows with certainty that no deception can occur. This state of pure love can in no way include worldly love.

In connection with the above, I, brother scribe, told her the story of Moses striking the rock with his staff,[104] but before I finished—in fact, right when I began—Christ's faithful one explained its meaning.

There is another way, she said, in which God permits spiritual persons to be deceived. It is this: When a person feels loved by God, experiences spiritual benefits, does spiritual works, and speaks about them, but is too self-assured and oversteps proper limits, God, as a consequence, justly permits some deception to occur in order to make that person realize the transgression. —After I had finished telling her my story about Moses, she told me that this was her understanding of what had happened to him.

There is still another way, she said, in which spiritual persons can be deceived. This occurs when you have a strong feeling of God's presence, your love is good, your heart is pure and at its best, and you fully intend no longer to please the world but Christ alone. As a result, you find yourself totally within Christ, in supreme and inexpressible joy, and feel yourself totally embraced by Christ. Nonetheless, so that the soul may know how to preserve that which belongs to it, and to render to God what belongs to God, God sometimes permits some deception to take place in you in order to preserve your integrity, for he is solicitous that you not overstep your proper limits. And still all this is not enough for the soul, until it has been led to complete knowledge of itself and complete knowledge of the goodness of God. Once this is attained, absolutely no deception is possible for then the soul has been led to the full knowledge of truth.[105]

This "full knowledge of truth" is to be understood in this way: The soul is first of all so filled with knowledge of itself that it does not seem to it that it could be filled more fully, nor can it be aware of anything else or remember anything else. And at that moment, it suddenly comes to the awareness of the goodness of God. It sees both together in a totally undescribable way. All this still does not seem sufficient, so God's zeal for this soul sees to it that it undergoes trials.

All deceptions in love are eradicated by the power of the virtue of poverty, which is the root of all virtues and the "school of divine wisdom"

Christ's faithful one also said that God had spoken to her and from him she had heard poverty praised as such a lofty teaching and such a great good that it totally exceeds our capacity to understand it. God had told her: "If poverty were not such a great good, I would not have loved it. And if it were not so noble I would not have assumed it."[106]

Christ's faithful one likewise related the following to me: Pride can exist only in those who believe that they possess something. The fallen angel and the first man became proud and fell only because they imagined and believed that they possessed something. For neither angel nor man nor anything else has being; only one has it, God.

Humility exists only in those who are poor enough to see that they possess nothing of their own. In every case when God permits evil to happen, he makes it benefit the growth in being of those who are good. For this reason he saw to it that his Son—who possessed being more than one can say—became more poor than any saint or any person had ever been. He saw to it that he became so poor that it was as if he had no being, but it seemed thus only to sinners who were deprived of the true light; to those with understanding it did not—and does not—seem thus.

This said truth is so profound—namely, the truth about the virtue of poverty, how it is the root and mother of humility and every good— this is so profound that it cannot be written about. Whoever possessed this virtue could never fall into ruin and deception. They could never retain anything for themselves, and would also perceive how God loved true poverty.

Divine wisdom teaches this truth about poverty: It makes a person first see one's own defects, then discover one's own poverty and how truly one is poor in being. Thus illumined by the gift of divine grace, one sees the goodness of God. Then all doubt concerning God is immediately taken away, and one loves God totally; and loving with this love one performs works in accordance with this love, and then all self-reliance is taken away. When somebody possesses this truth, not all the devils there are, nor all the things we could possibly say, could ever deceive them. For the soul receives therein the most clear and luminous teaching on everything about this life, and in such a way that as long as it possesses this truth, it can never be deceived. This is why I understand that poverty is the mother of all virtues and the teacher of divine wisdom.

This divine wisdom taught the Blessed Virgin through the incarnation of Christ. It granted her, first of all, knowledge of herself; and after she knew herself, all doubt concerning God was removed, and she immediately entrusted herself to divine goodness; and knowing herself and the goodness of God, she said: "Behold the handmaid of the Lord; may it be done to me according to your word."[107] Divine wisdom grants us this same teaching in the humanity of Christ: he who, although he was God, nonetheless wished that his humanity be bound in obedience to the Father and to every will of the Father. This is why all the wisdom of the world, unless it is incorporated into this truth, is absolutely nothing and turns into its own condemnation. Likewise all the wise ones in the world, unless they are brought to this truth, are as if nothing and led to their own condemnation. When the soul understands this truth, then it can perform works without any intention and without concern for any merit.[108]

CHAPTER VIII
THE SIXTH STEP CONTAINS THE MANY AND UNBEARABLE SUFFERINGS
—A VERITABLE PASSION AND MARTYRDOM—
WHICH ANGELA ENDURED,
WHICH WERE CAUSED AS MUCH
BY BODILY AILMENTS
AS BY COUNTLESS TORMENTS OF BODY AND SOUL
HORRIBLY STIRRED UP IN HER BY MANY DEMONS

Brother scribe introduces the theme of the torments of body and soul that afflicted Angela

As useful and noteworthy as I thought they were, I, brother scribe, did not take great care, nor could I, to write down, in this sixth step, the full account of the many sufferings which Angela endured, and which were caused as much by bodily ailments as by countless torments of soul and body which many demons horribly stirred up in her. But I did manage, from the words of Christ's faithful one, to write some small part of her testimony of the sufferings she endured, as well as I could grasp them while she was speaking, sketching them rapidly because I could not understand them sufficiently to write a more complete account.[109]

Christ's faithful one told me, brother scribe, that she thought that the bodily ailments she endured were beyond description, and the ailments and sufferings of her soul were even more beyond any kind of comparison. In short, concerning the sufferings of the body, I heard her say that there was not one part of her body which had not suffered horribly.

Concerning the torments of the soul which demons afflicted upon her, she found herself incapable of finding any other comparison than that of a man hanged by the neck who, with his hands tied behind him and his eyes blindfolded, remains dangling on the gallows and yet lives, with no help, no support, no remedy, swinging in the empty air. She added that the demons pushed her to despair even more cruelly than this.[110]

I, brother scribe, also heard it said, and learned that a certain friar wearing the habit of the Friars Minor, and to my mind trustworthy, was greatly astonished and moved to compassion as he heard how Christ's faithful one was so horribly tormented; and this said trustworthy friar also perceived through a revelation from God that everything she said, and more, about the martyrdom she endured from these horrible torments was true. Thereupon, this friar was willed with a great and wonderful compassion and devotion toward her.

Angela's words, which I, brother scribe, could rapidly sketch were the following.

Account of the horrible torments of body and soul which Angela endured and their effects on concupiscence

a. First, a description of how demons suspend the activities of her soul so that her vices are revived and her virtues sapped away

Christ's faithful one said: I perceive that demons hold my soul in a state of suspension; just as a hanged man has nothing to support him, so my soul does not seem to have any supports left. The virtues of my soul are undermined, while my soul sees it and knows it and watches it happening. And when it perceives all its virtues being subverted and departing, and it can do nothing to prevent this process, the pain and the anger that it feels pushes it to such a point of despair that at times it cannot weep and at other times it weeps inconsolably. There are even times when I am so overwhelmed with rage that I can hardly refrain from tearing myself apart, while at other moments I cannot refrain from horribly beating myself and I raise welts on my head and various parts of my body. When my soul sees all its virtues fall and leave, then it is overcome with fear and grief. It wails and cries out to God repeatedly and unceasingly: "My son, my son, do not abandon me, my son!"[111]

Christ's faithful one also said that there was no part of her body which was not beaten and afflicted by demons. Because of the horrible nature of these afflictions, she asserted that the bodily ailments she suffered, like those of the soul, were beyond description. She also added that in this state all her past vices were revived, and even though this was only temporary, it caused her great torment. Even vices which she never knew existed entered her body, and though, likewise, these did not last, they too caused her great torment. And when these past vices were put to death again, she found consolation in her awareness that she had been handed over to many demons and they were responsible for the reawakening of these past dead vices as well as the addition of unknown ones. Then, remembering that God was afflicted, despised, and poor while on earth, she desired that all her ills and afflictions be doubled.

b. Second, a description of how vices, especially those contrary to chastity, which seemed to have been extinguished in the soul, are reawakened in the body by temptations from the devil

Christ's faithful one also said: While I am in this most horrible darkness caused by demons it seems to me that there is nothing I can hope for. That darkness is terrible; vices which I knew to be dead are reawakened from the outside by demons, and along with those, some vices which had never been there before come alive in my soul. My body (which nonetheless suffers less than my soul) experiences such burning in three places—the shameful parts—that I used to apply material fire to quench the other fire, until you forbade me to do so.[112] When I am in that darkness I think I would prefer to be burned than to suffer such afflictions. I even cry out for death to come in whatever form God would grant it. I beseech him to send me to hell without delay. "Since you have abandoned me," I tell him, "make an end to it now and completely submerge me."[113] I understood then that all this is the work of the demons and that these vices do not live on in my soul because even if they do violence to the body, my soul never consents to them. As for the body, it is in such pain and so weary of life that it is ready to give itself up to death rather than suffer so. But the soul, perceiving that all its powers have been taken away, even if it does not consent to these vices, nonetheless does not have the strength to resist them. And even if it perceives that they are contrary to God's will, it nonetheless falls into them.

c. Third, a description of how, God permitting, she is assailed
by a previously unknown vice and overcomes it
through a special virtue granted to her

Christ's faithful one likewise said: God clearly permitting it, a certain vice was transmitted to me which was never mine before. I know clearly that God permitted this vice to enter into me. This vice is so great that it surpasses all the others. But there is likewise a certain virtue, which was also clearly granted to me by God to counter this vice, and it is so powerful that it immediately overcame the vice. If, for other reasons, my faith in God was not so firm, the power of this virtue alone would make my faith in God certain and secure and remove all possibility of doubt. This virtue remains with me always, and it has the power to overcome the said vice. It sustains me and prevents me from falling into it. And it is so powerful that it not only sustains me, but gives me such strength that I truly recognize God at work in it. For nothing which the eye has seen, nor which the ear has heard, nor anything else could induce me to rescind from this virtue and succumb to sin. Likewise, even if everyone in the world and all the demons in hell were to contend against me with all the means at their disposal, in no way could they induce me to commit the least sin.[114] And this is why my faith in God remains so firm. This vice I am referring to is so great that I am ashamed to speak of it. It assails me so powerfully that when the said countervailing virtue does not make its presence felt and seems to fade from me, then there is nothing left to sustain me and, as a result, there is nothing shameful enough nor any punishment great enough to prevent me from hurling myself immediately into sin. And yet when the power of the aforesaid virtue intervenes, it is so liberating that it seems to me I could not sin for all the good or evil that is in this world.

Arnaldo points out how steps six and seven overlap, and makes an observation on the state Angela is in

I, brother scribe, observed Christ's faithful one suffer more horribly in this sixth step than can be described. This sixth step, however, lasted but a short while, that is, about two years. It concurs with the seventh, the most wonderful step of all, which began shortly before it and which follows in my account. I also observed that what took place in this sixth step faded in a brief space of time but not totally or completely,

199

especially in regard to her numerous bodily ailments. I further observed that while Christ's faithful one was in the seventh step, divine life grew in her beyond my capacity to describe it.[115] Though she was always very ill and could eat only very little, she was quite plump and rosy-cheeked. But she was also so full of pain, and all the limbs and joints of her body were so swollen that it was only with great difficulty that she could move, walk, or even sit. Notwithstanding, she believed that the punishments her body suffered were very light.

A description of the torments which arise from the struggle between humility and pride, and which have effects on the irascible power of the soul

a. First, the effects of humility

Everything which precedes was written when Christ's faithful one was in the seventh step, and the sixth had already come to an end. Speaking about the sixth step, Christ's faithful one told me, brother scribe, the following: A certain kind of humility was in continual conflict in my soul with a certain kind of especially vexing pride. It is humility because I perceive myself as fallen from every good and devoid of every virtue and grace. In this state, I perceive myself as so full of sins and defects that it is impossible for me to imagine that God could henceforth ever wish to have mercy on me. I perceive myself as the house of the devil, a worker for and a dupe of demons, their daughter even. I perceive myself devoid of rectitude and virtue, indeed, worthy only of the lowest part in hell. This, I want to specify, is not the same humility that is sometimes mine, which brings contentment to my soul and makes me come to the awareness of the goodness of God. Rather, this humility is accompanied with countless ill effects. It gives me the impression that my soul is surrounded by demons and makes me aware of the defects of my body and soul. I am completely closed off from God in such a way that I cannot recall God's presence, have any remembrance of him, or even be aware that he is the one who allows this to happen. I see myself as damned, but I am in no way preoccupied with this damnation; rather, what concerns me and grieves me most is having offended my Creator, for I do not want to offend him or to have offended him for all the good or evil that can be named.[116] Perceiving my innumerable offenses, I fight with all my strength against the demons so that I may conquer and prevail over the aforesaid vices and sins. But there is no way I can do so. I cannot find any ford to cross to safety, not even a small window through which I could escape; I find no remedy which could be of any help to me. It weighs heavily on me to have fallen so low.

b. Second, the effects of pride

After this, pride begins its assault, and its effect is to make me full of anger, sadness, bitterness, and conceit. I even derive extreme bitterness from the favors God granted to me in the past. Now when I remember them, I derive no comfort from the memory. Now these gifts offend me and, to my astonishment and dismay, I even entertain the conviction that there never was any true virtue in me. Nor do I see any reason that God could have allowed virtue to exist in me. Every good is so closed off and hidden from me that I become full of anger, sadness, bitterness, conceit, and affliction beyond what I can say. And even if all the consolers, all the wise of the world, and all the saints in paradise would try to offer words of solace and would promise me every imaginable good and consolation, and even if God himself would speak to me (unless he were to alter the present state of my soul or his mode of operation), I would draw no consolation or healing from it; nor would I believe anything of what they said. Even more, all their words would only serve to increase my ills, anger, bewilderment, sadness, and pain more than I can say. In exchange for these torments and in order that God might take them away, I would willingly choose and would prefer to undergo all the afflictions, ailments, and pains which have existed in the bodies of everyone at once. I think these would be less than the above torments. Finally, in exchange for them I would regard every imaginable kind of martyrdom as consolation.

c. Third, an explanation of how this struggle purifies the soul

These torments, which were frequent, began sometime before the pontificate of Pope Celestine[117] and lasted for more than two years. Toward the end of this period I was not fully and entirely liberated from them; I still felt some of their outer effects but not their inner ones. But now that I have entered another state, I am aware that through this struggle with the aforesaid humility and pride extreme purgation and purification have taken place in my soul. I have realized that without humility no one can be saved. The greater one's humility, the greater is the perfection of the soul. I have become aware also that caught in this struggle between humility and pride, the soul has passed through fire and undergone martyrdom. The truth of this humility is such that the soul truly becomes aware of its own offenses and defects as they are brought to light through punishment, martyrdom, and purgation by the said pride and demons. For this reason, I also became aware that the more a soul is laid low, abased, impoverished, and thoroughly humiliated, the more it is prepared, purged, and purified for a greater elevation. For the extent of the soul's elevation corresponds to the extent of its humiliation and abasement. The matters mentioned above are a beautiful illustration of this truth.

CHAPTER IX
SEVENTH SUPPLEMENTARY STEP

The seventh step is the revelation about which one can only say that it cannot be conceived, for whatever one can conceive, it is not that

Long discourse on the various ways of seeing God and living with him

a. Explanation of the experience of seeing God "in and with darkness"[118]

Christ's faithful one said the following: Once my soul was elevated, and I saw the light, the beauty, and the fullness that is in God in a way that I had never seen before in so great a manner. I did not see love there. I then lost the love which was mine and was made nonlove.

Afterward, I saw him in a darkness, and in a darkness precisely because the good that he is, is far too great to be conceived or understood. Indeed, anything conceivable or understandable does not attain this good or even come near it. My soul was then granted a most certain faith, a secure and most firm hope, a continual security about God which took away all my fear. In this good, which is seen in the darkness, I recollected myself totally. I was made so sure of God that in no way can I ever entertain any doubts about him or of my possession of him. Of this I have the utmost certitude. And in this most efficacious good seen in this darkness now resides my most firm hope, one in which I am totally recollected and secure.

Once I, brother scribe, questioned her about a theme treated by the blessed Augustine in a book I had read wherein he is questioned by his disciples concerning whether the saints are, or will be, standing up in heaven.[119] These disciples allude to what blessed Stephen had seen, namely, Jesus standing at God's right hand. They question this and seem to want to prove that there cannot be in heaven any place to stand or to sit; and the arguments they advance are subtle. While I was questioning her, Christ's faithful one was suddenly swept up in ecstasy and seemed not to understand what I was saying. At that moment she was granted a wonderful grace. After a short delay, I pressed her to respond to the question, which she seemed unable to understand. Instead of answering it, she related the following: My soul has just been elevated to a state of joy so great that it is totally unspeakable. I cannot say anything about it. In this state I knew everything I wanted to know and possessed all I wanted to possess. I saw the All Good.

She also added: In this state the soul can never even think of the withdrawal of this good, or about withdrawing from this good, or that it might ever have to be separated from it from then on. For the soul finds all its delight in this All Good. Furthermore, the soul sees absolutely nothing that the lips or even the heart could afterward speak about. It sees nothing and everything at once.[120] Continuing to speak in this way, she said: Henceforth, there is no good which could be described or even conceived in which I can place my hope. My hope rather lies in this secret good, one most certain and hidden[121] that I understand is accompanied with such darkness.

As I, brother scribe, resisted what she said about this darkness and did not understand her, Christ's faithful one told me by way of explanation: The All Good was all the more certain and superior to everything the more it was seen in darkness and most secret. This is why I see the All Good accompanied with darkness: because it surpasses every good. All else, in comparison, is but darkness.[122] No matter how far the soul or heart expands itself, all that expanse is less than this good. What I related until now—that is, when the soul sees all creation overflowing with God's presence, when it sees the divine power or the divine wisdom (all of which Christ's faithful had said she had already seen in such a marvelous and indescribable way)[123]—all this is inferior to this most secret good, because this good which I see with darkness is the whole, and all other things are but parts.[124]

She further explained: Even though all these previous experiences of God are totally inexpressible, they nonetheless are a source of great joy. But when God is seen in darkness it does not bring a smile to the lips, nor devotion, fervor, or ardent love; neither does the body or the soul tremble or move as at other times; the soul sees nothing and everything;[125] the body sleeps and speech is cut off.[126] And all the signs of friendship, so numerous and indescribable, all the words which God spoke to me, all those which you ever wrote—I now understand that these were so much less than that which I see with such great darkness, that in no way do I place my hope in them, nor is there any of my hope in them. Even if it were possible that all these previous experiences were not true, nonetheless, that could in no way diminish my hope—the hope that is so secure and certain in the All Good which I see with such darkness. Christ's faithful one told me, brother scribe, that her soul had been elevated only three times to this most exalted and altogether ineffable way of seeing God with such darkness, a vision which was a superlative and utterly wonderful grace. On many—indeed, innumerable—occasions, she had seen the All Good, and these visions were always experienced with darkness, but they were not as exalted nor did they include darkness as great as the one we have been speaking of.

b. A twofold experience: The world repels Angela; and God draws her to himself in order that she may lie in the divine abyss[127]

Once when Christ's faithful one was sick, she told me, brother scribe: On the one hand, the world with its thorns repels me, for when I think of the world I perceive that it is for me only a place of thorns and bitterness. Likewise, devils pursue and harass me in many ways, and almost continually persecute me. They have power over me because God has placed my soul and body in their hands. But no matter how much they may be able to afflict my body, they cannot torment and inflict pain on my soul to the same extent, for the soul is more closed to their attacks than the body. It seems to me that I can almost see them in bodily form with their horns set to assail me.

On the other hand, God draws me to himself.[128] But if I say that he draws me to himself with gentleness or love or anything which can be named, conceived, or imagined, that is completely false; for he does not draw me by anything which can be named or conceived by even the wisest in the world. Even if I say that it is the All Good which draws me, I destroy it. For in this state, it seems to me that I am standing or lying in the midst of the Trinity, and that is what I see with such darkness. This draws me more than anything else I have experienced so far, more than any good I have ever spoken of before. So much more so that there is nothing to compare to it. Everything I say now about it seems to say nothing or to be badly said. Afterward she added: It seems that whatever I say about it is blasphemy. And when you asked me if this darkness drew me more than everything I had ever experienced, what I answered seems to me to be blasphemy. That is why I fell very sick when you asked me those questions and I answered them the way I did.

c. Angela, totally immersed simultaneously in the love of God and of Jesus Christ crucified, lies in God and on the "bed" of the cross

When I am in that darkness I do not remember anything about anything human, or the God-man, or anything which has a form. Nevertheless, I see all and I see nothing. As what I have spoken of withdraws and stays with me, I see the God-man. He draws my soul with great gentleness and he sometimes says to me: "You are I and I am you."[129] I see, then, those eyes and that face so gracious and attractive as he leans to embrace me. In short, what proceeds from those eyes and that face is what I said that I saw in that previous darkness which comes from within, and which delights me so that I can say nothing about it.[130] When I am in the God-man my soul is alive. And I am in the God-man much more than in the other vision of seeing God with darkness. The soul is alive in that vision concerning the God-man. The vision with darkness, however, draws me so much more that there is no comparison. On the other hand, I am in the God-man almost continually. It began in this continual fashion on a certain occasion when I was given the assurance that there was no intermediary[131] between God and myself. Since that time there has not been a day or a night in which I did not continually experience this joy of the humanity of Christ.

At this moment, my desire is to sing and praise:

> I praise you God my beloved;
> I have made your cross my bed.
> For a pillow or cushion,
> I have found poverty,
> and for other parts of the bed,
> suffering and contempt to rest on.[132]

When I, brother scribe, asked her for a better explanation of what she had said, Christ's faithful one added: This bed is my bed to rest on

205

because on it Christ was born, lived, and died. Even before man sinned, God the Father loved this bed and its company (poverty, suffering, and contempt[133]) so much that he granted it to his Son.[134] And, in concord with the Father, the Son wanted to lie in this bed and continued to love it. This is why this bed is my bed, namely, the cross where Christ suffered in his body and much more in his soul, and on it I have placed myself and I have found my rest. On this bed I believe I die and through this bed I believe I am saved. I cannot describe the joy which I expect from those hands and feet and the marks from the nails which pierced them on that bed.[135] Humming, I say to the Son of the Blessed Mary: "What I feel there are no words for; what I see I never want to depart from. Because for me to live is to die. Oh, draw me then to yourself!"[136] But when I remembered of whom and to whom I was speaking while I was saying these words, I immediately became speechless.

When I am away from these experiences for any length of time, all that I find in the world repels me so that I desire even more to return to them. This is why my desire to die is such a deathly torment. However, I, brother scribe, observed and also heard Christ's faithful one tell me that this torment over her desire to die, which so crucified her (as she had said), was removed; not that she no longer desired to die, but that now this desire was not as tormenting.

d. Angela asserts that her daily life was filled with mystical elevations

Her soul was often elevated into God. And this prompted her to say that sometimes these elevations blended with one another. She also added that there were almost always new ones, so that what she experienced in one, she did not experience in another, for there was almost always something new or different about each one. Neither eating, nor speaking, nor anything else stood in the way of the frequent elevations of her soul or spirit. But her companion did take care to assist her when she was eating, for sometimes she forgot to eat and often she could only eat a very little. I observed that she could hardly recall from one day to the next what she was telling me. Even within the space of an hour, she could already have forgotten what she had just said and could not repeat it. These elevations occurred, it seems to me, during the seventh step.

After what has just been written, Christ's faithful one told me, brother scribe, that her soul found its delight and swam[137] in these bliss-filled elevations, because in them she perceived that both love and the Spirit are granted in measure. She repeated that her soul found delight and swam in these elevations. As I, brother scribe, objected to these statements, opposing them with arguments drawn from the Holy Scriptures, she responded that what the Holy Scriptures affirmed was true and not contrary to what she had said. She added: What it says is true, namely, that God does not grant his Spirit according to measure, but what my soul swims and takes delight in is in the awareness that God gives according to measure even to his Son and all the saints.[138]

Introduced into the highest counsel of God's justice, Angela understands the divine judgments

She also told me: Nothing gives me such a complete knowledge of God as my recognition of him through his judgments. At night or in the morning, when I recite a litany, praying to God as follows: "Lord, deliver me by your coming, and deliver me by your nativity, and your passion," there is nothing that delights me more than when I reach the invocation in which I proclaim joyfully and confidently: "By your holy judgments deliver me, O Lord."

Christ's faithful one added: The reason why I proclaim with such joy and confidence to God, "By your holy judgments deliver me," is because I do not recognize God's goodness more in one good and holy person, or even in many good and holy people, than in one or many who are damned. This profound truth was shown to me only once, but the memory and the joy of it never leave me. Even if all the other truths of faith were shaken, I would still be sure of this one, namely, the justice of God's judgments. What depths are found there! All of them serve to benefit the good, for every soul which has—or will have—the knowledge of these judgments and their depth will reap benefits in everything that happens to them from their awareness of this attribute of God.

At this point, I, brother scribe, heard her say wonderful things about the world.[139] I understood some of the things she was telling me but she could not explain what she meant fully enough for me to totally understand her, nor could I grasp what she meant well enough to put it into writing.

Also, at this point, one should note and commit well to memory words which were revealed to Christ's faithful one almost immediately after I had begun to write. I, brother scribe, decided to place these words where she had related them to me, that is, in the second step, the one on divine unction. At that moment, Christ's faithful one had told me that she had heard God say: "Have it written at the end of your narrative that thanks should be given to God for all that you have written. Also, whoever wants to remain in a state of grace should not take the eyes of their souls away from the cross, whether it be joy or sadness that I bestow on them or allow to happen to them."[140]

Christ's faithful one also said: No matter how far the understanding of the soul is able to stretch itself, that is nothing in comparison to what it experiences when it is lifted beyond itself and placed in the bosom of God. Then the soul understands, finds its delight, and rests in the divine goodness; it cannot bring back any report of this, because it is completely beyond what the intelligence can conceive, and beyond words; but in this state the soul swims. As a fruit of this state, my soul can now understand the meaning of the sayings of Christ that sometimes seem harsh and difficult. Likewise, my soul understands why in the soul of Christ there was unmitigated pain, for when my soul is transformed into the passion of Christ it discovers such pain in Christ's passion that it too suffers unmitigated pain. As a consequence, when my soul recalls the passion suffered by Christ's soul no joy at all is possible, which is not what happens when it recalls the passion suffered by Christ's body, because then, after a moment of sadness, it rediscovers joy. My soul understands the explanation of this in the way that I have just mentioned. In the same way, it understands the acute pain that was in the soul of Christ when he lay in the womb of his mother, which was the same as later on in his life, except that, at that moment, he had not yet had the actual experience of it. From all this, my soul understands the judgments of God.

Five locutions or consolations or visions which occur while Angela is participating in the celebration of the Mass

Once while the conventual Mass was being celebrated, Christ's faithful one heard God speaking to her, but what he told her at this time is not recorded here. But on another occasion, when the priest who was celebrating the Mass was close to the time of communion, she did hear God speaking to her as follows: "There are many who break, and even draw blood from my back." She saw and perceived that these words were coming from the host which the priest had just broken. Then, Christ's faithful one, after having meditated on these words, prayed to

God as follows: "May he not be such a one." To this God responded: "He shall not be, for all eternity."[141]

Christ's faithful one also said that her soul was in a state of great joy as it experienced itself to be within the Trinity and to be within the ciborium wherein the body of Christ is deposited. The soul understood that Christ was at once in the ciborium and yet present everywhere, filling everything. Great was the soul's wonder to find such delight in that ciborium! It was so delighted and in such immense jubilation that it was moved to ask: "Why do I find such delight in this ciborium? Since you, Lord, are everywhere, why do I not find the same delight everywhere?" And God answered me with words I do not fully recall. I do remember him saying: "Through the words that the priest says, I am enclosed in this ciborium. And I do this by a special miracle."

On another occasion, I, brother scribe, was the one to give her communion. Because at each communion, Christ's faithful one used to receive a special grace, I, brother scribe, as I had often done many times, asked her if this communion had brought her satisfaction. She answered by saying that, if she could, she would like to receive communion daily.[142] She also told me that in this communion she had been granted a grace or a divine consolation through which she perceived and felt with the utmost certitude that receiving communion purifies, sanctifies, consoles, and preserves the soul.[143] She had felt and perceived these four effects of communion in her soul more than usually. She also told me that God had told her about these four effects, and how useful they were.

Christ's faithful one went on to say that once, during a Mass I was celebrating, a great joy had entered her soul at the moment of the elevation of the body of Christ and she had heard God telling her: "Behold the man who was crucified." And her soul saw him. But immediately upon hearing these words, her soul passed on to another vision, and did not remain in this one. What had suddenly taken place in her soul was a wonderful transformation, a silent one, for it was impossible to describe. In this new state, into which she had suddenly passed over, her soul found itself enwrapped within Christ's divinity. And while this was happening, she was told: "Behold, the total joy of angels and saints, and your own total joy." But truly, this was told to me in a far more pleasant a way than how you are presently reporting it. I can hardly recognize what you are now saying about it.

Again during Mass, on another day, she had heard God speaking to her, but did not remember everything he had said. But she did remember that she had heard him tell her that it was not so much the great commentators on the Scriptures who were to be commended, but rather those who put them into practice. She added that all of Holy Scripture finds its fulfillment in the example of Christ's life. This much she understood.

On still another occasion, while she was in the church of St. Francis in Assisi, after brother Apicus[144] had celebrated a Mass, and I was speaking with her, she related the extremely great, new, and most wonderful revelations which she had just received during the Mass. Since these were especially noteworthy, a certain friar to whom Christ's faithful one and I had communicated these secret revelations, and who was with us when she related them, told me that I should write them down. But as I was just passing by, I could not write them down at the time. When, a few days later, I wanted to write them down, I asked Christ's faithful one to repeat them for me, but neither she nor I could remember everything. As a result, I can only relate a small part of what she had previously told me: My soul was then elevated into a state of joy so great and so new that I have never known joy so great nor experienced it in such a manner during my entire life's journey. God spoke to me in this state. And blessed Francis also spoke to me in a similar new and most sweet way. While Mass was being celebrated, my soul stood and took delight in the same joys which I have experienced when out of the body, or so it seemed to me. There was such a great and ineffable joy in my soul that if I did not know that God makes everything according to measure, I would say that this joy greatly surpasses all measure. At the same time, the following words were addressed to me: "I am Francis sent by God. The peace of the Most High be with you!" Addressing me directly he added: "Light, daughter of the light who is light of lights"; and much more that is unrecorded. Then he said: "Recommend the manse to them, that is the possession which I have left behind me"—which I understood as meaning the poverty which he had left to be observed—and recommend it also to those who follow me, who will love it because I have loved it." When I perceived that it was the blessed Francis who was speaking, my joy became greater still. After he had spoken to me at length, a divine working, similar to those I am accustomed to, also confirmed what the blessed Francis had said to me. During the whole time I was in Assisi, that is, during more than nine days, the blessed Francis spoke to me every day.

On the same day, I experienced such a lofty elevation and such a clear perception of how Christ comes in the sacrament of the altar that never before or after has it been so clearly demonstrated to me. It was shown to me how Christ comes accompanied by a mighty throng, or host. Usually I find delight only in Christ, and so I was amazed that this time I found delight in both him and his host, and this was a source of great wonder for me. My perception of him alone was one thing, that of his host another, and I found delight in both of them. And I was told that his host were the Thrones, but I did not understand what this word meant.[145] This host formed an array so imposing, a militia of such great number, that if I did not know that God does all things according to measure, I would believe that the number of this host was without measure, indeed countless. Then she heard God telling her: "There are souls in which I come and I go, but throughout a great number of cities, there is no soul in which I rest as I rest in yours." He then told me the number of cities, but I do not remember it. I, brother scribe, asked her if that militia, for it was a militia, could be measured either by its length or its breadth. She answered that it could not be measured either by its length or its breadth. It was ineffable.

By the workings of divine grace, Angela is elevated to a state of most high union with God

Shortly after the preceding was written, I questioned Christ's faithful one, and she responded as follows:[146] Last Lent imperceptibly I found myself totally immersed in God even more profoundly than usual. Moreover, it seemed to me that I was in the midst of the Trinity and receiving greater gifts than ever before, and these were continuous. To be so immersed in God filled me with joy and delight. As I felt myself in this richness of God and benefiting from these great and unspeakable delights, so totally beyond any I had ever experienced, the divine and ineffable workings which were realized in my soul were such that no saint or angel could tell of them or explain them. I am convinced that there is no saint, angel, or creature which has anywhere near the capacity to understand these divine workings and that extremely deep abyss.[147] And everything I am saying now is so badly and weakly said that it is a blasphemy against these things.

I was and am now drawn out of everything I had previously experienced and had taken such delight in: the life and humanity of Christ; the consideration of that very deep companionship which the Father from eternity in his love had bestowed on his Son (in which I had taken such deep delight), namely, the contempt, the suffering, and the poverty experienced by the Son of God; and the cross as bed to rest on. I was also drawn out of the vision of God in the darkness in which I used to take such delight. Every previous state was put to sleep so tenderly and sweetly that I could not tell it was happening. I could only recall that now I did not have these experiences. For in the cross of Christ in which I used to take such delight, so as to make it my place of rest and my bed, I find nothing; in the poverty of the Son of God, I find nothing; and in everything that could be named, I find nothing.

In these divine workings God manifests himself to Angela in two ways

In all these totally ineffable workings which take place in the soul, God initially makes his presence felt in the soul through these ineffable workings. Then he manifests himself by disclosing himself to the soul and by bestowing ever greater gifts on it, accompanied by ever greater clarity and ineffable certitude. The two ways that he initially makes his presence felt are the following.

a. *First God, on the one hand, makes the soul understand how he is present in every creature and, on the other hand, totally recollects it to himself*

In the first mode, God presents himself in the inmost depths of my soul. I understand not only that he is present, but also how he is present in every creature and in everything that has being, in a devil and a good angel, in heaven and hell, in good deeds and in adultery or homicide, in all things, finally, which exist or have some degree of being, whether beautiful or ugly. She further said: I also understand that he is no less present in a devil than a good angel. Therefore, while I am in this truth, I take no less delight in seeing or understanding his presence in a devil or in an act of adultery than I do in a good angel or in a good deed. This mode of divine presence in my soul has become almost habitual.[148] Moreover, this mode of God's presence illuminates my soul with such great truth and bestows on it such divine graces that when my soul is in this mode it cannot commit any offense, and it receives an abundance of divine gifts. Because of this understanding of God's presence my soul is greatly humiliated and ashamed of its sins. It is also granted deep wisdom, great divine consolation, and joy.

Another mode of God's being present to my soul is much more special and quite different from the previous one; and the joy that he grants to it is also different, for in this state he gathers me totally into himself. God produces in my soul many divine workings accompanied by much greater graces, and there is so deep and ineffable an abyss that this presence of God alone, without any other gifts, is that good that the saints enjoy in eternal life. Of these gifts of Paradise, some saints have more, others less. And these gifts—even though I cannot find words to describe them, for my words blaspheme and make hash of what they should express—I affirm that they are expansions of the soul through which it is rendered more capable of possessing God.

b. Second, God discloses himself to the soul with the fullness of his tenderness, wisdom, truth, and plenitude

And immediately upon presenting himself to the soul, God likewise discloses himself and expands the soul and gives it gifts and consolations which the soul has never before experienced, and which are far more profound than earlier ones. In this state, the soul is drawn out of all darkness and granted a greater awareness of God than I would have thought possible. This awareness is of such clarity, certitude, and abysmal profundity that there is no heart in the world that can ever in any way understand it or even conceive it. Even my own heart cannot think about it by itself, or ever return to it to understand or even conceive anything about it. This state occurs only when God, as a gift, elevates the soul to himself, for no heart by itself can in any way expand itself to attain it. Therefore, there is absolutely nothing that can be said about this experience, for no words can be found or invented to express or explain it; no expansion of thought or mind can possibly reach to those things, they are so far beyond everything—for there is nothing which can explain God. I repeat there is absolutely nothing which can explain God. Christ's faithful one affirmed with utmost certitude and wanted it understood that there is absolutely nothing which can explain God.

Holy Scripture, she added, is so sublime that there is no one in the world wise enough, not even anyone with learning and spirit, who would not find it totally beyond their capacity to understand Scripture fully; still, they babble something about it. But of these ineffable workings which are produced in the soul when God discloses himself to it, nothing at all can be said or babbled.[149] Because my soul is often elevated into the secret levels of God and sees the divine secrets, I am able to understand how the Scriptures were written; how they are made easy and difficult; how they seem to say something and contradict it; how some derive no profit from them; how those who do not observe them are damned and Scripture is fulfilled in them; and how others who observe them are saved by them. I see all this from above. Thus when I return to myself after perceiving these divine secrets, I can say some words with security about them, but then I speak entirely from outside the experience, and say words that come nowhere near describing the divine workings that are produced in my soul. My statements about them ruin the reality they represent. This is why I say that I blaspheme in speaking about them.

She said: If I were given all the spiritual joys and all the divine consolations and delights which all the saints who have existed from the beginning of the world until now have said they have received from God; and even if you were to add the countless other things they could have spoken of but did not; and even if on top of this were added all the pleasures of the world, good and evil, and the latter were transformed into good and spiritual pleasures; and they lasted long enough for me to go all the way to their completion and thus led me to the unspeakable good of that manifestation of God which I experienced; nonetheless, even for all these benefits, I would not give up, change, nor trade even a moment, the twinkling of an eye, of the experience of this totally unspeakable good. I speak to you in this fashion so as to somehow put it in your mouth and enable you to swallow it, for this unspeakable good I experienced infinitely surpasses any I have previously spoken about; and it is mine not only for the twinkling of an eye, but often for a good while and very often in this most efficacious manner; as for the other mode, which is not as efficacious, it is with me almost continually.

Even if at times I can still experience outwardly some little sadness and joy, nonetheless there is in my soul a chamber in which no joy, sadness, or enjoyment from any virtue, or delight over anything that can be named, enters.[150] This is where the All Good, which is not any particular good, resides, and it is so much the All Good that there is no other good. Although I blaspheme by speaking about it—and I speak about it so badly because I cannot find words to express it—I nonetheless affirm that in this manifestation of God I discover the complete truth. In it, I understand and possess the complete truth that is in heaven and in hell, in the entire world, in every place, in all things, in every enjoyment in heaven and in every creature.[151] And I see all this so truly and certainly that no one could convince me otherwise. Even if the whole world were to tell me otherwise, I would laugh it to scorn. Furthermore, I saw the One who is and how he is the being of all creatures.[152] I also saw how he made me capable of understanding those realities I have just spoken about better than when I saw them in that darkness which used to delight me so. Moreover, in that state I see myself as alone with God, totally cleansed, totally sanctified, totally true, totally upright, totally certain, totally celestial in him. And when I am in that state, I do not remember anything else.

On one occasion, while I was in that state, God told me: "Daughter of divine wisdom, temple of the beloved, beloved of the beloved, daughter of peace, in you rests the entire Trinity; indeed, the complete truth rests in you, so that you hold me and I hold you." One of the effects of that state in my soul is to greatly increase my delight and understanding of how God comes into the sacrament of the altar accompanied by his host.

When I leave that supreme state in which I do not remember anything else, I come back and see myself in those good things I have just spoken about, but at the same time I see myself completely full of sin and obedient to it, devious, impure, totally false and erroneous, and yet I am in a state of quiet. For what remains with me is a continual divine unction, the highest of all and superior to any I have ever experienced in all my life.

God is the one who leads me and elevates me to that state. I do not go to it on my own, for by myself I would not know how to want, desire, or seek it. I am now continually in this state. Furthermore, God very often elevates me to this state with no need, even, for my consent; for when I hope or expect it least, when I am not thinking about anything, suddenly my soul is elevated by God and I hold dominion over and comprehend the whole world. It seems, then, as if I am no longer on earth but in heaven, in God. This state I am in far surpasses all others, for it is a state of such great fullness, clarity, certainty, ennoblement, and expansion that I feel no other previous state came anywhere near it. Christ's faithful one told me, brother scribe, that she had experienced this unspeakable manifestation of God more than a hundred times, even thousands and thousands of times, and each time her soul had received something fresh, and what it experienced was always novel and different.

On the feast of the Purification of Mary, Angela's soul experiences its presentation to God simultaneously with the aforesaid divine manifestation

She likewise narrated the following: During the period when that unspeakable manifestation of God was occurring in my soul, one day, on the feast of St. Mary of Candlemas,[153] while blessed candles were being distributed for the celebration of the presentation of the Son of God in the temple, and at the very moment when this unspeakable manifestation of God was taking place, my soul experienced its own presentation. And it saw itself so noble and elevated that, henceforth, I cannot conceive or even imagine that my soul or even the souls in paradise could be or are endowed with such nobility. My soul then could not comprehend itself. If the soul, which is created, finite, and circumscribed, cannot comprehend itself, will it not be far less able to comprehend God, the creator, who is immense and infinite? My soul, then, immediately presented itself before God with the utmost assurance and without any fear. This presentation was accompanied with greater delight than I have ever experienced, with a new and most excellent joy, and with new miracles, so much so that I cannot imagine that my soul ever experienced anything so miraculous, so clear, and so new. Such was this encounter with God. In this encounter I simultaneously perceived and experienced both that previous unspeakable manifestation of God to my soul, and this new manifestation of my soul and its presentation to God. In this I found new delights different from all previous delights, and I was told most high words which I do not want to be written.[154]

After this, when I returned to myself, I discovered that I was glad to suffer every injury and pain for God, and that nothing anyone could say or do could henceforth separate me from him. And I cried out: "Lord, what can henceforth separate me from you?" In response, I was told that there was nothing that could separate me from God.[155] Furthermore, I delighted in the thought of my death. One cannot imagine the delight that is mine when I think of the day of my death.

After everything written above, Christ's faithful one also told me, brother scribe, that she had heard God speaking to her in words too wonderful to relate. She was told that this unspeakable good mentioned above is the same good and none other than that which the saints enjoy in eternal life, but there the experience of it is different. In eternal life the least saint has more of it than can be given to any soul in this life before the death of the body.[156] Christ's faithful one said that she understood this.[157] Thanks be to God always. Amen.

Appendix concerning the Holy Eucharist

Christ's faithful one also told me, brother scribe, that once she had asked God the following question: "I see that you are present in the sacrament of the altar, but where are your faithful?" Opening the understanding of my soul, he answered: "Wherever I am, the faithful are also with me." And I myself perceived that this was so. I also very clearly discovered that I was everywhere he was. But to be within God is not the same as to be outside of him. He alone is everywhere encompassing everything. Addressing herself to me, brother scribe, she said: "I do not understand about each and every one of the faithful," but she gave me to understand that she was talking only about the faithful who were saints. Thanks be to God always. Amen.[158]

Epilogue of the brother scribe establishing the authenticity of everything that had been written

After I, brother scribe, had written almost everything which can be found in this small book,[159] I asked and requested Christ's faithful one to beseech God and pray that if I had written anything false or superfluous he would, in his mercy, reveal it and show it to her, so that we would both know the truth from God himself. Christ's faithful one responded by saying: Before you made this request, I myself often asked God to make known to me if in what I said or what you wrote there was any word of untruth or anything superfluous, so that I could at least confess myself of it. God answered me that everything I had said and you had written was completely true and contained nothing false or superfluous. She also told me that I had tempered what God had told her, for there was much that he had told her which I could have put into writing but did not. God, she said, even told me: "Everything which has been written is in conformity with my will and comes from me, that is, issues forth from me." Then he added: "I will put my seal to it." Since I did not understand what he meant by these words "I will put my seal to it," he clarified these words by saying: "I will sign it."

I, brother scribe, wrote my narrative with great reverence and fear, and in great haste, just as I heard it from Christ's faithful one. I wrote everything as well as I could, while she was present, not adding anything of my own from the beginning to the end, but, however, omitting many of the good things she told me simply because I did not understand them well enough to write them.

She spoke to me about herself in the first person, but because I was in a hurry, I sometimes wrote my text in the third person, and I have not yet corrected it. From the beginning to the end, I hardly wrote anything except when she was speaking to me in person.[160] I had to write her words very rapidly just as she was saying them, for I was forced to make haste because of the obstacles and prohibitions I encountered from my fellow friars.

Nonetheless, I took the greatest care to note accurately her very own words, as well as I could grasp them, not wanting to write anything more after I had left her. I did not know how to go about writing anything afterward, for I was very careful and fearful lest I might perhaps add something, even a single word, that she had not really said. Furthermore, I always reread to her what I wrote, repeating it many times, so that I would be sure to take down only her very own words.

Furthermore, the Lord saw to it that two other trustworthy friars, acquainted with Christ's faithful one, read the text and heard directly from her everything which I had written.[161] They examined everything and even engaged in frequent discussions with her. And what is more, God granted them the grace to be certain of its validity, and, by word and deed, they bear faithful witness to it.

PART TWO

The *Instructions*

INSTRUCTION I:
ANGELA CONFESSES TO BE A GREAT SINNER

I was plunged into an abyss of deep humility, the depths of which began to open to me, but only briefly, on the second Sunday of Lent.[1] On the following Monday, at Compline, in the abyss of this humility, I saw so clearly the superabundance of my malice, iniquity, and sins that it seemed impossible for me to disclose them and make them known, by any method, or by means of any creature in this world. I was not ashamed, however, to confess in front of everyone all the sins I had committed. I even enjoyed imagining how I could make public my iniquities, hypocrisies, and sins.

I wanted to parade naked through towns and public squares with pieces of meat and fish hanging from my neck and to proclaim: "Behold the lowest of women, full of malice and deceit, stinking with every vice and evil." I observed Lent enclosed in my cell to impress people and win esteem. Whenever anyone invited us, I made sure they were told: "I do not eat flesh or fish." But in reality, I fancied fine foods and was full of gluttony; I was a great eater and a guzzler. I pretended I wanted only what was necessary for me, but I had things put away for another day. I affected outward poverty and feigned to sleep on hard surfaces, but what I really wanted was to stay in bed and sleep all day; and what I did in fact was sleep under many blankets which were removed in the morning so that no one could see them.

See what a devil I am and what malice is in my heart! Listen to how proud I am, hypocritical and an abomination before God. While I pretended to be a daughter of prayer, I was a daughter of wrath, pride, and of the devil. And while I pretended to possess God in my soul and receive divine consolations while I was in my cell, in fact, it was the devil who was in my soul and in my cell. Know that, during all my life, I studied how I could be admired and honored and enjoy a reputation for sanctity. Know also that because of the malice, lies, and hypocrisy hidden in my heart, many were deceived. I am responsible for the death of many souls, including my own.

Afterward, sunk in the abyss I have mentioned, I turned to those who are called my sons and said to them: Do not believe me any more! Do you not see that I am possessed by the devil? You who are called my sons, pray that God in his justice may chase the demons from my soul and uncover my most wicked deeds, so that God may no longer be dishonored because of me. Do you not see that everything I have said to you was false? Are you not aware that if suddenly the whole world was empty of malice the abundance of mine would suffice to fill it all? Do not believe me any more! Stop adoring this idol. The devil is in her, and everything she has told you was a pack of lies and diabolical! Pray that God in his justice may make this idol fall and smash in pieces, and the falseness, duplicity, and pretense of her deeds and words be brought out in the open! For I used the words of God to paint myself in false colors so that I would be the one honored instead of him. Finally, pray to God that he expel the demons from this idol so that the world be no longer deceived by this accursed woman!

And for this, I myself pray to the Son of God, whose name I dare not mention, that if he himself does not wish to manifest my iniquity he make it known by having the earth open and swallow me up, so that, seeing this, men and women would say: "What a sham this woman was, painting herself on the exterior with false colors, while within she was a total fraud." What I would like to do is to tie a rope around my neck and be dragged through towns and public squares and have children escort me, crying out: "Here's the woman whose entire life was one big lie!" And men and women around would say: "Look at the great miracle God has done! He has made this woman disclose the iniquities, malice, hypocrisies and sins which she had concealed so well all her life!" But all this outcry against me would still not satisfy my soul.[2]

Know that I am sunk into a state of despair the likes of which I have never experienced before. I despair of God and his gifts. This is a battle between him and me. For my part I am convinced that there is no one in the world as full of malice as I am and as deserving of damnation. This is so because everything which God has bestowed on me and granted to me serves only to increase my sense of despair and damnation. I beg all of you to pray that God in his justice may delay no longer in expelling the devil from this idol so that her most wicked inner faults be revealed. My body feels faint; I have a splitting headache from having shed so many tears; and all my limbs are disjointed because it is impossible for me to make known the lies and malice that are in my soul. Yet I rejoice that in part, at least, these are becoming public.

And I saw all these things in truth, without any humility. And you, who have written this, know that it is but a small part of all my faults, iniquities, and abuses. For I began to do evil when I was but a child.

INSTRUCTION II:
THE PERILS OF SPIRITUAL LOVE

Appropriate weapons for the defense of good love

Christ's faithful one had been asked many times to say something about God. She began one of her answers by naming the errors, perils, and illusions which can be detected in spiritual and good love: There is nothing in the world, neither man nor devil nor any thing, that I hold as suspect as love, for it penetrates the soul more than any other thing.[3] Nothing exists that so fills and binds the heart as love does. Therefore, unless you have the weapons to regulate it, love can easily make the soul fall into utter ruin. I am not speaking about evil love, which of course all must shun as dangerous and a thing of the devil, but about good and spiritual love between God and the soul, neighbor and neighbor.[4]

It often happens that two or three people, men and women, love one another very intensely and harbor such heartfelt and special affection for one another that they want to be almost always together. Whatever one wishes, the other also wishes. Unless it is regulated with the weapons just mentioned, this type of love is very reprehensible and dangerous, even if it is spiritual and conceived for God's sake. For if the love the soul has for God is not forearmed it will be swept away by its own fervor, soon decrease or fall into some disorder, and not be able to last. Unless it is regulated by the proper weapons, true love of neighbor, that of devout men and women, either becomes carnal or gets lost in wasted conversations. For hearts bound to one another in this type of imperfect love are extremely indiscreet. This is why for fear of wrongful love, I am willing to suspect the love that is good.[5]

Weapons to regulate spiritual love are presented. These are acquired through a triple transformation of the soul

The weapons by which good love ought to be regulated are found and transmitted through transformations which take place in the soul. There are three kinds of transformations: sometimes the soul is transformed into God's will; sometimes it is transformed with God; and sometimes it is transformed within God and God within the soul.

The first transformation occurs when the soul strives to imitate the works of the suffering God-man[6] because God's will has been and is being manifested in them. The second transformation occurs when the soul is united with God, feels deeply the consolations of God's presence, and can express these with words and thoughts. The third occurs when the soul, by a most perfect union, is transformed within God, and God within the soul; then it feels and tastes God's presence in such a sublime way that it is beyond words and conception.

The first transformation has nothing to do with the type of love we are considering. The second suffices to regulate love if it is truly alive in the soul. The third is the most efficacious.[7]

Description of the third transformation, and some aspects of the second, including their link with the first

In the third transformation (and even in the second, but not so perfectly), the soul is infused with the grace of a wisdom by which it knows how to regulate the love of God and neighbor. The soul then knows how to harmonize the sentiments, sweetnesses, and fervor that it receives from God so wisely that love is stabilized and can persevere in what it undertakes without any outward show of laughter, bodily movements, or gestures.[8] Likewise in love of one's neighbor or friends the soul brings to it such wisdom and maturity that it expresses love when it is appropriate, and does not when it is not appropriate. The reason for this is that while God is unchangeable, the soul is not; but the more the soul is united to God, the less it is subject to change. From such a union the soul acquires wisdom, maturity, depth, discernment, and enlightenment, and armed with these it knows how to regulate the love of God and neighbor so well that it cannot be deceived or fall into disorder. Whoever does not feel infused with such wisdom should never extend special love or heartfelt affection toward any man or woman, for even if it is done for God's sake and with the best intentions, one runs the risk of encountering the dangers inherent to love. One should never bind oneself to another until one has first learned to separate oneself from others.

Love has various properties. Because of love, and in it, the soul first grows tender, then it pines and grows weak, and afterward finds strength. When the soul feels the heat of divine love, it cries out and moans. It is like a stone flung in the forge to melt it into lime; it crackles when it is licked by the flames, but after it is baked makes not a sound. Thus the soul in the beginning seeks divine consolations, but if these are withdrawn, it grows tender, and even cries out against God and complains to him: "You are hurting me! Why are you doing this?" and so forth. Assurance of God's presence engenders tenderness in the soul. In this state it is satisfied with consolations and other similar gifts. But in the absence of these, love grows and begins to seek the loved one. If it does not find him, the soul pines. It is then no longer satisfied with consolations, for it seeks only the Beloved. The more the soul receives consolations and feels God, the more its love grows, but the more, likewise, it pines in the absence of the Beloved.[9]

But once the soul is perfectly united to God, it is placed in the seat of truth, for truth is the seat of the soul.[10] It then no longer cries out nor complains about God, nor grows tender or pines away. On the contrary, it acknowledges itself to be unworthy of every good and every gift of God, and only worthy of a hell more horrible than the one which exists. Wisdom and maturity are established in the soul. As a result the soul becomes ordered and so strengthened that it can face death.[11] It possesses God to the fullness of its capacity. And God even expands the soul so that it may hold all that he wishes to place in it. The soul then sees the One who is, and it sees that all else is nothing except insofar as it takes its being from him.[12] In comparison, everything up until now seems as nothing to it—as, indeed, all created reality. Nor are death, infirmity, honor, or dishonor of any concern to it. The soul is so satisfied and at rest that it desires nothing; it even loses the capacity to desire and to act effectively because it is bound to God.[13] In this light it sees so well that God does everything with order and appropriateness that even in his absence, it does not pine. Likewise it becomes so conformed to God's will that even in his absence it is content with everything he does and entrusts itself totally to him.[14]

The following then is true, namely, that when the soul is strengthened and finds its rest in this state of perfect love, it loses its capacity to desire. Nor can the soul act when it is in possession of the full vision of God. But when this vision is withdrawn—for it is not granted to anyone to remain always in this vision—the soul is stirred by a new, effortless desire to perform even greater works of penance than before. The reason for this is that this state is more perfect than all others. The power of this perfection is such that the greater it is the more the soul is driven to imitate the master of perfection, that is, the suffering God-man.[15]

But for all of his life the suffering God-man knew only one state: that of the cross. His life began on the cross, continued on the cross, and ended on the cross. He was always on the cross of poverty, continual pain, contempt, true obedience, and other harsh deeds of penance. Since the heritage of the father should be handed down to his sons, God the Father handed the heritage of the cross and penance to his only Son. As a consequence, it is fitting that all the sons of God, the more they reach perfection, assume this heritage and adhere to its implications all their life. For the entire life of the suffering God-man was filled with the most bitter effects of the cross and penance. How long does penance last, and how much of it is there? As long as one lives. And as much as one can bear. This is the meaning of being transformed into the will of God. But when the soul is truly transformed into God or within God and is in that state of perfect union and enjoys the full vision of him, it seeks nothing more. When, however, it is not in this state it strains to transform itself into the will of the Beloved until it recovers this state. And the suffering God-man demonstrates his will by the works of the cross and of penance which are always with him.

The more perfect one is and the more one loves God, the more one tries to do what the suffering God-man does and avoid whatever is contrary to God's will. Does not someone who loves another perfectly try to conform to the other's ways and do those things that please the loved one more?

If there are any (such as those who say they have the "spirit of freedom") who claim they live without desires and have no longing, and in no way and at no time are responsible for any actions, they should not be believed, for what they claim is not true.[16] They should reflect on the wrongfulness of what they are doing. They are perfectly able to dance, play, eat, and drink sumptuously and excessively, behave dishonestly, and engage in illicit behavior. If they can and do engage in these and other similar evil activities, and can desire and perform these actions, how much more, if they truly love God, should they desire and do what is good and pleasing to God. They should take a good look at our father, the blessed Francis. He was a mirror of holiness and every perfection, the model for all those who wish to live the spiritual life.[17] When he was near the end of his life, even though his state of perfection was so excellent and his union with God so ineffable, nonetheless, he said: "Brothers, let us begin to do penance for until now we have made little progress."[18]

Of imperfect and suspect love

There are many who believe themselves to be in a state of love who are actually in a state of hatred.[19] And there are many who believe they possess God while in reality they love the flesh, the world, and the devil. Hence some love God so that he will protect them from sickness, bodily ailments, and temporal dangers. Such persons even love themselves in such a disorderly way that they treat their bodies as though they were souls and gods. They even love material things to put these at the service of the gods they have made of their bodies. They love their friends and relatives inordinately as a way of benefiting from them and being honored by them. They love spiritual persons not for their goodness but to cover themselves with the mantle of their holiness. Because such a love is not pure, its fruit is the flesh with all its carnal and spiritual vices. They love to possess special talents such as knowing how to read and sing well so that they might please others. They love to possess great learning so that they can persuade others not through love but by force of reason and arrogantly correct others so as to appear important.

There are others who believe they love God, and they do love him, but their love is infirm and imperfect. They love God, for instance, so that he will remit their sins, preserve them from hell, and grant them the glory of Paradise. They love God so that he will preserve their goodness, and so that they will not offend him any longer and not lose paradise. They love God to receive consolations and sweetnesses from him. They love God to be loved by him. They even love their friends and relatives with a spiritual love because they desire to be spiritual and good and they desire this for their own sake, to gain honor and profit from it. Those who are literate love God to receive from him the meaning, knowledge, and understanding of the Scriptures. Those who are illiterate desire to have the capacity to speak usefully and spiritually for the benefit of others so that they may be more loved and more honored. They love spiritual persons so that they may be considered one of them and be loved by them for their own spiritual benefit and honor. They even love poverty, humility, obedience, contempt, and other virtues because they wish to excel in these over others and because they hope that no one can match them in perfection. They wish to have no equal in the ways of the spirit. In this they resemble Lucifer's sin, for he too did not want anyone to achieve his perfection. There are others who lavish praise on all, whether they be spiritual persons or not, because they wish to enjoy a universal reputation of holiness and be praised by all, good and bad alike, for their holiness.

There are others who love their spiritual brothers or sisters with a spiritual and perfect love, that is, they love them as themselves, totally in God. As their love grows they seek the presence of their beloved. If the beloved is absent, their love pines and sickens, and when the beloved is present, it grows. As it grows, it prepares the way for greater sickening whenever the loved one is again absent. This growth in love also leads to complete identification with the beloved, so that everything that pleases one, pleases the other, and everything that displeases one likewise displeases the other. Because their souls are not sufficiently armed to regulate the fervor of their love which keeps growing and is not perfectly ordered, this type of love inevitably becomes disorderly.

And if the love of the beloved person is in a similar state of disorder, lacks the necessary weapons to protect it, and is likewise pierced with the same sword of love, this state is greatly to be feared, for it is then that lovers begin to reveal their secrets to one another. Among other things they reveal how much they love one another, for they feel the need to express their feelings for one another. They say to one another: "There is no one in the world that I love more and carry more in my heart." And their mutual devotion leads to the desire to touch one another, and they even believe this will be spiritually beneficial because they think this is harmless. Reason, however, since it is not totally stifled, initially protests; but later on even reason and spirit see—or rather, believe—that touches of this kind do no harm, and so permission is granted to go ahead with this type of behavior. This is the soul's downfall. From this moment on, it weakens and gradually falls from its state of perfection.

And since the power of reason is somewhat stifled, it begins to think: "This can be done because it is not a serious sin."[20]

Afterward, swept away by the ardor of love, all capacity to say no to whatever the beloved wants is taken away. But because of this state of disorder, the beloved can will to do wrong. Thus if one of the lovers wishes to do wrong, the other cannot refuse the invitation to do so; and if there is no invitation from one, the other does the inviting. What follows is an abandonment of prayer, abstinence, solitude, and all the virtues they were accustomed to practice, and all the divine love which was theirs is converted into disordered love. Furthermore, the ardor of their love for one another grows to such a degree that neither words nor the presence of the beloved satisfies them as it did at first, for the lover then desires to know whether the beloved is also stricken as deeply by the same arrow of love. And if this is known to be the case, there is danger for both of them for, afterward, neither words nor presence any longer suffice and, as a consequence, both fall into all kinds of depravity. This is why I assert that love is more suspect than anything for it contains all possibility of evil. Therefore, whoever has not attained the state of perfect love should hold all other forms of love in suspicion.[21]

The love that is perfect and above suspicion finds its source in the vision of the supreme Being and the uncreated Good

The perfect and highest form of love, one without defects, is the one in which the soul is drawn out of itself and led into the vision of the being of God.[22] For when the soul is so drawn out of itself and led into this vision, it perceives how every creature has its being from the one who is the supreme Being; how all things and all that exists come to be through the supreme Being; how God is indeed the only one who has being, and that nothing has being unless it comes from him. The soul drawn out of itself and led into this vision derives from it an ineffable wisdom, one that is deep and mature. In this vision, the soul discovers that only what is best comes from the supreme Being and it cannot deny this, for it sees in truth that all things that are from him are excellently made; things are done badly when we have destroyed those things he made. This vision of the supreme Being also stirs up in the soul a love corresponding and proportionate to its object, for it teaches us to love everything which receives existence from the supreme Being. It likewise teaches us to love everything which has being, that is, every creature, rational and nonrational, with the supreme Being's own love. It teaches us to love rational creatures, especially those we know are loved and cherished by him. When the soul sees the supreme Being stoop down lovingly toward creatures, it does likewise. Thus the supreme Being makes me love those who love him. The latter are recognized through certain signs.

This is the sign of those whose friendship with the supreme Being is divine and who are true followers of his only Son: Those who are in this state always have the eyes of their spirit turned toward him so that they love him, follow him, and transform themselves completely and totally according to the will of the Beloved, that is, the supreme Being. Their souls have learned (from possessing the vision of the supreme Being) to love this being; this vision stirs up the soul's love, and because it knows how to love the supreme Being, it knows how to love creatures appropriately: that is, more or less, according to the extent of the supreme Being's love toward them; and in no way can it transgress these limits. This is why, once again, in everything which touches upon love, the soul ought to be suspicious and cautious until it has been given this perfect love from God. Once, however, the soul has attained this vision of the supreme Being of God and is in the state of love which corresponds and is proportionate to that being, the soul's love is so solid that even if it experiences new visions or elevations, it is not affected by them. Furthermore, it is not even necessary for the soul to be in the state of this ineffable vision of the supreme Being of God, for merely thinking about him would be enough to expel every malice of every other love and even enable one to withstand the knife of love.

The soul is also given a vision of the Uncreated.[23] This vision deposits an uncreated love in the soul. In this uncreated love the soul cannot act; it is without works, but love itself acts. When the soul possesses this vision of the Uncreated, it can do nothing, because it is completely absorbed in this vision; it can contribute nothing to uncreated love. It is to be noted, however, that when the soul is given this vision, it has been actively working, in that with its whole being it desired to be united with the Uncreated, and with its whole being sought how to be better united with him. Indeed, it is the Uncreated himself who operates in the soul and inspires it to withdraw from all created things to be better united to him. It is the uncreated love, then, which is at work and the one producing the works of love. At the source of this work is an illumination which sets ablaze a new desire and a powerful love to which the soul both contributes and does not contribute, for it is the uncreated love that does all the work. It is responsible for all the good and none of the evil that we do.[24] True annihilation consists in becoming aware that we are truly not the authors of any good.[25]

Those who possess the spirit of truth are aware of this truth. Furthermore, true love causes neither laughter[26] nor inordinate eating and drinking, nor frivolity. It does not say: "I am not held to any law," but always subjects itself ever more to the law; and when there is no law, it makes its own law. For the love of God is never idle, even when it follows the way of the cross through bodily penance. The sign that true love is at work is this: The soul takes up its cross, that is, penance as long as one lives, penance as great and harsh as possible.

When love is done with the works of the cross and penance in me, that is, after it has pushed these to their final limits, as long as I live and as harsh as possible, then I will become aware that in truth I am an unprofitable servant. And if I wish to ask God for something, I will do it in the name of the penance he did in me and for me. This is the sign of the spirit of truth:[27] to realize that God's being is total love and to acknowledge oneself as total hate.

Once the soul has this knowledge, it follows that it must commit itself to perform bodily penance. When the soul does penance, it may find the burden of penance heavy and even at times impossible to carry. As a result, it may have the impression that the soul is the one doing the work; but in truth, this is not the case, for it is the Uncreated that is at work in it and for it. At times, the Uncreated may make the penance seem light, but even this is for the soul's benefit. We should not be surprised if the soul is weighed down with penance because the true Teacher came to do penance for us: Throughout his entire life he experienced the bitterness of penance and the cross for us. Those who are elevated to the vision of the Uncreated and the being of God will find rest in the cross and in virtuous deeds wherever they occur. Their love will be constantly renewed, and they will be set ablaze to act more courageously. Those who are not in this spirit of truth will make idols for themselves out of the virtuous deeds they perform. And their first idol will be the divine light given to them.

INSTRUCTION III:
THE GREAT "BOOK OF LIFE," NAMELY,
THE SUFFERINGS OF CHRIST,
PRAYER, AND POVERTY

PART I
MEDITATIONS ON THE MYSTERY OF SUFFERING
IN THE LIFE OF THE LORD

God, whose plan is ineffable, foreordained that the heart of Jesus would be stricken with seven afflictions

Christ's sufferings were unspeakable, manifold, and hidden.[28] And his unspeakably acute sufferings originated in the ineffable wisdom of the plan of God, who foreordained it and bestowed it on him. From all eternity, in an ineffable manner, Christ was united to this divine plan, and it culminated in his experiencing the supreme degree of suffering. The more wondrous the divine plan, the more acute and intense Christ's suffering. The painful effects of the divine plan were so acute and the sufferings so unspeakable and extreme that there is no intelligence comprehensive or large enough to ever be able to understand them. The divine plan, then, was the source and origin of all the sufferings of Christ. In it they begin and end.

Some of Christ's sufferings were a consequence of the ineffable divine light granted to him. God, who is ineffable light, enlightened Christ ineffably.[29] It was part of the divine plan for Christ to be so ineffably united to God and transformed into his divine light that the suffering he was given to endure was altogether ineffable. Christ saw in the divine light the measure of suffering allotted to him. Because of its very excessiveness and ineffability, this suffering was concealed from all creatures. This suffering, a consequence of the light given to him, had its source and origin in the divine plan.

Christ also suffered most intensely and acutely from his most wonderful compassion toward the human race he loved so much. His compassion and suffering for each person was directly in proportion to each one's offenses and the punishments which he knew with utmost certitude each was incurring or had incurred. Because Christ's love for each of his elect was so ineffable and visceral, he continually felt, as if present to him, the offenses they were going to commit or had committed, as well as the corresponding pain and punishment they would have to suffer for each of their great offenses. Out of his compassion he took upon himself the punishments due to them, and this was for him a source of extreme suffering. The more visceral Christ's love for his elect, the more did his compassion and suffering increase as he took on their punishments and sufferings. The cause of these sufferings of Christ is to be found in the divine plan.

Some of Christ's suffering also came from his compassion toward himself. This was because he foresaw the indescribable suffering that would inevitably befall him. Because he perceived himself as the one sent by the Father to bear in his own person the sufferings and pains of all the elect, and because he knew that he could not be wrong about these indescribable and acute sufferings that would fall upon him—for he was sent to give himself totally for this purpose—Christ's compassion for himself was the source of extreme suffering. For if someone knew with absolute certainty that he would inevitably have to endure the greatest and most indescribable pain and suffering, and had the sight of this suffering constantly before him, would he not have compassion for himself in proportion to this coming suffering? (At this point mother,[30] as I was writing, you told me: "It was different from what I said; it was deeper. But I say it this way because you are so slow to understand." This is indeed what you told me.) Christ, foreseeing, then, the undescribable suffering that he would inevitably have to endure, had compassion for himself at the thought of being transformed into such a state of suffering.

Some of Christ's suffering also reflects his compassion for his most dear mother. Christ loved her more than any other creature—from her alone he had received his very flesh. Christ suffered extremely because he saw the extreme suffering that was hers. For endowed with the noblest and deepest qualities, superior to any other creature, she grieved over her own true son, in her own special way, more than any other creature grieved for him. Seeing her in such great pain, Christ suffered all the more out of compassion for her. The mother of God suffered in the extreme, and Christ continually bore this suffering in himself. The foundation for this suffering is the divine plan.

Christ also suffered as a result of his compassion for his apostles and disciples, because of the intense suffering that they would have to undergo when the sweetness of his physical presence, the source of such joy, was withdrawn from them. His physical presence was truly so loving and delightful that his mother and his disciples were afflicted with indescribable suffering when he was taken away from them at the time of the passion. All these sufferings Jesus, the God-man, bore continually within himself.

Finally, Christ suffered extremely and acutely because of the gentle, most noble, and sensitive nature of his soul. The intense and acute suffering he endured was torment in direct proportion to his soul's nobility and innate sensitivity. This noblest of souls afflicted on itself the greatest suffering. And all these sufferings of Christ originate at the highest and totally ineffable levels of the divine plan. (At this point, mother, you also said: "Because of the ineffable union between soul and body, all these sufferings dispensed by the divine plan tormented Christ's soul so terribly and intensely that each of its pains reverberated in his body, and the body, too, was most keenly afflicted.")

Five kinds of knives with which Christ's enemies tried to destroy him

There were five kinds of knives that pierced Jesus, the God and man.[31]

The first kind of knife was the perverse cruelty of those whose hearts were set against him. Their hearts were so continually and obstinately set against him that their constant concern was to eliminate him from the face of the earth by the most shameful and ignominious means imaginable.

The second kind of knife was the knives of those who clamored against him with most vicious tongues. Because of the constant anguish of their hate-filled and obstinate hearts, they continually spoke against him with the venom and poison of their vicious and deceitful tongues.

The third kind of knife was the immense and boundless rage directed against him. From obstinate and murderous hearts, and deadly and biting tongues intent on tearing Christ apart, came forth the most cruel rage, continually directed at him. The many thoughts directed against him were like so many knives driven into his soul. The words spoken against him and the most cruel rage and anger were like so many knives which continuously pierced his soul.

The fourth kind of knife was the perfect fulfillment of all the evil intentions of Christ's enemies, for they did with him whatever they wanted.

The fifth kind of knife with which Christ was stabbed was the terrible nails with which they nailed him to the cross. They used the largest of nails, blunted, rusty, and square, because this shape causes the most extreme pain. They did this so as to better satisfy their malice.

The triple meaning of the sufferings of Christ for our salvation

To show us something of the excessive and ineffable pain that he suffered on our behalf, and to teach us to always grieve from the depths of our hearts over his sufferings, Christ as God and man had three reasons for saying what he did when he cried out on the cross: "My God, my God, why have you abandoned me?"[32]

He cried out so that, in his prayer, who God was—and who he, God's Son was—would become manifest. God cannot be abandoned, but Christ showed that he was human when in his sufferings he cried out like one abandoned by God.

He cried out also to make known the most acute and unspeakable suffering he endured for us. God, the Father of Christ, knew full well the sufferings of Christ; Jesus himself also knew them since he was the one who endured them. Therefore it was only for us that he cried out these words on the cross. He did so to show us the continual and acute sufferings he had endured (not for himself but for us), and also to admonish us always to weep over them ourselves. The creation and makeup of the body of Christ, the infusion of the soul into the body and its union with the Word, occurred once and for all, simultaneously. By virtue of this most wonderful union, the soul of Christ was filled with the highest and most ineffable wisdom and was thus able to make everything infallibly present to itself in a totally unspeakable way. As a result, from the instant of its creation until the moment of its separation from the body, the soul of Christ endured, continually and totally, that most acute and unspeakable suffering which he saw he was inevitably destined to sustain according to the divine plan. His own words testify to this, for he often said that he was carrying the cross and bore its burden.[33] Likewise, so that we might gain our salvation from it, he also said—not for himself but for his disciples and us—"My soul is sad unto death,"[34] thus suggesting that everyone, especially his legitimate followers, should always weep over his sufferings.

Christ, then, cried out "My God, my God," and so forth, in order to give us hope and comfort, so that if we are afflicted, if we undergo tribulation, or even feel abandoned in our sufferings, we shall not be overwhelmed by despair, but see very clearly by his example that he ultimately profited from temptation; and that he, as God, is ready to come quickly to our aid.

PART II
MEDITATION ON THE SUPREME NECESSITY
OF PRAYER ACCORDING TO THE "BOOK OF LIFE"

Prayer is necessary for the soul's sanctification, which the divine light brings to perfection

No one can be saved without divine light. Divine light causes us to begin and to make progress, and it leads us to the summit of perfection. Therefore if you want to begin and to receive this divine light, pray. If you have begun to make progress and want this light to be intensified within you, pray. And if you have reached the summit of perfection, and want to be superillumined so as to remain in that state, pray.

If you want faith, pray. If you want hope, pray. If you want charity, pray. If you want poverty, pray. If you want obedience, pray. If you want chastity, pray. If you want humility, pray. If you want meekness, pray. If you want fortitude, pray. If you want some virtue, pray.

And pray in this fashion, namely, always reading the Book of Life,[35] that is, the life of the God-man Jesus Christ, whose life consisted of poverty, pain, contempt, and true obedience.

Once you have entered this way and are making progress in it, tribulations, temptations from demons, the world, and the flesh, will plague you in many ways and afflict you horribly; but if you want to overcome these, pray. And when the soul wants to improve its prayer, it must enter into it with a cleansed mind and body, and with pure and right intention. Its task is also to turn evil into good, and not, as many of the wicked do, convert good into evil. A soul thus exercised in cleansing itself goes with greater confidence to confession to have its sins washed away. And so that nothing impure may remain, it puts itself to a kind of scrutiny. It enters into prayer and examines the good and evil it has done. As it tries to determine the intentions behind the good things it has done, it discovers how in its fasts, prayers, tears, and all its other good deeds, it has behaved deceitfully, that is, inadequately and defectively. You are not to behave, therefore, like the wicked, but rather confess your sins diligently and grieve over them, for it is in confession that the soul is cleansed. After this, you are to return to prayer and not let yourself become preoccupied with anything else. As a result, you begin to feel the presence of God more fully than usual because your palate is more disposed to savor God's presence than before. It is through prayer, then, that one will be given the most powerful light to see God and self.

Exhortation to be on guard against false teachers of prayer

Beware of giving yourself to another unless first you learn to separate yourself from others. Beware also of those who flatter you with sweet words and seek to make themselves especially attractive to you by what they say, and make a show of their revelations, because these are the snares of the wicked who try to lure others after them. Beware also of those who have merely the appearance of holiness and of good works, lest they drag you along their way. Beware also of your own fervor, that is, the spirit which accompanies this fervor; before following its lead, look, look again, examine it and determine its origins, its means, and its end. Follow its lead only to the extent that it corresponds to the way of the Book of Life and no further.[36]

Again, beware of those who say they have the "spirit of freedom,"[37] but whose ways are openly contrary to the life of Christ. God the Father willed that his Son—who was not subject to the law but was, on the contrary, above the law and was the author of the law—be made subject to the law; and he who was free became a slave. Thus, it is necessary that those who wish to follow Christ conform themselves to the life of Christ, not in seeking freedom by dissolving the law and divine precepts, as many do, but by subjecting themselves to the law, to divine precepts, and even to counsels. Such followers of Christ form an association and give themselves a set of regulations,[38] that is, the Holy Spirit gives them a set of regulations which tells them how they should live, and it binds them. And there are many things that are permissible and not contrary to God's will, which the Holy Spirit does not allow them to do, under this rule which he has given them. Therefore, those who wish to be bound by this rule must pray.

Be careful not to give way to your enemies, who are continually watching you. For you will yield to your enemies if you stop praying.

The more you are tempted, the more you should persevere in prayer. And by the very fact that you persevere in your prayers, you put yourself in a position to be tempted. Must not gold be purified and melted down? But by the very perseverance of your prayers you will be freed from temptations. Finally, it is through prayer that you will be enlightened, liberated, cleansed, and united with God.

Definition, nature, degrees, and effects of the "Book" of prayer

The purpose of prayer is nothing other than to manifest God and self.[39] And this manifestation of God and self leads to a state of perfect and true humility. For this humility is attained when the soul sees God and self. It is in this profound state of humility, and from it, that divine grace deepens and grows in the soul. The more divine grace deepens humility in the soul, the more divine grace can grow in this depth of humility. The more divine grace grows, the deeper the soul is grounded, and the more it is settled in a state of true humility. Through perseverance in true prayer, divine light and grace increase, and these always make the soul grow deep in humility as it reads, as has been said, the life of Jesus Christ, God and man. I cannot conceive anything greater than the manifestation of God and self. But this discovery, that is, this manifestation of God and self, is the lot only of those legitimate sons of God who have devoted themselves to true prayer.

Those who possess the spirit of true prayer will have the Book of Life, that is, the life of Jesus Christ, God and man, set before them, and everything they could want, they will find there. Thus they will be filled with its blessed teaching—which does not puff anyone up—and will find there every doctrine they and others need. Hence if you wish to be superenlightened and taught, read this Book of Life. If you do not simply skim through it but rather let it penetrate you while reading it, you will be taught everything needed for yourself and for others, no matter what your state of life. Also, if you read it carefully and not casually, you will be so inflamed by divine fire that you will accept every tribulation as the greatest consolation. It will even make you see that you are most unworthy of these tribulations, and what is more, if success or human praise should come your way because of whatever quality God has placed in you, you will not become vain or put on airs because of it. By reading in the Book of Life, you will see and know that, in truth, the praise is not meant for you. Not boasting or feeling superior about anything but always remaining humble is one of the signs by which one can detect that one is in the state of divine grace.

There are three kinds of prayer: bodily, mental, and supernatural.[40] Divine wisdom is most orderly and it imposes its order on all things. Through its ineffable wisdom it has ordained that one does not attain mental prayer unless one has first passed through bodily prayer, and likewise, one does not attain supernatural prayer unless one has first passed through bodily and mental prayer. Divine wisdom also wills and has ordained that the canonical hours be said at the hours assigned for each one of them unless one is totally unable to do so because of some serious bodily ailment or because one is so absorbed in a state of mental or supernatural prayer and experiencing such joy in that state that one is totally speechless. Divine wisdom likewise teaches that when possible the hours should be said with the mind in a state of quiet and, as is fitting, with the body attentive and in a recollected state.[41]

The more you pray the more you will be enlightened; and the more you are enlightened, the more deeply and exaltedly you will see the supreme Good and what this supreme Good consists of; the deeper and more perfect your vision, the more you will love; the more you love, the more you will delight in what you see; the more you find delight, the more you will understand and be made capable of understanding. Afterward, you will come to the fullness of light because you will understand that you cannot understand.

Outstanding examples of prayer: Jesus and the glorious Virgin Mary

The Son of God, Jesus Christ in his human nature, himself gave us the example of the wonders of prayer and the need to persevere in it. He taught us how to pray in many ways through word and deed. Through words, he advised us to pray when he told his disciples: "Watch and pray lest you enter into temptation."[42] You will find in many other places in the gospel the many ways he taught us how to say this venerable prayer, and how he let us all know, by recommending it again and again, how dear it was to him. Loving us from the bottom of his heart, he wanted to take away every pretext we could have for neglecting this blessed prayer. This is why he said it himself, so that drawn by his example, we would love this prayer above all others. The evangelist, in fact, says that through the intensity with which he said this prayer, his sweat became like drops of blood falling to the ground.[43] Put this mirror before your eyes and strive with all your might to reproduce something of this prayer, for it was for you that he prayed, and not for himself. He was also teaching us how to pray when he said: "Father, if it is possible, remove this chalice from me. Yet thy will be done and not mine."[44] Notice how Christ always preferred the divine will to his own. Follow his example. He also taught us how to pray when he said: "Father, into your hands I commend my spirit."[45] What more can one say? Jesus' whole life was a prayer because he was in a continual state of manifestation of God and self. Did Christ then pray in vain? Why, then, do you neglect prayer, when without prayer nothing can be obtained? Christ Jesus, true God and true man, prayed for you and not for himself so that you could have an example of true prayer. If you wish to obtain something from him, you must necessarily pray, for without prayer you cannot obtain it.

We also have the example of the glorious Virgin, mother of Jesus Christ, God and man. Shall we condemn her prayer and that of her son, Jesus Christ, God and man? If we do not condemn the Virgin Mary's prayer, why do we not follow her example? For she taught us to pray by the example of her own most holy prayer. She prayed when she promised God to remain a virgin. While she prayed, making this promise, divine light abounded in her more fully and made her consecrate her virginity, and even her whole body and soul, more gloriously to God.[46] In this same divine light she was granted the most perfect manifestation of who God is and who she was. This prayer, that is, this manifestation of God and herself, was the content of her contemplation, which was ineffable.

We pray in two ways the glorious Virgin Mary had no need of. We pray that God may deliver us from eternal damnation, which we deserve because of our sins, and that God in his abundant mercy may cleanse us of our sins. The mother of God had no need of this kind of prayer. We pray also to be enlightened, to grow in virtues and divine gifts—all things which the mother of God possessed in the greatest degree. Although she was of our corrupted flesh, she was, nonetheless, personally chosen by God the Father and adorned by him with a privilege so unique, glorious, and perfect that she never needed to be purified or freed from the penalty of sin. The mother of God was adorned with privileges and virtues so unique, and with gifts so ineffable, that nothing could separate her, not even for a moment, from divine union.[47] She was so ineffably united to the supreme and absolutely ineffable Trinity that she enjoyed something in this life of what the saints enjoy in the heavenly homeland. The joy of the saints is a joy of incomprehension; they understand that they cannot understand. It was in this type of understanding that the soul of the blessed and glorious Virgin Mary swam. The full experience of the heavenly homeland, however, could not be hers in this life.

PART III
MEDITATION ON PERFECT POVERTY
AND SOME EXAMPLES OF IT

God redeems the false poverty of fallen man with divine poverty which is its opposite

It was on the path of poverty that the first man fell, and on the same path the second man, Christ, God and man, raised us up. The worst poverty is that of ignorance. Adam fell because of his ignorance, and all those who have fallen or are falling do so through ignorance. This is why it is fitting that the sons of God should rise and be restored through the opposite kind of poverty.

Three examples show us true poverty: Christ, the Virgin Mary, and the good thief crucified with Jesus

We have an example of true poverty in Jesus Christ, God and man. This God and man Jesus Christ raised us up and redeemed us by poverty. His poverty was truly ineffable, for it concealed so much of his total power and nobility. He let himself be blasphemed, vilified, verbally abused, seized, dragged, scourged, and crucified, and through it all, he always behaved as one powerless to help himself. His poverty is a model for our life; we should follow this example.[48] For our part, we do not have to hide our power, for we have none; but we must manifest and be aware of our great powerlessness.

We have another example of true poverty in the glorious Virgin Mary, the most holy mother of God. She taught us this poverty clearly when, in response to the news of the great mystery of the incarnation, she declared herself to be of our corrupted flesh and referred to herself as most lowly when she adopted as her own the lowliest of titles: "Behold the handmaid of the Lord!"[49]—and this was indeed the most lowly name she could call herself. Such acknowledgment of one's poverty is always most acceptable to God.

We have yet another example of true poverty in the good thief who was crucified with the God and man Jesus Christ. He had lived an evil life and had done wicked deeds, but once he received divine light and truly saw the goodness of God, he immediately saw his own poverty, acknowledged it, and answered his companion, who was insulting Christ: "You are under the same condemnation as this man. Is there no fear of God in you? We are receiving what we deserve, but he has done no wrong." And turning to Christ he said: "Remember me, Lord, when you come into your kingdom."[50] At that moment he was saved.

For us sinners, I see no better satisfaction we can make to God for our sins than by fully acknowledging our poverty. When the soul becomes fully aware of its poverty, it does not wait for God to judge it; it judges and condemns itself. It is given the grace to immediately seek out new forms of penance in order to make satisfaction to God for its sins. In all this the soul sets no limits to its penance and suffering.

Blessed Francis was a perfect follower of poverty, and taught us two special dimensions of it

What a perfect example is given to us by our glorious father, blessed Francis, who possessed the ineffable light of the truest poverty! He was so filled, and more than filled, with this light, that he opened up a very special way and showed it to us all. I cannot think of any saint who demonstrated to me more remarkably than he did the way found in the Book of Life, the model being the life of the God-man, Jesus Christ. I know no other saint who more remarkably set himself to follow this way. He set himself with such determination along that path that his eyes never left it, and the effects could plainly be seen in his body.[51] And because he set himself with such total determination to follow this path, he was filled to overflowing with the highest wisdom, a wisdom with which he filled and continues to fill the whole world.

There are two things which our blessed and glorious father Francis taught us in a remarkable way.

One is to recollect ourselves in God, that is, to recollect our whole soul within the divine infinity.[52] He was so filled to overflowing with the Holy Spirit that the grace of that Spirit animated all his works and actions. Having cleansed him in body and soul, the Holy Spirit sanctified him within and without, strengthened him in every way, directed all his actions, purified him within and without, and joined him to God in constant and ineffable union. Finally, the Holy Spirit—or the wonderful power of the Holy Spirit, by which all things are put in order—which wonderfully ordered his soul and made it the seat of God, also, at the same moment, likewise ordered his body in a singular manner. I see him as remarkably poor and as an unrivaled lover and follower of poverty. He was indeed poor within and without, so that it seems to me that he was totally transformed into poverty. He not only imposed poverty on himself, but prescribed it for the whole world; and he derived this injunction from the Book of Life, that is, from the life of the God and man Jesus Christ. Let us trust St. Francis because he was not a hypocrite, nor did he pray in vain.

The second lesson blessed Francis taught us was poverty, suffering, contempt, and true obedience. He was poverty personified, inside and out. He lived in this way and persevered in it to the end. Everything that Jesus, God and man, despised, he despised most perfectly. Everything that Jesus, God and man, loved, he loved most intensely and supremely. With inexpressible perfection he followed in the footsteps of Jesus in order to become conformed to him as much as he could in all things. Because the blessed Francis saw God perfectly in an ineffable vision, he loved him with an ineffable love, and, correspondingly, he received from this vision of God the most complete effects of its power of transformation. For what one loves intensely, one desires very much to possess; the stronger the love, the stronger the desire to possess. All that Jesus Christ, God and man, loved, Francis, the poorest of the poor, loved. He had one cleansing and purification after another, and was continually being cleansed because of the pure vision that was continually his. The God who gave him a unique vocation also gave him unique gifts for the benefit of himself and others. The uncreated God wanted to demonstrate in our holy father, the blessed Francis, veritable plenitude, a plenitude beyond our comprehension. The blessed Francis came into possession of these unique gifts and this plenitude as a result of true and constant prayer.

When, therefore, you find someone who claims to have the "spirit of freedom," saying: "How dare you judge me! What do you know about what is in my heart?" You are to respond to such persons firmly and reproach them boldly by saying that the Holy Spirit teaches us to judge the wrongfulness of our deeds. For the Holy Spirit, when poured into the soul, immediately puts it into the most perfect order, and then orders the body in the same way as the soul, with the same kind of perfect order. Whatever is contrary to this teaching is false!

St. Francis teaches that the poverty of fallen man is healed by imitating the contrary poverty of Jesus in his humanity and by contemplating his divinity

The more perfectly and purely we see, the more perfectly and purely we love. As we see, so we love. Therefore, the more we see of Jesus Christ, God and man, the more we are transformed into him by love. And to the extent that we are transformed into him by love, we will in turn be transformed into the suffering which the soul sees in Jesus Christ, God and man. As I said of love that the more the soul sees, the more it loves, I say the same of suffering, that is, the more the soul sees of the unspeakable suffering of Jesus Christ, God and man, the more the soul suffers and is transformed into his suffering. Likewise, the more the soul sees of the greatness and sensitivity of Jesus Christ, God and man, and the sharper its vision of him, the more it is transformed into him through love. Likewise, again, the more the soul sees of the suffering of Jesus Christ, God and man, and the sharper its vision of this unspeakable suffering, the more it is transformed into it. Thus, the transformation of the soul into Jesus Christ, God and man, through love, is directly in proportion to its transformation into his suffering.

And then, when the soul sees the superinfinity or the superloftiness of God—when I name it, it seems to me I blaspheme rather than name—and when the soul sees, also, the incredibly wretched beings with whom this totally ineffable and superlative divinity deigned to establish friendship and kinship—the more clearly and deeply the soul sees this, the more viscerally and profoundly is it transformed into the suffering of Jesus Christ, God and man. Swimming in an unspeakable manner[53] in the utterly ineffable and superabundant goodness of the divinity, the soul sees itself as a creature so full of defects that it goes blind, as it were, in seeing them because it sees that what it understands of these defects is nothing in comparison to what they really are. The more lucid the soul's vision, the more painfully it is transformed into the suffering of Jesus Christ, God and man.

Afterward, the divine light having expanded its capacity to see, the soul becomes aware that it and it alone was the cause of the excessive and almost infinite suffering of Christ, and it in turn is transformed into this excessive suffering. Seeing, then, the absolutely infinite and superabundant goodness of the divinity deigning to stoop down for such a totally wretched creature as itself, stooping down so low as to become a mortal man, and seeing the one who was creator of heaven and earth willing to be continually so cruelly tormented during his life with unspeakable sufferings and dying such a foul death, the soul in turn is transformed into even more extreme sufferings. If at any time during life, one has sought to serve the needs of others, these efforts are redoubled at the time of death. Similarly, the King of kings—even though the inexpressible and continual suffering he endured had made of his whole life an unspeakable cross—at the time of his death, instead of a chamber of gold and a scarlet bed, had an abominable cross, one so wretched that, had he not been nailed to it, it could not have held him.[54] Nails held him to the cross by the hands and feet, otherwise he would have fallen. And instead of servants solicitous to care for him, there was a whole array of demons so set to afflict him cruelly and wound him viciously and without ceasing that at the moment of death they refused him even a drop of the water he cried out for to quench his thirst. The more the soul has a clear and sharp vision of all these sufferings, the more it is intimately and profoundly absorbed and transformed into the continual and totally unspeakable sufferings of Jesus Christ, God and man.

Finally, the soul seeing that poverty caused its fall, and seeing that Jesus, God and man, raised it up by the opposite poverty; seeing that it incurred eternal sufferings, and seeing that Jesus, God and man, wanted to suffer continually and almost infinitely to deliver it from these sufferings; seeing that it had fallen into a state of contempt and derision, away from the supreme and totally ineffable deity; and seeing that Jesus Christ, God and man, wished to be despised, ill-treated, and to appear to all in such an extreme state of derision for the very purpose of removing it from this state of derision—the soul is transformed into the immense suffering of Jesus, God and man, which is totally unspeakable.

All this was perfectly realized in the person of our father, blessed

Francis, on whom we should fix our gaze so that we might follow his example.

INSTRUCTION IV:
ON PILGRIMAGE TO ASSISI, ANGELA RECEIVES EXTRAORDINARY REVELATIONS AND GRACES

Writer's introduction to the theme

In the name of the most blessed Trinity and the most reverend mother of our Lord Jesus Christ.

The following is a description of the transformations which took place in the soul of Christ's faithful one as a result of the various gifts which the Most High bestowed upon it. Although I was united to her by deep bonds of friendship and Christian charity, it was only with great difficulty, many prayers, and powerful arguments that I, the writer, could get her to tell me about them. For she maintained the most astonishing and absolute reserve about the divine gifts she had received. As far as I can see, I would never have been able to know of them if I had not let her know how upset I was that I had to leave suddenly for a long trip with little hope of ever seeing her again. This moved her to compassion.[55]

She had already told me many times that she did not think it at all proper to speak of these divine gifts, and had advanced many good and virtuous reasons for not doing so, especially her inability to describe these gifts properly, for indeed no human words can be found to correspond with what is presented below concerning her experiences in the body or in her imagination. Even less can be said of what she experienced in her soul, about not only those friars of whom we shall speak shortly, but also her own ecstasies. These experiences are totally indescribable except for the few that I will mention here, as I heard them from her, and as the Lord grants me to remember them. The illuminations which this blessed soul received kept her continually absorbed in God and, in a manner incomprehensible to us, they were indeed continual and unceasing. Moreover, from the infinite and limitless ocean of divine riches, this blessed soul often received ever new and unprecedented gifts, superior to previous ones, which led her ever deeper into the fathomless abysses of God.

What took place during the celebration of the sacrifice of the Mass on the Sunday before the feast of the Indulgence

a. How Angela is led into the abyss of the divinity and simultaneously, during a vision of the Crucified, is transfixed by the sword of compassion

On the Sunday before the feast of the Indulgence, a Mass was being celebrated at the altar of the most reverend Virgin Mary in the upper church of the basilica of blessed Francis.[56] At about the time of the elevation of the body of the Lord, while the organ was playing the angelic hymn "Holy, holy, holy," Angela's soul was absorbed and transported into the uncreated light by the majestic power of the sovereign and uncreated God. The result of this ecstasy was such fruition and illumination as is totally indescribable. What is said here of this experience captures absolutely nothing of it, for no human words are eloquent enough to express the way the uncreated and omnipotent God powerfully draws the soul to himself. After her absorption into the fathomless depths of God and while she was still under the impact of this continuing vision, the image of the blessed crucified God and man appeared to her, looking as if he had just then been taken down from the cross. His blood flowed fresh and crimson as if the wounds had just recently been opened. Then she saw how the joints and tendons of his blessed body were torn and distended by the cruel stretching and pulling of his virginal limbs at the hands of those who had set upon him to kill him on the gibbet of the cross. The bones and sinews of his most holy body seemed completely torn out of their natural position; and yet his skin was not broken.

At this heartrending sight she was transfixed to the marrow with such compassion that in truth it seemed to her that she was totally transformed in spirit and body into the pain of the cross. At the sight of the dislocated limbs and the painful distension of the sinews, she felt herself pierced through even more than she had been at the sight of the open wounds. For the former granted her a deeper insight into the secret of his passion and the harsh cruelty of his executioners. The sight of the crucified body of the good and beloved Jesus stirred her to such compassion that when she saw it, all her own joints seemed to cry out with fresh laments, and her whole body and soul felt pierced anew from the painful impact of this divine vision. She was in a daze, because on the one hand, the uncreated God was refreshing and restoring her soul with the ineffable radiance of his most sweet divinity's fathomless splendor,

245

but on the other hand, the same blessed crucified God and man, Jesus, pierced her whole being with his compassionate crucifixion and his cruel death pains which he showed her. Thus the blessed and glorious Jesus, by an invisible act, had fittingly bestowed upon her soul, in a perfect manner, the double state of his own life. He did this by granting her a certain intuition which, through the transformative power of her compassion over his death, allowed her full contemplation of his life and crucifixion. For more than any one I have ever seen, she strove to outwardly conform herself totally to the life of Christ. But let us refrain from trying to praise her—for no words can be found to match her virtues—and proceed with our narrative.

b. In that vision she also contemplates the embrace, blessing, and exhortation which her spiritual sons received from Christ

While she was thus both totally absorbed in the experience of the sweetness of God and also crucified as a result of the vision of Christ crucified; while she was filled with joy and sorrow, sated with myrrh and honey, quasi-deified and crucified, suddenly a multitude of the sons of this holy mother appeared around the blessed and sorrowful Jesus. And he embraced each one of them with great love, and his hands drew each one's head close to himself as he made them kiss the wound at his side. The joy engendered in the soul of this mother by such deep love for her sons on the part of the blessed and crucified God and man made her forget the inner pain that had penetrated her soul at the sight of such harsh torments inflicted on him.

There seemed to be varying degrees of intensity in the way her sons were embraced and placed to Christ's side. He thrust some of them into his side more, some less, some more than once, and some he absorbed deep into his body. The redness of his blood colored the lips of some, and the whole face of others, according to the varying degrees mentioned. To each one he extended abundant blessings and said: "My sons, make manifest the way of my cross, my poverty, and my contempt—for especially now, those abound who keep these concealed. I have chosen each of you especially for the purpose of manifesting, by your example and word, my truth which is trampled on and hidden." This blessed soul also understood that even as each of the signs of Christ's love just mentioned appeared to her with varying degrees of intensity, likewise, the words spoken fitted the various degrees of Christ's intimacy with each of the sons. Although she had seen the degree each one was in, she did not wish to divulge it of any of them individually. And it did not seem to me to be appropriate to ask, for only one thing matters: that each one strive to the utmost to be joined to the blessed Crucified One and embrace his command to follow the way of contempt, poverty, and the cross with all their strength. She added that it was totally impossible to express the deep and tender love for his sons, which shone in the eyes of the blessed face of the God and man Jesus Christ as he embraced them and pressed them to his sacred wound, as well as in the many other signs of love, blessings as well as words, which he gave to them.

c. *The writer's reflections concerning the above visions*

I believe that the friars whom the Most High gave her as sons of her heart should pay close attention to what this holy mother told me. Generally speaking, the gifts she received—that is, the kind just mentioned—begin in her own elevations and her being set afire, and find their fulfillment in our reproduction of them. By such means, the blessed God clearly shows us that in her is the root from which comes everything we receive, and we are her crown and joy in the Lord. Thus the root of her fervent love may blossom and grow in us as if sending off shoots.

Moreover, we must ponder with great care what she also said, namely, that the elevations into the Uncreated and the transformation into the Crucified placed her in a continual state of being plunged into the fathomless depths of God and of being transformed into the Crucified, a state which she believes will be hers forever. These words and many others like them—though I do not know if I understand them correctly—seem to me to mean that this blessed soul was placed anew in a process of continual transformation in God and in his most infinite light and, in a way not previously experienced by her, into feeling the pain of the Crucified. Although for her this experience is continuous and uninterrupted as if it were an ongoing process, nonetheless, I believe this same experience grows with new ardor, joy, sweetness, and savor, but in the same mode as the original and continual illumination. That is, while the process is continual, it may change in intensity. Because of this, one can say that this process remains the same, and yet as far as the kinds of representations and the increase of ardor and sweetness go, what happens is new. But on this point she is the one who should be questioned, for having experienced this state she can speak of it better than I, who fumble for words and perhaps do not describe it accurately. I say this because she presented what occurred during the procession as something new. Given the resemblances between both these experiences, I can only understand her in the way I have just explained and which demonstrates their continuity.

For the total state of her soul is so beyond description that we can hardly stammer anything about it. This is not surprising since she herself, an expert and a teacher of these things, asserted that she could say absolutely nothing about them because their modality is totally beyond description. It seemed to her a kind of blasphemy to try to express the inexpressible. But her maternal instincts swayed her, and our persistent requests won her over, to some extent. Still, it must have been extremely painful for her. More than anyone else I ever knew, she was in the habit of saying: "My secret is mine."[57]

On the day of the procession to the church of St. Mary of the Angels, the same vision is repeated, with further development. During this vision, the Virgin Mary also embraces Angela's spiritual sons

On the day of the procession itself, while Angela was in the procession, going to the Church of Our Lady, she felt in a wonderful and totally undescribable way the unfathomable attraction of the uncreated God, as described above.[58] She saw the blessed triune God dwelling with all his majestic splendor in the souls of her sons, transforming them in diverse ways, according to the degrees mentioned previously. For her it was like being in paradise to see the divinity dwell in them in this way. God poured out his love so deeply and tenderly upon them that she found endless satisfaction in looking at them.

I who write this saw, with my own eyes, her face completely transformed and beaming with angelic, wondrous, and glorious joy. The blessing which the uncreated God showered upon her sons was so great, so sweet, and so heartfelt that it is better to be silent about it, because it is ineffable. Then God made this demand of the sons: "My beloved sons, offer yourselves to me as a holocaust, a total sacrifice, body and soul."—Consider, my brothers, how much we ought to love, by our affection and deeds, the one who so wholeheartedly gave himself to us, who claims us for himself so lovingly, and wishes to possess us so totally.

Then she also saw the crucified God and man in the manner just mentioned, and she was moved to such pain and compassion at the sight of his disjointed limbs (as previously indicated) that I pass over the description of it, for it is totally indescribable. During the entire procession, this image of the crucified Christ was held aloft before her eyes—and not by somebody carrying it. At the wish of the mother, all her sons, present and absent, gathered before the blessed Crucified One and, in the manner mentioned, he held them close to himself, embraced them, and pressed them to his side. He then said to them: "I am the one who takes away the sins of the world.⁵⁹ I have born the burden of all your sins, and these will not be imputed to you in eternity. For this is the bath which cleanses you, this the price of your redemption, this your dwelling place. Therefore, my sons, do not be afraid to defend and to manifest the truth of my way and life which is under attack, for I am always with you as your helper and defender."

On this occasion she was also shown, as so often in the past, the purification of all her sons according to three degrees. There is the general purification of every fault. There is also a special purification granted to a few, which consists of a great grace and the strength to avoid sin easily. Every purification adorns the soul with much beauty, but the beauty of the second purification is very great and very attractive, and the third gives such an extraordinary beauty that she absolutely refused to tell me anything about it, except that it was totally indescribable. As I kept insisting, she finally told me: "What do you want me to say? My sons seem to be so transformed in God that it is as if I see nothing but God in them, in both his glorified and suffering state, as if God had totally transubstantiated and absorbed them into the unfathomable depths of his life."

Then, as we approached the church of the most blessed mother of God she, the queen of mercy and mother of every grace—who had before appeared exalted on high—now leaned down toward her sons and daughters, and in a new and most gracious manner redoubled her most sweet blessings. She kissed them all on the breast, some more, some less, and some she held closely in her arms, as well as kissing them. Her love for them was so great that, as she appeared, totally numinous, she seemed to absorb them into the almost infinite light within her breast. It did not seem to Christ's faithful one that she saw arms of flesh, but a wonderful and very soft light into which the mother of God absorbed them as she hid them within her breast and held them with a great and deeply felt love.

During the sacrifice of the Mass, on the morning of the feast of the Indulgence, there is added to the preceding vision one in which St. Francis blesses, praises and exhorts Angela's spiritual sons

On the morning of the feast of the Indulgence[60] during the first part of the Mass celebrated near the ambo, the Lord did many things for Angela. Among other things, the blessed Francis appeared to her, glorified, and greeted her in his usual fashion: "May the peace of the Most High be with you." He always greeted her with a most pious, very humble, gracious, and affectionate voice. He then highly praised the intentions of those of his sons who burned with zeal to observe the poverty prescribed by the Rule, and he exhorted them to grow in deeds. Then he said: "May the eternal, full, and abundant blessing which I received from the eternal God descend upon the heads of these most beloved sons, yours and mine. Tell them that they are to help me by following the way of Christ and making it manifest in word and deed. And they should have no fears, for I am with them and the eternal God is there to help them." Francis praised these sons very affectionately for their good intentions and encouraged them to proceed with confidence, for he himself would assist their resolve. He then blessed them so lovingly that he seemed to pour himself totally out in his love for them.

After the pilgrimage, Angela herself applies the message of the visions to her spiritual sons

She had many other ineffable visions which concerned her and her sons but which I could not extract from her. As for the little I have written—which is rich in meaning and substance—even if it loses something as I tell it I have nonetheless written it as faithfully as I could. Finally, however, overcome by my importuning she finally told me, with much difficulty and distress, Why do you want to know so much? The blessed God himself has poured himself totally out in love for you, and so has his most sweet mother. They wish to bear all the burden of your penance. They only ask that you be shining examples of their pain-filled, very poor, and despised life. Their will and their desire is that they might see you dead to this life; that your dwelling place be in heaven; and that you have only the use of your body in this world. And as someone dead is not affected by either honors or insults, so you too must be unperturbed by any outer events and preach to others more by the mortification of your lives than by contentious discourse.[61] They likewise wish that all you do be directed toward heaven and the blessed and uncreated crucified God and man so that while outwardly you work, speak, and eat, inwardly you are always immersed in the blessed God who wants to bear you always within himself and assist you in all your actions.[62]

May he who, in his mercy, saw fit to ask this of us also see fit to fulfill his plan in us through the merits of his glorious mother and through the intercession of his beloved servant, our mother. On her merits, as onto a root, he has been willing to graft us like saplings, so that through her, that is, with her salutary examples and these same merits as our ladder,[63] we may ascend without ceasing to the heights of her most excellent life and the transformation of ourselves into the most holy passion of the Crucified. May we continue our ascent until we enter together with the blessed Jesus into the bosom of the Father, and find our rest there, the rest of those who are blessed for ever and ever. Amen.

INSTRUCTION V:
CONCERNING HUMILITY AND THE REASONS FOR ACQUIRING IT

A humble heart entails the imitation of the life of Christ and the Virgin Mary and is the foundation of all virtues as well as the light for the knowledge of God and self

Behold, my blessed sons, and observe the model of your life, the suffering God and man, and learn from him the form of all perfection.[64] Observe his life, be attentive to his teachings, and with all your affection, run after him, so that led by him you may successfully attain the cross. He gave himself as an example and exhorts us to look at him with the eye of the spirit as he says: "Learn from me for I am meek and humble of heart and you will find rest for your souls."[65]

My sons, be attentive, look with your most profound gaze into the depths of this doctrine, the sublimity of this teaching. Note its basis and its roots. Christ did not say: "Learn from me to fast," although as an example to us and for our salvation, he fasted forty days and forty nights.[66] He did not say: "Learn from me to despise the world and to live in poverty," although he lived in very great poverty and wished that his disciples live in the same way. He did not say: "Learn from me to perform miracles," although he himself performed miracles by his own power and wished that his disciples do so in his name. But he said simply: "Learn from me because I am meek and humble of heart."

The truth of the matter is that he set forth humility of heart and meekness as the foundation and firmest basis for all the other virtues. For neither abstinence, severe fasting, outward poverty, shabby clothing, outward show of good works, the performance of miracles—none of these amount to anything without humility of heart. Rather, abstinence will become blessed, austerity and shabby clothes will become blessed, good deeds will become blessed and full of life, when they are solidly founded in humility. Humility of heart is the matrix in which all the other virtues and virtuous works are engendered and from which they spring, much as the trunk and branches spring from a root. It is because this virtue is so precious, because this foundation is so firm and solid, upon which is built the perfection of all spiritual life, that the Lord wished especially that we should learn it from him. And it is because humility of heart is the root and guardian of all the other virtues that the Virgin Mary, as if forgetting the many other virtues which abounded in her soul and body, commended herself only for humility and affirmed it as the principal reason for the incarnation of God in her, saying: "Because he has looked upon the humility of his servant, etc."[67] Be eager, therefore, my sons, to get yourselves a firm base in humility, and in every way to entrench yourselves in it, so that, as members united to the head, in nature and in truth, you can, in humility and through it, find and possess rest for your souls.

O my sons, where can a creature find rest or peace if not in him who is the sovereign rest and peace, the sovereign source of peacefulness and tranquility for your souls? But no soul will be able to attain him if it is not grounded in humility. For without humility of heart all the other virtues by which one runs toward God seem—and are—absolutely worthless. This humility of heart that the God-man wished us to learn from him is a life-giving and clear light which opens the understanding of the soul so that it perceives both its own vileness and nothingness and the immensity of divine goodness. The more the soul realizes the magnitude of the divine goodness, the more it advances in the knowledge of itself. The more it perceives and knows that it is nothing, the more it will rise up to know and praise the ineffability of the divine goodness which its humility makes it perceive and understand so fully. And from this, all the other virtues begin to blossom.[68]

As the first of all virtues, the love of God and neighbor, springs from humility, so do all the other virtues originate in the light of humility

Indeed, the primary virtue of all, which is the love of God and neighbor, originates in the light of humility. For the soul, perceiving its own nothingness, and perceiving God lowering himself for such vile nothingness and even united to this nothingness, is set ablaze with love for God, and in this burning love is transformed into God. And thus transformed by love, is there any creature who would not return this love with all its strength? Truly, the soul thus transformed loves, with the love of God, every creature as is fitting, because in every creature it perceives, understands, and recognizes God's presence. Hence the soul finds joy and delight in the good fortune of a neighbor and grieves and is saddened at anyone's misfortune. This is so because of the kindness of its disposition.

Seeing the spiritual or corporeal misfortunes of a neighbor, those who lead the spiritual life do not become puffed up by their own well-being and presume to judge or despise that person. For enlightened by the light of humility the soul sees itself perfectly, and seeing itself, it becomes aware and even knows that it has fallen in the same plight as its neighbor; or, if it has not fallen, it knows and understands it was not able by itself alone to resist falling, but by the help of God's grace and grace holding the soul in its hand making it strong in the face of evil. For such a soul, judgment of one's neighbor is not a source of pride but rather a reason for becoming more humble. Perceiving the defects of its neighbor makes it look at itself and makes it see very clearly its own evil and defects in which it has fallen or would have fallen had it not been for the supporting hand of God. When it sees the bodily ills of its neighbor, the transforming love of God makes it consider them as its own. It grieves and feels the compassion of the apostle, who said: "Who is weak that I am not affected by it?" and so forth.[69] Thus, just as I said that the virtue of love takes its origin from the root of humility, so the same can be said for faith, hope, and all the other virtues. For all of them, according to the particular nature of each, are initiated by and spring from humility as their foundation. It would take too long to demonstrate this for each one in particular; perhaps one can reflect on this more profitably in silence.

Humility provides peace for individual souls and peace in society. It brings security to every union and is conducive to self-control in speech

I tell you all this, my sons, so that you may stand firm on this foundation, find your strength in it, and strive to grow in it. For the life of those who are established in this humility is very angelic, pure, kind, and peaceful. And because humble persons are most kind, they are affable and loving to all, especially toward the predestined,[70] for whose conversions they are set up as a light and as an example; for it is through kindness and meekness that the predestined are most quickly converted. And because the peace of humble persons is an interior peace, no adversity can trouble them, for they can say with the apostle: "Who can separate us from the love of Christ? Can trial, or distress or hunger," and so forth.[71]

Run then, my blessed sons, and do not rest in your search until you have achieved your foundation in this humility without which you cannot progress in the way of God. I see this search as very useful and necessary for you, for without humility all the other virtues seem to me to be worthless. My sons, satisfy my desire and stand firm upon this virtue. Quench, my sons, the thirst I have to see you deepen to the very depths the knowledge of yourselves and your own vileness. Satisfy, my sons, my desire which causes me such anguish, such a thirst and a hunger—namely, that from this deep knowledge of yourselves you may be plunged into the fathomless depths of the immense goodness of God. If you are thus immersed in the depths of the immensity of God and the knowledge of yourselves then you will acquire a solid foundation in this said humility.[72]

As a result you will no longer be prone to disputes and quarrels. Instead, like the suffering God-man, you will be like the deaf who do not hear, the mutes who do not speak; and you will become a true member of the body of Jesus Christ, who, according to the word of the apostle, was not in the habit of getting involved in quarrels.[73] How much good is accomplished by humility! It renders peaceful and quiet the souls of those who are filled with it. The exterior peace which they have as a result of their inner peace is so great that if they hear harsh words addressed to them or perhaps against some truth, they do not seek to justify themselves with excuses; their only response is a brief and submissive one. If a false charge is laid against them, they prefer to confess their ignorance of it and claim that they do not understand what they have been told, rather than respond contentiously. As to this mode of curbing the tongue, I can see no other source from which it proceeds than this twofold immersion in the fathomless depths of the divinity, that is, in the immensity of the goodness of God and in the knowledge of one's own vileness; and this is found in the light of the said humility.

True humility is acquired through prayer and meditation on "The Book of Life," that is, the passion of Christ in his soul, his body and each of his members, which has atoned for the sins of all

But I ask you, where does one find this humility, this feeling of one's vileness, this light, this immersion into the depths, this curbed tongue? Which path leads to it? Most definitely, all these are found in fervent, pure, and continual prayer.[74] It is mainly in such prayer that the soul learns to look at and read the Book of Life, that is, the life and death of the crucified God and man. The sight of the cross gives the soul perfect knowledge of its own sins, which leads to humility. In that same cross it sees the multitude of its sins and how it has offended God with all its members. And in the cross it sees the ineffable outpouring of God's mercy toward it and how for the sins of each of its members, the God-man endured the most cruel suffering in each member of his blessed body.[75]

The soul, when it gazes upon the cross, considers how it has offended God with its head by washing, combing, and perfuming it in order to be admired by others to the displeasure of God. Then it perceives that as penance for these sins, the head of the God-man was wounded and suffered great pain. It is because of the soul's abuses in washing, combing, and perfuming that his hair was pulled out from his most holy head, his head was pricked and pierced with sharp thorns which cruelly bloodied him all over with his precious blood, and then beaten with a reed.

The soul also sees how it offended God with its whole face, and in particular with its eyes, nose, ears, mouth, and tongue. Then it considers how, as penance for these sins, the face of Jesus was covered with opprobrium. Because of the sins the soul perceives it has committed through washing, it sees Christ badly battered and filthy with spittle.[76] Because it gazed with impropriety, resting its eyes on empty and harmful objects in which it took pleasure against God's will, for these sins of our eyes the soul sees the eyes of Christ bleared by the blood which ran over them from his head so cruelly pierced with thorns, and sees his eyes bathed with tears from his weeping on the cross. Because it has also offended God with its ears, by hearing empty and harmful conversations, and because it took pleasure in these, it sees the most horrible penance Christ endured for this kind of sin. He heard with his ears the horrible shouts of his enemies: "Crucify him, crucify him."[77] He heard himself condemned by a wicked man[78] for the redemption of humanity, and heard mockery and blasphemy directed at him by impious men. Because, also, the soul has offended God with its mouth and tongue by uttering empty and death-dealing words, and by delighting in fancy foods, the mouth of Christ was soiled with spittle and his lips and mouth made to taste the bitterness of vinegar and gall. Because, also, it has offended God by taking pleasure in fragrant perfumes, the soul realizes that Christ's own nostrils smelled the terrible stench of spittle for us.[79]

By looking at the cross, the soul also considers how its neck offended God by swaying to and fro in fits of anger and pride and for such sins it sees Christ buffeted by the most cruel blows.[80]

It sees, too, that it has offended God by illicit embraces and movements of its shoulders, and for these it considers how Christ did penance by embracing the cross with his holy arms, carrying it on his shoulders while the crowds jeered.[81] It also perceives that its hands and feet have offended God by illicit caresses and advances, by things it has touched and places it has walked, and because of this Christ was stretched out on the cross, extended in every direction, spread out like a skin; his holy hands and feet nailed to the cross, cruelly wounded and pierced by the points of horrible nails.[82]

The soul also considers how it has offended God by its affected and precious style of dress, and because of this it sees Christ stripped and shamefully raised on the cross while the soldiers divided his clothing among themselves.[83]

The soul also perceives that it has offended God with its entire body; and for such offenses it sees Christ's whole body suffer repeated flagellations and horrible torments; it sees him pierced with a lance and his entire body bloodied with his precious blood.[84] Because the soul took inward pleasure in each of its sins, it sees the most holy soul of

Christ endure a multitude of diverse and horrible pains: that is, the passion which his body endured tortured and crucified his soul unspeakably; so did his compassion for his most holy mother; the violation of divine reverence caused by sin; and also his compassion for our misery. All these pains and sufferings put together, horribly and unspeakably, crucified Christ's soul.[85]

The need to go to the cross of the Lord and to gaze upon it so as to receive a contrite and humble heart as well as the abnegation of the use of the senses, or "spiritual circumcision"

Come then, my blessed sons, let us look at the cross, weep with me for Christ who died on it for our iniquities, for we are the ones responsible for his great suffering.

Those who have not offended God with all their members and all of themselves, as I have, who am nothing but sin, should not grieve or weep less, for they would not have resisted sin had not the grace of God come to their defense; and for this defense they have not been grateful. Hence they too should be grieving.

And if some have not offended God mortally, they should nonetheless grieve and weep. For in their state of purity and virginity they have not striven to please God as much as they should have done; and likewise they have not offered the example to others they should have offered. They have in this fashion tarnished their purity.

Hence it is fitting that all should weep and all should grieve while lifting the eyes of their souls toward the cross on which the God-man Jesus Christ did such horrible penance and endured such harsh affliction for our sins. As has been said, the sight of the cross, toward which only a true and continual prayer can lead the soul, will bestow upon the soul full knowledge, awareness, sorrow, and contrition for sins, and the light of the said humility.

When the soul sees its sins, each and every one, from the point of view of the cross and sees Christ tormented, afflicted, and sorrowful for each and every sin, it too grieves and is similarly saddened over them. And in this grief, it begins to punish and discipline each of its members and all the senses with which it used to offend God. It thus receives a real and spiritual circumcision, of which Christ, in his own circumcision, wanted to be an image. For the main reason for Christ's circumcision was to give us an example of what spiritual circumcision consists, the one bestowed on the soul, as has been said, from looking at the cross.[86]

Strive, my blessed sons, to acquire this circumcision so that those who took pleasure in offending God with their eyes by looking at empty and harmful things now circumcise their eyes by forbidding them every illicit glance and washing them clean by weeping every night. Let those who see they have offended God by their gluttony now circumcise and punish their mouths by abstaining from the pleasures of the table and maintaining sobriety of soul and body. As for those who have offended God with their mouths and tongues by speaking arrogantly, spreading scandal, slandering others, indulging in vain discourse, or perhaps blaspheming, let them now circumcise and punish their tongues by confessing their sins, by addressing their neighbors with words of peace and holy exhortations, by devoting themselves especially to the praise of God in continual prayer, and by observing holy silence as much as possible. Apply yourselves, my blessed sons, and consecrate to Christ the Lord all your members, all your senses, all the movements of your soul, and all things with which you remember having offended him, in order to convert the number of your sins into an accumulation of merits.

In order to do better, examine your life carefully every day; recollect yourselves for this purpose at least once a day; and pass in review before the eyes of your soul all the time that has gone by. If the time has been well spent, praise the Lord, and if to the contrary, moan and grieve for the evil you have done. This is the true circumcision of the soul prefigured in Christ's own circumcision. Let us give thanks to God.

INSTRUCTION VI:
THE SIGN OF TRUE LOVE, NAMELY, CARRYING OUT THE WILL OF THE BELOVED, ADMITS OF THREE STAGES AND DISTINCTIONS

The first sign of true love is that the lover submits his will to that of the Beloved. And this most special and singular love works in three ways.[87]

First, if the loved one is poor, one strives to become poor, and if scorned, to be scorned.

Second, it makes one abandon all other friendships which could be contrary to this love, and leave behind father, mother, sister, brother, and all other affections contrary to the will of the Beloved.

Third, one can keep nothing hidden from the other. This third action, in my opinion, is the highest one and completes all the others. For in this mutual revelation of secrets, hearts are opened and bound more perfectly to one another.

INSTRUCTION VII:
THE CAUSE AND THE REASONS FOR TEMPTATIONS;
THEIR ROLE IN PURIFYING THE SOUL
OF ITS FAULTS, CULPABILITY, AND INDEBTEDNESS

Temptation is an instrument of God's justice, and its salutary effect is to punish us for our past sins

I am blinded, filled with darkness, and without any truth. Therefore, my sons, suspect, as from an evil person, all the words you hear from me. Carefully evaluate everything I say, and do not believe any of my words unless they match those of Jesus Christ.[88]

I find no pleasure in writing to you now. I am compelled to do so because of the many letters you have written to me.[89] However, I will write what has been freshly stamped in my heart: If someone offends God by a certain vice, that person should be punished by this same vice.[90]

I speak first of the vice of pride, which is the root of all evil.[91] When by the grace of God a soul is made humble, it makes every effort to expel pride from itself. When it is born again in God, it does indeed become humble and desires with its whole heart to be without pride. Nonetheless, pride comes to the soul in spite of itself. And when pride comes to it in this way and the soul takes pleasure in it, it is culpable. And when pride comes without giving pleasure, the soul is filled with bitterness and affliction. Ultimately, however, when pride comes without giving pleasure, the soul is established on the seat of truth and is no longer capable of any pride. Thus pride comes without the soul's assent in order to punish it for its past consent. Therefore, console yourselves, my sons, and take strength from the fact that God wants to punish the defect in you by means of the same defect.

The same thing applies to the vice of avarice. The sight of God's bounty expands the soul. This vice, nonetheless, stimulates it to punish itself for past faults. So it is with vice of the flesh. Not only the souls

259

who have fallen into committing actual deeds of the flesh should be punished, but even those who through their own negligence have fallen by the most fleeting thought. Therefore, my dear sons, do not be surprised if we are punished by temptations, because every fault must receive its due punishment.

Are you not aware that no one can drive away vainglory and hypocrisy from oneself? And this is so because of a past fault or for the sake of the soul's increase in merit. Therefore, whatever happens, let us be content if we come out victorious.

Are you not also aware that when you recite the Divine Office and are not totally present to it as you ought to be, you deserve to be punished? Thus when you recite the Office you do and you do not, because you are not totally present to it. This troubles you and you start over again from the beginning, and this very struggle is your just punishment. And when you want to go back and meditate on what you have just said, you are immediately distracted and do not remember anything about it. This happens as a punishment for our malice. For when we pray God wants us to be totally present and not divided. Therefore when we pray, let us keep our heart totally present to God, and not divided, because when our heart is divided we lose the fruit of true prayer. But we do not need to be totally present in our other activities, such as eating and drinking, our comings and goings, and the like. If we wish to feel the fruit of true prayer, while at the same time performing our various other occupations, we are to keep our heart totally present to God. If we are tempted while praying, it is because our hearts are not totally committed to prayer.

When we are tempted we should consider two things. We should first consider the justice of God, who exercises his vengeance upon us. Let us greatly rejoice when we see this justice of God in action against us, for whatever God does, he does justly. Second, when we are tempted we should consider it just, because it is our own fault. Let us greatly grieve over this because we have indeed offended God shamefully.

Temptations arise from imperfections of the soul and are eradicated by God's love, which gradually and profoundly transforms the soul

If we wish to be freed from our temptations, we should be transformed completely into the loving God and seek his will; and seeking it, be united to it; and united to it, examine all its qualities; and in doing so, put them into practice. When we have put them into practice with strength and courage, no vice can remain in us.

There are three qualities necessary for lovers.

The first is to become transformed according to the will of the Beloved.[92] This will seems to me to be revealed by his example: poverty, suffering, contempt, humiliation, and true obedience. When the soul devotes itself completely to putting these qualities into practice, no vice nor temptation can find room in it.

A second transformation occurs when the soul has a great desire to be transformed into the qualities of the Beloved. I will cite only three of these, for you know them better than I. The first is love, which consists of loving all creatures according to what is appropriate to each. The second is to become truly humble and kind. The third quality is the one God grants to his legitimate sons, namely immutability. For the closer the soul is to God, the more immutable does it become. This is why we should be ashamed when we are disturbed by any vile occurrences; in such cases we should recognize our miserable condition.

The third transformation consists in the total transformation into God. The soul is then outside the scope of all temptations because it is no longer in itself but in the One who is. But when we return to our miserable condition, let us be on our guard against all creatures and ourselves. I beg you, be master of yourselves and do not hand yourself over totally to any creature. Rather, give yourself totally to the One who is.

Exhortation to beware of certain temptations in pastoral ministry, that is, giving way to flattery and empty discourse rather than proclaiming the holy truth

When one of you preaches, hears confessions, or gives counsel, he should not keep his mind on creatures, but on the Creator. Do not behave like fools, for whatever the fool has his eye on, there is his whole heart. When you come across flatterers, men or women, who tell you: "Brother, your words have converted me to penance," do not pay any attention to them but rather turn to the Creator and thank him for this blessing. There are many preachers of falsehoods whose preaching is full of greed, and out of greed they preach for honors, money, and fame. My beloved sons, I wish with all my heart that you preach the holy truth and that the book you rely on be the God-man.[93] I do not tell you to give up your books, but that you should always be willing to do this, whether you keep them or abandon them.[94] I do not want you to be like those who preach only with words of learning and dryly report the deeds of saints, but rather speak about them with the same divine savor as they had who performed these deeds. Those who have first preached well to themselves with this divine savor know how to preach well to others.

A very special remedy for all temptations is the meditation on the virginity of Mary, the mother of God

There is another very special remedy for all temptations. It consists in vividly calling to mind the virginity and uprightness which the mother of God possessed to a most singular degree. Keep in mind too how perfectly she loves these virtues, and how she loves to see them brought to perfection in all the sons of God. And we should look at how these virtues were loved by the God-man himself. The sight of this does two things: It chases away all temptations from us, and it teaches us to be totally circumcised inside and out. Therefore, my sons, may the memory of these virtues of the mother of God be always in your soul. Amen.

INSTRUCTION VIII: TO SERVE, LOVE, AND SUFFER BECAUSE OF THE KINDNESS OF GOD

O my son, I desire with all that I am that you be a lover and disciple of suffering.[95] I also desire with all that I am that you be deprived of every temporal and spiritual consolation. For such is the source of my consolation, and I ask you that it be yours. I do not intend to serve or love for any reward, but I intend to serve and to love because of the incomprehensible goodness of God. I desire that you grow anew and be reborn in this desire so that you are deprived of all consolation for the love of the God and man Jesus Christ who was likewise deprived. I am not sending you any other greeting than this one, namely, that you always grow in divine union, and that you be always in a state of tribulation, hunger, and thirst for as long as you live.

INSTRUCTION IX:
TO ACHIEVE UNION OF MIND AND HEART
IT IS NECESSARY TO BECOME LITTLE

O you who are dearest to my soul, I desire for you what I desire for my companion and myself: that you always be of one mind and that there be no divisions among you.[96] I desire that you have in your souls what leads from discord to unanimity, namely, becoming little. When you are little, you do not consider yourself self-sufficient because of your knowledge or natural abilities, but rather you are always inclined to acknowledge your defects and your miserable condition; you question yourself and contend against yourself so as to convince yourself of your defects and strive to correct them. To be little also means that you are not a threat or a burden to others; nor are your words contentious, even if your life strikes a powerful blow to all those who are opposed to this littleness. This is what I desire from you, my dearest ones, that by following this way of littleness and poverty, disciplined zeal and compassion, your life may be, even when your tongue is silent, a clear mirror for those who wish to follow this way, and a sharp-edged sword against the enemies of truth.

O my beloved, forgive me my pride—I who am the proudest of all and a daughter of pride—if I dare to admonish you and lead you in the direction of humility, even though I am the very contrary of humility.[97] It is my zeal for you and my confidence in you which makes me speak this way. I speak with you with as much assurance as I do to my own soul. Please, although I have spoken arrogantly, forgive me, because of the confidence with which I speak to you.

My dearest ones, my soul will be greatly put at ease if I hear from you that having become little has made you of one heart and soul, for without this unity, in truth, I do not see how you can please God.

INSTRUCTION X:
ON FLEEING THE MANIFOLD SNARES OF AMBITION
IN ORDER TO BE MORE ATTENTIVE TO GOD

The only thing necessary for us is God.[98] Finding God consists in recollecting our souls in him. For the soul to better recollect itself in God, it must cut off every superfluous practice, familiarity with others, useless talk, and the search for novelty. In short, one must separate one's soul from all which disperses it and bring it to know the abyss of its miseries. The soul must think about what it did in the past, what it is doing in the present, and, finally, consider attentively how much good it can ascribe to God. Let us not let a day pass without mulling over these thoughts; and if the day goes by, at least let us not let the night go by. Turn, O soul, toward knowing the mercy of God, how Jesus Christ behaved toward you in all your miseries. Be on your guard against ingratitude and do not forget the blessings you have received.

Be on guard against pride. Fight against honors and every source of vanity—spiritual as well as temporal honors, gluttony, and avarice. Do not seek anything, be it small or great, which can make you greedy. Try to live without cares[99] and without any desire to be self-sufficient. For all these are indeed daughters of pride, which prevent the soul from reaching the heights.

INSTRUCTION XI:
ON PUBLIC AND PRIVATE PENANCE

On another occasion, she said that if all by yourself you performed all the penances which everyone in the world has performed, this would not suffice for you to merit those things which are promised and awaited. Therefore, you should try to do in private as much penance as possible and even desire to do those penances which you cannot do and are beyond your capacity. You should also do penance in public, provided your motive is not to be seen doing it. To abstain from doing something good only in order not to be seen is to be lukewarm. You should never abstain for such a motive. In these things we have the example of the Master who did many things which were never known and yet his love was so great that he also did many things in public.[100]

INSTRUCTION XII:
THE NECESSITY OF ENDURING TRIBULATIONS
IN ORDER TO CARRY OUT THE WILL OF GOD
WITH A LOVE THAT IS PURE

She also said: The tribulations of this world mean eternal consolations.[101] Therefore you should not worry too much about temporal tribulations, for they will come to an end.

Poor me, I am asking something of you, dear, and I am embarrassed —because you know in your sleep, better than I do wide awake, the meaning of the tribulations you are telling me about—although if I were really a good Christian, tribulations would be consolations for me.[102]

I beg you not to be concerned with outer activities which now are so inviting to you, and by means of which the world continually invites you. You know better than I that the sons who are sons only through creation act differently than those who are sons through grace. There is no doubt that the one who loves much wants to be loved much; and the one who gives all wants all in return. I beg you, also, dear son, that you do God's will in all that you do. For I believe that you wish to become the beloved son of God, who wants you not only partially, but totally. I therefore beg you not to be carried away by the thought of either gaining or losing honors and temporal advantages, but to do all things according to the will of the Supreme Good.

My son, bear the fact that others afflict you rather than you afflict them. This the Master teaches, who sustained all things and did not want to return the like to others.

Fill your sensitive soul, dear son, with the presence of the un-created God. Work at, and consider well, the noble vocation to which God has called you. And if the uncreated God has established himself in you, I beg you that you establish yourself in him. Grow! Grow! Grow!

May all my salutations and well-wishing find their fulfillment in the one who is the source of all salvation and well-being! Help fulfil my desire: I hunger for your progress. Pray the supreme Good that I be sated with the knowledge of your progress.

The light, the love, the peace of the Most High be with you! I am not worthy to grant you a blessing, nor do I deserve one. But if out of his goodness, God wishes to grant me his blessing, I want to let go of it on your behalf and grant it to you according to God's wishes.

INSTRUCTION XIII:
THAT TRIBULATIONS ARE OPPORTUNITIES
AND BLESSINGS IN THE LIFE
OF THE SONS OF GOD

Once, as a response to a group undergoing tribulations, she said the following to console them.[103]

Concerning the tribulations which you are suffering, I extend to you my heartfelt sympathy and envy. When you are afflicted and tested within and without, it is most certainly a sign that you are among the loved ones of the Beloved. This was the lot of our Teacher, as you know better than I. My tongue cannot express nor my heart imagine the extent of the tribulations which our Master endured in his soul. Our own tribulations, however, come from a different source than his. When our lesser troubles come, let us strive with all our strength to struggle through them victoriously, endure them patiently, even rejoice in these temporal tribulations which have an end, and love them with all our heart. For if we suffer tribulations, it is a sign that we are loved by the beloved God and he is giving us a pledge of his inheritance. Consider the pain of the suffering Christ and it will be a remedy for all your suffering. The Son of God was afflicted by evil for our benefit.

There are three things which these most holy, and misunderstood, tribulations accomplish in the soul. First, they make the soul turn to God, or if it has already done so, they prompt it to greater conversion and closer adherence to him. Second, tribulations make the soul grow. When rain comes on well-prepared soil, it germinates and bears fruit; so, likewise, when tribulations come, the soul grows in virtue. Third, tribulations purify, comfort, and quiet the soul, and give it peace and tranquility.

These most holy tribulations are very appropriate for us. Therefore, you should not try to change what God is doing in you, for tribulations are very useful, not only for you, but for many others. I believe with all my heart that these most holy and misunderstood tribulations are sure signs, worthy and noble advocates, trustworthy witnesses by which we are more strongly accredited before God. I likewise firmly believe that nothing unites us so well to God, keeps us united among ourselves, and leads us to God the way these most holy tribulations can. Do not be astonished, then, if I have a holy envy of you.

I ask that you do not forget me, for you are never away from my thoughts. I am also firmly convinced, my sons, that we do not really know what noble effects emerge from holy tribulations. Because if we did, we would go after them avidly.

May the light of those who suffer trials be with you. May the love and peace of the Most High be with you. May the blessing of the most high God be with you forever, my sons, and also with us. May all our salutations and well-wishing be fulfilled in him who is our salvation and well-being. Farewell, stay with the thought of the suffering God-man and his virgin mother, and do not be ungrateful to him. Pray for my companion Masazuola, who is more ill than usual, and for me, the vilest of creatures.

INSTRUCTION XIV:
TRUE KNOWLEDGE OF GOD AND SELF IS THE BASIS AND GUARDIAN OF ALL PIETY

Do not be surprised, my dearest sons, if I have not answered the several letters you have written to me.[104] It is because I have been bound to God that I have not been able to write to you or to any others, nor could I give you any spiritual advice except the very ordinary words which follow. There are only two things in the world that I find pleasure in speaking about, namely, knowledge of God and self, and remaining continually in one's cell and never leaving it. If you leave your cell, you should strive to return to it with sorrow and true contrition. I believe that anyone who does not know how to stay put and remain in a cell ought not to go anywhere; it is not for them to seek out any other kind of good, and they ought not to probe into things which are above them.

O my dearest sons, of what use are revelations, visions, feelings of God's presence, sweetnesses from him? Of what use are gifts of wisdom, elevations? Of what use even is contemplation? Indeed all these are useless unless one has a true knowledge of God and self. That is why I am surprised that you expect letters from me, because I do not see that my letters or my words should or could console you, nor can I see how you could receive consolation from them unless they bestow upon you the kind of knowledge I am referring to. I find delight in speaking about this truth and nothing else; and silence has been imposed on me for everything else.

I ask you, my dear sons, to pray to God to give us this light, to me and to all my offspring, and to make us always remain in it.

I would add that the vision of the Uncreated, the love that springs from the vision of the Uncreated, is itself the guard and protection for this vision. But love and charity sometimes do not keep guard well, and reveal the secrets of this vision—love being made to expand. Therefore, another guard has been posted: It is the holy zeal which is born of this true vision of the Uncreated and this guards it better than love. Because of the strict guard this zeal sets up, it makes what is certain, uncertain, and what is black, white. Then the vision itself rises up, puts aside both love and zeal, and is its own protection.

This is why, my sons, I ask you to forgive me, because this is the bond that the vision of the Uncreated has put on me, and it has imposed silence upon me.[105] To whatever extent I need to apologize I accuse the rightness of this vision which knows well its rightness; thus it speaks and it will make me say everything which will be necessary for you and others.

May all our salutations find their fulfillment in the resurrection of the Lord and in the renewal he realizes in his most perfect loved ones.

INSTRUCTION XV:
THE LEGITIMATE SONS OF GOD THE FATHER NEED THE TEACHINGS OF THE "BOOK OF LIFE," THE CRUCIFIED, IN ORDER TO BE TRANSFORMED INTO HIM

O dearest son, if you wish to have the light of divine grace, and a heart free from all care, if you wish to curb all harmful temptations, and to be made perfect in the ways of God, do not tarry in running to the cross of Christ.[106] Truly there is no other way for the sons of Christ to manage to find God, and having found him, to hold on to him, but in the life and the way of the suffering God and man which, as I have been in the habit of saying and which I reaffirm here, is the Book of Life, the reading of which no one can have access to except through continual prayer. Continual prayer elevates, illumines, and transforms the soul. Illumined by the light perceived in prayer, the soul sees clearly the way of Christ prepared and trodden by the feet of the Crucified; running along this way with an expanded heart, it not only distances itself from the weighty cares of the world but rises above itself to taste divine sweetness. Then it is set ablaze by divine fire. Thus illumined, elevated, and set ablaze, it is transformed into the God-man. All this is achieved by gazing on the cross in continual prayer.

Hence, my dearest son, fling yourself upon this cross, ask him who died on it for you to enlighten you to know yourself fully, so that plunged deep in the knowledge of your own defects, you can be uplifted to know fully the sweetness of divine goodness which seemed incomprehensible to you when, so full of defects as you were, God lifted you up to divine sonship, and promised to be your Father. Do not, therefore, be ungrateful toward him, but strive to accomplish in everything the will of so great and so lovable a Father. For if legitimate sons cannot accomplish what pleases the Father, how will the adulterous ones be able to do so? Adulterous sons are the ones who stray from the discipline of the cross through concupiscence of the flesh. Legitimate sons, on the other hand, are the ones who strive to conform themselves in every way to their teacher and Father who suffered for them. They do so by following him in poverty, suffering, and contempt. For certainly, my dear son, these three things are the basis and the fulfillment of all perfection. For in these three, the soul is truly enlightened, perfected, purged, and most fittingly prepared for divine transformation.

INSTRUCTION XVI:
THE SIX SIGNS BY WHICH GOD MANIFESTS HIS LOVE

There are six signs by which the Father shows his love.[107] The first sign is his blessing; God the Father first blesses the soul he loves. Second, he communicates his riches to it. Third, he admonishes it. Fourth, he corrects it. Fifth, he guards and defends it. Finally, sixth, he preserves it.

INSTRUCTION XVII:
THE EXPECTATION OF THE NATIVITY
OF THE CHILD JESUS BESTOWS
TRUE KNOWLEDGE OF SELF AND
LOVE OF TRIBULATIONS

O dearest one, part of my soul, I desire with my whole self that I might hear tell of you, that in your soul you desire, as the saints did, and do now, the Child who is soon to come and be born; and that he be born in your soul according to my desire.[108]

O dearest one to my soul, strive to know yourself, because, in truth, I do not believe that there is a greater virtue on earth. Try to rid yourself of every thought, every imagination harmful to your soul. Prepare yourself, as is my desire, to receive this Son about to be born, because, in truth, he is the one who will grant you knowledge of yourself. He will be the salvation of your soul, which I desire from the depths of my soul. And now may the Consoler console you, my soul!

I am astonished by what you wrote me concerning the tribulations which you endured when you were at Spello. I am not unedified but rather edified by what you wrote, for what you consider to be signs of hatred, I consider as signs of love. But then I thought that this was the same envy that I sometimes feel toward Masazuola when I believe she is more united to God than I. Know, my soul, that I became indignant only out of compassion for you. Your tribulations moved me more than my own. I ask you, therefore, as strongly as I can, not to worry any more about these tribulations. Forget them completely for know that when they are gone from you they will have gone from me as well. I experienced tribulation in reading the letter you wrote me.

Keep in mind, my dearest son, that no creature has ever bound me through hatred or love—or ever will. Do not pay attention to exterior signs, because they are not always true. There is a love that can be demonstrated by signs, and a love which cannot be demonstrated by signs. I ask you, my dearest son, to become infused with the love that is totally inexpressible, the love that has no exterior signs.

I desire with my whole self that you be renewed in the love and pain of the suffering God-man. I also desire with my whole self that you feel my love without my need to express it.

May the divine love, divine peace, and eternal blessings be with you. Amen.

INSTRUCTION XVIII:
IN BOTH TRIBULATION AND CONSOLATION,
THE PRAYING HEART
SHOULD ALWAYS BE UNITED WITH GOD
AND THE CRUCIFIED ONE

**Angela exhorts one of her spiritual sons that,
whatever the circumstances, he should pray,
keep vigils, and perform good works**

I desire very much, my beloved son, that you be reborn and renewed.[109] I also desire, my son, that you rid yourself completely of negligence and laziness. Furthermore, my son, I desire that you do not pray less, or keep vigils less often, or do any other good works any the less when divine grace is withdrawn from you than when it is in your possession.

It is a good thing and very acceptable to God, my son, if you pray, keep vigils, and perform other good works when the fervor of divine grace is with you, but it is altogether most pleasing and acceptable to God that, when divine grace is lacking or has been withdrawn from you, you do not pray less, keep vigils less often, or perform fewer good works. Act without grace just as you do when you have grace.

Therefore, my son, if divine fervor or warmth impels you sometimes to pray, keep vigils, and devote yourself to spiritual discipline and exercises, then, when it is God's pleasure to withdraw this fervor or warmth from you—either because of some deficit in you or, which is most often, to amplify and increase his grace in you—strive to do your utmost not to pray less, or keep vigils less often, or be less persistent in doing good works. Even if you suffer tribulations or temptations, which serve to punish and purify the sons of God, and grace is taken from you, strive nonetheless not to pray less, keep vigils less often, or be less persistent in doing good works; likewise, strive to resist and fight against temptations just as much as ever, in order to overcome them. Thus by your continual prayers, vigils, tears, spiritual discipline and exercises, and every kind of importuning, may you at least force God to deign to restore to you at some time the fervor and warmth of his grace.

Do your share, my son, for God will do his part well. Forced prayers, my son, are particularly pleasing to God.[110]

Angela, in her great love for her spiritual son, commends him to God, and exhorts him never to abandon prayer

When I gaze upon the uncreated God the experience is indescribable, most sweet, and consoling. Because of this, God, out of his indescribable kindness, makes me return to myself and turn and direct my gaze toward you. It seems to me that he shows me almost everything in you, inside and out, so that with a new and undescribable joy, I am made an entirely new person in you, so much so that I cannot take my eyes off you. You should know, my son, that this love is so intense that I ask him who produced it to moderate it, because it seems to me that I am no longer myself but you. This makes me say to myself: "I wonder to whom

I am writing, since I am you and you are me." If you could see my heart, my son, you would be entirely bound to do what God wants, because my heart is God's heart and his mine. I am beginning to smile about you. I want that smile to grow, for it will have its fulfillment in paradise.

What makes the soul stronger in God and fortifies it is love, and what makes it more tender is love. Each of these is appropriate in its own way. But I think you know this, so I need not explain it. Let me tell you, my son, that I live in a state of great languor. Love has done this, because the more something is loved, the more one desires that it be possessed. Therefore, because with my whole being I desire to have you before the divine majesty, I languish. Moreover, this love, my son, generates a great zeal in me, one which is painful and makes me suffer, because I continually fear with all my being that there might be something in you which impedes your way to God.

This is why, my son, I beg you with all my being not to turn the eyes of your soul away from this suffering God-man. If you keep your eyes fixed on him, your entire soul will be set ablaze. But if you are not doing so, strive with all your being to fix your eyes on him and keep them there. Moreover, my son, I desire with all my heart that your soul be elevated to see this suffering God-man, for this pleases me very much. But if your soul is not thus elevated, go back to yourself, start from the beginning and review from head to foot all the ways in which this suffering God-man was afflicted and crucified. If you cannot regain and rediscover these ways in your heart, repeat them vocally, attentively and frequently; because what the lips say and repeat grants fervor and warmth to the heart.

My dear son, poor fool that I am, I beg you not to find your support in this world nor to depend on this world, because whoever depends on this world will find himself deceived, for this world is full of illusion.[111] Find your support rather in the suffering God-man. For whoever sees this suffering God-man, so poor and full of continual and indescribable pain, so despised and totally annihilated—to see this is an effect of grace—I am sure such a person would follow him in poverty, and continual suffering, contempt, and vileness. No one can be excused for not having and finding divine grace. The most bountiful God distributes his grace abundantly to all, that is, to all who wish and seek it.

I also desire, my son, that you fill yourself with this uncreated God, and that in your soul there be no other fullness except this one. If you cannot be filled with the uncreated God, be at least filled and hold on to the fullness of what I have said above, namely, that of the suffering

God-man. If either is withdrawn from you, my son, do not rest until you rediscover and regain one of these fullnesses, because no one can hold on without one of them.

May the light, love, and peace of the most high God be with you. May the blessing of the most high God be with you forever, my son. Farewell in the God-man Christ and in his Virgin Mother. I ask you not to be ungrateful to the Blessed Virgin who has so much solicitude for you. Pray for my companion, who is very sick, and carefully attend to what she promised you. Pray also for me, most vile creature, and for all your brothers and sisters.

We are forever obligated to our venerable father and yours, Brother John, the minister general, who has been of such help to us, vile and abject persons.[112] May he to whom it belongs to bestow rewards, reward him and you, my son!

INSTRUCTION XIX:
IN A VISION ON THE FEAST OF THE
PURIFICATION OF MARY,
ANGELA CELEBRATES HER TRUE "OFFERTORY"

Angela sees the mother of God offering her son and then placing him in her arms

On the morning of the feast of the Purification of the Blessed Virgin, I was in the church of the Friars Minor in Foligno when candles were being distributed.[113] And I heard God telling me: "This is the hour when Our Lady came into the temple with her son." When my soul heard this I felt such great love welling in me that it is impossible for me to say or understand anything about it.[114]

Then my soul was elevated and saw Our Lady enter. I moved toward her with great reverence and fear. Our Lady totally reassured my soul, and she held forth her son to me and said: "O lover of my son, receive him." While saying these words she extended her arms and placed her son in my arms. He seemed to have his eyes closed as though asleep, and was wrapped in swaddling clothes. As if wearied from her journey, Our Lady sat down. Her gestures were so beautiful and gracious, her manner and behavior were likewise so gracious that it was exceedingly sweet and delightful for me to look at her and admire her. So much so that I turned again and again to look at the child, whom I held closely in my arms. And I likewise turned again and again to look at Our Lady herself, so beautiful was she to admire.

Then, suddenly, the child was left naked in my arms. He opened his eyes and raised them and looked at me. I saw and felt such a love for me as he looked at me that I was completely overwhelmed. I brought my face close to his, and pressed mine to his. There was such a fire that emanated from the opening and raising of the eyes of that child, who remained naked in my arms, and the effect on me of this child and his opening his eyes in that way was a benefit so totally unspeakable that although I felt it, I can in no way speak about it.[115]

Inspired by this vision, Angela offers herself and all her spiritual sons to God, who kindly receives this offering

Then suddenly God, in his immense majesty, appeared to me and said to me: "He who has not seen me as little will not see me as great." And he added: "I have come and I have offered myself to you, now it is your turn to offer." But he did not say what or how or to whom I was supposed to offer myself.

But immediately, my soul, in an indescribable and marvelous way, offered itself to him. Then I offered specifically and by name some of my sons. I offered myself and them perfectly and totally, withholding nothing for myself or for them. After this, I offered all my sons together. My soul perceived and understood that God accepted this offering and received it with great joy. I cannot describe the ineffable joy, delight, and sweetness I felt when I saw God receive and accept this offering with such kindness.[116]

On the following day, God heard Angela's desire to accomplish everything that was pleasing to him

On the Friday morning immediately following this feast, I said to God: "I know you are my Father, my God, and my Lord, teach me what you want me to do, instruct me in those ways which please you, because I am ready to obey." I stayed with these words and others like them until

Terce. Then I heard a voice tell me: "I know what pleases me." I heard these words clearly, but I am at a loss to express what I saw and understood and what God showed me. (Although, however, I will more willingly tell what I understood than what I heard.) There was a totally ineffable abyss. He showed me [my son] what you yourself are, and who are the ones who live in God and who are the ones who do not. He said: "In truth I say to you that there is no true way other than following in my footsteps, for in my way there is no deception whatever." He used the words "in truth" very often in numerous conversations with me.[117]

INSTRUCTION XX:
ON THE FEAST OF THE ANGELS,
THROUGH THEIR INTERCESSION,
ANGELA IS GRANTED AN ECSTATIC VISION
OF THE CRUCIFIED

On the feast of the angels during the month of September, I was in the church of the Friars Minor in Foligno and wanted to receive communion.[118] When the time for communion arrived, I prayed as I had before to the angels and especially St. Michael, and I asked them the following: "O ministers of God, you have the office and the power to administer and present him to others, make the God-man present to me and make him present in the same way that the Father gives him to humanity, first of all as alive, poor, suffering, in contempt, wounded, bloodied, and crucified. Afterward, make him present to me as dead on the cross."

Then the most holy angels spoke to me with indescribable graciousness: "You, who are most pleasing and delightful to God, behold, it has been granted to you, and you have him present; furthermore, it is given to you that you have the power to administer and make him present to others." And, in truth, he was present to me just as I had asked from the most holy angels. I saw him very clearly with the eyes of the soul, at first alive, suffering, bleeding, and crucified. Afterward, I saw him dead on the cross.

Then I felt such an acute pain at the sight of such a painful spectacle that my heart was ready to burst. On the other hand, I felt such a great delight, such a great joy at the presence of the angels and at the discourse they held with me, which was so very pleasing that I had never experienced any pleasure as tremendous as I derived from the discourse of the angels. I would never have believed that the most holy angels could cause me such pleasure and bestow such delight upon my soul.

Because I had prayed to all the angels, and especially the Seraphim, the most holy angels then said to me: "Behold, that which the Seraphim have is given and communicated to you."[119]

INSTRUCTION XXI:
CHRIST AND ST. FRANCIS ASSIST ANGELA IN HER SICKNESS

The friars refusing to do so, Christ himself, exercising his priestly ministry, administers the sacrament of the sick to Angela

Once when I lay sick in bed, I heard these words said by the suffering God-man: "Come to me you who are aglow with every agreeable color." And he added: "I want you to be my little martyr."[120]

When I asked to be anointed, the friars told me there was some grumbling among them on this subject because my companion had just been anointed and it was said that we resorted too frequently to anointing. I was somewhat troubled by this response. While I lay in bed, with this troubling response on my mind, I suddenly heard these words: "I with all my priests will anoint you; you will indeed be anointed."

During this same sickness Christ and St. Francis come to Angela's aid

On another occasion during this same illness, while I lay in bed very weak and afflicted in body, the God-man Jesus appeared and consoled me very pleasantly. He began by showing me what is generally so pleasing to the sick, that is, a great compassion, with which, it seemed to me, he was greatly moved. Then he said to me: "I came here to serve you, and I want to serve you." The service he rendered to me was the following. He sat next to my bed and he was so pleasant to me that it is totally unspeakable. I can say absolutely nothing of the indescribable joy and delight that was mine to see and hear him. I saw him with the eyes of my soul far more clearly than the eyes of the body can see another body.

This most clear and delightful vision bestowed on my soul a joy and a delight which is totally indescribable.

After this, he showed me the blessed Francis and said: "Here is the one whom, after me, you have loved so much. I want him to serve you." Then the blessed Francis showed me the kinship and intimate love that was his for me, and it was great in every way. Great was my delight in the kinship and love which the blessed Francis demonstrated toward me. Afterward, he spoke most secret and most high words to me. Finally, he said: "You are the only one born of me."

INSTRUCTION XXII:
ON THE LEGITIMATE SONS OF GOD

The true sign of authentic sons of God is their faithful response to the faithful love of the suffering Jesus Christ

O sons of God, transform yourselves totally into the suffering God-man who loved you so much that he deigned to die a most ignominious and altogether unspeakably painful and bitter death for you.[121] And all this, O man, only because of his love for you!

Hence the true sign of the legitimate sons of God is their perfect love of God and neighbor.[122] The one [Christ] who loves very much to be served in turn serves others very much. Consider, O sons of God, how most pure and faithful was the suffering God-man's love for you, how he did not spare himself but spent himself completely, solely out of his love for you. In return, O man, he absolutely wants his legitimate sons, in the measure possible for a created being, to respond with something of the same purity of love and the same most humble fidelity. This is why he always wanted and always had sons, whose faith was alive, to faithfully serve him, the most faithful God. Now, O sons of God, this suffering God-man is telling me almost continually that I should admonish you to be faithful to the one who has been most faithful to you. And one who is faithful to God is also faithful to his neighbor.

How the suffering God-man loved us with a very pure and very faithful love he clearly showed us through his birth, life, and death. But because we are unfaithful we do not perceive vividly and continually that, for us, he was born in a state of utmost poverty, suffering, and contempt. We likewise do not perceive with heartfelt emotion that, for us, he led a life that was most meek, divine, poor, humble, salutary, and laborious. And therefore, the fact that, for us, he died a most poor, humble, painful death, one in which he was held in utmost contempt and ignominy, does not make us continually die to ourselves.

Who is the one who will respond with a lively and continual faith, no matter how little it is, to the one whose fidelity to us was most divine and faithful? But no, as if it were of no concern to us, we turn our backs on all this.

The motive of our fidelity and love is that, for our instruction, God gave creatures power over his son

Let us consider, therefore, O sons of God, what should motivate us to be very faithful, with all of our being, to the suffering God-man who was most faithful to us. Because of his very pure and very faithful love for us he willingly and humbly subjected himself totally not only to rational creatures, but also to nonrational and insensible ones. Even though he has placed everything under the subjection of rational creatures, nonetheless, as it should be, everything remains subject to the Creator. This same Creator purely out of love for you so annihilated himself and abased himself that he gave the fullness of power not only to rational creatures but even to nonrational and insensible ones, to exercise their authority over him.

a. He gave power to the thorns and ropes

He gave thorns the power to enter and pierce most cruelly his most divine head. He likewise gave ropes the power to tie him to the pillar, the power to restrain him and to keep him fastened in one place.

Make me happy, O sons of God, and prove yourselves faithful to this God who is most faithful to us. May the most humble fidelity and faithful humility he showed us move you to your very depths. It is solely for you that he abased himself, (in order to exalt you) to the point where he permitted insensible objects to hit and lacerate him, the author of life; and, likewise, to hold him in one place, though he is altogether without limits or boundaries.

b. He gave power to a veil, to whips and nails, to the gibbet and the sponge

He who is totally light, and from whom all light comes, and without whom there is only darkness, gave a veil the power to cover him. He bestowed upon whips the power to beat him unmercifully. He bestowed upon nails the power to enter and pierce the most divine hands and feet of the God who made everything. He gave power to the gibbet, called the cross, to hold up its maker and Lord, pierced and bloodied. He bestowed upon the sponge, the vinegar, the gall, and many insensible creatures, the power to insult their God and maker and have full dominion over him. Finally, he bestowed upon the lance the power to enter, open, and pierce his most divine side.

These created things should have and could have been obedient to their own Lord and maker, and not to the creature who was misusing them. But the most profound, most faithful, and totally extraordinary humility of this most high and majestic God deflates and confounds our pride-filled nothingness! The very author of life, who alone is, wished to be annihilated and made subject to all creatures, even the insensible ones, so that you, who were dead and had become insensible to divine realities, might have life through his humility and abasement. And you, O man, who were nothing, know that he, who alone is, has loved you with a love so pure and so faithful that solely out of love for you he wished to be annihilated, in order to give you most perfect being.

The nails and the lance should and could have bent and not obeyed a creature's misuse of them; and not pierced and wounded the most divine hands, feet, and side of their own Lord and maker. They, and other insensible objects, obeyed a creature in opposition to their Lord and maker, only because they had received power over him.

c. He granted power to the devil, and to the heart and senses of humans

Moreover, he gave to the devil the power to tempt him, and even to lead him about. He gave to humans full power over his person. He bestowed upon their hearts the power to form perverse and murderous thoughts against him. Finally, he bestowed the power upon their senses to blaspheme against him, hold council to arrange everything according to plan, strike him, lacerate him, and most painfully crucify and kill him.

d. Final exhortation

Therefore, O sons of God, never take your eyes off this most faithful humiliation which the suffering God-man underwent for your sake. Oh, with what most faithful fidelity did the uncreated God serve his creature, when solely because of him, he made himself obedient even to insensible creatures!

O man, it was only for you that he was submissive[123] to all tribulations. Only for you was he submissive to all injuries. Only for you was he submissive to all opprobrium. Only for you was he submissive to every pain. Only for you was he submissive to every suffering. Only for you was he submissive to death.[124]

INSTRUCTION XXIII:
ANGELA'S INTIMATE DIALOGUE
WITH THE SUFFERING JESUS CHRIST

On Wednesday of Holy Week, I was meditating on the death of the Son of God incarnate, and trying to empty my soul of everything else so I could be more recollected in his passion and death. I had only one care, only one desire, and that was to find the best way to empty my soul from everything else in order to have a more vivid memory of the passion and death of the Son of God.[125]

My love for you has not been a hoax[126]

Suddenly, while I was engrossed in this effort and desire, a divine word sounded in my soul: "My love for you has not been a hoax." These words struck me a mortal blow. For immediately the eyes of my soul were opened and I saw that what he had said was true. I saw his acts of love, everything that the Son of God had done, all that he had endured in life and in death—this suffering God-man—because of his inexpressible and visceral love. Seeing in him all the deeds of true love, I understood the perfect truth of what he had said, that "his love for me had not been a hoax," but that he had loved me with a most perfect and visceral love. I saw, on the other hand, the exact opposite in myself, because my love for him had never been anything but playing games, never true. Being made aware of this was a mortal blow and caused such intolerable pain that I thought I would die.

I did not love you in appearance only, or from afar, but in the intimacy of your soul

Suddenly other words came to increase my sorrow. After he had said, "My love for you has not been a hoax"—and I had perceived that this was true on his part but quite the contrary on mine, and I had felt such pain that I thought I would die—he added: "I have not served you only in appearance" and then "I have not kept myself at a distance, but have always felt you close to me."

These words increased my mortal pain and suffering even more. My soul cried out: "O Master, that which you assure me is not in you, is totally in me. My love for you has never been anything but a hoax and a lie. Nor have I ever really wanted to come close to you and feel the sufferings which you felt and endured for me. Furthermore, I have never served you, except in appearance and not truly." I perceived all the signs and marks of the truest love in him; how he had given himself wholly and totally to me, in order to serve me; how he had come so close to me: He had become human in order to truly feel and carry my sufferings in himself. When, on the other hand, I perceived the exact opposite in me, I had such suffering and pain that I thought I would die. I felt my ribs dislocate in my chest under the weight of my pain, and it seemed as though my heart would burst.

While I was thinking especially about the words he had said, "I have not kept myself at a distance, but have always felt you close to me," he added, "I am deeper within your soul than your soul is to itself."[127] These words increased my suffering even more, because the more I perceived how deeply present he was to my soul, the more I knew that, for my part, I was far from him.

Whoever wants to feel my love, speak with me, and follow me, I will not keep at a distance, because "these are my sons"

Afterward, he added other words demonstrative of his deeply felt love. He said: "I would not withdraw my presence from anyone who wants to feel my presence deeply. It would also give me the greatest pleasure to grant a sight of me to anyone who wants to see me. I would likewise take great delight in speaking with anyone who wants to speak with me." These words stirred in my soul the desire not to feel, see, or say anything which could offend God. This is what God especially requires from his sons, because inasmuch as he called and chose them to feel his presence, see him, and speak with him, he wants them to be completely on their guard against everything to the contrary.[128]

In the beginning[129] when he had shown me the specific characteristics of his sons he had said to me: "All those who are lovers and followers of my poverty, suffering, and contempt are my legitimate sons; and these are likewise your own sons, and no others."

INSTRUCTION XXIV:
IMITATION OF THE PASSION OF CHRIST IS EASY

Christ's faithful one once told me that she had heard God tell her that it is easy for those for whom Christ died to die for him; it is easy for those for whom he suffered to suffer for him; it is easy for those for whom he was despised to be despised for him.[130]

INSTRUCTION XXV:
THE LIBERTY THAT GOD GRANTS
IS PART OF HIS PLAN

Concerning the liberty God grants to the soul, Angela once said the following.[131]

When God grants liberty to the soul, it perceives that it understands him with the fullness of truth, without any falsehood. The soul not only understands, it also sees and feels him. Sometimes the soul even hears God telling it that liberty is granted to it so that it can do whatever it wants. God says to it: "I want nothing more than what you want." The will of God and the will of the soul are then made one. God also speaks to the soul and gives it the mission to do and say everything it wishes to do and say; there is nothing God does not entrust to it completely. This is liberty with regard to external practices.[132]

But the liberty which is given to the soul when God elevates it to himself cannot be described. In this liberty, God elevates, seizes, and holds onto the soul; and the soul is endowed with such complete security that it can do and say whatever the body and the soul want. Immediately, the soul and body are wisely ordered and with an ordering they miraculously receive from God. The body is so circumscribed by this orderliness of wisdom that it cannot fall into any disorder. Not because fear or love restrains it, but because the soul, forming but one single will with God, wants nothing other than what God wants. Therefore if God has granted an ordinary ordering to the sick and to sinners, so, the more liberty he grants to elevated souls, the more strict, wise, and great is the order by which he binds and holds them.

INSTRUCTION XXVI:
REVELATIONS AND VISIONS CONCERNING ANGELA'S SPIRITUAL SONS AND THE PORTIUNCULA

In a vision Angela rejoices in hearing and seeing how much her spiritual sons are loved and blessed by God

On the feast of St. Peter in Chains, I wanted to receive communion at the Mass one of you was to celebrate at the altar near the pulpit on the right side of the church of the blessed Francis.[133] And suddenly I heard: "Behold, Brother So-and-so is coming."—These words referred to one of her sons, one of the nine of us who were around her in front of that altar.—When the voice said "Brother So-and-so is coming," I doubted and did not wish to raise my head to see him; but when I returned from the altar I did see him. I was told many things specifically concerning him.[134]

Then I was told of all my spiritual sons in general: "These and all the others will be sources of joy for you." I had prayed that they would all be purified and be sources of joy for me. God himself purified them all and he said: "To your sons present and absent I will bestow the fire of the Holy Spirit who will set them ablaze and, through love, will transform them completely into my passion. This transformation, however, will vary greatly from one to another. The more they keep in mind my passion, the more they will have of my love; and the more of such love they have, the more they will be united to me." He added other things about these different degrees of transformation, but I no longer remember them. All this delighted me very much.

Then my soul was suddenly elevated and I saw the majesty of God in an utterly unspeakable way, more than I had ever seen him. I saw him embracing all my sons. He held some at his side, others close to his breast or his face, and still others he embraced totally. He did so according to the degree of their transformation into the passion of Christ and his love. All of them, the first, the second, and the third, rejoiced to be in God's presence, but those who were totally embraced and faced God directly rejoiced indescribably more than the others. My own joy over this was also indescribable.

In another vision, while entering the Portiuncula, Angela saw, to her amazement, God's power expanding the Portiuncula into a great church

The next morning, when I was about to enter the church of the glorious Virgin of the Portiuncula in order to receive the Indulgence, I was holding the hand of a certain woman who wished to help me. The moment I placed my foot over the threshold of the church, I was suddenly enraptured with such an impact that my body just stood there and did not move, and I let go of the woman who was going ahead of me to help me.[135]

I saw the church expanding, by the power of God, into one of an astonishing magnitude and beauty.[136] There was nothing material in this church; everything about it was totally indescribable. My soul was amazed at how it expanded as soon as I set foot in it, because I knew that the church of St. Mary of the Portiuncula was extremely small.

A message from God concerning Brother A.

Again, when Brother A. was celebrating Mass at an altar in another part of the church, I was told: "May my son and now yours receive the blessing of God the Father, the Son, and the Holy Spirit; this will be a source of great joy for you."[137]

And he said: "You will have sons, and all of them will receive this blessing, for all my sons are yours, and yours, mine."

While I was back in Foligno, after I had received communion at the last Mass Brother A. celebrated, I was told concerning him: "This intimate son of yours will be a source of great joy for you; I confirm the eternal blessing I gave him. I am the one who takes away sins; none but I can do so. I have removed from him the guilt and the penalty." As I did not understand any of these words, I related them to the said brother after he had finished his Mass. When he heard the words "I have removed from him the guilt and the penalty," he took off his capuche,[138] bowed his head, and wept.[139]

Also, the blessed Francis said of this friar: "Sister, remember me to my brother, Brother A."

INSTRUCTION XXVII:
THE SEVEN GIFTS OF GOD WHICH TRANSFORM
THE SOUL INTO CHRIST JESUS

Whoever has been able to obtain these most sweet gifts of God should know that he has reached consummation and perfection in the most sweet Lord Jesus Christ; and, likewise, has become this same most sweet Lord Jesus Christ through transformation. The more one grows in these gifts, the more the being of the most sweet Jesus will grow in him.[140]

The first gift is the love of poverty by which the soul strips itself of the love of every creature; does not want to possess anything other than our Lord Jesus Christ; does not place its hope in the help of any creature in this life; and shows this by its deeds.

The second gift is the desire to be despised, vilified, and covered with opprobrium by every creature. The soul wants everyone to believe that it is worthy of such treatment, so that it receives no sympathy from anyone. It wants to live in the heart of none except God, and receive no esteem whatsoever from anyone.

The third gift is the desire to be afflicted, burdened, filled, submerged, with all the sufferings of the body and heart which the most sweet Lord Jesus and his most sweet mother endured. Furthermore, with this gift the soul wants every creature to inflict these sufferings on it without intermission. If you cannot want these three—poverty, suffering, and contempt—you should know that you are far from resembling the blessed and most sweet Christ. For poverty, suffering, and contempt accompanied him in the highest degree, everywhere, all the time, and in everything that he did. They likewise accompanied his mother in the highest degree.

The fourth gift is that you know you are unworthy of receiving such a great benefit and, likewise, totally incapable, by yourself, of possessing these—that is, poverty, suffering, and contempt. For when you presume too much that you possess the one you love, you lose love. Therefore you never feel that you have succeeded in attaining this gift, but it seems to you that you are always just starting anew, that you have never done anything until now, and that you have never had any of these three.

The fifth gift is to constantly strive to think how these three [poverty, suffering, and contempt] existed in the Lord Jesus Christ and, in continual longing prayer, to cry out to the Lord that he might give you these three that were his garments, his companions, and send them deep into your heart, and not to ask anything for yourself. It is in this perfect transformation into poverty, suffering, and contempt that you should place all your joy in this life. You should strive to lift yourself to the level of imagining how the heart of the most sweet Jesus was filled and overflowed with all these three, infinitely more than what was visible in his body.

The sixth gift is to flee like the worst pestilence all those, be they spiritual or carnal persons, who impede the soul from acquiring these three; and, likewise, to hold in horror, despise, and flee, as if it were a serpent, all that in this life seems to be different from or opposed to these three.

The seventh gift is not to pass judgment on any creature, nor to get bogged down trying to judge others, as the gospel says, but rather to esteem yourself as more vile than the others, no matter how wicked, and as unworthy of any grace from God.

Because the soul is still weak and cannot yet serve God without the hope of a reward,[141] it is given to know that these gifts merit possessing God fully in the heavenly homeland, or rather, that the soul, through the transformation realized by these gifts, becomes God totally.[142] This is true to such an extent that even in this life God bestows a great deal of this full transformation to souls who are thus transformed into his contempt, poverty, and suffering. The soul, however, should not seek and desire in this life the consolations that accompany these gifts, unless perhaps when, in its weakness, it needs strengthening.[143] The soul's one desire should be to attain the perfect crucifixion of Christ, his suffering, poverty, and contempt.

INSTRUCTION XXVIII:
TRANSFORMATION INTO CHRIST THROUGH THE EXERCISES OF PRAYER AND PENANCE

In the name of our suffering Lord Jesus Christ. Amen.

The three schools of prayer—bodily, mental, and supernatural —by which the soul is transformed into the Beloved

It is in prayer that one finds God.[144] There are three schools, that is three types of prayer, without which one does not find God. These are bodily, mental, and supernatural.[145]

Bodily prayer takes place with the sound of words and bodily movements such as genuflections. I never abandon this type of prayer. For sometimes when I want to devote myself to mental prayer, I am impeded by my laziness or by sleepiness. So I turn to bodily prayer, which leads to mental prayer. It should be done with attention. For instance, when you say the Our Father, you should weigh carefully what you are saying. Do not run through it, trying to complete a certain number of them, like little ladies doing piece work.

Prayer is mental when meditating on God so occupies the soul that one thinks of nothing but God. If some other thought comes to mind I no longer call such prayers mental. Such prayer curbs the tongue and renders one speechless. The mind is so totally filled with God's presence that it cannot think or speak about anything except about God and in God. From mental prayer, then, we move on to supernatural prayer.

I call prayer supernatural when God, bestowing this gift upon the soul and filling it with his presence, so elevates the soul that it is stretched, as it were, beyond its natural capacities. In this type of prayer, the soul understands more of God than would seem naturally possible. It knows that it cannot understand, and what it knows it cannot explain, because all that it sees and feels is beyond its own nature.[146]

In these three schools of prayer you come to know who you are and who God is. From the fact that you know, you love. Loving, you desire to possess what you love. And this is the sign of true love: that the one who loves is transformed, not partially, but totally, into the Beloved. But because this transformation does not go on without interruption, the soul is seized by the desire to seek all the ways by which it can be transformed into the will of the Beloved, so it can return again to that vision. It seeks what was loved by the Beloved. God the Father provided a way for us to attain this transformation and this way is through the Beloved, that is, through God's own Son, whom he made the Son of poverty, suffering, contempt, and true obedience.

The life of prayer is strictly bound to the way of the poverty, suffering, contempt, and true obedience of Christ. The soul must follow this way in order to be transformed into him

a. The triple poverty of Christ

The greatest poverty is not to know God. This was the pride that caused the fall of the first man. Therefore God found another kind of poverty which we should practice. There are three kinds of poverty that we should make our own.

The first poverty is the lack of temporal goods, which Christ practiced perfectly. Each of us ought to imitate him in this poverty, and perfectly, if we can. Those who cannot do so perfectly, either because they belong to the nobility[147] or have a family, should at least have a sincere love of poverty and renounce affection for worldly belongings.

The second poverty is that of friends, which Christ experienced to such an extent that none of his friends, nor any of the people he was related to through his mother, could shield him from a single blow. Thus we too must be poor in terms of friends and any creatures which interfere with imitating Christ.

The third poverty of Christ was that he was poor in terms of his own self. Even though he was omnipotent, he willed to become weak so that we might imitate him—not by hiding power as he did, which we cannot do because we do not have his power, but by attentively considering and weeping over our defects, vileness, and misery.[148]

Therefore, the soul seeking to do the will of the Beloved, which he showed us by the example of his poverty, should strive to be transformed into this poverty as perfectly as it can.

b. The continual sufferings of Christ

The soul also wants to be transformed into the sufferings Christ endured.[149] God the Father made him the Son of suffering; Christ always lived in suffering. From the moment of his conception he was in extreme suffering, because divine wisdom had shown him all that he was to suffer. The suffering began at that moment and lasted until the separation of his soul from his body. This is demonstrated by his prayer: "My soul is sorrowful unto death."[150] Because he said that death would be the end of his suffering, we are given to understand that its beginning was the moment of his conception.

Since we are responsible for these sufferings of Christ, we ought to be transformed into them. We do this according to the measure of our love. Hence, because of the sufferings of Christ, we should pursue all forms of suffering so as to be always in a state of suffering. We should desire sufferings and bear them patiently whatever happens: whether they come through words or deeds which offend us; or through temptations (so, without consenting to them, let us patiently bear the temptations which God allows to come our way); or through whatever form of tribulation, sadness, or anything else. We also ought to desire what we do not have in the way of suffering in order to imitate the Beloved, who was always in a state of suffering. However, we should not bring suffering upon ourselves through blameworthy deeds.

c. Contempt in the life of Christ

Christ was also the Son of contempt because he was subjected to contempt, reproach, and abandonment by everyone.[151] We ought to imitate him in this if we love him, since love makes one seek the same things as the Beloved. Whoever is truly attentive to poverty and is truly poor will be afflicted, and, as a consequence, be subject to contempt. Thus, true poverty is the root of all these things.

d. The true obedience of Christ

Christ was also a Son of obedience, and this led him to leave the bosom of his Father, and to obey him unto death.[152] In this we should imitate him, and be obedient not only to divine precepts and to religious superiors, if we have them, but even to the messengers of his will, that is, to the inspirations which God sends to our soul. May our obedience be prompt and without delay.

To be transformed into Christ, the soul must imitate him in all the other virtues as well, such as peace and meekness

We should imitate our Lord Jesus Christ not only in those things just mentioned, but also in the other virtues.[153] Peace is one, and we should be peaceful in words and deeds and in our way of life. But as to those defects and other things which threaten our soul, we should be like lions in expelling them. We should practice kindness and meekness not only among ourselves but with everyone in the measure fitting to each one. On the other hand, we should avoid too great a familiarity with the wicked, unless there is something in their behavior to call them to order on, and thus be of service to them. Let us, finally, be kind and meek, not returning evil with evil, but bearing it patiently.

Let us be indulgent toward those who offend us by word or deed, respond calmly, and not oppose them by taking note of the injury. It is with a calm exterior and a soul at rest that we must exercise indulgence to those who offend us, like a certain person who would willingly kiss the feet of those who offend him. To acquire this virtue one should look at Christ and see how he bore offenses with kindness. His example gives us strength not to hold a grudge.

Finally, we should imitate Christ so as to remain straightforward in word and deed, without deception or duplicity.

INSTRUCTION XXIX:
THE KNOWLEDGE OF GOD AND SELF

On another occasion, when she was asked why one should embrace poverty, suffering, and contempt, she replied: "One must know God and oneself."[154]

Knowledge of God presupposes knowledge of self in the following manner: One must consider and see who is the offended, and then consider and see who is the offender. From the insight derived from the second consideration, one is granted grace upon grace, vision upon vision, light upon light.

And from these, one begins to attain knowledge of God. The more one knows, the more one loves; the more one loves, the more one desires; the more one desires, the more one grows in the capacity to act accordingly. How one acts is the sign and measure of love. And the test of pure, true, and upright love is whether one loves and acts in accordance with the love and action of the loved one.

Christ, the Beloved, always had, always loved, and always practiced poverty, suffering, and contempt. Therefore, like Christ, the one who loves him should always love, put into practice, and possess these three things, as said above.

INSTRUCTION XXX:
THE THREE ASPECTS OF THE EUCHARIST

**Three aspects must be considered in the holy sacrifice
of the altar: The mystery of the love of Christ,
the mystery of his suffering, and how the soul
must enter into both and be transformed**

We must perceive and pay close attention to three aspects of the holy sacrifice, for these contain great truths.[155] I have no doubt—on the contrary, I am certain—that any soul who truly perceives these three aspects, no matter how dry its love, must immediately be infused with love when it becomes aware how much it has been loved.

In order to become aware of these three aspects, the soul must enter into the God-man and look at the holy ordering which he realized in this holy sacrifice. One must also look at the ineffable love which led the God-man to seize every possible means to remain with us totally. He instituted this very holy sacrifice, not only as a memorial of his death (through which he saves us), but also as a way of remaining with us totally and forever. Whoever wishes to enter and penetrate these depths must have good eyes.

Now I want to begin speaking to you about these three aspects of the holy sacrifice which we should look at, namely, the two with which the God-man was concerned when he instituted it, and third, how the soul is brought in to see these two. In the first aspect we see the ineffable love he had for us; how his deep love for us poured into us totally; how he handed himself over to us totally and for always. In the second we see the unspeakable and deadly pain he suffered for us; how at the moment of his death he had to leave us, and leave us through such a most painful death; how he had to pass through such indescribably acute suffering, which had to include feeling abandoned.

It seems to me that these are the truths which must be studied in depth by those who wish to celebrate the holy sacrifice and participate in its benefits.

The mystery of the love of Christ who of his own accord remains with us and offers himself to the soul in this sacrament so that the soul may be transformed into him

The soul, then, must not simply quickly pass over the first aspect, but should stop and dwell upon it. This first aspect, namely, what the God-man accomplished for the human race, is so full of his kindness for us that we do well to take notice of the ineffable love that was his when he ordained to hand himself over totally to us in this holy sacrifice. Note well and perceive who is the one who wishes to remain with us in this holy sacrifice! It is the "One who is," and he who is remains with us in this most holy sacrifice in his entirety. Let no one be surprised that he can be on so many altars at once, both here, and across the seas, there just the same as here, and here just the same as there. For he has said: I am God and I am beyond your comprehension. And, also, I am God and I have created without you; I do my work without you; and nothing is impossible for me.[156] Bow before what you do not understand.

What soul could be so cruel as to see this aspect that shows the God-man's love for us, such a filial love, and not be immediately transformed into love? What soul could see in this aspect so much suffering, such bitter pain, how it required such submission to all forms of suffering, visible and invisible, and not be immediately transformed into a state of suffering? What soul could be so incapable of love as to see how Christ loved it, how he decided to remain with us in this most holy sacrifice, and not be transformed totally into love?

This aspect of Christ's love for us was such that even though he saw his death as imminent and experienced such unspeakably acute, deadly, and totally unconceivable sufferings—for every type of suffering converged on his body and soul—still, as if not thinking of himself, he never renounced his intentions, so great was his love for us. Indeed, such is the plan of divine love that its purpose is always to draw back to itself that which it loves; it draws everyone out of themselves and out of all created reality, and totally into the uncreated. Then the soul is made capable of understanding that the whole Trinity was involved in planning this very holy sacrifice.

The mystery of the suffering of the "abandoned Lover" proposes itself to the soul so that it might be transformed into the same suffering

The soul then turns to see another aspect of the God-man's love, that which has to do with the presence of his death and all his sufferings. Just as the sight of Christ's love transformed the soul into love, likewise, the sight of the pain-filled countenance of the abandoned Lover transforms the soul into suffering. The effect of looking at the Lover's countenance filled with such suffering and bitter pain is to transform the soul totally into suffering. No divine consolation can ease the pain, but, rather, it becomes part of the pain itself.

The soul is transformed into these two mysteries when it looks at and possesses both of them simultaneously and continually

Those who wish to be the very faithful sons of this holy sacrifice should constantly consider this truth. When the Beloved turned his gaze toward us and his countenance was filled with such bitter pain, he was totally and solely in us. Likewise when he turned his gaze to us and his countenance was filled with such filial love, he was totally and solely in us. In the same way, therefore, let us be totally and solely in him. If the soul did not see the pain-filled and suffering countenance of the Beloved at the same time that it sees his loving countenance, it would be overwhelmed by too much joy and gladness. Likewise, if it did not see the filial and loving countenance of the Beloved at the same time that it sees his pain-filled and suffering countenance, it would be overwhelmed by too much pain and suffering. One tempers the other.

INSTRUCTION XXXI:
THE USEFULNESS OF CONSOLATIONS

On another occasion Angela began to speak as follows: God in his overflowing love for the soul grants it caresses, that is, consolations, feelings of his presence, and other similar favors which I also call caresses. The soul should not seek these. But neither should it spurn them, because they make the soul speed along to God and are its food. It is as a result of these consolations that the soul makes its ascent in the love of God and strives to be transformed into the beloved.[157]

INSTRUCTION XXXII:
RESPONSES TO THREE QUESTIONS
CONCERNING THE EUCHARIST
AND THE APPROPRIATE WAY TO PREPARE
ONESELF TO RECEIVE IT

Angela's response to the first question: In the mystery of the Eucharist there is a greater matter—that is, the goodness of the uncreated God—and a lesser matter— that is, the charity of God having become human. These two are united in the person of Christ

Once Angela was questioned concerning the body and the blood of our Lord Jesus Christ which the priest offers as a sacrifice on the altar and she replied as follows.[158]

If the soul wants and desires to understand and to say something about God, ordainer, sovereign, uncreated and incarnate; and it wishes to know something about matters concerning him; and especially if it wants to know something concerning this most high and holy sacrament which God, as ordainer, ordains to be celebrated daily through the words of his priest, his minister, then such a soul ought to be transformed totally in God through love. Once transformed into him, the soul should place itself in his presence, stay there, and enter within God himself and not remain outside him. The following is what I mean by "being in the presence of God" and "entering within him": to consider and perceive him, who is the ordainer and highest uncreated good.

Let the soul consider, first of all, who and what God is in himself. Then, elevated out of itself into God, it can see him who is invisible, know him who is unknowable, feel him who is imperceptible, comprehend him who is incomprehensible. And this is so because the soul sees, knows, feels, and comprehends God as invisible light, incomprehensible and unknown good. Comprehending, seeing, knowing, and feeling God, the soul, according to its capacity, expands in him and becomes filled with him through love. It finds its delight in God and God finds his delight in it and with it. The soul, then, experiences and possesses God's sweetness more from what it does not comprehend than from what it comprehends, more from what it does not see than from what it sees, more from what it does not feel than from what it feels, more, finally, from what it does not know than from what it knows. It seems to me that this is the reason that no matter how perfect the soul, even if it is as perfect as that of the Blessed Virgin, it comprehends nothing of God, the ordainer, uncreated and infinite. From looking at what it sees, feels and knows, it sees, feels, and knows that it cannot see, feel, and know. Therefore, concerning, and in, this mystery and most high sacrament the soul must ponder over, see, feel, and know its uncreated ordainer, and who he is.

It should also see and consider what it is concerning him and in him which creates order, that is, what he did and does to be ordainer of this mystery. I do not know what name to give it unless it be "love without measure," for he is the ordainer, the good God, infinite love.

The soul, finally, should also see and consider the order itself, that is, to what end this mystery is ordered, what final purpose the sovereign and infinite goodness wills for it: God's desire is to unite us to himself, incorporate us in himself, and himself in us. Furthermore, he wishes that we carry him within ourselves as he himself carries us, consoling and strengthening us.

Such is the first rationale of this mystery and most high sacrament which the soul sees and ought to see when it enters into God.

Afterward, the soul turns away from considering the greater reality within this mystery and proceeds to ponder over and see a lesser one so well bound to the greater one that the soul sees, feels, and knows the lesser in the greater and the greater in the lesser. This is so because in this mystery the soul discovers God as uncreated and God as man, that is, the divinity and humanity in Christ united and conjoined in one person. Sometimes, in this present life, the soul receives greater delight in the lesser reality than in the greater one. For the soul is more suited and conformed to the lesser reality which it sees in Christ, as the incarnate God, than it is to that which it sees in Christ as the uncreated God; because the soul is a creature which is the life of its flesh and of all the members of its body. Thus it discovers both God as man and God as uncreated, Christ the creator and the creature. It also discovers in Christ a soul united with flesh, blood, and all the members of his most sacred body. And this is why when the human intellect discovers, sees, and knows in this mystery Christ as man and Christ as God, ordainer of this mystery, it feels delight, and expands in him, because it sees, as I have said, God as man and God as uncreated, made in the same form and almost like itself—that is, the human soul sees the soul of Christ, and the eyes, flesh, and body of Christ. But while considering, seeing, knowing, and understanding this lesser reality, the soul should not lose sight of the greater one. For it discovers and sees in this abyss of human and divine realities not only the infinite goodness of God, but also the supreme and unheard-of human charity of Christ, God made man, the ordainer as man of this mystery.

The soul, I say, discovers supreme divine goodness and supreme human charity. But it can discover and see this infinite goodness and supreme charity when, from within this mystery and concerning it, it ponders and reflects upon that which is near, long, and hard. Looking and pondering, the soul sees when the mystery was ordained, and discovers the near juxtaposed with the long, and the long not only juxtaposed but conjoined with the hard. For the soul discovers and sees that this mystery was ordained at the Last Supper of the Lord, quite late, near to night. By "long" I refer to the long-lasting passion of Christ. Finally, the soul discovers the long-lasting passion of Christ conjoined with the hardness of his death. This is what I call the near, the long, and the hard, which the soul can and should consider and see in the hour at which this mystery was ordained. It was, in truth, the great charity and supreme goodness of Christ, God and man, that ordained and produced at such a time and at such an hour a mystery so new, wonderful, unheard of, unique, perfect, full of love, and precious, for the purpose of consoling the souls of all the faithful and providing comfort and help to the whole church militant in the present life.

Angela's response to the second question:
The Eucharistic sacrifice is ancient in its foreshadowings,
new in the truth contained in this sacrament itself

Because Angela had used the word "new," she was asked whether there was anything new in God, ordainer of this mystery.

She replied: Nothing new occurs in God because he does not vary or change. The novelty of this work of God can be and is on the part of the creature who receives the newness, a new and unaccustomed operation. Thus, this mystery was and is new, even though from all antiquity it was foreshadowed in the Holy Scriptures. One can call it a new and ancient sacrament—ancient in that it was foreshadowed in the Scriptures, new as to the truth of this sacrament itself, in which the creature always receives something very new.[159]

We know well, and by faith we see most certainly, and without any possible doubt, that the bread and the blessed wine, through the infinite power of God—at the most holy words which Christ, the ordainer and God made man, pronounced, and which, in turn, the priest ought to and does pronounce—do become Christ in their substance. Thus, in this mysterious consecration, the substance of the bread and wine are transubstantiated and become Christ, God and man. The color of the bread and wine, their taste, virtue, form, mode, all their properties subsist. But they do not subsist in Christ, they subsist in themselves through the power of God raising them above their nature. The color subsists in itself, the savor in itself, the form in itself, the property in itself.[160]

Truly great, therefore, is this new thing that God's wisdom, in his sovereign goodness and immense charity, has wrought in his creature, besides many other special and unique new effects that this same most holy body and blood of our Lord Jesus Christ produces for his friends and elect.

Angela's third response: The angels and the saints in heaven rejoice with the church in the celebration of the Eucharist

When Angela was also asked if the angels and the saints find and receive some new joy or sweetness in this most blessed mystery, she replied: The angels and the saints do indeed find, see, feel, and taste a new joy and sweetness in it. Furthermore, they not only stand in its presence, but are also within it, in God, the infinite good, the cause of their blessedness. This is so because they always have present before them the uncreated God, the God made man.

If in this new mystery the angels and the saints receive a new joy, a new sweetness, a new reason to be elated, I believe this is possible because of the communion they enjoy with the head and with his members, that is, with Christ, God and man, as head, and with his members, the just and the faithful. They see, feel, and know that Christ finds his delight in this most high mystery. Christ himself shows them that he finds a very special satisfaction in this mystery by reason of the benefits it provides for and in his devout and faithful friends. This is why, with Christ, all the blessed saints find special delight in this mystery. They are elated anew by it, and in their own way honor Christ in how he manifests himself in these new workings. For what pleases the head ought to and can please the members; what pleases the Father should please the sons; what pleases the good Lord can and ought to please his whole family. Hence all the saints, in their own way, rejoice in and with everything that pleases their head, Father and Lord, uncreated God, God become man.

All the saints who reign in the heavenly homeland can and do also find joy in this mystery because of the good and the benefits this sacrament procures for the holy souls of the militant church. The most high favors granted to humanity in this mystery are not only the cause, matter, and means of joy and sweetness for the devout and holy souls who are part of the church militant in this present life, but they are also the cause of the joy, the sweetness, and the gladness for all the saints who reign with God in glory.

**Angela concludes her discourse on the Eucharist
by warmly exhorting everyone to dispose themselves
to receive this sacrament as worthily as possible**

One should really do some serious thinking before going to receive the great favors accorded in this most high mystery. One should keep in mind whom one is approaching, what state one is in, and how and why one approaches it.

For one is going to a good which is the All Good, the cause of every good, the giver, producer, and possessor of every good. Hence it is the only good, for without this good there is no other good. This good suffices, fills, and satisfies all the saints and the blessed spirits, all the just justified by grace, and the souls and bodies of all the blessed who reign in glory.

One is also going to receive the Good, God made man, the one who satisfies, abounds, overflows, and enjoys himself in all creatures, above all creatures, and beyond all creatures, without mode or measure. The creature cannot know or possess this Good except to the extent that this Good itself wishes. This Good wishes it as much as the creature, according to the degree of its being, is able to receive it from the one who is being, who bestows being to all, and who is above all being.

One goes to this Good, beyond and outside of which there is no other good. O neglected, unknown, unloved Good, discovered by those who totally desire you and yet cannot possess you totally. If one looks and ponders with utmost care the small piece of bread which the body eats, how much more should the soul not look and ponder before receiving this eternal and infinite good, created and uncreated, this sacramental food which is the sustenance, treasure, and fountain for the life of both soul and body. This is truly the Good which in itself contains every good. One must, therefore, approach such a table, and such a great and wonderful Good with great respect, purity, fear, and love. The soul must approach it all cleansed and adorned, because it is going to that which, and the one who, is the Good of all glory. It is going to that which, and the one who, is perfect blessedness, eternal life, beauty, loftiness, sweetness, all love and the sweetness of love.

Why should one go to this mystery? I will tell you what I think. One should go to receive in order to be received, go pure in order to be purified, go alive in order to be enlivened, go as just in order to be justified, go united and conjoined to Christ in order to be incorporated through him, with him, and in him, God uncreated and God made man, who is given in this most holy and most high mystery through the hands of the priest. Thanks be to God always. Amen.

INSTRUCTION XXXIII:
THE FREQUENCY OF THE RECEPTION
OF THE EUCHARIST

Once Angela was questioned by two trustworthy Friars Minor concerning a phrase from St. Augustine: "Receive the Eucharist every day," and so forth.[161] She replied as follows.

Blessed Augustine was holy and wise. Seeing good persons mixed with evil ones, in order not to embolden the latter, he did not praise such a practice. And in order not to hinder the good, he did not blame this practice. For evil persons draw their boldness from the praise of others. The good find their security in a good conscience and this must not incur the blame of a saint.

INSTRUCTION XXXIV:
THE WAYS IN WHICH LOVE LEADS TO GOD

Perfect love consists in the total gift of oneself to God, the supreme Good, who hands himself totally over to us

God, our uncreated, incarnate, supreme, and perfect Good, is total love.[162] He loves totally and wants to be loved totally. Hence, he wants his sons to be totally transformed into him by love.

The ones I call his special and beloved sons are those who live in grace and charity in this good and perfect God, with the perfection of love. We are all his sons in the order of creation, but his special chosen sons are those in whom God, the supreme Good, takes special delight because he discovers in them his own likeness. Only divine grace and divine love, which is perfect love, deposit, realize, and shape this likeness in the soul of every son of God.

Therefore God, noble by nature, wants the heart of his son not partially but totally, without intermediary, and without any rival companion. Our God, however, is so full of courtesy toward the soul that if a soul gives its heart to him totally, he accepts it totally, but if it gives it to him only partially, he accepts that, even though it is in the nature of perfect love to want all and not just a part. We know that a husband who loves his wife cannot bear the thought that in her secret heart he might share her affections with another. But if a son of God would only get to know and taste the love that is divine—that of the uncreated, incarnate, and suffering God, who is the supreme Good—he would give himself totally to him, and take leave not only of himself but of other creatures as well. He would love this loving God so totally that he would transform himself completely into this God-man, the supreme Good, and beloved one.

This is why, if a soul wishes to attain this perfection of love—in which it gives itself completely and serves God without the thought of a reward in this world, or even in the next, but gives itself to God and serves him for himself alone, as the one who is totally good and the total good, and worthy to be loved for himself alone—such a soul must enter through the straight path and walk along it with a love that is pure, upright, fervent, and ordered.

The first degree of perfect love is to know God in truth

The first degree to be attained, or step that the soul must take when it enters the way of love, through which it desires to reach God, is to know God in truth.[163]

By "to know God in truth" I mean to know him not just from the externals—such as the tone conveyed by writing, words, signs, images, or resemblances to anything created—for this way of knowing something according to the way we speak about it gives a kind of simple knowledge about God. To know God in truth is to know him as he is in himself, to understand his worth, beauty, sweetness, sublimity, power, and goodness, and the supreme Good inherent in him who is the supreme Good. For the way in which a wise person knows something in truth differs from the way a simple person knows only the appearance of truth. To illustrate this, perhaps the following example or comparison might be useful. Suppose two florins, one of gold and one of lead, were lying in the road. A simple person might pick up the gold florin because it was beautiful and shiny, but would not know about the value of gold. The wise person, knowing the truth about gold and lead, would avidly go for the gold florin and pay little attention to the lead one. Similarly, the soul, knowing God in truth, is aware and understands him as good, and not only as good, but as the supreme and perfect Good.

When the first degree of love has been attained, the others follow, the greatest being the degree of transforming love

Discovering that God is good, the soul loves him for his goodness. Loving him, it desires to possess him; desiring him, it gives all that it has and can have, even its own self, in order to possess him; and in possessing him, the soul experiences and tastes his sweetness. Possessing, experiencing, tasting God himself, the supreme and infinite sweetness, it enjoys him with the greatest delight.[164]

Then, enamored with the sweetness of the Beloved, the soul desires to hold him; desiring to hold him, it embraces him; embracing him, it binds and weds itself to God, and finds God bound and wedded to itself in the sweetest form of love. Then the power of love transforms the lover into the Beloved and the Beloved into the lover. This means that, set ablaze by divine love, the soul is transformed by the power of love into God the Beloved whom it loves with such sweetness. Just as hot iron put into the fire takes on the form of fire—its heat, color, power, force—and almost becomes fire itself, as it gives itself completely and not partially while retaining its own substance, similarly, the soul, united to God and with God by the perfect fire of divine love, gives itself, as it were, totally and throws itself into God. Transformed into God, without having lost its own substance, its entire life is changed and through this love it becomes almost totally divine.[165]

For this transformation to happen, it is necessary that knowledge come first, and the love follows which transforms the lover into the Beloved.[166] This is how the soul which knows God in truth and loves him with fervor is transformed into the Good it knows and loves with such fervor.[167]

The said knowledge of God and transformation of love are the work of grace and granted immediately in prayer, especially while reading the "Book of Life"

The soul cannot have true knowledge of God through its own efforts or by means of any created thing, but only by divine light and by a special gift of divine grace. I believe there is no quicker or easier way for the soul to obtain this divine grace from God, supreme Good and supreme Love, than by a devout, pure, humble, continual, and violent prayer.

By prayer I mean not merely prayer from the mouth, but of the mind and heart, of all the powers of the soul and senses of the body. This is the prayer prayed by the soul who wills and desires to find this divine light, studying, meditating, and reading without cease in the Book and the more-than-a-book[168] of Life. This Book of Life is the entire life of Christ while he lived as a mortal on earth.

Hence, God, the Father most high, shows and teaches the form, the manner, and the way by which the soul can have knowledge of him, and can come to him through love. This way and teaching, this same God, the Father most high, shows and teaches through his most loving Son.[169]

The rule of perfect love consists in being in the companionship of the Lord, that is, a life of penance with him

I say more, and I say it firmly convinced of its truth, that the Son of God and of the Father most high, through his always-loving plans and out of his immense love for rational creatures—souls capable of relationship with him—himself provided and still provides himself as the way in this world. By this I mean the truest way, a direct and short way, by which every soul which so desires can walk to God and in God for a small price, and by means of a limited and light penance.

How small and light is this penance, considering the fault which is ours and the punishment we deserve and considering the reward we hope for and the glory promised us! Every soul which has faith can know and see this truth. Our fault was, and is, infinite, just as the divine majesty of God we offend is infinite. The punishment should correspond to the fault. But the divine majesty, wishing to call the soul back into the bosom of its mercy, puts a limit to this infinite punishment and says: "Do penance, so that you can come to me, the same kind of penance that I, the Son of God, did on earth to save you. I forgive you your fault, strike out your offenses, and absolve you from the punishment due to them." In truth, this is a great bargain which the divine goodness makes with the soul: "Do not do for me more than I have done for you; it is not for my faults that you do penance, but I do penance for yours. I do so without expecting any benefit from you; you do so in the hope of obtaining an infinite reward from me."

Therefore, O soul, if you wish to know the small, limited, and short penance which God wishes from you, I tell you this: He wishes you to do the most fitting penance possible, one that fits your condition, a penance as long as you live, and no longer. If you live one hour, you do penance for one hour. If you live longer, do a longer penance. In his just and ordered will God wishes you to do penance only as long as you live and no more.

The example, the method, and the form of how the soul should do penance is perfectly and truly demonstrated and taught in the life of Christ, the penance which he did, the special companionship which accompanied him during his life on earth. From the moment his soul was created and infused into his most holy body in the womb of his most pure mother until his last hour on earth when his soul left his body through his most cruel death on the cross, he never lived apart from this companionship; it never left him while he was in this world. This much cannot be said of any of his apostles, his other followers, John the Evangelist, or even his most holy mother, the Virgin Mary.[170]

The three companions of Christ which led him to perfect love of God: poverty, contempt, and suffering

What kind of a companionship was it, then, that accompanied Christ faithfully, continually, and lovingly? It seems to me it was the one that God the Father on high, according to his plan, destined for his Son for his earthly existence; the most perfect, continual, and highest poverty; the most perfect, continual, and highest contempt; the most perfect, continual, and highest suffering. Such was the companionship which accompanied Christ continually in his continual penance. This penance lasted as long as he lived on earth. Through it he, in his humanity, traveled toward heaven. And through it the soul can and should walk toward God and in God. There is no other way. It is necessary that the way the Head followed, the members should follow; and the companions that accompanied the Head should likewise accompany his members.[171]

a. The first companion of Christ: voluntary poverty

A companion of our head, Christ, was, as I have already said, voluntary, continual, highest, and most perfect poverty. This poverty was of three kinds: The first was great; the second was greater, joined to the first; and the third was most perfect, united to both the first and second. Christ's poverty included all three degrees, but in him they subsisted in the highest and most perfect manner as one.[172]

Christ, the way, the guide of our souls, exemplified the first degree of the most perfect poverty by choosing to live poorly and be poor, bereft of all earthly possessions. He kept nothing for himself: no house, land, vineyard, coins, money, estate, dishware, or any other possessions. He neither accepted any earthly goods, nor wanted to accept anything but a life of extreme bodily neediness, with scarcity, hunger, thirst, cold, hard labor, austerity, and hardship. Neither would he accept anything elegant or refined, but only such coarse and common items as were found at the place, time, and season where he was living his life of strictest poverty.

The second degree of poverty, greater than the first, was that he wanted to be poor with regard to relatives, friends, and all earthly affections. As a result, he did not have any friends or relatives who could intervene to spare him even one piercing by the nails, one lash of the rod or whip, or a single rebuke or insult. He so stripped himself of the love of his relatives and parents that not for the sake of mother, nor brother, nor any friend, did he omit to do, or even want to omit to do, anything which pleased or could please the will of his most high Father.[173]

The third and supreme degree of poverty was that Christ stripped himself of his very self, became poor with regard to his own power, wisdom, and glory. The uncreated God, the God-made-man, the incarnate and suffering God wanted to appear and live in this world as a little poor man: powerless, simple, and weak, devoid of glory and human wisdom.[174]

O poverty, how you are scorned! In our day, you are trumpeted out of town by almost every class of people in this world. Who can be found today to glory in such a perfect companion? Blessed the creature who can glory in having such a companion in his penance. For Christ, in order to teach us, wanted poverty as his companion. But we know our own behavior only too well. For not only do we grasp at temporal goods with a perverse sense of their necessity, but also we are not satisfied with our fair share, we go after what is superfluous.

Alas, alas, we know what kind of clothing the Son of God wore! We know what kind of bed he slept on, what kind of bed the cross was! We know what kind of drink he was given to slake his thirst! We know how much he was protected, defended, and helped by his friends and relatives, and we know what kind of company he kept! We know how much he wanted to defend himself, how he wanted to exalt himself, how he wanted to glory in his own power and wisdom! And indeed he could have done this in all honesty, for he possessed in himself the power to do whatever he wanted by his very essence, by grace and by nature. But we, dishonestly, wish to snatch at what we do not have, and cannot achieve through our own powers, and we display to others what we do not really have at all. Thus our penance does not proceed along the right path, because it withdraws from and dismisses Christ's own companion, holy poverty.[175]

b. The second companion: willingly suffering others' contempt

The second companion of Christ's life in this world was contempt; voluntarily and perfectly, he became an object of contempt. He wanted to live and did live in this world like a servant who had been cast aside, sold, and not ransomed. And not just as an ordinary servant but as one considered evil, iniquitous, and as one vituperated, derided, bound, struck, beaten, whipped, and finally condemned and killed for no reason. When someone, by chance, wished to confer some worldly honor on him, he always opposed it by either word or deed. He always fled worldly honors and sought after shame and contempt in this world, but not by giving any cause or reasonable motivation by any fault or lack on his part.[176]

Can such a person be found today, who loves this kind of companionship so much as to flee honor and love shame, who wants to be vilified, debased, and despised for any good deeds done, rather than praised and commended? Believe me, there is no faithful person to be found, except the one who is joined to Christ, the head, through a love that is perfect. For a soul, fully in love with Christ, which perceives that Christ, as head, loves and wants such companionship, will love and want it in a similar manner. There are some who say: "I love Christ, I want to love him, and I do not care if the world does not honor me; but I do not love him to the point of wanting or desiring to be shamed and despised for I live in a continual struggle and fear of what someone might do to me and what God might permit."

This is clearly a sign that this soul has little faith, little justice, little love, and is very lukewarm. Either the soul has or has not committed deeds for which it deserves to be confounded, chastised, and shamed— and very few can justly be excused on such counts. If the soul has committed such deeds, publicly or secretly, it should be prepared to bear the consequences with patience and joy, and with calmness of both body and soul. The soul should do so for two reasons: First, the chastisement and shame purge the soul of the punishment it ought to receive because of its own iniquity; second, the chastisement and the shame endured and born with patience render satisfaction for the debt to God and neighbor in conformity to the will of divine justice. But if the soul has not committed such deeds, either in desire or action, it should, if God permits, bear chastisement, shame, and abasement with a hundredfold greater patience and joy, for these are meant for our growth in grace. And as the merit of grace grows, so do our reward and what is given to us in glory. But we, for our part, fear that the good God might make us grow. We do not fear that our faults might make us lesser and weaker.—In truth this is how holy souls, the friends of God, grow.

Thus Christ, who had committed no faults, loved shame, shunned honors, and in conformity with the divine plan, freely chose to be debased and held in contempt in his life in order to teach his friends how they can grow in merit and in grace through love.

Such, therefore, is the second companion which continually accompanied Christ during his whole life. He had such a love for this companion that he never wished to be separated from it. If we wish to see the beginning, the middle, and the end, in short, the entire life of Christ, the Son of God, it was all humility, living without the honors of this world, and being the object of extreme contempt.

c. The third companion: extreme suffering

The third companion, more deeply experiential and continual, was the extreme suffering which, from the very beginning, accompanied the soul of Christ; for his holy soul, united with his body to his divinity, was filled with highest wisdom.[177] He became, all in an instant, both a pilgrim on life's way, and one who comprehended what that way entailed. Already in the womb of his mother, his holy soul began to feel the most extreme suffering as perfect reparation to God, and this not for his own faults but for the faults of humanity. For Christ saw, felt, knew, and understood, together and separately, all the torments and each one in detail which he would have to endure, soul and body, with deepfelt pain.

The holy soul of Christ knew beforehand each of the knife-like tongues, that is, each of the sharp words which would cut him up in the future.[178] Christ knew when, how, by whom, and where he would be attacked. He knew and saw how he, as man, was to be betrayed, sold, arrested, abandoned, renounced, bound, derided, beaten, whipped, judged, condemned as a thief, led to a cross, stripped, crucified, put to death, blasphemed, pierced by a lance which opened a wound in his holy side. He also knew beforehand all the hammer blows and all the nail wounds. His holy soul knew in itself and had before itself all the sufferings, the groans, the wailing, and the pain-filled lamentations of his mother. It is thus that the whole life of Christ was accompanied by continual sufferings.[179]

How will the unhappy soul which only wishes to receive consolations in this world go to him, who is the way of suffering? In truth, the soul perfectly enamored of Christ, its beloved, would not wish to have any other bed or state in this world than the one he had. I believe that even Mary, watching her beloved son lamenting and dying on the cross, did not ask of him then to experience sweetness but rather suffering. It is in a soul the sign of very weak love to want from Christ, the Beloved, anything in this world but suffering. It should certainly be possible for the soul to understand that a good master is more pleased by the services of a poor servant who serves him faithfully out of love, without pay or benefits, than the services of someone rich, who receives good wages every day and serves in the hope of receiving special benefits. Similarly, if a soul, fattened on the great sweetness of its experience and taste of God, runs lovingly toward him, it does not have as much merit as the one who runs to God and serves him with an equal and similar love, but without consolation and in a state of continual suffering.

d. Concluding exhortation

This, it seems to me, is what I am taught by divine light, which comes from the life of Christ, who is the way by which we go, by means of love, in God and to God. This was the way Christ, our head, went, and it is by this way that the hands, arms, shoulders, feet, legs, and all the members of the body should go. The soul will discover that by going by the way of temporal poverty it will obtain eternal riches; through contempt and shame, highest honor and great glory; through a light penance accompanied with pain and suffering, the possession of the supreme

Good, God eternal, accompanied by an infinite amount of sweetness and consolations. But the soul should not forget, as has been said, that it should serve God for himself alone, for he is worthy of being loved and served by every rational creature because of his own supreme goodness. Thanks be to God.

INSTRUCTION XXXV:
THANKSGIVING FOR THE MYSTERIES IN THE LIFE OF THE SAVIOR AND THE GIFTS OF THE CREATOR

This is the last letter our mother, the most holy Angela of Foligno, wrote before her final illness.[180] She said that it would be her last letter, for she foresaw her happy passage from this life long before it happened. She spoke with much affection and had almost to force her disheartened scribe to write what she said.

Angela, in prayer, praises God's great love made visible in the incarnation

My God, make me worthy of knowing your highest mystery— brought about by your most ardent and ineffable charity, with the charity dispensed by the Trinity—that is, the most high mystery of your most holy incarnation which you accomplished for our sake. The incarnation was the beginning of our salvation and it does two things for us: First, it fills us with love; second, it makes us certain of our salvation.

O incomprehensible charity! There is indeed no greater charity than the one by which my God became flesh in order that he might make me God. O heartfelt love poured out for me! When you assumed human form, you gave of yourself in order to make me. You did not let go of anything in yourself in any way that would lessen you or your divinity, but the abyss of your conception makes me pour out these deep, heartfelt words: O incomprehensible one, made comprehensible! O uncreated one, made creature! O inconceivable one, made conceivable! O impalpable one, become palpable!

O Lord, make me worthy of seeing the depth of the charity which you communicated to us in your most holy incarnation. O happy fault, which merited that we discover the most hidden depths of the divine

charity until then hidden from us. Oh, in truth, I cannot imagine anything greater to contemplate! O most high, make me able to understand
this most high and ineffable charity.

Angela contemplates the five mysteries in the life of the Savior and begs God to be able to know fully their greatness

O Lord, there are five mysteries which you wrought for our sake.
Enable us, O Lord, to understand them. The first is the mystery of the
incarnation; the second, the mystery of the nativity of the Son of God;
the third, the death of the Son of God for us; the fourth, the resurrection; the fifth, the ascension into heaven.

There are three things we should consider concerning the incarnation of the Son of God.

The first is love. O highest and transformed love! O vision divine!
O ineffable one! When will you, Jesus Christ, make me understand that
you were born for me? Oh, how glorious it is to truly understand—as I
now see and understand—that you were born for me. This fills me with
every conceivable delight. The same certitude that we derive from the
incarnation we also derive from the nativity; the reason he became incarnate is the same as the reason he was born. O admirable one! How
wonderful are the mysteries which you have brought about for us!

The second mystery is what the incarnation of the Son of God does
for us: It grants us certitude of our salvation. We can be very certain that
the purpose of his incarnation was the same as that of his birth because
we have evidence of the birth of Jesus Christ in poverty, suffering, and
contempt, for in this state he was born, lived, and ended his life.

The third is the mystery of his death. He was born to die for us.
There are five things to consider about the death of Jesus Christ. The
first is its declaration of the certitude of our salvation. The second is its
strength and victory over our enemies. The third is the fullness and
superabundance of the love of God made manifest by his death. The
fourth is that he fills us with the most high truth, poured out from the
profound depths of his heart, that is, the knowledge, sight, and understanding of how God the Father shows, teaches, makes clear, and declares his Son to us through his most holy incarnation, his nativity, and
his death. The fifth is the consideration of how the Son of God manifests his Father to us by his obedience through his whole life, an obe-

dience which he brought to a conclusion with his death. Through such obedience he answered to God the Father on behalf of the human race.

Make me worthy, O uncreated God, to know the depth of your love and of your most ardent charity. Make me worthy of understanding the ineffable charity you communicated to us when you showed us your son Jesus Christ in the incarnation, and when he, your Son, manifested you, the Father, to us. O admirable and joyous love! In truth, in you is to be found all that is pleasant, agreeable, and delightful. This is the contemplation which elevates the soul from the world, lifts it above itself, and brings it peace and tranquility.

The fourth is the mystery of the resurrection, and, in particular, two effects of this mystery: the first, that the resurrection gives us a firm hope of our own resurrection; second, that it makes us know spiritual resurrection. This God accomplishes through divine grace when he brings the dead back to life and restores the sick to health. O most high, admirable, unknown mystery, ineffable and sacred, you have fulfilled all our needs and aspirations. Make me worthy, Lord, to know this most high mystery.

The fifth is the mystery of your ascension. O Lord, make me worthy to know this most high mystery. O Love, make me worthy and capable of understanding this mystery, for in your ascension is fulfilled and brought to completion our whole salvation. O my Lord Jesus Christ, you have placed us in possession of God your Father!

These five mysteries are the school for those who are true scholars. The true school, in which these five mysteries are learned, is the school of continual prayer. Make me worthy, Lord, to know and to understand the spiritual charity with which you created me. Enable me, O incomprehensible one, to know and to understand the inestimable and most ardent charity which was yours, the deep and heartfelt love with which you, from all eternity, chose the human race to see you, and with which you, the most high, have deigned to want to see us. Make us worthy, Lord, to know our guilt so that through it we can come to know the God-made-man whom you sent to us to remove our guilt.

Angela praises the seven gifts of the Creator and gives thanks to God, beseeching him that she might understand these gifts fully

After this, Angela spoke of the seven gifts, or very special benefits, bestowed on us by the goodness of God. She began by saying: Make me capable and make me worthy of understanding these seven gifts which, among many others, you have bestowed upon us.

The first is the ineffable gift of creation.

The second is the wonderful election by which you have deigned to choose us to be in your presence.

The third is the inestimable gift you bestowed on us when you sent your Son to his death in order to give us life. This is the gift of gifts.

The fourth is the highest gift of your goodness: You deigned to make me a sensible and rational creature, not an irrational beast. O admirable one, the power of reason which you have placed in me does three things for me. First, it makes me know you, the admirable one! Second, it makes me know my sins. Third, this same power of reason, which is mine by your grace, makes me oppose evil with my free will. O incomprehensible one, you have given me no greater gift than this. O form-without-exemplar, you formed us from your own form when you made us rational creatures. You have indeed vested us with yourself and with your own power of reason.

The fifth is the gift of understanding. Make me worthy, Lord, to know this gift, for you have given it to us so that we may know you, my God.

The sixth is the gift of wisdom. O Lord, make me worthy to know the most ardent charity with which you have given us this gift of your wisdom. Oh, in truth, this is the gift of gifts: to savor you in truth.

The seventh gift is love. O supreme Being, make me worthy to understand this gift, which is greater than any other gift. For all the angels and the saints have no other gift than that of seeing you, their Beloved, and loving you and contemplating you. O gift above all other gifts, because you are that gift and you are love. O highest good, you have made us to know you, love itself, and make us love such love. All those who come into your presence will be satisfied according to the love they have. Nothing leads contemplatives to contemplate, except true love. O admirable one, you have done wonders in your sons! O supreme Good! O incomprehensible and most burning charity! O divine person, you have deigned to sustain us within your own substance! Oh, this is a wonder above all wonders that you have accomplished for your sons! Certainly, there is no human intelligence which is not found wanting before the presence of your substance, but with divine intelligence we experience your divine substance! It is the pledge granted specifically to those who are true solitaries. It is the occupation of all the choirs of angels. And those who are true contemplatives are occupied in this way. Afterward they become solitaries and are separated from the earth. Their conversation is in heaven.

INSTRUCTION XXXVI:
ANGELA'S HAPPY PASSAGE INTO HEAVEN, AND HER LAST WORDS

"In the name of our Lord Jesus Christ, the crucified Nazarean, may his name be blessed forever and ever. Amen." These were the last words uttered by Angela of Foligno, the legitimate spouse of Christ, as she neared her happy passage from this life.[181]

Stricken by illness, on the feast of the Holy Angels, Angela, in ecstatic contemplation in their presence, is finally wedded to the Divine Spouse

First of all, at the beginning of her illness, on the feast of the Angels in September,[182] Angela said: I wanted very much to receive communion on this feast of the Angels, but there was no one available to bring me the most sacred body of Christ. I became very sad. Then in the midst of this sadness and this desire to receive communion, I began to think about this feast and the praise of the angels, that is, their function and activity of praising God.

Suddenly, my soul was elevated and a great multitude of angels appeared to me. They led my soul to an altar and told me: "Here is the altar of the angels." On the altar they showed my soul the praise of the angels, that is, the one whom they praise and who is the praise of all. The angels then said to my soul: "In the one who is on the altar is the perfection and fulfillment of the sacrifice which you are seeking." And they added: "Prepare yourself to receive the one who has espoused you with the ring of his love. This union with him has already been realized. Now, he wishes to renew it."

My soul truly experienced all this, and it was much more than words could express. These are but a shadow of what I experienced; my memory of it is only a shadow of the truth my soul experienced. But that shadow gladdens my soul more than I can say.

THE BOOK OF BLESSED ANGELA (*INSTRUCTIONS*)

Near the feast of the Nativity of our Lord, Angela,
while sick, is freed from the storms which assail the soul

After this, while Angela lay shattered by her last illness, her mind was more than usually immersed and absorbed in the abyss of the divine infinity. She spoke only at intervals, a few brief phrases at a time, and rarely. We, who were present, tried to grasp what she said as best we could. We have briefly assembled her words as follows.

Once, near the feast of the Nativity of Our Lord, at about the time she passed away to Christ, she said: "The Word was made flesh!" And, after a long delay, as if coming from another world, she added: "Oh, every creature is found wanting! Oh, the intelligence of the angels is likewise not enough!" We asked her: "How are creatures found wanting, and for what is the intelligence of angels not enough?" She responded: "To comprehend!"

Afterward, she said: "Behold, the moment has arrived in which my God fulfills his promise to me. Christ, his Son, has now presented me to the Father." But before this she had also said: "You know how when Christ was in the boat, there were great storms? Truly, it is sometimes like that with the soul. He permits storms to assail it, and he seems to sleep." And another time, she said: "In truth, God at times allows a person to be completely broken and downtrodden before he puts an end to the storm. He behaves in this way especially with his legitimate sons."

At the end, Angela blesses her spiritual sons,
greatly commending them to love one another

On another occasion, she said: "My sons, I would be glad to tell you some things if I knew that God would not deceive me." She was referring to the promise of her approaching death, because having a great desire to die, as she said, she feared very much that God would restore her to health. Then she said: "What I wish to say, I say to you only in order that you might put into practice what I myself did not. I say it only for the honor of God and for your own profit. I do not want to take to the grave something that could be of help to you."

Here is what God told my soul: "Whatever is mine is yours, and whatever is yours is mine." Who can deserve that all the riches of God should belong to her, that our riches should be God's and his ours? In truth nothing can deserve this except charity! O my dear little sons, fathers, and brothers, strive to love one another and to truly possess divine charity. Because by this charity and mutual love the soul deserves to inherit divine riches. I do not make any other testament except that I wish for you to have love for one another, and I leave you all that I have inherited: the life of Christ, that is, his poverty, suffering, and contempt.[183]

She placed her hand on the head of each of us saying: May God bless you, as I do, my dear sons, you and all the others who are not here. As Christ has showed to me an eternal blessing and indicated its meaning to me, so do I bestow that blessing, with all my heart, on you, both present and absent. And may Christ himself bestow it to you with that hand which was nailed on the cross. Those who will possess this inheritance, namely, the life of Christ, and become true sons of prayer, will without doubt later possess the heritage of eternal life.

Later she said: I have nothing to do with what I wish to say, for all of it is from God. For it pleased the divine goodness to place in my care, under my solicitude, all his sons and daughters who are in the world, who are on this side of the sea or beyond it. I have kept them in my care and suffered for them, and my sufferings were more than you could know. She then added: O my God, I now place them once again in your hands; keep them and preserve them from all evil.[184]

Afterward she added: My little children, strive to be charitable toward everyone, because I say to you that my soul truly received more from God when I wept and suffered with all my heart over the sins of others than when I wept over my own sins. Truly, there is no greater charity on earth than to suffer for the sins of others. The world could mock what I say, because it seems to be contrary to nature that someone could suffer and weep over the sins of one's neighbor more than for one's own. But the charity which does this is not of this world. My children, strive to have this charity.

Judge no one, even when you see someone commit mortal sin. I do not tell you that sin should not displease you, or that you should not abhor sin, but I say that you should not judge sinners, because you do not know the judgments of God. For many seem to us to be saved and are actually damned before God, and there are many who seem to us to be damned and are saved by God. I can tell you that there are some whom you have despised, who stray, that is, who are destroying the good things they have begun, but about whom I entertain a strong hope that God will lead them back to his way.

Like a spouse prepared for her wedding, Angela has a foretaste of the coming of her divine spouse

On another occasion, Angela said that her soul had been washed, cleansed, and immersed in the blood of Christ, which was fresh and warm as if it flowed from the body of Christ on the cross. Then it was said to my soul: "This is what cleansed you." And my soul replied: "My God, will I be deceived?" "No," she was told.

My soul then heard these words: "O my spouse, my beautiful one, I love you with great affection. I do not want you to come to me burdened with these pains and sorrows, but jubilant and filled with ineffable joy. For it is only fitting for a king to wed his long-loved bride, clothed in royal garments." He showed me the robe which the bridegroom shows to the bride he has loved for so long. This robe was neither of purple, nor of scarlet, nor of sendal, nor of samite, but of some marvelous light which clothed her soul.

Then God showed me the Word, so that now I would understand what is meant by the Word and what it is to speak the Word. And he said to me: "This is the Word who wished to incarnate himself for you." At that very moment the Word came to me and went all through me, touched all of me, and embraced me.

Before this, he had also said: "Come to me, my beloved, my beautiful one, my dearest, whom I love so much. Come, for all the saints are waiting for you with great joy." And he added: "I do not entrust to either the angels or any other saints the task of bringing you to me. I will come for you in person and I will take you with me." A long time before this he had also said: "You have become suitable to be with me and have attained a most high place before my majesty."

Final admonition to her disciples that they be little and humble whatever the advantages, spiritual or temporal, they may attain in life

On another occasion she said: Cursed be the advantages in life which inflate the soul: power, honor, and ecclesiastical office! My little children, strive to be small.

And then she cried out: O unknown nothingness! O unknown

nothingness! Truly, a soul cannot have a better awareness in this world than to perceive its own nothingness and to stay in its own cell. There is greater deception in spiritual advantages than in temporal ones—that is, to know how to speak about God, to do great penances, to understand the Scriptures, and to have one's heart almost constantly preoccupied with spiritual matters. For those who are taken by them fall many times into errors and are more difficult to lead back to the right way than those who have temporal advantages. And again she cried out: O unknown nothingness! O unknown nothingness!

Angela commends her soul to God and, as if gently falling asleep, she dies in peace and joy

When she was near death, the very day before she died, she frequently said: "Father, into your hands I commend my soul and my spirit." One time, after she said this, she told us: "I have just received this answer to what I said: That which is imprinted on your heart in life, it is impossible not to have in death." Then we asked her: "Do you want to go away and leave us?" She replied: "I have kept it hidden from you, but now no longer. I must go."

That very day, all her suffering ceased. For many days before she had been horribly tormented and afflicted in every single part of herself, internally and externally. But now her body lay in such a state of rest and her soul in such happiness that she seemed to taste already some of the joy promised to her. We asked her then if this promised state of jubilation had indeed been granted to her. And she responded that, true enough, she was already in this said joy-filled state. She remained lying with her body and mind at rest and in a jubilant mood until Saturday night after Compline. She was surrounded by many friars who celebrated the Divine Office in her presence. It was during the last hour of that day, on the octave of the Feast of the Holy Innocents that, as if gently falling asleep, she died peacefully.

Thus, her most holy soul, freed from the flesh and absorbed into the abyss of divine charity, received from Christ, her spouse, the stole of immortality and innocence to reign with him forever. Where she is, may we too be led by the power of the most holy cross, the merits of Christ's most holy mother, and the intercession of our most holy mother, Angela, by Jesus Christ himself, the Son of God, who lives and reigns with the Father and the Holy Spirit, forever and ever. Amen.

OBITUARY

The venerable spouse of Christ, Angela of Foligno, passed from the shipwreck of this world into the joys of heaven—promised to her a long time before—in the year of our Lord 1309, January 4, during the reign of Pope Clement V. Thanks be to God. Amen.[185]

EPILOGUE

Lest worldly wisdom—which is animal, earthbound, and diabolically inspired, coming from pride-filled teachers who talk big but do nothing—remain forever unconfounded by God's eternal wisdom, God raised up a woman of lay state, who was bound to worldly obligations, a husband and sons, possessions and wealth, who was unlearned and frail.[186] By means of the power divinely infused in her through the power of the cross of Christ, God and man, she broke these worldly bonds and ascended to the peaks of gospel perfection. By the holy foolishness of the cross of Christ, she renewed the wisdom of gospel perfection. She showed us the way of Jesus Christ. This way had become overgrown and obliterated, and the high and mighty had told us, by their words and their deeds, that it could not be followed. But Angela showed us not only that Jesus' way was possible and easy, but also that it leads to the highest delights for virtuous souls.

O heavenly wisdom of gospel perfection, oh, how you have, with the eternal God, rendered foolish the wisdom of this world! And you, eternal God, through Angela, have raised up against men, a woman; against the proud, someone humble; against the clever, someone simple; against the lettered, someone unschooled; against religious hypocrisy, the holiness of someone who condemned and despised herself; against empty talkers and idle hands, a marvelous zeal in deed and silence in words; and against the prudence of the flesh, the prudence of the spirit, which is the science of the cross of Christ. Thus, a strong woman brought to light what was buried under by blind men and their worldly speculations.

Therefore may all shame be gone from all the offspring of this holy mother. Learn from Angela the great counsel, the wisdom of the way of the cross and its riches, namely the poverty, suffering, contempt, and the true obedience of the good Jesus and his most sweet mother. Teach it to men and women and all creatures through the language of efficacious

317

deeds. So that you may be proud in being called to such a school, know, dear ones, that she herself is the teacher in the discipline of God and the one chosen for this work.

She is truly a shining light of God, a mirror without blemish of God's majesty, and an image of his goodness. Although she is only one person, she can do all things. Even though she remains in herself, she renews all, and her influence extends itself to holy souls throughout the world. She makes all her sons prophets of truth and friends of God. Truly, anyone who fights against Angela—or rather, against the way of Christ, and his life, and his teachings—has no love for anyone. This is taken from the seventh and eighth chapter of the book of Wisdom.[187]

Remember, most dearly beloved ones, that the apostles, who first preached Christ's life of suffering, learned from a woman that his life was raised from the dead. In a similar manner, most beloved sons of our holy mother, our rule has been dead in carnal men since the suffering-filled observance of it by our first apostolic parents, Francis and his companions. Now, learn along with me that this rule, preached by the observance of our holy mother, is immortal![188] It is not against the order of providence that God, to men's shame, made a woman a teacher—and one that to my knowledge has no match on earth. For St. Jerome said of the prophetess Huldah, to whom crowds ran, that the gift of prophecy had been transmitted to the female sex to shame men who are doctors of the law but who transgress the commandments of God.[189] Thanks be to God always. Amen.

Notes to the Introduction

1. The statue (sixteenth century), which also serves as the art cover for this volume, is by an anonymous Umbrian sculptor, who incorrectly dresses Angela as a religious. Until 1856, a cavity within the statue contained Angela's relics. These were later placed in the wax reproduction of Angela that now lies on the altar dedicated to her in the church of San Francesco in Foligno. See Fabio Bisogni, "L'iconografia della Beata Angela da Foligno," in *Sante e Beate Umbre tra il XIII e il XIV secolo* (Foligno: Edizioni dell'Arquata-Foligno, 1986), 144. On the history of this reliquary, and the controversy between the Friars Minor Conventual and the commune of Foligno over the ownership of Angela's remains (1544–1909), see M. Faloci-Pulignani, "La Beata Angela da Foligno: Memorie e documenti," *Miscellanea Francescana* 25 (1925): 117–24.

2. M. J. Ferré, "Les principales dates de la vie d'Angèle de Foligno," *Revue d'histoire franciscaine* 2 (January 1925): 31–34. His chronology awaits further verification.

3. The title on the cover of one of the earliest manuscripts (cod. Assisi, ca. 1315–1381) of Angela's writings reads: *Liber sororis Lellae de fulgineo de tertio ordine sancti francisci*. During this period, saints were often called by diminutives as a sign of humility.

4. The original documents, on which the assumptions (based on unverifiable local traditions) in the text about Angela's life prior to her conversion are made, have been lost. The main source for the records of these local traditions is Ludovico Jacobili's seventeenth-century biography of Angela, "Vita della B. Angela da Foligno," in *Vite dei SS. e BB. di Foligno* (Foligno 1628), 16–24. For further documentation related to Angela's life, see M. Faloci Pulignani, *La Beata Angela da Foligno: Memorie e documenti* (Gubbio 1926); idem, *Miscellanea Francescana* 25 (1925): 75–80, 113–32; 26 (1926): 78–81.

5. Ferré, "Les principales dates," 11.

6. In the Middle Ages, most letters were dictated by their author, taken down and copied by a scribe or secretary. See Giles Constable, "Letters and Letter Collection," in *Typologie des sources du moyen âge occidental* 17 (Paris: Brépols, 1976), 13–14.

7. Instructions 7, 14, 17, clearly indicate that Angela received many letters from her disciples, which she read and to which she responded. Scholars remain divided on her ability to write. Ferré and Blasucci deny it; Thier and Calufetti, editors of the critical edition of Angela's writings, are not convinced; Andreoli affirms it. See M. J. Ferré, *Le livre de l'expérience des vrais fidèles* (Paris: Editions E. Droz, 1927), xiii; A. Blasucci, *Il libro della Beata Angela da Foligno* (Rome: 1950), 263, n. 9; L. Thier and A. Calufetti, eds., *Il Libro della Beata Angela da Foligno* (Rome: Editiones Collegii S. Bonaventurae ad Claras Aquas, 1985), 26 and note 8 (hereafter referred to as *Il Libro*); S. Andreoli, "La Beata Angela era analfabeta?" *Gazetta da Foligno*, 15 January 1975.

8. Toward the end of instruction 5. Instruction 1 contains an even more vivid confession by Angela of the waywardness of her past life, although this may well be a medieval exaggeration, perhaps not written by Angela, but by an anonymous scribe after her death.

9. Faloci Pulignani concludes that prior to her conversion "Angela's life was not scandalous, at least not publicly so" ("Memorie e documenti," 77); Blasucci reaches the same conclusion (*La Beata Angela da Foligno* [Foligno: Edizione Chiesa di S. Francesco, 1978], 10), as do Thier and Calufetti (*Il Libro*, 27); Ferré asserts that "her sin was of the flesh" (*Sainte Angèle de Foligno: sa vie, ses oeuvres* [Paris: Librairie Plon, 1936], 3). For less substantiated opinions, see P. Leone, who claims that "she had forgotten the most holy obligations of wife and mother" (*Aureola Serafica*, vol. 1 [Quarachi, 1898], 769); R. P. Hostachy: "She lived with a man" (*Joie et sainteté* [Lille, 1924], 90); J. K. Huysmans: "Married, she practiced adultery. Lovers tumble from her bed in succession, and when spent, she sheds them like scales from her flesh" (*En route* [Paris, 1895], 109).

10. Note also that the common opinion among theologians and canonists during this period was that marital sex was free from sin only so long as no one enjoyed it. Both law and morality also required a higher standard of sexual restraint from women than from men. See James A. Brundage, "Sex, Marriage, and the Legal Commentators, 1234–1348,"

in *Law, Sex, and Society in Medieval Europe* (Chicago: The University of Chicago Press, 1987), 417–87.

11. Ferré's argument for setting 1285 (after July) as the date of Angela's conversion is based on the fact that before this date the bishop of Foligno, Paparone of the Papereschi of Rome, O.P., was a Dominican, who probably would not have requested a Franciscan as his chaplain, given that there was a Dominican friary in Foligno. See "Les principales dates," 30. The argument is not conclusive.

12. According to Ferré, Berardo II of the counts of Attignano was bishop of Foligno from 12 July 1285 to 1296: "Le opere autentiche di Angela da Foligno ritrovate dopo sei secoli di dimenticanza," *Studi Francescani* 10 (1924): 114, n. 1.

13. The manuscripts identify him, and only a few times, as "Fra. A." It is also uncertain whether the confessor in question is the same person as the friar who later was to serve as Angela's scribe and confessor. For further details see my subsequent discussion of "Fra. A." (sec. II, A).

14. Ferré, "Les principales dates," 30.

15. This is assuming that Arnaldo was also the same friar who previously had heard her conversion-confession in Foligno. See above, n. 13.

16. About half a year separates the redaction of the first twenty steps from the seven supplementary ones. Ferré dates the supplementary steps as follows: "First step: 1291. Very probable. Second step: 1291 and beginning of 1292. Very probable. Third step: Summer of 1292. Certain. Fourth step: Beginning of August 1292–end of Summer 1293. Certain. Fifth step: Lent 1294. Morally certain. Sixth step: Spring 1294–Spring 1296. Certain. Seventh step: First months 1294–end of Summer 1296. Certain" ("Les principales dates," 26).

17. Cited in Faloci Pulignani, "Memorie e documenti," 115. The editors of the critical edition believe that this encounter, including the presence of Angela's companion falsely identified as Pasqualina, is fictional. See *Il Libro*, 32–33 and n. 37. The monastery of Valle Gloria was, after San Damiano, the oldest Poor Clare monastery. See Faloci Pulignani, "Le Clarisse di Vallegloria in Spello," *Miscellanea Francescana* 14 (1913): 165–70.

18. Faloci Pulignani, "Memorie e documenti," 116.

19. In 1930, the Chapter of the cathedral in Foligno, through Cardinal Ernest Dubois, archbishop of Paris, made a formal but unsuccessful request for Angela's canonization. See Faloci Pulignani, "Beata o Santa Angela" in *L'autobiografia e gli scritti della Beata Angela da Foligno*, trans.

Maria Castiglione Humani [Città di Castello: Casa Editrice "Il Solco," 1932], xxxi–xxxiii. A similar, and likewise unsuccessful, request was made to Pope John Paul II on the occasion of the celebration, in 1985, in honor of the seventh centenary of Angela's conversion in 1285.

20. Until now the nonmanuscript tradition has identified the companion's name as Pasqualina. According to the editors of the critical edition, chroniclers of Franciscan and Foligno history, including the *Martyrologium Franciscanum*, have falsely identified a certain Bl. Pasqualina (d., possibly, 1313), also a Folignate and member of the Franciscan Third Order, as Angela's companion. Their argument is not totally convincing. See *Il Libro*, 30–31, and n. 33–37.

21. Chap. 3, p. 141; chap. 7, p. 191.

22. Masazuola, for instance, is regularly mentioned as a recipient, along with Angela, of God's blessings, the most striking of which is suggested by the episode in which both of them drank water they had used to wash the sores of a leper: the water tasted so sweet that, Angela recalled, it was as if "we had received holy communion" (chap. 5, p. 163).

23. Instruction 17, p. 270.

24. Good general surveys of the Middle Ages that I have consulted include the following: Hubert Jedin, gen. ed., *History of the Church*, vol. 4: *From the High Middle Ages to the Eve of the Reformation*, by Hans-George Beck et al., trans. Anselm Biggs (New York: Seabury Press, 1980); Louis J. Rogier et al., gen. eds., *The Christian Centuries*, vol. 2: *The Middle Ages*, by David Knowles with Dimitri Obolensky (New York: Paulist Press, 1969); Léopold Genicot, *Le XIII siècle européen* (Paris: Presses Universitaires de France, 1968); Jacob Huizinga, *The Waning of the Middle Ages: A Study of the Forms of Life, Thought and Art in France and the Netherlands in the XIVth and XVth Centuries*, trans. F. Hopman (London: Arnold, 1924); R. W. Southern, *Western Society and the Church in the Middle Ages* (Harmondsworth: Penguin Books, 1970); and Jacques Le Goff, *Medieval Civilisation*, trans. Julia Barrow (New York: Basil Blackwell, 1988).

25. For the papacy in the Middle Ages, see Geoffrey Barraclough, *The Medieval Papacy* (New York: W. W. Norton & Company Inc., 1968); Daniel Waley, *The Papal State in the Thirteenth Century* (London: Macmillan & Co., 1961); and Walter Ulmann, *The Growth of Papal Government in the Middle Ages*, 3rd ed. (New York: Barnes & Noble, 1970).

26. See Henry Dwight Sedgewich, *Italy in the Thirteenth Century*,

2d ed. (Boston and New York: Houghton Mifflin Co., 1933); and Robert Brentano, *Two Churches: England and Italy in the Thirteenth Century* (Princeton: Princeton University Press, 1968).

27. *Purgatorio*, canto six, 76, Italian text and trans. with commentary by Charles S. Singleton, Bolingen series LXXX (Princeton: Princeton University Press, 1973), 197.

28. For the growth of medieval cities in Italy, see E. Ennen, *Storia della città medievale* (Bari: Ed. Laterza, 1978); L. A. Kotel'Nikova, *Mondo contadino e città in Italia dall'XI al XIV secolo* (Bologna: Il Mulino, 1975); and David Herlihy, *Cities and Society in Medieval Italy* (London: Variorum Reprints, 1980).

29. For demographic and commercial expansion, see David Herlihy, *Medieval and Renaissance Pistoia: The Social History of the Italian Town 1200–1430* (New Haven: Yale University Press, 1967); Armando Sapori, *The Italian Merchant in the Middle Ages* (New York: W. W. Norton & Co. Inc., 1970); and Francesco Valsecchi, *Commune e corporazione nel medioevo Italiano* (Milan: La Goliardica, 1949).

30. See Daniel Russo, "Saint François, les franciscains et les représentations du Christ sur la croix en Ombrie au XIIIe siècle," *Mélanges Ecole Française de Rome* 96 (1964): 548–717; see also Emile Mâle, *Religious Art: From the Twelfth to the Eighteenth Century* (New York: Pantheon Books, 1949), 61–123.

31. The following studies were especially helpful for the description of the spirituality of this period: G. Gracco, "La spiritualità italiana del tre-quatrocento, linee interpretative," *Studio Patavina* 18 (1971): 74–116; Dom Jean Leclerc, Dom François Vandenbroucke, and Louis Bouyer, *The Spirituality of the Middle Ages*, trans. The Benedictines of Holme Eden Abbey, Carlisle (New York: Seabury Press, 1982); Richard Kieckhefer, *Unquiet Souls: Fourteenth-Century Saints and Their Religious Milieu* (Chicago: The University of Chicago Press, 1984); Raffaelo Morghen, *Medievo Cristiano* (Bari: Editori Laterza, 1968); M. Petrocchi, *Storia della spiritualità italiana*, vol. 1 (Rome: Ed. di Storia e Letteratura, 1978); Francis Rapp, L'église et la vie religieuse en occident à la fin du moyen âge (Paris: Presses Universitaires de France); Jill Rait, ed., in collaboration with Bernard McGinn and John Meyendorff, *Christian Spirituality: High Middle Ages and Reformation* (New York: Crossroad, 1987); André Vauchez, *La spiritualité du moyen âge occidental: VIII–XII siècles* (Paris: Presses Universitaires de France, 1975); and Felix Verne, *Medieval Spirituality*, trans. The Benedictines of Talacre (London: Sands & Co., 1930).

32. For Innocent III, see Sidney Raymond Packard, *Europe and the Church under Innocent III* (New York: Russell & Russell, 1968), with a good bibliography; and M. Maccarrone, "Riforme e sviluppo della vita religiosa con Innocenzo III," *Revista di storia della chiesa in Italia* 16 (1962): 29–72.

33. Studies of religious and heretical movements of the Middle Ages consulted include the basic, Herbert Grundmann, *Movimenti religiosi nel medievo* (*Religiose Bewegungen im Mittelalter*, 1935 and 1961), trans. Maria Ausserhofer and Lea Nicolet Santini (Bologna: Mulino, 1974); also, Raoul Manselli, *L'eresia del male* (Naples: Morano, 1963); Gioccchino Volpe, *Movimenti religiosi e sette ereticali nella società volontaria nel medioevo* (Florence: Sansoni, 1975); Robert Moore, *The Origins of European Dissent* (New York: St. Martin's Press, 1977); and Malcolm D. Lambert, *Medieval Heresy: Popular Movements from Bogomil to Hus* (New York: Holmes & Meier, 1977).

34. See Leclerq et al., *The Spirituality of the Middle Ages*, 196–200; Ewert Cousins, "The Humanity and the Passion of Christ," in *Christian Spirituality: High Middle Ages and Reformation*, 75–91.

35. For poverty in the Middle Ages, see the fundamental M. Mollat, *The Poor in the Middle Ages: An Essay in Social History*, trans. Arthur Goldhammer (New Haven: Yale University Press, 1986).

36. Cf. Vauchez, *La spiritualité du moyen âge*, 136.

37. *St. Francis of Assisi: Omnibus of Sources*, ed. Marian A. Habig (Chicago: Franciscan Herald Press, 1972): I *Celano* 17, p. 243; 2 *Celano* 9, p. 369; Bonaventure, *Legenda major*, 1:6, p. 639, *Legenda minor*, 1:8, p. 798; *Legend of the Three Companions*, 4:11, p. 900. Hereafter, all quotations and references from the early biographies of St. Francis are from this edition, unless otherwise stated (referred to as *Omnibus of Sources*).

38. M.-D. Chenu, *Nature, Man and Society in the Twelfth Century*, sel., ed., and trans. Jerome Taylor and Lester K. Little (Chicago: The University of Chicago Press, 1968), 230.

39. Jean Sainsaulieu, "Ermites," in *Dictionnaire d'histoire et de géographie ecclésiastique*, vol. 15 (1963), cols. 771–87; see also Pierre Doyère, "Erémitisme en occident," *Dictionnaire de spiritualité ascétique et mystique* (Paris: Beauchesne, 1937 ff. [Hereafter abbreviated as *DS*]), vol. 4 (1960), cols. 936–82; L. Genicot, "L'érémitisme dans son contexte économique et social," in *L'eremitismo in occidente nei secoli XI e XII* (Milan, 1965), 45–69; L. Gougaud, "La vie érémitique au M.-Age," *Revue d'ascétique et de mystique* I (1920): 209–40.

40. On the nature and significance of medieval pilgrimages, see *Pellegrinagi e culto dei santi in Europa fino alla prima Crociata*, Atti del IV Convegno del Centro di Studi sulla Spiritualità Mediovale (Todi, 1963); Etienne Delaruelle, "Le pélerinage dans la vie religieuse médiévale," in *La piété populaire au moyen âge* (Torino: La Bottega d'Erasmo, 1975), 477–555; and Victor Turner and Edith Turner, *Image and Pilgrimage in Christian Culture* (New York: Columbia University Press, 1978), 177–203.

41. For medieval Eucharistic piety, see Josef Jungmann, *The Mass of the Roman Rite: Its Origins and Development*, trans. F. A. Brunner, vol. 1 (New York: Benziger, 1951), 119–21; and Caroline Walker Bynum, "Fast and Feast: The Historical Background," in *Holy Feast and Holy Fast: The Religious Significance of Food to Medieval Women* (Berkeley: University of California Press, 1987), 31–69.

42. On the medieval practice of the sacrament of Penance, see C. Vogel, *Le pécheur et la pénitence au moyen âge* (Paris: Ed. du Cerf, 1969); and Henry Charles Lea, *A History of Auricular Confession and Indulgences in the Latin Church* (New York: Greenwood Press, 1968), vol. 3.

43. On the central role of the Bible in the Middle Ages, see Beryl Smalley, *The Study of the Bible in the Middle Ages*, 2d ed. (South Bend, Ind.: University of Notre Dame Press, 1964).

44. A useful bibliography on the veneration of the saints in the Middle Ages can be found in *Saints and Their Cults: Studies in Religious Sociology, Folklore and History*, ed. Stephen Wilson (Cambridge: Cambridge University Press, 1983); on Marian devotion, see Theodore Koehler, "Marie (Sainte Vierge)" *DS*, vol. 10 (1980), cols. 450–55; also, Elizabeth A. Johnson, "Marian Devotion in the Western Church," in *Christian Spirituality: High Middle Ages and Reformation*, 392–414.

45. For a basic bibliography on Bonaventure, see Jacques Guy Bougerol, ed., *Bibliographia Bonaventuriana (c. 1850–1973)*, vol. 5 of *S. Bonaventura 1274–1974* (Grottaferrata: Collegio S. Bonaventura, 1974).

46. See Raoul Manselli, *La religion populaire au moyen âge: Problèmes de méthode et d'histoire* (Paris: J. Vrin, 1975), 204–15; and Giovanni Miccoli, "La storia religiosa," in *Storia d'Italia*, vol. 2 (Torino: Guilio Einaudi, 1274), 840–45.

47. *Medieovo cristiano*, 12. See also *L'attesa dell'età nuova nella spiritualità della fine del medioevo*, Atti del Convegno del Centro di Studi sulla Spiritualità Mediovale (Todi: Cyprian, 1960).

48. On Joachim of Fiore, see Bernard McGinn, *Visions of the End: Apocalyptic Traditions in the Middle Ages* (New York: Columbia Univer-

sity Press, 1979); idem, *The Calabrian Abbot: Joachim of Fiore in the History of Western Thought* (New York: Macmillan, 1985); idem, *Apocalyptic Spirituality* (New York: Paulist Press, 1979); Marjorie Reeves, *The Influence of Prophecy in the Later Middle Ages: A Study in Joachimism* (New York: Oxford University Press, 1969); and Henri de Lubac, *La posterité spirituelle de Joachim de Fiore, I. De Joachim à Schelling* (Paris: Editions Lethielleux, 1978).

49. See A. Frugoni, "Il giubileo di Bonifacio VIII," *Bolletino dell'Istituto Storico Italiano per il Medioevo e Archivio Muratoriano* 62 (1950): 1–103.

50. On the Flagellants, see G. Cecchini, "Flagellanti," *Dizionario degli Istituti di Perfezione* (Rome: Edizioni Paoline, 1974ff. [hereafter abbreviated as *DIP*]), vol. 4 (1977), cols. 60–72; also, *Il movimento dei disciplinati nel settimo centenario del suo initio*, Atti del Convegno Internazionale (Perugia, 1960).

51. See Gordon Leff, *Heresy in the Later Middle Ages*, 2 vols. (Manchester: Manchester University Press, 1967); Robert Lerner, *The Heresy of the Free Spirit in the Later Middle Ages* (Berkeley: University of California Press, 1972); and Raoul Manselli, *Eretici e ribelli del XIII e XIV* (Pistoia: Telini, 1974).

52. Dante, *Paradiso*, canto XI, 120.

53. The literature on Francis and the early Franciscans is voluminous. The most significant recent biography of the Poverello is Raoul Manselli's *St. Francis of Assisi*, trans. Paul Duggan (Chicago: Franciscan Herald Press, 1988). The social and economic implications of the early Franciscans are well explored by David Flood, O.F.M., *Francis of Assisi and the Franciscan Movement* (Quezon City, Philippines: The Franciscan Institute of Asia, Contact Publications, 1989); see also David Flood, O.F.M., and Thaddée Matura, O.F.M., *The Birth of a Movement: A Study of the First Rule of St. Francis*, trans. Paul Schwartz and Paul Lachance, O.F.M. (Chicago: Franciscan Herald Press, 1975); *Francis and Clare: The Complete Works*, trans. Regis Armstrong, O.F.M. Cap., and Ignatius Brady, O.F.M. (New York: Paulist Press, 1982).

54. A study of Francis as mystic, one based on his own writings and amplified by the accounts of his early biographers, remains to be written. For an introductory essay with an extensive bibliography, see Octavian Schmucki, O.F.M. Cap., "The Mysticism of St. Francis in the Light of His Writings," *Greyfriars Review* 3, no. 3 (December 1989): 241–66; also, *L'esperienza di Dio in Francesco d'Assisi*, ed. Ettore Covi, O.F.M. Cap. (Rome: Laurentianum, 1982). The expression of Francis's

stigmata as "incorporated mandala" is taken from Ewert Cousins, *Bonaventure and the Coincidence of Opposites* (Chicago: Franciscan Herald Press, 1978), 193.

55. For the rise and expansion of the Franciscan movement, see Théophile Desbonnets, O.F.M., *From Intuition to Institution: The Franciscans,* trans. Paul Duggan and Jerry Du Charme (Chicago: Franciscan Herald Press, 1988); Cajetan Esser, *Origins of the Franciscan Order,* trans. Aedan Daly and Trini Lynch (Chicago: Franciscan Herald Press, 1970); Gratien de Paris, *Histoire de la fondation et de l'évolution de l'Ordre des Frères Mineurs au XIIIe siècle* (Paris, 1925; reprint, Rome: Instituto Storico dei Cappucini, 1982); John Moorman, *A History of the Franciscan Order: From its Origins to the Year 1517* (London: Oxford University Press, 1968; reprint, Chicago: Franciscan Herald Press, 1988); Lazaro Iriarte, O.F.M. Cap., *Franciscan History,* trans. Patricia Ross (Chicago: Franciscan Herald Press, 1982); Wayne Hellman, O.F.M. Conv., "The Spirituality of the Franciscans," in *Christian Spirituality: High Middle Ages and Reformation,* 31–50; *L'espansione del francescanesimo tra Occidente e Oriente nel secolo XIII,* Atti del 6 Convegno Internazionale, Società Internazionale di Studi Francescani (Assisi, 1979). For the growth of the establishments of the Franciscans in cities or along major trade routes, see Luigi Pellegrini, *Insediamenti francescani nell'Italia del duecento* (Rome: Ed. Laurentianum, 1984).

56. Moorman, *A History of the Franciscan Order,* 94.

57. On the clericalization of the Order, see L. C. Landini, O.F.M., *The Causes of the Clericalization of the Order of Friars Minor, 1209–1260, in the Light of Early Franciscan Sources* (Chicago: Franciscan Herald Press, 1968); Raoul Manselli, "La clericalizzanione dei Minori e San Bonaventura," in *S. Bonaventura Francescano,* 14 Convegno del Centro di Studi sulla Spiritualità Medievale (Todi, 1974), 181–208.

58. On the generalate of St. Bonaventure, see Desbonnets, *From Intuition to Institution,* 127–32; H. Roggen, "Saint Bonaventure, second fondateur de l'Ordre des Frères Mineurs?," *Etudes Franciscaines* 17 (1967): 67–69; E. R. Daniel, "St. Bonaventure a Faithful Disciple of Saint Francis. A reexamination of the question" in *S. Bonaventura, 1274–1974,* vol. 1 (Grottaferrata, 1973), 170–87; and G. Miccoli, *Bonaventura e Francesco,* Atti del 14 Convegno del Centro di Studi sulla Spiritualità Mediovale (Todi, 1973), 47–73.

59. Referring to the disservice done to the Franciscan Spirituals, David Flood writes: "Briefly, the Spirituals held to Francis' ideals in disregard for the easing adaptations others (the community) sought in

the interests of pastoral effectiveness. The term became a party label in the early fourteenth century. In the thirteenth century it was used to designate a quality. Modern historiography has pushed the former, substantial meaning back into the thirteenth century. The result has been at best confusion, at worst history by ready category" (*Peter Olivi's Rule Commentary*, ed. Franz Steiner Verlay [GMBH, Wiesbaden, 1972], 2, n. 5).

60. On the Spiritual-Community controversy, studies consulted include the following: David Burr, *The Persecution of Peter Olivi* (Philadelphia: The American Philosophical Society, 1976); idem, *Olivi and Franciscan Poverty: The Origins of the Usus Pauper Controversy* (Philadelphia: University of Pennsylvania Press, 1989); Frédégand Callaey, *L'idéalisme franciscain spirituel au XIV siècle: Etude sur Ubertin de Casale* (Louvain: Université de Louvain, 1911); Charles Davis, "Ubertino da Casale and His Conception of 'altissima paupertas,'" *Studi Medievali* 22 (1981): 1–56. *Chi erano gli spirituali*, Atti del 3 Convegno Internazionale, Società Internazionale di Studi Francescani (Assisi, 1976); David Flood, "Le projet franciscain de Pierre Olivi," *Etudes franciscaines* 23 (1973): 367–79; *Franciscains d'Oc.: Les Spirituels, ca. 1280–1324* (Toulouse: Edouard Privat, 1975); Malcolm Lambert, *Franciscan Poverty: The Doctrine of the Absolute Poverty of Christ and the Apostles in the Franciscan Order* (1210–1323) (London: S.P.C.K., 1961), chap. 7–10, 149–246; Duncan Nimmo, *Reform and Division in the Franciscan Order: (1226–1538)* (Rome: Capuchin Historical Institute, 1987), 109–201; Clément Schmitt, "Introduzione allo studio degli Spirituali e dei Fraticelli," in *Picenum Seraphicum* 11 (1974): 7–23; idem, "Fraticelles," *Dictionnaire d'histoire et de géographie ecclésiastique*, vol. 18 (1977), cols. 1063–1108; Gian Luca Potestà, *Storia ed escatologia in Ubertino da Casale* (Milano: 1980); Mario Sensi, *Le osservanze francescane nell'Italia centrale (secoli XIV-XIV)* (Rome: Istituto Storico dei Cappucini, 1985), 1–17; Lydia von Auw, *Angelo Clareno et les spirituels italiens* (Rome: Edizioni di Storia e Letteratura, 1979); and Michael Cusato, O.F.M., "La renonciation au pouvoir chez les frères mineurs au 13e siècle (Ph.D. Diss., Université de Paris, Sorbonne, 1991).

61. See Raoul Manselli, *La 'Lectura super Apocalipsum' di Pietro di Giovanni Olivi: Ricerche sull'escatologismo mediovale* (Rome: Laurentianum, 1971).

62. See Stanislao da Campagnola, *L'Angela del sesto sigillo e l'alter Christus* (Rome: Laurentianum, 1971).

63. "Historia septem tribulationem," in *Archiv für Literatur und*

Kirchengeschichte des Mittelatle, ed. Denifler & Ehrle (Berlin, 1886), vol. 2, p. 302.

64. Burr, *Olivi and Franciscan Poverty,* 27.

65. Ubertino of Casale, *Arbor vitae crucifixae Jesu* (Venice: Andrea de Bonettis, 1485; reprinted, Charles T. Davis, ed.: Monumenta politica et philosophica rariora 4 (Turin: Bottega d'Erasmo, 1961), chap. 5, 465a. For the development of the application of the Antichrist concept to Boniface VIII, Benedict XI, and John XXII by the Spirituals, see Raoul Manselli, "L'anticristo mistico: Pietro di Giovanni Olivi, Ubertino da Casale e i papi del loro tempo," *Collectanea franciscana* 47 (1977): 5–25.

66. From Laud 58(83) "Third Letter from Jail to Pope Boniface VIII," in *Jacopone da Todi: The Lauds,* trans. Serge and Elizabeth Hughes (New York: Paulist Press, 1982), 182. Here and in subsequent references to Jacopone, the numeration of the Lauds follows the one adopted by the Hugheses with, in parenthesis, the one in the new edition by Franco Mancini, *Jacopone da Todi: Laude* (Rome: Guis. Laterza & Figli, 1974). On Jacopone see also George Peck, *The Fool of God: Jacopone da Todi* (University of Alabama Press, 1980); *Iacopone e il suo tempo,* Atti del Convegno del Centro di Studi sulla Spiritualità Mediovale (Todi, 1959).

67. *Quorundam exigit* condemned the entire *zelanti* movement, and in particular those in Provence; *Sancta Romana* expressly condemned "certain men of the profane multitude, who are commonly called *fraticelli* or *frates de pauperre vita bizzochi* or *beghini,* or other names," and "who claim to belong to the First and Third (Franciscan) Order, and live in various parts of Italy, in Sicily and in Provence, especially at Narbonne and Toulouse, but also in dioceses and provinces on both sides of the ocean." This bull was directed against two distinct groups, dissident Spirituals (in particular Angelo of Clareno's congregation, the Clareni or *fraticelli della povere vita,* and the Beguines or *bizzochi* (the equivalent term in Italian). Both groups subsequently were referred to as *Fraticelli* (friars who formed associations of their own outside the parent body). *Gloriosam ecclesiam,* issued less than a month after *Sancta Romana,* was directed specifically against the dissident Spirituals of Tuscany who had taken refuge in Sicily. In this battle with the Spirituals, as in the entire conflict, leaders of the Community—in this latter instance, Raymond of Fronsac, procurator of the Franciscan Order, and Bonagrazia of Bergamo, ex-procurator—played prominent roles.

68. The term *"Fraticelli"* is an umbrella term covering various dissident Franciscans. Although some received episcopal approbation,

most of them sought, or were forced by sanctions of the Church, to form associations outside the Order. On the Fraticelli, see D. L. Douie, *The Nature and Effect of the Heresy of the Fraticelli* (Manchester, 1932); Nimmo, *Reform and Division*, 241–99; Sensi, *Le Osservanze Francescane*, 14–17; and C. Schmitt, "Fraticelles," *DS*, vol. 5 (1965), cols. 1167–88.

69. For this final part of our rapid sketch of this thorny moment in Franciscan history I have relied mainly on the following studies: Burr, *The Persecution of Peter Olivi*, 73–92; idem, *Olivi and Franciscan Poverty*, 107–96; Lambert, *Franciscan Poverty*, chaps. 7–10, pp. 149–246; Raoul Manselli, *Spirituali e Beghini in Provenza* (Rome, 1959); Nimmo, *Reform and Division in the Franciscan Order*, 51–201; Jacques Paul, "Les spirituels, l'église et la papauté," in *Chi erano gli spirituali*, 221–62; and Sensi, *Osservanze Francescane*, 1–17.

70. Good overviews of popular religious movements and the emerging laity during this period can be found in Raoul Manselli, *La religion populaire au moyen âge: Problèmes de méthode et d'histoire* (Montréal: Institut d'Etudes Médiévales Albert-le-Grand, 1975); Etienne Delaruelle, *La piété populaire au moyen âge* (Torino: Bottega d'Erasmo, 1975); and André Vauchez, *Les laics au moyen âge: pratiques et expériences religieuses* (Paris: Editions du Cerf, 1987).

71. For a recent study on the origins of the Franciscan Third Order and the medieval penitential movement, see Raffaele Pazzelli, *St. Francis and the Third Order: The Franciscan and Pre-Franciscan Penitential Movement* (Chicago: Franciscan Herald Press, 1989). Also, Ida Magli, *Gli uomoni della penitenza: Lineamenti antroplogici del medioevo italiano* (Bologna: Cappelli, 1967); *I laici nella "societas christiana" dei secoli XI e XII*. Atti della 3 settimana internazionale di studio (Mendola, 1965; Milan: Vita e Pensiero, 1968); *L'Ordine della Penitenza di san Francesco d'Assisi nel sec. XII*, Atti del 1 Convegno di Studi Francescani (Assisi, 1972), ed. O. Schmucki (Rome: Istituto Storico dei Cappuccini, 1973); *I Frati Penitenti di san Francesco nella società medioevale*, Atti del 2 Convegno di Studi Francescani (Rome, 1976), ed. M. D'Alatri (Rome: Istituto Storico dei Cappuccini, 1977); *Il movimento francescano della penitenza nella società medioevale*, Atti del 3 Convegno di Studi Francescani (Padua, 1979), ed. M. d'Alatri (Rome: Istituto Storico dei Cappuccini, 1980); *Francescanesime e vita religiosa dei laici nel '200*, Atti del 8 Convegno Internazionale di Studi Francescani (Assisi, 1980; Assisi, Università degli Studi di Perugia, 1981); and *Prime manifestazioni di vita comunitaria maschile e femminile nel movimento francescano della*

NOTES TO THE INTRODUCTION

Penitenza, 1215–1447, Atti del 4 Convegno di Studi Francescani (Assisi, 1981), ed. R. Pazzelli and L. Temperini (Rome: Commissione Storica Internazionale TOR, 1982).

72. Théophile Desbonnets in the concluding remarks of the International Congress of Franciscan studies held in Assisi (1972) on this theme remarked: "It appears to me, in all due proportion, that the current state of this question strikingly resembles that of the 'Franciscan question' at the beginning of this century. One need only replace the name of Sabatier by that of Meerseman to discover an almost identical situation if one is to judge by the violence of opposing positions" (*L'Ordine della Penitenza*, 332). The same Desbonnets also observes: "If one cannot affirm that Francis was the 'founder' of the Third Order, one must at least declare that he instituted it, and was above all its Father" (ibid., 332). See also G. G. Meerseman, O.P., in collaboration with G. P. Pacini, *Ordo Fraternitatis: Confraternite e pietà dei laici nel medievo,* 3 vols. (Rome: Herder, 1977); and *Dossier de l'Ordre de la Pénitence au XIII siècle* (Fribourg: Presses Universitaires, 1966).

73. See André Vauchez, "Conclusion," in *I Frati Penitenti di San Francesco,* 375.

74. See Giovanna Casagrande, "Manifestazione comunitarie femminile in Umbria nel sec. XIII, XIV, XV," and Mario Sensi, "Comunità di penitenti Francescani nella valle Spoletana: Dai primi gruppi spontanei al tentative de centralizzione," in *Prime manifestazione di vita comunitaria,* 459–79, 482–505.

75. See *S. Chiara da Montefalco e il suo tempo,* Atti del 4 Convegno di Studi Storici Ecclesiastici, ed. Claudio Leonardi e Enrico Menestò (Florence: "La Nuova Italia" Editrice, 1981).

76. Roeggen, "Les relations du premier ordre franciscain avec le Tiers-Ordre au XIII siècle," in *L'Ordine della Penitenza,* 208–9.

77. Dante, *Purgatorio,* canto XIII, 138.

78. "In the face of such experiences [the tendency on the part of the Penitents to live their religious experience autonomously] the papacy, the hierarchy, the Franciscans and the Dominicans maintained, for some decades, an uncertain attitude, oscillating between diffidence and open support" (Giovanni Merlo, "Controllo ed emarginazione della dissidenza religiosa," in *Francescanesimo e vita religiosa,* 381).

79. The literature on the religious life of women in the later Middle Ages continues to proliferate. Among the studies I have consulted are the following: Marie-Thérèse d'Alverny, "Comment les théologiens et les philosophes voient la femme," *La femme dans les civilisations des*

Xe-XIIIe siècles: Actes du colloque tenu à Poitier les 23–25 septembre 1976, Cahiers de civilisation médiévale 20 (1977): 105–29; Vincenzo Bo, "Il problema antropologico-culturale del monachesimo femminile," under "Monachesimo" in *Enciclopedia delle Religioni,* vol. 4 (1972), cols. 628–39; Brenda M. Bolton, "Mulieres sanctae," in *Sanctity and Secularity: The Church and the World,* ed. Derek Baker, Studies in Church History 10 (Oxford: Blackwell, 1973), 77–95; Caroline Walker Bynum, *Jesus as Mother: Studies in the Spirituality of the High Middle Ages* (Berkeley: University of California Press, 1982); idem, *Holy Feast and Holy Fast: The Religious Significance of Food to Medieval Women* (Berkeley: University of California Press, 1987); idem, "Religious Women in the Later Middle Ages," in *Christian Spirituality: High Middle Ages and Reformation,* 121–39; Michael Goodich, "Contours of Female Piety in Later Medieval Hagiography," *Church History* 50 (1981): 20–32; Grundmann, *Religiöse Bewegungen im Mittelalter;* Richard Kieckhefer, *Unquiet Souls: Fourteenth-Century Saints and Their Religious Milieu* (Chicago: University of Chicago Press, 1984); Maria Consiglia De Matteis, ed., *Idee sulla donna nel medioevo* (Bologna: Patron Editore, 1981); Eleanor McLaughlin, "Equality of Souls, Inequality of Sexes: Women in Medieval Theology," in *Religion and Sexism: Images of Women in the Jewish and Christian Traditions,* ed. Rosemary Ruether (New York: Simon & Schuster, 1974), 213–66; idem, "Women, Power and the Pursuit of Holiness in Medieval Christianity," in *Women of Spirit: Female Leadership in the Jewish and Christian Tradition,* ed. Rosemary Ruether and Eleanor McLaughlin (New York: Simon & Schuster, 1979), 99–130; Régine Pernoud, *La femme au temps des cathédrales* (Paris: Editions du Seuil, 1977); and Vauchez, *Les laics au moyen âge.*

80. The patristic and scholastic theological view of women has been extensively researched—e.g., Kari Elisabeth Borresen, *Subordination and Equivalence: The Nature and Role of Woman in Augustine and Thomas Aquinas,* text and citations translated from the revised French original by Charles H. Talbot (Washington, D.C.: University Press of America, 1981). See also McLaughlin, "Equality of Souls, Inequality of Sexes"; and d'Alverny, "Comment les théologiens voient la femme." Concerning Bonaventure's concept of women, D. H. Maes observes: "In the works of Bonaventure, the inferiority of women is described in the same terms as in Thomas. For him, likewise, a woman is an imperfect, deficient man. The latter surpasses her in dignity, authority, strength and spirit. Woman, being rather passive, is necessary only for reproduction. Furthermore, she is more sensual and more easily inclined

to evil. The masculine sex is therefore superior from this point of view" ("La femme et le sacerdoce d'après Gabriel Vasquez," *Studio Moralia* 10 [1972]: 312; see also J. Rézette, "Sacerdoce et femme chez S. Bonaventure," *Antonianum* 51 [1976]: 520–27).

81. On the involvement of medieval women in heretical movements, aside from the classic account of Grundmann, *Religiöse Bewegungen im Mittelalter,* see Eleanor McLaughlin's more recent essay, "Women and Medieval Heresy: A Problem in the History of Spirituality," *Concilium* 111 (1976): 73–90; also, R. Manselli, *La religion populaire,* 117–24.

82. According to the masterful study of André Vauchez—and a subsequent one by Weinstein and Bell—on the evolution of the ideals of medieval holiness during the period 1198–1431, not only was there a greater tendency to raise lay people to the altar or bring them to canonization trials, but statistics indicate that most of these lay people were women. Furthermore, during the time span that Vauchez's study covers, five, or half, of the women brought to canonization trial were of Franciscan inspiration: St. Elisabeth of Hungary (1231), St. Rose of Viterbo (1251), St. Clare of Assisi (1253), St. Clare of Montefalco (1308), and Bl. Delphine of Puimichel (1360): *La sainteté en occident aux derniers siècles du moyen âge d'après les procès de canonisation et les documents hagiographiques* (Rome: Ecole Française de Rome, 1931), 243–49, 316–18, 402–10. According to Weinstein and Bell, whose statistics include not only those actually canonized but also those popularly revered as saints, the percentage of female saints doubled (from 11.8 percent to 22.6 percent) between the twelfth and the thirteenth century: Donald Weinstein and Rudolph Bell, *Saints and Society: The Two Worlds of Western Christendom: 1000–1700* (Chicago: University of Chicago Press, 1982), 220–21.

83. Peter Dronke, *Women Writers of the Middle Ages: A Critical Study of Texts from Perpetua (d. 203) to Marguerite Porete (d. 1310)* (Cambridge: Cambridge University Press, 1984), 202.

84. In the proliferation of writing by religious women during this period, the most outstanding examples are the *Letters, Poems, and Visions* of Hadewijch of Antwerp; the *Mengeldichten* of Hadewijch II; *The Seven Degrees of Love* of Beatrice of Nazareth; *The Flowing Light of the Godhead* by Mechthild of Magdeburg; and the *Mirror of Simple Souls* by Marguerite Porete—all written in the vernacular. Among those written in Latin, Mechtild of Hackeborn's *Liber Spiritualis Gratiae,* St. Gertrude the Great's *Legatus Divinae Pietatis,* and St. Clare's Rule (she was

the first woman to write one) and letters are among the most prominent. See Dronke, *Women Writers*, 202–28; also, *Medieval Women's Visionary Literature*, ed. Elizabeth A. Petroff (Oxford: Oxford University Press, 1986), 3–5, 20–38; *Medieval Women Writers*, ed. Katharina M. Wilson (Athens: The University of Georgia Press, 1984), VII–XXIX. On literacy among laywomen, especially in Italy, see David Herlihy, "The Natural History of Medieval Women," *Natural History* 87 (March 1987): 56–67.

85. Bynum, *Holy Feast and Holy Fast*, 14. Bynum also argues that it is misleading to interpret medieval women exclusively in terms of the notion of inferior femaleness. Although such notions are present in their writings, nonetheless, a predominant theme of their spirituality uses the "weakness" of the female body/flesh "not only as symbol of the humanness of both genders but also as a symbol of—and a means to approach to—the humanity of God" (ibid., 296).

86. Rusconi, "L'espansione del francescanesimo femminile," in *Movimento religioso femminile*, 311.

87. The basic study on the Beguines remains McDonnell's *The Beguines and Beghards in Medieval Culture, with Special Emphasis on the Belgian Scene* (New Brunswick, N.J.: Rutgers University Press, 1954). See also Robert E. Lerner, "Beguines and Beghards," *Dictionary of the Middle Ages*, vol. 2 (New York: Scribner, 1983), 157–62; A. Mens, "Beghine, Begardi, Beghinaggi," *DIP*, vol. 1 (1974), cols. 1165–80; and R. Guarnieri, "Pinzochere," *DIP*, vol. 6 (1980), cols. 1721–49.

88. For Beguines in southern France see especially Raoul Manselli, *Spirituali e beghini in Provenza* (Rome, 1950); in central Italy, see Mario Sensi, "Incarcerate e recluse in Umbria nei secoli XIII e XIV: Un bizzocaggio centro-Italiano," in *Il movimento religioso femminile in Umbria nei secoli XIII-XIV*, Atti del Convegno (Città di Castello, 1982), ed. Roberto Rusconi (Florence: "La Nuova Italia" Editrice, 1984), 35–121; idem, "La monacazione delle recluse nella valle Spoletana," in *S. Chiara da Montefalco e il suo tempo*, Atti del 4 Convegno di Studi Storici Ecclesiastici (Spoleto, 1981), ed. Claudio Leonardi and Enrico Menestò (Florence: "La Nuova Italia" Editrice, 1985), 71–121.

89. The most outstanding of the early Beguines was Marie d'Oignies (1177–1213) of Brabant-Flanders. Her biography was written by Cardinal Jacques de Vitry, who became her disciple, and was also a chronicler and defender of the *mulieres sanctae*. For a well-documented study showing the parallels between the spirituality of the Beguines and the Franciscans, see A. Mens, "L'Ombrie italienne et l'Ombrie bra-

NOTES TO THE INTRODUCTION

bançonne: Deux courants religieux parallèles d'inspiration commune," *Etudes franciscaines, Supplément* 17 (1967): XIV–78. For a suggestive essay showing the parallels between the early Beguines and Franciscan piety in central Italy, in particular a comparison between the life of Marie d'Oignies and Chiara da Montefalco, see Romana Guarnieri, "La 'vita' di Chiara da Montefalco e la pietà Brabantina del '200: prima indagini su un ipotesi di Lavoro," in *S. Chiara da Montefalco,* 305–367.

90. The expression is a traditional one and goes back to St. Jerome, but it frequently appears in the twelfth and thirteenth century to indicate the desire to live in complete poverty. See R. Grégoire, *"Nudus nudum Christum sequi; studi storici in onore di O. Bertolini* (Pisa, 1972), 395–409. On the links between Eucharistic devotion and ascetical practice, see Bynum, *Holy Feast and Holy Fast,* and Rudolf M. Bell, *Holy Anorexia* (Chicago: University of Chicago Press, 1985).

91. See Rusconi, "L'espansione del francescanesimo femminile," 308; also, J. Leclerc, "Il monachesimo femminile," in *Movimento religioso femminile,* 79; and Sensi, "Monacazione delle recluse," 2.

92. Le Goff, "Franciscanisme et modèles culturels," in *Francescanesimo e vita religiosa,* 102.

93. In chapter 12 of the first rule, the *Regula non bullata,* Francis warns his brothers "to avoid impure glances and association with women," and chapter 11 of his second rule, the *Regula bullata,* explicitly forbids entrance into women's monasteries except with special permission from the Holy See (*Francis and Clare: The Complete Works,* 119 and 144).

94. The best new study of St. Clare is Marco Bartoli, *Chiara d'Assisi,* intro. A. Vauchez with an iconographic appendix by Servus Gieben (Rome: Istituto Storico dei Cappuccini, 1989); see also *Claire d'Assise: Ecrits,* intro., Latin text, trans., notes, and index by Marie-France Becker, Jean-François Godet, and Thaddée Matura, O.F.M., *Sources Chrétiennes* no. 325 (Paris: Editions du Cerf, 1985); Chiara Augusta Lainati, "Una 'lettura' di Chiara d'Assisi attraverso le Fonti," in *Approccio storico-critico alle Fonti Francescane* (Rome: 1979), 155–177; *Clare of Assisi: Early Documents,* ed. and trans. Regis Armstrong, O.F.M. Cap., (New York: Paulist Press, 1988); Clare Gennaro, "Chiara, Agnese e le prime consorelle," in *Movimento religioso femminile,* 169–91. For a symbolic approach to the relationship between Francis and Clare, see Pierre Brunette, O.F.M., "Francis and Clare of Assisi: A Journey into Symbols of Growth," *Studia Mystica* 12, no. 1 (Spring 1989): 6–20.

95. In 1298, Boniface VIII imposed strict enclosure on all women's

monasteries; see Jean Leclerc, "Clausura," *DIP,* vol. 2 (1975), cols. 1166–74.

96. See Vauchez, "La sainteté féminine dans le mouvement franciscain," in *Les laics au moyen âge,* 189–202.

97. On medieval women mystics, see the overview by Valerie M. Lagorio, "The Medieval Continental Women Mystics: An Introduction," in *An Introduction to the Medieval Mystics of Europe,* ed. Paul Szarmach (Albany: State University of New York Press, 1984), 161–93; also Elizabeth Petroff, *Consolation of the Blessed* (New York: Alta Gaia Society, 1979) and *Medieval Women's Visionary Literature;* Bynum, "Women Mystics in the Thirteenth Century: The Case of the Nuns of Helfta," in *Jesus as Mother,* 170–262; *Temi e problemi nella mistica femminile trecentesca,* Atti del 20 Convegno del Centro di studi sulla spiritualità medievale (Todi: Presso L'Accademia Tudertina, 1983); Vauchez, "Prophétesse, visionnaires et mystiques dans l'occident médiévale," in *Les laics au moyen âge,* 239–49; and Emile Zum Brunn and Georgette Epiney-Burgard, *Women Mystics in Medieval Europe,* trans. Sheila Hughes (New York: Paragon House, 1989).

98. Vauchez, "L'idéal de sainteté," 336. Not counting those of Franciscan inspiration whom we have just mentioned in the text, the outstanding representatives of this mystical evolution in Italy would include Bl. Margarita of Castello (d. 1320), St. Umiltà of Faenza (d. 1310), Margarita of Faenza (d. 1330), and St. Catherine of Siena (d. 1380). In Germany, the most noteworthy examples were the three mystical religious of the Cistercian monastery of Helfta: St. Mechthild of Hackeborn (d. 1299), Mechthild of Magdeburg (d. 1297), and St. Gertrude the Great (d. 1301), successors of St. Elisabeth of Schönau (d. 1165) and St. Hildegard of Bingen (d. 1179); in the Low Countries: Mary of Oignies (d. 1213), St. Christina of St. Trond, called the "Admirable" (d. 1224), St. Lutgarde of Aywières (d. 1246), Hadewijch of Brabant (mid-thirteenth century), Bl. Juliana of Cornillon (d. 1258), Beatrice of Nazareth (d. 1268), Bl. Ida of Louvain (d. 1300), and a host of others; in France, Marguerite d'Oingt (d. 1310), Bl. Douceline d'Aix (d. 1274) and Marguerite Porete (d. 1310); in Sweden, St. Brigitta (d. 1373). It is likewise important to mention a few of the outstanding male mystics, many of whom were influenced by and in turn influenced women mystics: in the Rhineland, Meister Eckhart (d. 1328) and his spiritual heirs, Johannes Tauler (d. 1361), Bl. Heinrich Suso (d. 1366), and later, Bl. John Ruusbroec (d. 1381); in Italy, St. Bonaventure (d. 1274), Jacopone da Todi (d. 1306), and Bl. Giles of Assisi (d. 1262).

NOTES TO THE INTRODUCTION

99. For the ways in which some Beguines daringly innovated within the mystical tradition, see Zum Brunn and Epiney-Burgard, *Women Mystics in Medieval Europe*, xiii–xxxiv; Bernard McGinn, "Love, Knowledge and *Unio Mystica* in the Western Christian Tradition," in *Mystical Union and Monotheistic Faith: An Ecumenical Dialogue*, ed. Moshe Idel and Bernard McGinn (New York: Macmillan, 1989), 66–75.

100. This primacy of love, as Bernard McGinn observes, did not exclude "a form of intuitive 'knowing' (*intelligentia, intellectus*) superior to reason (*ratio*). This form of knowing subsumes the lower aspects of the reasoning process into the higher, transformed state" (*Mystical Union and Monotheistic Faith*, 68).

101. Canon 5 of the Council of Vienne is directed against Beguines, "some who, as if led by a peculiar insanity, argue and preach on the Holy Trinity and the divine essence and, in regard to the articles of faith and the sacraments of the Church, give expression to opinions that are contrary to Catholic belief." Canon 6 specifically condemns eight errors held by Beguines, central among which were antinomian tenets attributed to the Free Spirit heresy (*Disciplinary Decrees of the General Councils*, text, trans., and commentary H. I. Schroeder, O.P. [London: B. Herder Book Co., 1937], 388–90). Historians differ on their interpretation of the Free Spirit heresy. For the traditional view, see Gordon Leff, *Heresy in the Later Middle Ages*, 2 vols. (New York: Barnes and Noble, 1967), 1:308–407. For a challenge to this view, see Robert E. Lerner, *The Heresy of the Free Spirit in the Later Middle Ages* (Berkeley: University of California Press, 1972). Lerner doubts that a Free Spirit movement ever existed apart from the minds of church leaders. Romana Guarnieri argues that "the Free Spirit movement (whose contours are difficult to determine) should not be seen only in its extreme, let us say criminal, cases; it was also—and perhaps above all—a movement of poetry and spirit, in the highest meaning of these terms. It was above all a piety movement, interlaced here and there with impiety" ("Il movimento del Libero Spirito: dalle origini al secolo XVI," in *Archivio Italiano per la Storia della Pietà* [1965], 5). For Jean Orcibal, the term is best used to refer simply to a number of independent, though similar, phenomena: "Le 'Miroir des simples âmes' et la 'secte' du Libre Esprit," *Revue de l'histoire des religions* 176 (1969): 36. See also Guarnieri, "Fratelli del Libero Spirito," *DIP*, vol. 4 (1977), cols. 633–52; L. Oliger, *De secta spiritus libertatis in Umbria saec. XIV: disquisitio et documenta* (Rome: Storia e Letteratura, 1943).

337

102. Ewert Cousins, "The Humanity and the Passion of Christ," in *Christian Spirituality: High Middle Ages and Reformation,* 375–92; idem, "Francis of Assisi: Christian Mysticism at the Crossroads," in *Mysticism and Religious Traditions,* ed. Steven T. Katz (New York: Oxford University Press, 1983), 163–91; see also Kieckhefer, "Devotion to the Passion," in *Unquiet Souls,* 89–121.

103. Carolyn Bynum observes that if these women visionaries avidly sought out pain and suffering, it was not primarily an effort to destroy or escape from the body, an effort rooted in dualism and self-hatred, but rather an attempt "to plumb all the possibilities of the flesh" (*Holy Feast and Holy Fast,* 294). On the significance of embodiment for medieval women's piety see also by Bynum, ". . . And Woman His Humanity: Female Imagery in the Religious Writing of the Later Middle Ages," in *Gender and Religion: On the Complexity of Symbols,* ed. Bynum, Harrell, and Richman (Boston: Beacon, 1986), 257–88; "The Female Body and Religious Practice in the Later Middle Ages," in *Fragments for a History of the Human Body,* vol. 1, ed. Michel Feher et al. (Canada: Zone, 1989), 163–219.

104. Long attributed to St. Bonaventure, modern scholarship is converging on John of Calibus, a Franciscan living in Tuscany in the second half of the thirteenth century, as the probable author of this masterpiece of early Franciscan literature. For an introduction and English translation, see *Meditations on the Life of Christ: An Illustrated Manuscript of the Fourteenth Century,* trans. Isa Ragusa, completed from the Latin and ed. Isa Ragusa and Rosalie B. Green (Princeton, N.J.: Princeton University Press, 1961).

105. As a result of their profound identification with the suffering Christ, wounds imitating those of his feet, hands, side, or head, sometimes even the scourge marks on his back, appeared on the bodies of many female visionaries; several received the stigmata: Mary of Oignies, Ida of Louvain, Christine of Stommeln, Elizabeth of Spalbeek, Gertrude of Oosten, and later Catherine of Siena.

106. See Kieckhefer, *Unquiet Souls,* 107.

107. On the theological vision inherent in late medieval hagiography, see ibid., 8–15; also, Bynum, *Holy Feast and Holy Fast,* 113–49; Anna Benvenutti Pappi, "Frati mendicanti e pinzochere in Toscana: dalla marginalità sociale a modello di santità," in *Temi e problemi nella mistica feminile,* 109–35; Vauchez, "Patronage des saints et religion civique dans l'Italie communale," in *Les laics au moyen âge,* 169–86.

108. For the influence of the Franciscan presence on the cult of

saints in the thirteenth century, see Anna Imelde Galletti, "I Francescani e il culto dei santi nell'Italia centrale," in *Francescanesimo e vita religiosa*," 313–63.

109. There were important social and political repercussions as well, as the studies of Anna Benvenutti Papi on the Bl. Umiliana of Cerchi have indicated. See "Umiliana dei Cerchi: Nascità di un culto nella Firenze del duecento," *Studi Francescani* 77 (1980): 87–117.

110. Further examples include: For St. Elisabeth of Schönau, Brother Eckbert; St. Bridget, the Cistercian Peter Olafson; St. Catherine of Siena, Bl. Raymond of Capua; St. Frances of Rome, Canon Mattioti; Mechthilde of Magdeburg, the Dominican Henry of Halle.

111. In dealing with the context of Foligno, I am especially indebted to the work of Mario Sensi: "Foligno sul calare del secolo XIII," *Sante e Beate Umbre*, 35–41; "Angela nel contesto religioso folignate," in *Vita e spiritualità della Beata Angela da Foligno*, Atti del convegno di studi per il VII centenario della conversione della Beata Angela da Foligno (1285–1985), ed. Clément Schmitt, O.F.M. (Perugia: Serafica Provincia di San Francesco O.F.M. Conv., 1987); "Incarcerate e recluse in Umbria nei secoli XIII e XIV: un bizzoccaggio centro-italiano," in *Il movimento religioso femminile in Umbria nei secoli XIII–XIV*, Atti del Convegno Internazionale di studio nell'ambito delle celebrazioni per l'VIII centenario della nascita di San Francesco d'Assisi, ed. Roberto Rusconi (Florence: "La Nuova Italia" Editrice, 1984), 87–121; "Incarcerate e Penitenti a Foligno nella prima meta del trecento," in *I Frati Penitenti di San Francesco*, 291–308. See also M. Faloci Pulignani, *Perugia e Foligno nel secolo XIII* (Foligno, 1938); Ludovico Iacobili, *Croniche della città de Foligno*, Ms. 198, collection of M. Faloci Pulignani (Biblioteca Communale of Foligno).

112. In 1282, the Perugians were excommunicated and placed under interdict for behaving like an autonomous state. They retorted by first burning in effigy the pope and the cardinals in front of the walls of Foligno and then launching their assault. In the ferocious battle that ensued, they were routed by the Folignati soldiers, the latter accompanied by priests waving banners of San Feliciano, protector of the city, and by women dressed as men. The chronicles further report that the defeat was so complete that one of these valorous women singlehandedly took ten Perugian male prisoners.

113. Besides the already cited work of Mario Sensi, see Lydia von Auw, "Les 'spirituels' de Foligno dans trois lettres en langue italienne du Ms. OL. (Bibliothèque Oliveriana, n. 1942, A)," in *Il B. Tomasuccio da*

NOTES TO THE INTRODUCTION

Foligno, Terziario Francescano ed i movimento religiosi popolari Umbri nel Trecento, ed. Raffaele Pazzelli (Rome, 1979), 49–61; and L. Jacobili, *Le vite dei santi e dei beati dell'Umbria,* 3 vols. (Foligno: 1647–1661).

114. See Sensi, "Angela nel contesto religioso folignate," 45–48.

115. I Celano 4:8, *Omnibus of Sources,* 236; on the relationship between St. Francis and Foligno see the notices compiled by M. Faloci Pulignani, *Le relazioni tra S. Francesco d'Assisi e la città di Foligno* (Foligno, 1893).

116. For the flourishing of the eremitical movement among the Franciscans in Umbria during this period, see Ugolino Nicolini, "L'eremitismo Francescano Umbro nei secoli XIII–XVI," in *Il B. Tomasuccio da Foligno,* 79–96.

117. On the presence of the Spiritual party in Umbria, Stanislao Campagnola observes: "The uninterrupted thread of religious experience lived and suffered in Umbria allows us to speak with security not only of the presence of the Spirituals in Umbria, but also of Umbrian Spirituals as elaborators and depositories of a tradition of attitudes, themes and ideas constantly present in the various phases in which the vicissitudes and writings of the Spirituals structured themselves" ("Gli Spirituali Umbri," in *Chi erano gli Spirituali,* 105).

118. Lydia von Auw, *Angelo Clareni opera I: Epistole* (Rome, 1980), 351–64.

119. See especially Sensi, "Incarcerate e recluse in Umbria: un bizzocaggio centro-italiano"; also, "La monacazione delle recluse nella valle Spoletana," 4–7.

120. Sensi, "Le Clarisse a Foligno nel secolo XIII," *Collectanea franciscana* 47 (1977): 349–63.

121. Sensi, "Angela nel contexto religioso folignate," 56–63. Sensi documents the presence of the following numbers of Beguine-like communities of women in Umbria toward the end of the thirteenth century (in the space of not even ten years): 13 in Spoleto, 4 in Foligno, 4 in Montefalco, 2 in Bevagna, and 1 in Spello. See, "Incarcerate e recluse in Umbria," 107–8.

122. Also significant is the presence of old manuscripts written in Provencale and found in the libraries of Assisi and Todi. See Sensi, "Angela nel contesto religioso Folignate," 59.

123. On St. Clare of Montefalco's community (which was under Franciscan influence but adopted the Augustinian rule), see *S. Chiara da Montefalco e il suo tempo,* especially the article by Romana Guarnieri,

"La 'Vita' di Chiara da Montefalco e la pietà Brabantina del '200: Prime indagini su un 'ipotesi di lavoro,' " 305–67.

124. Evidence of official suspicion surrounding this approval is the fact that the Assisi manuscript, one of the earliest of Angela's writings, was immediately concealed, and was hidden under lock and key in the Sacro Convento library where it was received in the early fourteenth century with the following marginal notation: "This book (of sister Lella of Foligno of the Order of Continents) was given to me by an unknown person whose name I have not been able to discover" ("Angela nel contesto religioso folignate," 67, n. 88).

125. Romana Guarnieri points out that, "strictly speaking, texts which treat with precision of the *fratres de libero spiritu*, or of the *secta spiritus libertatis* are rather rare." Even the name of the sect "oscillates and is inconsistent." Sometimes it appears as "spirit" or "freedom," other times as "spirit of freedom" or "freedom of spirit," still other times as "liberty in the spirit (Holy)" or "spirit in freedom"—titles and terms that allow for a wide variety of interpretations, all of which are vague ("Il movimento del Libero Spirito," 357). Not precisely speaking a heresy, Guarnieri further argues, it is rather a "movement" encompassing diverse "minor movements" that, along with horrendous doctrinal and moral aberrations, also produced fruits of sanctity (ibid., 354). In Italy, where it was active in the beginning of the fourteenth century, one of these minor movements was generally known as the sect of the Spirit of Freedom (*Spiritu Libertatis*), and appears as such in Angela's *Book*. Its leader was Bentivenga of Gubbio, already a member of the Pseudo-Apostles of Gerardo Segarelli of Parma. After the supression of the Pseudo-Apostles (ca. 1286), Bentivenga entered the Franciscans of the Province of Umbria and quickly won over many disciples (mostly lay persons of both sexes), who, for a while, seemed to have operated underground. The first explicit mention of this group appears in 1304, but it is likely that their movement dates from before that. In 1306, St. Clare of Montefalco (see instruction 2, n. 13), whom these heretics tried to win over to their cause, denounced them to Cardinal Napoleone Orsini, pontifical legate for Tuscany, and he had them tried and condemned to life imprisonment. Immediately afterward, the Minister General of the Franciscans sent two inquisitors to Umbria and they netted, among others, Francesco da Borgo S. Sepolcro, who was later virtually acquitted. On 1 April 1311, Pope Clement V issued the bull *Dilectus Domini*, which definitively condemned these dissidents. He deputized Bishop

Rainerio "de Casulo" of Cremono, to whom the bull was addressed, to hunt them down in the Spoleto valley. According to the testimony of Arnaldo of Villanova, a contemporary, the adherents of the sect numbered more than 240, and about 10 were Franciscans, others Fraticelli or members of the Flagellanti. Among the more or less defined basic beliefs attributed to this movement: quietism (a state of perfection in which sin is no longer possible and works of penance are no longer necessary); indifference toward the passion of Christ and the needs of others; the denial of free will and eternal condemnation for whatever sin or vice committed; the necessity of the sacraments (except the Eucharist) only for the imperfect; identity of human passions with the devil; the possibility of experiencing the presence of God not only in works that are good, but also in various and illicit forms of sexual behavior. See Guarnieri, *Il movimento del Libero Spirito*, 404–8; L. Oliger, *De secta spiritu libertatis*, 150–55; Sergio Andreoli, *Angela, la poverella di Foligno* (Siena: Edizioni Cantagalli, 1984), 73–81; and *Il Libro*, 93, n. 32. On the Free Spirit heresy, see also above, n. 101.

126. Ubertino mentions the following aberrations (among others): "for these 'brutal pigs,' there is no relationship between doing penance and the state of perfection once this latter state has been achieved, and, as a consequence, fasting and other acts of penance are no longer necessary; with the same reasoning, they justify all kinds of immoral behavior, debauchery, and deviant sexual activity; in the state of quiet, '*habitus beatitudinis*,' they claim that efforts to avoid sin and to love one's neighbor are no longer necessary." For such nefarious conduct, "an affront to the life of Christ, and an act of infamy towards the Holy Spirit," Ubertino argues, there is only one solution: The adherents of this sect "do not deserve to be confuted, but should be burned" (*Arbor crucifixae Jesu*, 154–58, 381–87). See Damiata, *Pietà e storia nell'Arbor Vitae di Ubertino da Casale*, 127–31. Angelo of Clareno was likewise later to describe the errors of this sect in the "sixth tribulation" of his *Historia septem tribulationum ordini minorum*, Book 2.

127. See S. Campagnola, "Influsso del Giochimismo nella letteratura Umbro-Francescana del due-trecento," in *Il B. Tomasuccio*, 97–129.

128. For an overview of the recluse movement in central Italy, see Sensi, "Reclusione," *DIP*, vol. 7 (1983), cols. 1235–42; idem, "Incarcerate e recluse," 113–16.

129. See Sensi, "Angela nel contesto religioso folignate," 68–72. Other blessed contemporaries of Angela in "Umbria sancta" include Bl. Angelo (d. 1291), an Augustinian from Foligno; Bl. Giacomo (1220–

1302). A Dominican from Bevagna; Bl. Angelo di Norcera Umbra and Bl. Andrea (d. 1264), Franciscans from Spello. See Sergio Andreoli, "Guida al 'Libro' della Beata Angela da Foligno," L'Italia Francescana, n. 1–2 (1980), 37.

130. Sensi, "Communita di Penitenti nella Valle Spoletana," in *Prime manifestazione di vita communitaria*, 485.

131. Moorman, *History of the Order*, 373. For the role of Trinci and the evolution of the Observant reform movement (division without disunity), see Nimmo, *Reform and Division*, 353–428; and Sensi, *Le Osservanze Francescane*, 19–73, 205–35.

132. Sensi, "Incarcerate e Penitenti a Foligno nella prima età del Trecento," in *Frati Penitenti*, 291.

133. In the first supplementary step of the *Memorial*, Angela says that among the reasons for her pilgrimage to Assisi was to ask St. Francis "the grace of observing well the rule of the blessed Francis which she had recently promised."

134. Sensi, "Angela nel contesto religioso folignate," 75.

135. For a linguistic analysis of the role of the three narrators of the *Memorial* (God, Angela, and Arnaldo), see Beatrice Coppini, *La scrittura e il percorso mistico: Il 'liber' di Angela da Foligno* (Rome: Editrice Janua, 1986).

136. In two manuscripts found in Perugia (ca. fifteenth century), "Bro. A." is interpreted as "Bro. Adamo"; one manuscript found in Avignon (ca. fifteenth century) names him "Arnaldus." Subsequent authors writing on Angela differ in their interpretation of this abbreviation. The name "Arnaldo" appears for the first time in the title of the book by G. B. Boccolini, *B. Angelae Fulginatis vita et opuscula, cum duplici prologo, V. F. Arnaldi Ord. Minorum* (Foligno, 1714). M. B. Lavaud identifies him as "Aimé" (*La vie spirituelle* 32 [1927], 508); C. Bordoni as "Arnoldo" and "Arnolfo" (cf. *Angela da Foligno, Magistra Theologorum* [Foligno, 1209], 8); R. Pieau as "Armand" (cf. *Vie de sainte Angèle de Foligno* [Paris, 1863]); G. Joergensen as "Arnoldo" (cf. *In Excelsis*, 2nd ed. [Florence, 1925], 94). The most recent hypothesis is that of Mario Sensi, who identifies him as Bro. Andrea, a Franciscan who played a key diplomatic role in the wars between Foligno and Perugia during Angela's lifetime ("Angela nel contesto religioso folignate," 43).

137. Most of the available information on Arnaldo and his redactional procedure is found in chapter two of the *Memorial*.

138. It is important to note that even though Arnaldo does say when

he begins his redaction that he was Angela's scribe and confessor, we cannot be absolutely certain that he was the same person who was her confessor at the time of her conversion.

139. See chapter 6, p. 170 and note 65.

140. Chap. 6, p. 176.

141. Instruction 26, p. 284.

142. Concerning the influence of the Umbrian dialect on the Latin of the *Memorial*, Georgio Petrocchi writes: "As far as our limited readings in this area can tell, no other religious prose from this century is so obviously permeated by the spoken vernacular as the *Liber de vera fidelium experientia* ("Sul 'Liber' della B. Angela da Foligno," in *Ascesi e Mistica Trecentesca* [Florence: Felice le Monnier, 1957], 6); for a list of Umbrian expressions in the *Memorial*, see P. Doncoeur, *Le livre de la Bienheureuse Angèle de Foligno*, Latin text (Toulouse: Editions de la Revue d'Ascétique et de Mystique, 1925), xvii.

143. See Faloci Pulignani, *L'Autobiografia e gli scritti della Beata Angela da Foligno*, xiii; Doncoeur, *Le livre de la Bienheureuse Angèle de Foligno du Tiers Ordre de S. François* (Paris: La Librairie de l'Art Catholique, 1926), 10; Ferré, "Les principales dates," 32–33; and *Il Libro*, 35.

144. See *Il Libro*, 115.

145. See *Il Libro*, 50; *Martyrologium Franciscanum* (Rome, 1938), 266; Lucas Wadding, O.F.M., *Annales Minorum seu trium Ordinum a S. Francisco institutorum* (Quaracchi, 1931 ff.), vol. 6 (yr. 1309), 182, and vol. 6 (yr. 1313), 244; and L. Jacobili, *Vite dei santi e beati del Umbria*, vol. 3 (Foligno, 1647), 394.

146. Petrocchi, "Sul 'Liber' della Beata Angela," 8, for example, the pages narrating the washing of the feet of lepers on Holy Thursday in the third supplementary step. Petrocchi also points to the two different styles in evidence in the *Memorial*: "I see in the *Liber* a poetry of asceticism distinct from a poetry of ecstasy; the former is more calm, relaxed and discreet and the latter, a perpetual state of feverish excitement allowing free reign to Angela's fiery imagination . . . the ecstatic tone is by nature antirealistic and abstract while the ascetic tone is material and concrete" (*Ascesi e mistica trecentesca*, 10–11).

147. L. Leclève (pseud. for Ferré), *Sainte Angèle de Foligno: Sa vie-ses oeuvres* (Paris: Librairie Plon, 1936), 43.

148. In the critical edition, where the first and second redactions agree with one another, the critical text is printed in roman typeface. What pertains exclusively to the second redaction is printed in italic. I

have not followed this procedure in my text. Since many of the insertions of the second redaction consist of words, short phrases or sentences, such italics would be more intrusive than informative in a reading translation. Whenever appropriate, however, I have indicated in my notes important modifications supplied by the second redaction.

149. This Italian manuscript (M) is published alongside the Latin one in the critical edition of Angela's *Book*.

150. According to Thier and Calufetti, it is likely that toward the second half of the fourteenth century, an anonymous redactor decided to systematize a codex from the second redaction (second family) according to themes, e.g., selections on the passion of Christ in one chapter, those on prayer in another, etc. Biographical, historical, and explanatory data were synthesized and placed at the beginning. Further stylistic adaptations transformed the codex into a work of spiritual doctrine. The lost exemplar of this codex, a very old one, is at the origin of the third family of manuscripts, and, as such, useful for establishing the critical text. The wide distribution of this type of codex is due to the fact that, in 1643, Bollandus published one of them, and it became the key text for subsequent editions of Angela's works. Manuscripts from the sixth and seventh families were also useful in establishing the critical text. Those of the fourth and fifth families were manuscripts written in the vernacular based on one or the other of the existing Latin ones, and freely adapted to popularize Angela's teachings. See *Il Libro*, 51–73.

151. See the "ratio editionis" in *Il Libro*, 108–15.

152. See *Il Libro*, 112.

153. Ernesto Menestò, among others, thinks that the question of the two-redaction theory "is still far from being completely resolved." Among the criticisms he raises against the Thier-Calufetti effort is their failure to establish the necessary parental relationships among the components of the seven families of manuscripts. The existence of a second redaction, he also argues, would seriously compromise Arnaldo's affirmation that he wrote only what Angela dictated to him. Menestò still finds acceptable the Ferré hypothesis that "the original redaction was the major one (the second family) and the minor one (the first family), a later redaction, an extract/summary of the first one, due to some copier." See "Beate e sante dell'Umbria tra Duecento e Trecento: una ricognizione degli scritti e delle fonti agiografiche," in *Sante e Beate Umbre*, 71.

154. For an introduction and step-by-step commentary of Angela's

writings, see my thesis: *The Spiritual Journey of the Blessed Angela of Foligno according to the Memorial of Frater A.* (Rome: Pontificium Athenaeum Antonianum, 1984).

155. For further commentary and variations on these three basic transformations, see instructions 3, 7, 22, and 24.

156. Dante, *Inferno*, Canto 1, p. 3.

157. On the social origins and situations of mystic speech, Michel de Certeau observes: "[Mystics] do not reject the ruins around them. They remain in them; they go to them. . . . More generally, their solidarity with the collective, historically based suffering—which was demanded by circumstances but also desired and sought after as a test of truth—indicates the place of mystic 'agony,' a 'wound' inseparable from the social ill" ("Mystic Speech," in *Heterologies: Discourse on the Other,* trans. Brian Massumi [Minneapolis: University of Minnesota Press, 1986], 86).

158. Petruccio is mentioned in the eighteenth step as someone Angela used "to make fun of," before deciding to give away her belongings.

159. "The mystic's familiarity with abjection is a fount of infinite jouissance. One may stress the masochistic economy of the jouissance only if one points out at once that the Christian mystic far from using it to the benefit of a symbolic or institutional power (as happens with dreams, for instance) displaces it indefinitely within a discourse where the subject is resorbed (is that a grace?) into communication with the Other and with others. One recalls Francis of Assisi who visited leproseries 'to give out alms and left only after having kissed each leper on the mouth'; who stayed with lepers and bathed their wounds, sponging pus and sores. One might also think of Angela of Foligno" (*Powers of Horror: An Essay on Abjection,* trans. Leon S. Roudiez [New York: Columbia University Press, 1982], 127).

160. "Everything which precedes was written when Christ's faithful one was in the seventh step, and the sixth had already come to an end" (chap. 8, p. 199).

161. But later on, toward the end of the sixth step, Angela will say that the torments of this step "began sometime before the pontificate of Pope Celestine V and lasted for more than two years" (chap. 8, p. 201).

162. Angela herself will say that "toward the end of this period I was not fully and entirely liberated from these torments: I still felt some of their outer effects but not their inner ones" (chap. 8, p. 201).

163. *Il Libro*, 98, n. 51; 355, n. 2; 381, n. 34.

164. The first explicit sounding of the chords of the theme of dark-

ness occurs toward the end of the fourth supplementary step. At this previous stage of her itinerary, Angela, seeking to discover more about God's salvific plan, had fallen into a state of ecstasy and her soul was plunged "into a darkness" unable "to move forward or go back to itself." Afterward, she acceded to an even higher state, one of "greatest illumination," in which all "previous darkness" was withdrawn (whether a positive or a negative darkness is not clear from the context, probably the latter), and she was filled with divine light and supreme joy over her newfound understanding of God's power, will, and justice. Words failed her then to express this state, except to say that it gave her a peace, a quiet, and a stability she had not known before. Then she was drawn and uplifted to an even higher state where neither the power nor the will of God was seen as before, but rather something "stable, firm, and so indescribable" that she could say nothing about it save that "it was the All Good." She further reported not "seeing love" therein but "something indescribable." Finally, she was drawn away from even this stage and placed into a still higher and greater one. In it, she did not know whether she was in the body or out of it. The term "darkness" is not found in earlier steps, nor in the next one, the fifth supplementary step, which precedes the two we are looking at now.

165. The Latin: *abyssalem absorptionem in Deum.* "Abyss" terminology is found throughout this instruction either as a noun (*abyssus, inabyssatio*), an adjective (*abyssalis*), or even as a verb (*inabyssasse, inabyssari*). It also appears in the final step of the *Memorial,* as well as in a number of places in other instructions to describe Angela's peak experiences. Cf. also instructions 1, 5, 19, 25. In this same instruction 4, it is used as a verb—"*transsubstantiasse et inabyssasse*"—to describe the transformations of Angela's sons. In instruction 1, it is likewise used as a verb: "*istae est quedam humilitas in qua sum inabyssata.*"

166. Lillian Silburn, writing about the mystical experience of "annihilation and nothingness" (which has parallels with Angela's experience), comments: "If in the emptying out which makes of the mystic someone 'poor and naked,' the unconscious absorptions during which he is reduced to nothing without even knowing it, the annihilation in God and access to Nothingness, are very precise and clearly distinct experiences for the one undergoing them, these do not constitute strictly successive phases. One can be initiated before the end of the preceding one; many progress in parallel fashion and often there are flashes of future realization. This need not surprise us, for in the spiritual experience leading to the atemporal and the undifferentiated, every-

thing is present at every moment. It is very difficult to establish stages as if these evolved in temporal sequence. Moreover, as soon as the mystic lives in Nothingness—dwelling nowhere—empty spaces previously traversed tend to blend with one another so as to become one; in the forgetting of self, in the forgetting of forgetting itself, the mystic constantly loses himself in an abyss about which he knows nothing" ("Le Vide, le Rien, l'Abime," in *Hermes* 6 [1969]: 43).

167. Hans Urs Von Balthasar, *Pâques: le Mystère*, trans. R. Givord (Paris: Editions du Cerf, 1981), 76.

168. In his seminal study *Les structures anthropologiques de l'imaginaire* (Paris: Bordas, 1969; pp. 217–433), Gilbert Durand argues that darkness belongs to the nocturnal register of symbols and carries an ambivalent meaning. Such symbols are constantly "under the sign of conversion and euphemism." If, on the one hand, they evoke the descent or regression into the horrors of depression, chaos, and death; on the other hand, by what he calls a process of "progressive euphemization," by a sort of antithesis ("*antiphrase*"), a radical inversion of their affective meaning takes place. Thus, it is not only that within the very darkness of night itself the spirit seeks the light, nor even that the night precedes the day and bears within it the seed-time of light, but, even more radically, by a process of double negation and inversion, darkness itself discharges a positive meaning. As Durand puts it, "the most radical attitude of the nocturnal register of the imaginary consists in plunging oneself anew in substantial intimacy and establishing oneself by a negation of the negative into a state of cosmic quietude whose values have been inverted and whose terrors have been exorcised by euphemism" (ibid., 321). The multivalent meaning of the symbol of darkness is also brought out by a study of primitive religions. In a key article on the subject, "Le symbole des ténèbres dans les religions archaiques," Mircea Eliade indicates the positive and negative resonances of darkness: "One can understand not only that darkness precedes forms and periodically engulfs them, that 'being' rises from and returns to 'non-being,' that death precedes life and conquers it, but also that this return to darkness is beneficial; more than that: in certain cases (initiation, founding of a new mode of being), it is even indispensable. Ultimately, darkness symbolises the universal *Urgrund,* the primordial totality, the paradoxical fusion of being and non-being, the sum total, then, of all possibilities. A provisionary regression to darkness is equivalent to an immersion in the inexhaustible source where all modalities of being are found in *potentia*. . . . In fact, in the symbolism of darkness, we discover the note of 'atemporality,' of 'eter-

nity,' of the suspension of becoming. . . . Return to the darkness implies, then, an immersion in the pre-formal, a contact with what has not been used by time" (in *Polarité du Symbole*, Etudes Carmelitaines [Paris: Desclée de Brouwer, 1962], 27).

169. On the development of the theme of divine darkness in the tradition prior to Angela, see chapter 5 of my thesis, *The Spiritual Journey of the Blessed Angela*, 244–300. On the influence of Thomas Gallus on the early Franciscans, P. G. Théry points out: "Thomas Gallus, through the intermediary of St. Anthony, will have an enormous influence on the first Franciscan generation, of which he (Gallus) is perhaps the main spiritual director" ("Denys au moyen âge: à l'aube de la 'nuit obscure," *Etudes Carmelitaines* 23, vol. 2 [October 1938]: 71).

170. In a poem entitled "L'Archangélique" with Angela in mind, George Bataille writes: "Love is a parody of non-love/Non-love is the truth/In the absence of love everything is a lie/Nothing exists which does not lie/Compared to non-love/Love is lax/And does not love" (*Oeuvres Complètes*, vol. 3 [Paris: Gallimard, 1971], 76).

171. "Uncreated" love and the vision of the "uncreated" God (expressions not found in the *Memorial*) is the terminology used in some of the instructions that seem to comment on and parallel Angela's experience of the divine darkness. E.g., instruction 2: "The soul is also given a vision of the Uncreated. This vision deposits an uncreated love in the soul. In this uncreated love the soul cannot act, it is without works, but love itself acts. When the soul possesses this vision of the Uncreated, it can do nothing, because it is completely absorbed in this vision; it can contribute nothing to uncreated love. It is to be noted, however, that when the soul is given this vision, it has been actively working, in that with its whole being it desired to be united with the Uncreated, and with its whole being sought how to be better united with him. Indeed, it is the Uncreated himself who operates in the soul and inspires it to withdraw from all created things to be better united to him." See also instructions 14, 18, 22.

172. In describing her entrance into the divine darkness, Angela makes use of two prepositions, *in* and *cum*, in a manner not found elsewhere in the literature I have looked at in my research on the mystical experience of divine darkness. *In* conveys the sense of a condition, a deep identification and indwelling, as well as a place or location. It is when she sees God "in darkness" that Angela is totally recollected and finds her firmest faith, hope, and security. Gathered into God by the very act through which he transforms her to unite her to him, she shares

in God's own consciousness of himself, in virtual identity with him. This state is totally unlike any other state, for (resorting to traditional apophatic language) she says that this "most efficacious good" seen "in darkness is far too great to be conceived or understood." It is a "dark" condition because it far exceeds the soul's ordinary capacities of thinking, understanding, or loving. Finally, in the darkness, the soul paradoxically sees "nothing and everything at once." *Cum* implies accompaniment, association, union: It can mean such things as "characterized by," "under the influence of," "by means of." It is "with darkness" that Angela is extracted from the negative dimensions of this image and drawn into the mysterious abyss of the Trinity. It is under the influence of the attraction of this "great darkness," "which surpasses every other good," that all previous forms of her experience of God are negated: the All Good, the God-man, all images, intermediaries, and forms. Finally, it is by means of the darkness that proceeds from within the Trinity that the mystical marriage with Christ takes place and she is associated in the very movement in which he reveals and shows the Father, the unmanifested and undifferentiated side of God. The vision "with darkness" then transmits a heightened awareness of God's transcendence, his hidden and secret life within the Trinity, and a union with him characterized by sharing his own mode of being, loving, and knowing. Before this mystery, the soul is completely passive and still, for it is the "uncreated" that operates, yet fully "alive." What the soul sees "with darkness" is "the whole, and all other things are but parts." The experience is so ineffable that for Angela whatever she says about it "is blasphemy." In my research on this theme I have checked the Latin translations of the Pseudo-Dionysius found in Phillipe Chevallier et al., eds., *Dionysiaca*, vol. 1 (Paris: Desclée de Brouwer, 1937–1959), 566–717; Joseph Maréchal's collection of texts in the chapters "Sur les cimes de l'oraison" and "Témoignage médiévaux sur la nature de la haute contemplation" of his *Etudes sur la psychologie des mystiques,* vol. 1 (Bruges, Belgium: Desclée de Brouwer, 1937), 41–197, 257–99; and a series of texts assembled by the Carmelites of Amiens, "Expérience de Dieu dans l'obscur," in *Ma joie terrestre ou donc es-tu?,* Etudes Carmelitaines (Bruges, Belgium: Desclée de Brouwer, 1947), 317–77. Significant also are a number of other shifts in vocabulary that distinguish Angela from other writers who have developed the divine darkness theme. Almost completely absent are the many terms of eminence prefixed by the Latin *super* or *hyper* in Greek, e.g. superluminous, supra-unknown, found commonly in the Pseudo-Dionysius's descriptions of the objective transcendence of God. Likewise absent is the term "*excessus*" so prevalent in medieval descriptions (e.g., Bonaventure) of the soul's being lifted out of itself as it enters the darkness and the summits of contemplation. Neither does Angela ever use the term *caligo*, which is the technical term used in all the translations and commentaries of the Pseudo-Dionysius (including Bonaventure) that I know of. See my thesis, *The Spiritual Journey of the Blessed Angela of Foligno*, 376–79.

173. Commenting on the necessary fading of the passion of Christ at the summits of mystical experience, Stanislas Breton writes: "The passion is like an objectification of what in the deepest part of the soul, is faceless and stands naked before God. But this image is still too sensible. It has value only as a stage of development. It corresponds to a level which must be transcended. As necessary as it is at lower degrees, it reduces itself little by little to either a phenomenon of accompaniment or a remembrance of the past. To it must be applied the ascetics of representations which it has helped to educate. The base of support must be rejected when the thrust reaches its term. The raft no longer has any meaning when one reaches the other shore" (*Mystique de la Passion: Etude sur la doctrine spirituelle de Saint Paul de la Croix* [Tournai, Belgium: Desclée & Co., 1962], 37).

174. Henri De Lubac expresses well the interpenetration of mystical experience and Scripture: "There is ... a connaturality between the Scriptures and the soul. Each is a temple in which the Lord dwells, a paradise in which he strolls. Each is a fountain of living waters ... and the same living waters. The Logos, which is in the one as Word, is in the other as Reason. Both harbor the same mystery in the depths of the self. The experience of one is also in preliminary accord with the doctrine of the other; each is suited to express and rediscover itself in the other ... and likewise mutually enlighten each other" (*Histoire et Esprit* [Paris: Aubier, 1950], 347).

175. Instruction 2 describes a similar experience: "Once the soul is perfectly united to God, it is placed in the seat of truth, for truth is the seat of the soul. ... [In this state] it possesses God to the fullness of its capacity. And God even expands the soul so that it may hold all that he wishes to place in it. The soul then sees the One who is and it sees that all else is nothing except insofar as it takes its being from him. ... The soul is so satisfied and at rest that it desires nothing; it even loses the capacity to desire and act effectively because it is bound to God."

176. Some of the instructions were written before the second redaction of the *Memorial*, others after, and still others are undated. For the

dates proposed by the editors of the critical edition, see the notes accompanying each of the instructions.

177. This statement was written by the anonymous author of the epilogue. A recent tradition gives Angela the title "Magistra Theologorum" (teacher of theologians), probably taken from a quotation by M. Sandaeus ("*Talis fuit Angela, Theologorum Magistra*") in 1624 and quoted by J. Bollandus, *Acta Sanctorum*, 1 (Antwerp, 1643), 234. See also Celestino Bordoni, '*Magistra Theologorum,*' *Angela da Foligno* (Foligno: 1909).

178. In one of these letters Angela enjoins her sons to remain in their cells and never leave them (instruction 14). For the questions addressed to her from friars living in the Marches, see the final paragraphs of chap. 5.

179. *Il Libro*, 519, n. 16. The first twelve instructions (on which the others are largely dependent) are the following: 18, 22, 7, 9, 14, 10, 3, 6, 4, 11, 26, 8, according to the sequence in the B group of manuscripts (see note 181 below). See *Il Libro*, 519, n. 16.

180. For instance, a brief fourteenth-century compendium of Angela's teaching written in Italian contains many traces of the original redaction. Its author is unknown, probably one of Angela's later disciples. Faloci Pulignani even thinks that it should be considered part of Angela's writings. The editors of the critical edition have not retained it as authentic because the text has been too obviously manipulated. Reprinted on numerous occasions, bearing the title either of *Via della Salute* or *Via della Croce*, it can be found in *Prosatori Minori del Trecento I, Scrittori di religione*, ed. G. De Luca (Milano: Ricciardi, 1954), 857–67; and in English translation by Joseph R. Berrigan, "A Lovely and Useful Instruction by Angela da Foligno," in *Vox Benedictina* 2, no. 1 (January 1985): 24–41. See *Il Libro*, 47, n. 21, and 86, n. 47.

181. The B group (the first family of manuscripts) contains the text of the first redaction and probably the first collection of the instructions. See *Il Libro*, 51. The order of the instructions in B, and the chronological order, is as follows: 18, 22, 7, 9, 14, 10, 3, 6, 4, 11, 26, 8, 28, 31, 29, 27, 5, 2, 30, 32, 34, 35, 36. For the contents and sequence of the instructions in each group of manuscripts, see the table in *Il Libro*, 112.

182. See especially chapters 3, 4, 5 of *Holy Feast and Holy Fast*, 73–186.

183. There is an undocumented legend that for twelve years Angela's only food was the Eucharist. See the chronicles of Luke Wadding (an. 1309, n. 15 [VI, 178]), and Arturo da Moustier, *Martyrologium Franci-*

scanum (Paris, 1653), col. 9 (January IV). Cf. Abele Calufetti, "Angela da Foligno e l'Eucaristia," in *Vita e spiritualità della Beata Angela*, 338, n. 51–52.

184. Also, instruction 20 records that on the Feast of the Angels, Angela had a vision of Christ crucified and bleeding on the cross, and she heard angels tell her: "You, who are most pleasing and delightful to God, behold, it has been granted to you, and you have him present; furthermore, it is given to you that you have the power to administer and make him present to others." For similar examples of medieval women mystics claiming priestly functions, see Bynum, *Holy Feast and Holy Fast*, 231–33.

185. For an excellent and well-documented introduction to the influence of the Scriptures in Angela's spirituality, see Guiseppe Betori, "La scrittura nell'esperienza spirituale di Angela," in *Vita e spiritualità della Beata Angela*, 171–98.

186. For a more complete catalogue of biblical citations and reminiscences, see ibid. 192–98.

187. Ibid., 86–88.

188. Ferré points out that the times of anguish and incertitude lasted for ten out of the twenty-four years after Angela's conversion. The first period: toward the end of 1285 until the summer of 1293, followed by five or six months of certitude and happiness; then, the springtime of 1294 to that of 1296, the two years in which Angela experienced almost simultaneously the desolation of abandonment and the summits of her mystical experience; finally, a period of torment of undetermined length toward the end of her life. See *La spiritualité de sainte Angèle*, 96–97.

189. I Celano, chap. 6, n. 103 (*Omnibus of Sources*, 318).

190. Her clearest description of the Christocentric spiritual poverty characteristic of the Spirituals is found in instruction 27: "The first gift [of seven gifts from God which transform the soul into Christ] is the love of poverty by which the soul strips itself of the love of every creature, does not want to possess anything other than our Lord Jesus Christ, does not place its hope in the help of any creature in this life, and shows this by its deeds." Instruction 34 contains the concrete and detailed application of what it means to share in "the first company of Christ," namely poverty—an enumeration of examples in consonance with the *usus pauper* criterion developed by the Spirituals. See also in this same instruction, Angela's lament that "poverty is scorned" and "trumpeted out of town by almost every class of people in the world," a lament worthy of an Ubertino of Casale or an Angelo of Clareno; see

also instruction 3, where Francis is described as the personification of perfect interior and exterior poverty and poverty as the key to open and understand the story of salvation. Both of these themes were dear to the Spirituals. Support for the Spirituals is likewise in evidence in instruction 4, where Francis appears to Angela and praises the sons "who burn with zeal to observe the poverty prescribed by the rule."

191. For an approach that takes into account the chronological and thematic development of Angela's understanding of poverty, see Constanzo Cargnoni, "La povertà nella spiritualità della Beata Angela da Foligno," in *Vita e spiritualità della Beata Angela*, 342–54.

192. Further study would be needed to establish the similarities and differences between the theme of poverty as found in Angela's *Book* and as treated in other spiritual writers of the period: Bonaventure, Olivi, Ubertino of Casale, Angelo of Clareno, Jacopone da Todi, Marguerite of Cortona, Clare of Montefalco, U. Panziera, G. Colombini, Marguerite Porete, and Eckhart. In the notes that accompany this text, I indicate a few of these parallels.

193. For further information on the tenets and practices of this sect, see sec. I i, n. 101, J, n. 125.

194. It was a common topos among medieval mystics to try to clear themselves from suspicion of heresy by intense and sometimes exaggerated attacks on the Free Spirits, even though the Free Spirits' language was at times very near to their own. Among the Franciscans: Ubertino of Casale, Angelo of Clareno, Ugo Panziero of Prato (a follower of Clareno), Alvaro Pelayo, and, in the fifteenth century, Bernardino of Siena. Among the northern mystics: Suso, Tauler, Ruusbroec, Groote, and the Brethren of the Common Life, and in England, Walter Hilton. For a summary of their attacks see Lerner, "The Predicament of the Mystics" in *The Heresy of the Free Spirit*, 183–99; and Guarnieri, "Il movimento del Libero Spirito," 355–499.

195. For this kinship with heretical terminology and practices, see the footnotes accompanying these moments in our text (esp. chap. 9, nn. 116, 121, 122, 127, 133, and instruction 2, nn. 13, 16, 21, 27).

196. Chap. 4 and 7, pp. 157–58, 185–87.

197. Jean-Nöel Vuarnet, *Exstases féminines* (Paris: Arthaud, 1980), 77.

198. Ferré, *La spiritualité de sainte Angèle*, 59.

199. In an innovative study of the role of images in the shaping of Western Christianity and culture, Margaret Miles observes that in the paintings of Giotto and his successors, "a new relationship is created

between viewer and painted figures: The viewer is placed *within* the depicted event through the intensity of feeling he or she shares with the human beings of the painting" (*Image as Insight: Visual Understanding in Western Christianity and Secular Culture* [Boston: Beacon Press, 1985], 73); see also, Chiara Frugoni, "La mistica femminile nell'iconografia delle visioni," in *Temi e Problemi nella mistica femminile trecentesca,* Convegni del centro di studi sulla spiritualità medievale (Todi: Presso l'Accademia Tudertina, 1983), 139–79; and Carolly Erickson, *The Medieval Vision: Essays in History and Perception* (New York: Oxford University Press, 1976).

200. See Mariano D'Alatri, "Francesco d'Assisi visto dalla Beata," in *Vita e spiritualità della Beata Angela,* 147.

201. For this example showing the parallel between medieval paintings depicting Christ in the sepulcher and Angela's vision, see Frugoni, "Le mistiche, le visioni e l'iconografia," 170–71.

202. See instruction 2, p. 226, n. 16.

203. *Sainte Angèle de Foligno,* 137. Doncoeur: "[Angela] is a spiritual high point of the Catholic church and the world" (*DS*, vol. 1 [1938], col. 570). I. Colosio, O.P., former director of *Rivista di Ascetica e di Mistica:* "[Teresa of Avila] is the great phenomenologist of the mystical life while Angela is the great metaphysician" ("Beata Angela da Foligno: Mistica per autonomasia," 498); idem, "Angela is to mysticism what Dante is to poetry" ("Un nuova edizione delle opere della Beata Angela da Foligno," *Rivista di Ascetica e di Mistica* 10/2 [March–April 1965]: 193).

204. For the debate on Ubertino's chronology, see Philip Caliendo, *Ubertino da Casale: A Re-evaluation of the Eschatology in the Fifth Book of his 'Arbor Vite Crucifixe Jesu',* (Ann Arbor, Mich.: University Microfilms, 1979); also, Marino Damiata, *Pietà e storia nell'Arbor Vitae di Ubertino da Casale* (Florence: Edizioni "Studi Francescani," 1988), 14–15; G. L. Potestà, "Un secolo di studi sull '*Arbor vitae*': Chiesa ed escatologia in Ubertino da Casale," *Collectanea Franciscana* 47 (1977): 217–67; and *Il Libro,* 37, n. 46.

205. *Ubertinus de Casale: Arbor vitae crucifixae Jesu,* ed. Charles T. Davis (1485 edition reprinted Torino, 1961), pro. 5. Ubertino wrote this book while at Mt. La Verna, between 1304 and 1307; see F. Callaey, "L'idéalisme franciscain spirituel au XIV siècle: Etude sur Ubertin de Casale (Louvain, 1911), 20–22, 25. G. L. Potestà, *Storia ed escatologia in Ubertino da Casale* (Milan: Vita e Pensiero, 1980), 10.

206. "Une lettre importante d'Angèle de Foligno," *Revue d'histoire*

franciscaine 2 (1925): 361–75. Instruction 17 would be another letter possibly addressed to Ubertino.

207. *Il Libro*, 38–39, n. 47; 576–77, n. 1. Giacinto D'Urso, O.P., likewise doubts that any of Angela's letters were addressed to Ubertino. See his essay, "La B. Angela e Ubertino da Casale," in *Vita e Spiritualità della Beata Angela*, 155–70. Umberto Eco, in his best-selling novel *The Name of the Rose*, puts in the mouth of Ubertino (without citing the source) selections from Angela's writings, in particular from her teachings on the perils of love found in instruction 2 (trans. William Weaver [San Diego: Harcourt Brace Jovanovich, 1980], 230–31).

208. Fra. Giunta Bevegnati, *Leggenda Della Vita e Dei Miracoli di Santa Margherita Da Cortona*, trans. Eliodoro Mariani, O.F.M. (Vicenza: L.I.E.F., 1978), 353.

209. See Silvestro Nessi, "La fortuna del 'Libro' di Angela attreverso i secoli," in *Vita e Spiritualità della Beata Angela*, 101–5; M. J. Ferré, "Le opere autentichi di Angela da Foligno ritrovate dope sei secoli di dimenticanza," *Studi Francescani* 10 (1924): 124; F. Sarni, "Pier Giovanni Olivi e Ubertino da Casale, maestri di teologia a Firenze," *Studi Francescani* 11 (1926): 110–25; Damiata, *Pietà e storia*, 48–50; and *Il Libro*, 106.

210. *Pietà e storia*, 51–56.

211. Aside from the prologue to his *Arbor vitae*, Ubertino makes no explicit mention of Angela in his writings. Angelo of Clareno, likewise, doesn't say a word about her, either in his chronicles or in his letters. Her name is absent from the Franciscan chronicles of John of Winterthur (d. 1348), Arnaud da Sarrant (d. ca. 1383), Giacomo Oddi of Perugia (d. 1488), and Nicolò Glassberger (d. 1508), and from the list of Franciscan saints in Umbria between 1314 and 1322 compiled by Gualdo Tadino. See Clément Schmitt, O.F.M., "Il culto della Beata Angela in Italia e all'Estero," in *Vita e Spiritualità della Beata Angela*, 355–56.

212. As noted earlier, the Colonna cardinals had signed a manifesto declaring Boniface's election as pope illegitimate. Significantly, at the top of the list of the signers of this manifesto was Jacopone da Todi. Two other Franciscans were among those who signed it, and one of them was also from Umbria, Benedicto of Perugia. It is also known that Clare of Montefalco was once threatened with denunciation to ecclesiastical authorities by one of her contemporaries because of her connivance with the Colonna cardinals. As further evidence of the latter's strong ties to Umbrian resistance circles, Angelo of Montefalco, the

abbot of the prestigious Benedictine monastery of S. Croce di Sassovivo, was denounced by one of his monks for his public stand in favor of the Colonna position against Boniface. For fidelity and services rendered, James Colonna, after his reinstitution as Cardinal, named him his personal chaplain. See Nessi, "La fortuna del 'Libro' di Angela," 99–100.

213. Further evidence of the circulation of Angela's writings within Spiritual circles: The editors of the critical edition point to the strong resemblance of two prologues, one an introduction to the vernacular translation of John Climacus's *La Scala del Paradiso* attributed to the Augustinian Gentile of Foligno, confidante of Angelo of Clareno (a leader of the Spirituals and the Latin translator of Climacus's work); and the other, an introduction (unsigned) to a vernacular translation of Angela's writings, the important Milano codex (fourteenth century). That both introductions came from the same pen is certainly plausible, as, likewise, that Gentile was an early translator of Angela's writings. See *Il Libro*, 59–60.

214. There are many versions of how and where Ubertino died, all conjectural. See Caliendo, *Ubertino da Casale*, 71–72; also, Nessi, "La fortuna del 'Libro' di Angela," 104.

215. Subsequent mention of Angela's name and references to her writings among the Franciscans (until the seventeenth century) appear in the following: Bernardino de Bustis (d. 1513/1515) in his *Sermo de imitatione Christi quoad religionis ingressum et mundi contemptionem* (Bernardino is the source for the unsubstantiated report—found in some writings about Angela—that for twelve years the Eucharist was her only food); Mariano da Firenze (d. 1523), the first chronicler (*Compendium Chronicarum*) to truly and effectively propagate Angela's holiness; Marco da Lisbona (d. 1591), *Crónicas da Orden dos Frades Minores* (Lisbon, 1557–1562); Francesco Gonzaga, *De origine Seraphicae Religionis* (ca. 1579); Luke Wadding (d. 1657), *Annales Minorum seu trium Ordinum a S. Francisco institutorum*, 3d ed., vol. 6, no. 11–22 (Quaracchi, 1932), 175–82. See Schmitt, "Il culto della Beata," 356–57.

216. Our source for the circulation of Angela's writings during the period covered is Silvestro Nessi's "La Fortuna del 'Libro' di Angela," 97–115; for the manuscript tradition, *Il Libro*, 51–73.

217. For a list in chronological sequence of the editions and versions of Angela's writings, see *Il Libro*, 74–85.

218. See *Obras de Santa Teresa de Jesu*, ed. Silverio de Santa Teresa, *Libro de la vida*, (Burgos: El Monte Carmelo, 1915) ch. 20, 155, n. 2; *Franciscan Studies* 6 (1946): 316–31. The two following quotations

from Teresa's writings clearly bear the mark of Angela's influence: "I live without living in myself./And in such a way I hope./I die because I do not die" (refrain from her poem entitled "Aspirations," in *Collected Works of St. Teresa of Avila*, trans. Adrian Cooney, O.C.D., ed. Kieran Kavanaugh, O.C.D., and Otilio Rodriguez, O.C.D., vol. 3 [1985], 375; for the parallel and probably the source, cf. supplementary step 7 of Angela's *Memorial*: "I die because I do not die"); in speaking of the trials that occur in the sixth dwelling place in the *The Interior Castle*: "As for now, the reasoning faculty is in such a condition that the soul is not the master of it, nor can the soul think of anything else than of why it is grieving, of how it is absent from its Good, and of why it should want to live. It feels a strange solitude because no creature in all the earth provides it company, nor do I believe would any heavenly creature, not being the One whom it loves; rather, everything torments it. But the soul sees that it is like a person hanging, who cannot support himself on any earthly thing; nor can it ascend to heaven" (ibid, vol. 2, trans. Kieran Kavanaugh, O.C.D., and Otilio Rodriguez, O.C.D.), 423; in her experience of the "horrible darkness" of supplementary step 6 of the *Memorial*, Angela compares it with the image of a person "hanging without any supports."

219. "It is more than likely that he [Laredo] knew the Revelations of Angela of Foligno and the letters of Catherine of Siena, both of whom he names as among the great models of generous souls," Fidèle De Ros, *Le Frère Bernadin de Laredo: un inspirateur de sainte Thérèse* (Paris: J. Vrin, 1948), 233 (cf. Laredo's *Subida del Monti Sion* [Seville: 1535], vol. 3, chap. 7, 233.

220. According to Ubald d'Alençon, "it is very possible that St. Ignatius of Loyola was acquainted with the writings of Saint Angela" ("La spiritualité franciscaine," *Etudes Franciscaines* 39 [1927]: 291, n. 7). Balthasar Alvarez, S.J. (d. 1580), one of Teresa of Avila's confessors and spiritual directors, quotes entire chapters taken from Angela's writings in his *Exhortations* to his novices (referred to by P. Doncoeur, *Le livre de la bienheureuse soeur Angèle de Foligno*, 23, n. 2). In the seventeenth century, another famous Jesuit and mystic, Jean-Joseph Surin (1600–1665), was also a great reader and admirer of Angela, whom he interpreted as a forerunner of John of the Cross's theme of the dark night of the soul. See, for instance, the seventh part of his *Guide Spirituel* entitled "Du Purgatoire de l'âme, de l'Enfer de l'âme" (referred to by Jean-Noël Vuarnet, *Extases Féminines* [Paris: Arthaud, 1980], 93).

221. *Oeuvres de Saint François de Sales, Evêque de Genève et Docteur*

de l'Eglise, Edition Complète (Annecy: J. Niérat et al. (1892–1964), vol. 3, 108, 193, 295, 331; vol. 13, 314; vol. 14, 52; *Introduction à la vie dévote*, vol. 1, p. viii. See Antanas Liuima, S. J., *Aux Sources du traité de l'amour de Dieu de St. François de Sales*, 2 vols. (Rome: Librairie Editrice de l'Université Grégorienne, 1960), 236.

222. See Faloci Pulignani, "Memorie e documenti," 127.

223. Bollandus reproduces, substantially, a previous Parisian version, 1598 (probably based in turn on the Toledo edition of 1505), correcting it by selections from an older codex belonging to Cornelio Duijn of Amsterdam. Subsequently, in Foligno, G. B. Boccolini published the best of the more modern versions (1714), improving the Bollandus version by using, but only partially, the Assisi codex, which he had discovered and which was to later be recognized as basic for a more critical edition of Angela's writings. See *Il Libro*, 79 and 81.

224. *Opera Omnia*, ed. J. Sylvester (Prato: 1839), Book 2, chap. 26, n. 1, 261–62; chap. 31, n. 12, 293; Book 3 (1840), chap. 26, n. 7, 297; chap. 30, n. 8, 336; chap. 49, n. 11, 567; chap. 52, n. 7, 596; Book 4 (1841) part 2, nn. 5–6, 460–62.

225. *Riflessioni sulla Passione di Gesù Cristo*, in *Opere ascetiche* (Turin: 1880), vol. 1, 537–748; *Pratica di amar Gesù Cristo*, chap. 14, n. 12, in ibid, vol. I, 826; *Le glorie di Maria*, part 2, in ibid, vol. 1, 260; *La vera Sposa di Gesù Cristo, ovvero la monaca santa* (Turin-Rome, 1929), chap. 5, n. 8, 112; chap. 9, par. 1, n. 6, 305; chap. 10, par. 2, n. 9, 360; chap. 11, par. 4, n. 14, 423.

226. François de Salignac de la Mothe, *Les principales propositions du livre des maximes des Saints, justifiées par les expressions plus fortes des Saints Auteurs* (a work condemned by the church in the Quietist controversy) in *Oeuvres* (Paris: 1852), vol. 3, 268, 272, 273, 279, 366.

227. Jacques Bénigne Bossuet, *Instruction sur les états d'oraison*, Treatise I, Book 9, in *Oeuvres complètes*, vol. 9 (Paris: 1846), 177; ibid., vol. 18 (Paris: 1864), 562.

228. Quoted by Ubald d'Alençon in "La spiritualité franciscaine: les auteurs—la doctrine," *Etudes Franciscaines* 39 (1927): 290.

229. For a sampling of how Arndt used and expanded Angela's writings (notably her instructions), see *Johann Arndt: True Christianity*, trans. and intro. Peter Erb (New York: Paulist Press, 1979), 10–11.

230. *Angèle de Foligno: Visions et instructions*, 7th ed. (Stein Am Rhein, Switzerland: 1976), 22. According to this Swiss publishing house, their edition brought the number of Hello's translations in circulation to 61,000 or 65,000. Editions du Seuil, in Paris, has just published

a new edition, with intro. by Sylvie Duransti (1990). An Italian translation of Angela's writings by Luigi Fallacara, inspired by Hello's text, enjoyed three editions, *Beata Angela da Foligno: Il libro delle mirabile visioni e consolazioni* (Florence: Libreria Editrice Fiorentina, 1922; 1926; 1946). In Danish, selections from Angela's writings (based on Hello's version) appeared in a Copenhagen review: "Forsoninges Veie. Af den salige Angela af Foligno," *Katholiken* 2 (1899): 140–44. A year later, Johannes Joergensen, the noted biographer of St. Francis, inserted sections from the Angela corpus (again based on Hello's) in his novel *Var frue as Danmark* (Copenhagen: 1900), 221–25. The same Joergensen was to later write a brief spiritual biography of Angela, *In Excelsis* (Kempten-München, 1910), also translated into Italian (Florence: Biblioteca 'Florentia', 1925), and Polish (Poznan, 1914). For further information concerning Hello's translation, see Pierre Péano, O.F.M., "L'oeuvre d'Ernest Hello dans sa version française du livre de la B. Angèle" in *Vita e Spiritualità della Beata Angela*, 117–27.

231. *Elisabeth de la Trinité: J'ai trouvé Dieu, Oeuvres complètes,* ed. Conrad de Meester, vol. 1B (Dijon, France: Cerf, 1980), 264, 441, 507.

232. The Carmelite Blanche, a major character in the play, repeats the oft-quoted lines from Angela's writings: "Ce n'est pas pour rire que je t'ai aimé" (My love for you has not been a hoax) (*Dialogues des carmélites* in *Bernanos: Oeuvres Romanesques* [Paris: Gallimard, 1961], 1593).

233. Bataille's poem: "Love is a parody of non-love/non-love is the truth/in the absence of love everything is a lie/nothing exists which does not lie/compared to non-love/love is lax/and does not love" (*Oeuvres complètes,* vol. 3 [Paris: Gallimard, 1971], 76); references to and quotations from Angela are also found in ibid., "La somme athéologique," 248–51, "L'expérience intérieure," ibid, vol. 5, 7–189, 122–123; "Le coupable," ibid., translated as *Guilty* by Bruce Boone (Venice, Calif.: The Lapis Press, 1988), 11, 12, 16.

234. *Le livre de la bienheureuse Angèle de Foligno,* Latin text (Paris: Editions de la Revue d'Ascétique et de Mystique, 1925); and *Le livre de la bienheureuse soeur Angèle de Foligno du Tiers Ordre de S. François* (Paris: Libraire de l'Art Catholique, 1926).

235. *Sainte Angèle de Foligno: Le livre de l'expérience des vrais fidèles* (Paris: Editions E. Droz, 1927). Ferré also wrote two books on Angela's life and spirituality: *La spiritualité de Sainte Angèle de Foligno* (Paris: Mignard Frères, 1927) and, under the pseudonym Louis Leclève, *Sainte Angèle de Foligno: Sa vie-ses oeuvres* (Paris: Librairie Plon, 1936), and a

number of important articles, in one of which he establishes what until now has been accepted as the chronology of Angela's life (in need of review in the light of the new critical edition): "Les principales dates de la vie d'Angèle de Foligno," *Revue d'histoire franciscaine* 7 (1924): 136–48. Raymond Christoflour is another recent French translator of Angela's writings (incomplete): *Sainte Angèle de Foligno: Visions et révélations* (Namur: Les Editions du Soleil Levant, 1958).

236. *L'Autobiografia e gli scritti della Beata Angela da Foligno,* trans. Maria Castiglione Humani (Città di Castello: Casa Editrice 'Il Solco,' 1932).

237. Among Blasucci's many publications on Angela: *Il libro della Beata Angela da Foligno,* a reprint of the M. Castiglione Humani translation (see previous note), with intro. and notes by Blasucci and a preface by J. Joergensen (Rome: Angelo Signorelli, 1950); *Il Cristocentrismo nella vita spirituale secondo la Beata Angela da Foligno* (Rome: Miscellanea Francescana, 1940); *La Beata Angela da Foligno* (Foligno: Edizioni Chiesa di S. Francesco, 1978). Two other contemporary Italian editions of Angela's writings: *L'esperienza mistica della Beata Angela da Foligno nel racconto di Frater Arnaldo,* ed. Pasquala Valugani (Milan: Biblioteca Francescana Provinciale, 1964); and *L'esperienza di Dio Amore: Il libro di Angela da Foligno,* trans., intro., and notes Salvatore Aliquò (Rome: Città Nuova Editrice, 1972).

238. Among Andreoli's publications: *Angela, la poverella di Foligno* (Siena: Edizioni Cantagalli, 1984); two extensive bibliographies: "Bibliografia sulla beata Angela da Foligno (1248/49–1309)" and "Angela da Foligno: Bibliografia (1984–1987)," *L'Italia Francescana* 60 (1985): 75–92; 63 (1988): 185–200; the first translation of Angela's *Book* based on the new critical edition: *Il Libro della Beata Angela da Foligno* (Milan: Edizioni Paolini, 1990).

239. In this study I frequently refer to the proceedings of this congress: *Vita e spiritualità della Beata Angela da Foligno.* Likewise in honor of the centenary, there was an iconography exhibit of thirteenth- and fourteenth-century Umbrian saints with a special focus on Angela, which was published as *Sante e Beate Umbre tra il XIII e il XIV secolo* (Foligno: Edizioni dell'Arquata-Foligno, 1986); the sections dealing with Angela are on pp. 35–41, 45–46, 69–72, 129–216.

240. Augustine Baker, *Holy Wisdom: or Directions for the Prayer of Contemplation,* intro. by Dom Gerard Sitwell, O.S.B. (Whethampstead/Hertfordshire: Anthony Clarke Books, 1972). There is only one explicit quotation in Baker's book, but since it is a compilation made by the

Benedictine Sernus Cressy from a large number of Baker's manuscript treatises, it is likely, as implied in the quotation, that there are more: "To this purpose [the need to follow God's counsel as discovered in prayer] it is very observable, in the life of the same B. Angela, that God commanded her to set down in writing this passage (which is the only one for which she received such a command), to wit, that He would take away His light and grace from those who, being brought immediately to their internal master, would be so ungrateful as to forsake Him, and betake themselves to an external one; yea, and that moreover such should have a curse from Him, namely, if they did persist in receding from the divine conduct, constantly preferring human directions before God's" (p. 92). Since it differs from and amplifies the corresponding text of Angela's writings, this quotation obviously is either a free rendering or is based on an imperfect manuscript (the source is not mentioned).

241. *The Book of the Visions and Instructions of Blessed Angela of Foligno, as taken down from her own lips, by Brother Arnold* (London: 1871; Leamington: Art and Book Co., 1888); *The Book of Divine Consolation of the Blessed Angela of Foligno*, trans. Mary G. Steegmann, intro. by Algar Thorold (New York: Cooper Square Publishers, Inc., 1909, reprint in 1966). Most modern English translations or excerpts from Angela's writings (as well as some in other languages, e.g., Hello's) rely chiefly on the Bollandus Latin text published in 1643. Among its many limitations, it follows a different order in the steps (of which there are only 18). The result has been to create a great deal of confusion in contemporary attempts to understand Angela.

242. One of Underhill's earliest biographical pieces was on Angela, "A Franciscan Mystic of the Thirteenth Century: The Blessed Angela of Foligno," in *Franciscan Studies* by P. Sabatier (Aberdeen, Scotland: The University Press, 1912), 88–107, reprinted in E. Underhill, *The Essentials of Mysticism and Other Essays* (London: J. M. Dent and Co., 1920); see also, "Two Franciscan Mystics: Jacopone da Todi and Angela of Foligno" in *The Mystics of the Church* (London: James Clarke, 1925; reprint, New York: Schocken, 1964), 93–109. For the special place Angela occupied in Underhill's thinking, see Dana Greene, *Evelyn Underhill: Artist of the Infinite Life* (New York: Crossroad, 1990), 60, 61, 110.

243. Rudolph M. Bell, *Holy Anorexia* (Chicago: University of Chicago Press, 1985); Bynum, *Holy Feast and Holy Fast: The Religious Significance of Food to Medieval Women* (Berkeley: University of California

NOTES TO THE INTRODUCTION

Press, 1987); Elizabeth A. Petroff, *The Consolation of the Blessed: Women Saints in Medieval Tuscany* (New York: Alta Gaia, 1980); and *Medieval Women's Visionary Literature,* ed. Elizabeth A. Petroff (New York: Oxford University Press, 1986).

244. Simone de Beauvoir, "The Mystic," in *The Second Sex,* trans. and ed. H. M. Parshley (New York: Alfred A. Knopf, 1976), 670–78.

245. Julia Kristeva, *Powers of Horror: An Essay on Abjection,* trans. Leon S. Roudiez (Columbia University Press, 1982), 127.

246. Irigaray's only quote (from Hello's version) from Angela is an epigraph ("The Word was made flesh in order to make me God") inserted before a chapter on mystic language ("La Mystérique"), which, unless I am mistaken, teems with allusions to Angela's writings: in Luce Irigaray, *Speculum of the Other Woman,* trans. Gillian C. Gill (Ithaca, N. Y.: Cornell University Press, 1985), 191–202. For Irigaray, "This is the only place [mystic language] in the history of the West in which woman speaks and acts so publicly" (ibid., 191).

247. Umberto Eco, *The Name of the Rose,* trans. William Weaver (San Diego: Harcourt Brace Jovanovich, 1980), 230–31.

248. "Since the mammal brain commits a lot of its energy to sexual love, some students at this point in the 'road' become ascetic and celibate. They do so precisely in order to increase the speed of energy transfer. The women saints, also, such as Anna of Foligno, experience this same turn in the road, which usually involves an abrupt abandonment of husband and children" (Robert Bly, *Leaping Poetry: An Idea with Poems and Translations* [Boston: Beacon Press, 1972], 64). Cf. step 9 of the *Memorial,* where Angela expresses relief over the death of her husband and her sons.

249. From a cassette recording (accompanied by Merton's conference notes) graciously made available by the Thomas Merton Legacy trust via Robert E. Daggy, director of the Thomas Merton Studies Center (Bellarmine College, Louisville Kentucky). Merton, in his journal entry for Tuesday of Holy Week, April 13, 1965, refers to his conference on Angela as follows: "In the evening conference, I talked (foolishly) of Angela of Foligno and then back to Philoxenos. After supper and direction, I went up to bed in the hermitage feeling unwell. I woke up after an hour's sleep with violent diarrhea and vomiting, which went on for most of the night. Fortunately, the night was warm and moonlit. I was weak and nauseated all yesterday. I began to feel better in the evening and took a little supper. I slept last night in the infirmary and slept well too. Had a good breakfast of fried eggs and coffee. I felt a little

weak this morning, but on the whole I seem to have got off easy, unless it starts up again after supper, which I suppose it might. While it lasted, it was a miserable experience" (*Thomas Merton: A Vow of Conversation: Journals 1964–1965*, ed. and with a preface by Naomi Burton Stone [New York: Farrar, Straus, Giroux, 1988], 172).

Notes to the *Memorial*

1. Among Franciscans, "custody" is the term used for a territorial unit smaller than a province, and "custodian" or *custos* the term for the religious superior who presides over it.

2. Cardinal Colonna (d. 1318), protector of the Franciscan Spirituals, was excommunicated by Boniface VIII in 1296, after he had participated in a plot to declare Boniface's accession to the papal throne illegitimate. He was reinstated by Clement V in 1305. The other examiners are unknown.

3. Cf. Jn 14:23, 14:21. Ephrem Longpré, O.F.M., calls these texts from St. John the cornerstone of Franciscan—and Christian—mysticism. He comments: "The greatest mystics of the East and West recognize, notwithstanding occasional distinctions, that there exists a solemn promise of mystical experience in the discourse of the Last Supper (esp. Jn 14:21). For them 'the wonders' promised in the marvelous texts of the New Testament are realities. Everything that Christ promised at the Last Supper, that St. Paul teaches in his epistles, that the Holy Spirit postulates in the heart of the faithful, is literally fulfilled in the mystics" ("La contemplation dans l'école franciscaine," *DS*, vol. 2 [1953], col. 2080). Cf. also St. Francis in a key passage of the first Rule: "And let us make a home and dwelling place (cf. Jn 14:23) for Him who is the Lord God Almighty, Father and Son and Holy Spirit" (Armstrong and Brady, *Francis and Clare*, XXII, 27, p. 148); also, "The First Version of the Letter to the Faithful," ibid., I, 6, p. 63; "The Second Version of the Letter to the Faithful," ibid., 48, p. 70; St. Clare's "The Third Letter to Blessed Agnes of Prague," ibid., 23, p. 201.

4. The scribe, explaining the procedure of his redaction in chapter 2, mentions that although Angela spoke about herself in the first person, he himself transcribed her revelations in the third person. He confesses, however, that "in order to go faster," he did not take the time to make all

the corrections (to the first person) in his final draft. I have retained the switching of pronouns that occurs in his redaction.

5. On Angela's companion, for centuries named Pasqualina but now identified by the editors of the critical edition as Masazuola, see Introduction, sec. I B.

6. By designating thirty steps or transformations (*mutationes*) to her journey, Angela is following a very common medieval practice of constructing a numerical sequence of states of the soul. As for the number of steps, the only parallel I have found is the thirty steps of *The Ladder of Divine Ascent* of John Climacus. This work was translated into Latin by Angelo of Clareno between 1300 and 1305, and enjoyed a widespread circulation among the Franciscans in the early fourteenth century. An earlier version, perhaps around 1250, by an unknown translator, was soon lost. See Guarnieri, "Il movimento del Libero Spirito," 374; also, Ronald G. Musto, "Angelo Clareno, O.F.M., Fourteenth-Century Translator of the Greek Fathers: An Introduction and a Checklist of Manuscripts and Printings of his 'Scala Paradisi'" (*Archivum Franciscanum Historicum*, 76 [1983]: 589–645).

7. The biographical tradition on Angela identifies the chaplain as Bro. Arnaldo, her relative. There is, however, no documentary proof. See Introduction, sec. II A.

8. The theme of self-knowledge as a foundation stone for the spiritual life was quite widespread in the Middle Ages. The basic source for it was the widely read and copied *Confessions* of St. Augustine. See J. De Ghellinck, S. J., *Patristique et moyen âge: Etudes d'histoire littéraire et doctrinal*, vol. 2 (Paris: Desclée de Brouwer, 1947), 276; for the diffusion of this theme among medieval writers, see Pierre Courcelle, *Connais-toi toi-même: De Socrate à Saint Bernard*, vol. 2 (Paris: Etudes Augustiniennes, 1975).

9. Early biographies of St. Francis report that, as a sign of his conversion to a life of radical poverty, he stripped himself naked in front of his father, the bishop, and everyone, in the town square of Assisi (1 Celano, 15, in *Omnibus of Sources*, 241; 2 Celano, 12, ibid., 377; Bonaventure, *Legenda major*, chap. 2, no. 4, ibid., 642; *Legend of the Three Companions*, chap. 6, no. 20, ibid., 909). Francis's gesture, however, is more ideological than Angela's affective self-donation. Her stripping may also be related to the practice, among some heretical groups, of praying nude as a sign of a return to the primitive innocence of Adam and Eve before the Fall, because of a belief that such prayer was more

efficacious. This practice was noted and condemned by a bull from Boniface VIII, *Saepe Sanctam Ecclesiam,* issued in 1296. See Guarnieri, "Il movimento del Libero Spirito," 388–89. See also instruction 1 where Angela expressed the desire to parade naked through towns and public squares with pieces of meat and fish hanging from her neck.

10. The theme of spiritual nudity, "*nudus nudum Christum sequi,*" was common at the time. It basically entailed a desire to live in total poverty following the ideal set by Christ, who lived as a poor man and died naked on the cross. James of Vitry, the biographer of Marie d'Oignies, one of the early Beguines, says of her, "ut nudum Christum nuda sequentur" ("Vita B. Mariae Oignianensis" in *Acta Sanctorum* [Paris, 1867], vol. 5, p. 557). Bonaventure developed this theme, especially in his *Apologia Pauperum (Opera omnia),* vol. 8, pp. 233–320. It was also prominent among the Franciscan Spirituals. For the origins, meaning, and diffusion of this theme, see Réginald Grégoire, "Nudité," *DS,* vol. 11 (1982), cols. 500–18.

11. In contrast, Angela will later on declare, in a moment of anguish, that "to live was a source of greater pain than that caused by the death of her mother and sons" (chap. 3, p. 143). St. Birgitta of Sweden and St. Margaret of Cortona are two other medieval women visionaries, married and with children, who experienced a profound conversion after the death of their husbands. To be noted, also, that in the medieval context marriage was considered a handicap to salvation—a remedy for concupiscence and a concession to human weakness. The superior form of life was, therefore, virginity or continence. Moreover, the difference in ages between the spouses was considerable: the average age for men at the time of marriage was around thirty and for women fifteen. On the origins and evolution of the medieval ideal of virginity, see the excellent study by John Bugge, *Virginitas: An Essay in the History of a Medieval Ideal* (The Hague: Martinus Nijhoff, 1975); on the medieval concept of marriage, see Brundage, *Law, Sex, and Christian Society in Medieval Europe,* chaps. 8 and 9, 325–485. On the difference in ages between spouses, see David Herlihy, *Medieval Households* (Cambridge, Mass.: Harvard University Press, 1985), pp. 103–11.

12. Among the penances of medieval recluses were self-flagellation, repeated prostrations and genuflections, standing barefoot, standing only on one foot, or remaining with arms outstretched for long periods, as well as wearing iron chains or girdles. The hairshirt was a common instrument of penance. Fasting was frequent, during which the penitent

ate only bread and water. In exceptional cases the fast was absolute, the only food being the Eucharist. See Mario Sensi, "Reclusione," *DIP*, vol. 7 (1983), col. 1240.

13. L. Gougaud writes: "Mary and St. John were closely associated in the devotion of the Middle Ages" (*Dévotions et pratiques ascétiques du moyen âge* [Paris: Desclée de Brouwer, 1925], 77); also, Optatus Van Asseldonk, O.F.M. Cap., "Il crocifisso di San Damiano visto e vissuto da S. Francesco" *Laurentianum* 3 (1981): 457.

14. Devotion to the Sacred Heart of Jesus was quite current in the Middle Ages. It seems, however, that it was only in the thirteenth century that the heart of Jesus began to reveal itself in explicitly mystical visions; this happened especially among the women mystics: St. Margaret of Cortona, St. Ludgarde, St. Gertrude, St. Mechthilde, Ida of Louvain, Julianna of Norwich, to mention a few. See Auguste Hamon, "Coeur (sacré)," *DS*, vol. 2 (1953), cols. 1027–28.

15. Christine Ebner, St. Margaret of Cortona, St. Catherine of Siena, Aldobrandesca of Siena, Giacomo Bianconi, and Osanna Andreassi were other medieval mystics who placed their lips on Christ's side and drank his blood during visions. See Gougaud, *Dévotions et pratiques ascétiques du Moyen Age*, 125; also, C. Frugoni, "Le mistiche, le visioni e l'iconografia: rapporti ed influssi," in *Temi e problemi nella mistica femminile trecentesca*, 145.

16. What seems to be occurring in this step is Angela's definitive entrance and passage into the mystical state, the consciousness of being taken up by God and submitting more and more "passively" to his direction.

17. Medieval Christians observed three Lents of variable duration. The Great Lent consisted of the weeks prior to Easter. The second was during the season of Advent, and the third focused on Pentecost.

18. Angela owned two pieces of land in the vicinity of Foligno. One was next to Madonna delle Scuffiole near the S. Giacomo gate, and the other next to Palombaro near the Villa delle Sterpete. See M. Faloci Pulignani, *Memorie e documenti*, 16–18.

19. "Pietruccio" was the name commonly given to the Bl. Pietro Crisci (d. 1323), a nobleman of Foligno who had converted and distributed his goods to the poor. He became a Franciscan Tertiary and lived as a hermit in the tower of the Duomo in Foligno. See Mario Sensi, "Reclusione," *DIP*, vol. 7 (1983), col. 1239.

20. From this sentence to the end of the chapter belongs to the second redaction. It is the scribe's attempt to provide a bridge from the

end of the nineteenth step to the twentieth, which he restarts in chapter 3. See Ludger Thier, O.F.M., and Abele Calufetti, O.F.M., *Il Libro della Beata Angela da Foligno* (Grottaferrata [Rome]: Editiones Collegii S. Bonaventurae ad Claras Aquas, 1985), 154–55, n. 29. Hereafter referred to as *Il Libro*.

21. This holy man, who is also mentioned in chapter 2, is unknown.

22. Much of what is indicated in this chapter could serve as preface or introduction to the entire *Memorial*. It is inserted here because of the difficulties the scribe encountered in his redaction. The complex process he followed seems to be, roughly, the following: The first step he transcribed was the mystical event in Assisi, then the first nineteen steps of the *Memorial*. Since he ran into problems distinguishing what belonged in the remaining eleven, he condensed these into seven so-called supplementary steps. At the end of his first redaction, he wrote a brief schema or outline of each of these supplementary steps; he even corrected and elaborated it in the second redaction; and he then decided to put this material, along with other explanatory data, here between the nineteenth and twentieth steps in order to guide the reader. The repetitions, often confusing, are indicative of the successive and overlapping layers in the redactional process (*Il Libro*, 160, n. 2).

23. Cf. 2 Cor 12:3.

24. It is from this first and only reference to the text as a "memorial" that the first part of Angela's *Book* has been given its name.

25. See chapter one, p. 132.

26. This account of Angela's pilgrimage to Rome is taken from the first redaction and it belongs to the nineteenth step, probably before her entrance into the Franciscan Third Order. What seems to have happened is that the scribe had forgotten to mention it in his original draft and decided to insert it here in his second redaction because of its similarity with the Assisi pilgrimage. There must have been a brief lapse of time between the two pilgrimages. Date of the Roman pilgrimage: 1290–1291 (*Il Libro*, 178, n. 5).

27. Near this crossroads one can find to this day an ancient chapel dedicated to the Trinity, which Angela was surely familiar with.

28. In order to clarify the meaning of these two sentences, "I am the Holy Spirit . . . and "I am the one who was crucified," the redactor decided to insert a brief discourse on the presence of the Trinity in Angela later on in this step. See pp. 144–45.

29. Probable allusion to St. Paul's conversion on the road to Damascus. Cf. Acts 9:4 *et seq.*

30. Jerome Poulenc, O.F.M., describes this stained-glass window, which can be seen in the upper church of the Basilica of St. Francis, as follows: "Underneath the three angels of the bay on the left, the glorified Christ, sumptuously dressed, is represented standing on a pedestal. In front of him, St. Francis, about a third smaller than Christ, does not touch the ground and seems suspended in the air. The Lord holds him closely to himself by placing his left hand on his shoulder and by sustaining him with the other hand at the level of his right elbow. The founder of the Friars Minor is dressed in the habit of his Order, and carries a book and a small cross. The stigmata on his hands and feet are echoes of the wounds of the passion of the Lord and emphasize the theme of his union to the sufferings of Christ. The spatial vertical correspondence between the crossed nimbus of Christ and the cross of Francis further visually accentuates this participation" (p. 702). Poulenc finds the theological basis for this window in James of Milan's *Stimulus amoris,* a *vade mecum* of Franciscan medieval piety. As a result, he interprets it as depicting the spiritual motherhood of Christ, a theme current at the time (p. 713) ("Saint François dans le 'vitrail des anges' de l'église supérieure de la basilique d'Assise," *Archivum Franciscanum Historicum* 76 [1983]:701–13).

31. Cf. the prophet Daniel's vision as translated in the Latin vulgate: "Domine mi, in visione tua dissolutae sunt compages meae, et nihil in me remansit virtum" (Dn 10:16).

32. In step nine, Angela had said that the death of her mother, husband, and sons was a source of consolation for her. Here her husband is not mentioned.

33. This entire section is an attempt by the scribe in his second redaction to explain and theologically elaborate the advent of the Trinity into Angela. The text is obscure on many points (*Il Libro,* 190, n. 24).

34. Tradition interprets Brother A. as being the scribe Brother Arnaldo. See introduction, sec. II A.

35. With this passage the scribe resumes his first redaction, which had been interrupted in the nineteenth step (*Il Libro,* 192, n. 28).

36. This vision of Christ's throat undoubtedly draws its inspiration from a passage in the Latin vulgate version of the *Song of Songs,* 5:16: "Guttur illius suavissimum, et totus desiderabilis, talis est dilectus meus."

37. The Assisi pilgrimage probably took place in 1291 and the step that begins here in 1292 (*Il Libro,* 200, n. 2).

38. St. Syricus, whose name is linked to this symbolic unction, is

possibly the three-year-old child who was martyred in Tarsica along with his mother, St. Julitte. His cult was widespread in the Middle Ages. In 1389, the blessed Angelina of Marsciano, very devoted to our Angela, founded a monastery in honor of San Quirico (Italian for Syricus) near the walls of Assisi, which still exists today. No further traces of this popular devotion can be detected, but it is obvious that it was known in the thirteenth century, for Angela is sent to a certain Frater F. for further information about it (see Ferré, *Le livre de l'expérience des vrais fidèles*, 74, n. 1).

39. In one of the codices this brother's initial is "F." It could be one of the Franciscans close to Angela, and perhaps Friar Francis Damiani, brother of St. Clare of Montefalco, who was *custos* of the dukedom of Spoleto in 1308, and guardian of the friary in Foligno in 1309. It could also be the scribe himself (*Il Libro*, 211, n. 13).

40. The reference to God as the All Good, source of all that is, was a stereotyped formula of the period. In the Latin vulgate *"omne bonum"* is the name God gives to himself when speaking to Moses (Ex 33:19). Concerning St. Francis's use of it, Ottaviano Schmucki writes: "I must, however, specify that when the saint from Assisi speaks with such insistence of God as *plenum bonum, omne bonum, totum bonum*, he is far from Platonic, Pseudo-Dionysian, or Augustinian speculation on the metaphysical goodness of God. Rather, taking his inspiration very probably from selections, read or heard, of Benedictine or Cistercian writers of the twelfth century, he applied the concept of God the 'highest and unique good' to his meditation on the story of salvation" ("La visione di Dio nella pietà di San Francesco di Assisi," *L'Italia Francescana* 5 [September/October, 1982]: 517).

41. Cf. chap. 3, p. 140, and chap. 4, p. 152.

42. The removal of Angela's doubt concerning God's love for her, as narrated earlier in this step.

43. This ends the first part, the portion the scribe could write almost without interruption. Afterward, he could only write at intervals. This then could be an initial conclusion to his redaction (*Il Libro*, 218, n. 22).

44. The theme of Christ as "doctor of the soul" is strongly anchored in patristic and medieval literature, e.g., Hugh of St. Victor, St. Bernard, and St. Bonaventure. The latter's *Breviloquium*, part 6 (entitled *De medicina sacramentali*) contains a veritable treatise on Christ the doctor saving and healing through the *"medicamenta spiritualia,"* which are the sacraments (*Opera omnia*, vol. 5, 265–80). See also Gervais Du-

meige, "Médecin (le Christ)," *DS*, vol. 10 (1977), cols. 891–901. Cf. Lk 5:31–32; Mk 2:17; Mt 9:12–13.

45. In the Middle Ages three dimensions of the personality of Mary Magdalene struck the minds of the faithful: the converted sinner, the contemplative soul, the woman involved in the Paschal Mystery. See Victor Saxer, *Le culte à Marie-Madeleine en occident*, vol. 2 (Paris: Librairie Clavieul, 1959), 348.

46. The scribe will refer to and explicitly quote this passage toward the end of the seventh supplementary step as he is about to conclude his work (pp. 207–08). It probably belongs with preceding remarks in this step concerning the veracity of the redaction. Compare p. 154 and note 43 (*Il Libro*, 222, n. 26).

47. The fact that Angela's public blessing over alms has the power to take away sins in a context explicitly reminiscent of the Last Supper is highly irregular. In some heretical sects of the period, lay people, men and women, did claim the power to absolve sins, a practice explicitly condemned by Pope Boniface VIII in his bull *Saepe Sanctam Ecclesiam*, issued in 1296. See Guarnieri, "Il movimento del Libero Spirito," 388–89.

48. The theme of the "sons of God" dominates this step. The examples that illustrate it have obvious parallels in gospel parables (see Mt 22:1–14; Lk 12:35–48, 14:7–24, 15:3–32), but the main inspiration is drawn from Franciscan sources (see note 52). This theme also has striking similarities with the central theme of instructions 7, 18, and 22; and since most of this step is from the second redaction, it is possible that it was written at the same time as these instructions, around 1298, and inserted here at that date (*Il Libro*, 230, n. 2). According to Ferré, this step took place in the summer of 1292 ("Les principales dates," 11).

49. Cf. Rv 7:14, 14:1–5.

50. This aside is an insertion from the second redaction. The scribe will develop the theme of the sufferings of Christ more extensively in instruction 3.

51. Cf. Mt 22:1–14; Mk 10:39; Lk 22:30.

52. This is the first time in Angela's *Book* that the theme of the legitimate sons, inserted in the second redaction, occurs. It was used by Franciscans of the first generations in the debate on who were the legitimate sons of St. Francis. Its primary source seems to be a story in *The Legend of the Three Companions*, an early biography of the saint (1246). The Lord tells St. Francis a parable; in it a king espouses a poor woman, and he tells her sons when they have reached adulthood: "Fear nothing,

for you are my sons. If strangers are fed at my table, how much more you who are my legitimate sons" (*Omnibus of Sources,* chap. 12, n. 50, p. 934). In the 2 Celano version, another early biography, the story speaks of "privileged" sons instead of "legitimate," and adds that St. Francis himself was the fortunate spouse of the king (ibid., chap. 11, n. 16, p. 376). In a number of passages in his *Arbor vitae crucifixae Jesu,* Ubertino of Casale, a leader of the Franciscan Spirituals, mentions, as the "legitimate sons" of St. Francis, those who follow his Rule more rigorously, especially in regard to poverty (*Arbor vitae crucifixae Jesu,* Book 5, chap. 4, p. 435, chap. 7, pp. 449–50, chap. 9, p. 471). Likewise in Jacopone da Todi: "Bastard sons, cowardly in battle, / Surround me on every side— / How utterly unlike my true [*ligitimi*] sons, / Undaunted by sword or arrow! . . . Their [bastard sons] one concern is for ecclesiastical office; / They have sent Poverty into exile. / How utterly unlike my true [*ligitimi*] sons, / Who armed with austerity scorned the world!" (Laud 53 [35], "The Tears of the Church on Seeing Itself Reduced to a Shambles" in *Jacopone da Todi,* trans. Serge and Elisabeth Hughes [New York: Paulist Press, 1982], 171). Here and in subsequent references to Jacopone, the numeration of the Lauds follows the one adopted by S. and E. Hughes and, in parentheses, the one in the new edition by Franco Mancini, *Iacopone da Todi: Laude* (Rome: Guis. Laterza & Figli, 1974). For the scriptural basis of this theme, see Gn 27; Heb 12:1–17.

53. "Continents" was one of the terms used to refer to the Franciscan Third Order.

54. Probably, 3 April 1292.

55. The leprosarium in question was probably San Lazzaro di Corsiano, located outside the walls of Foligno. See Mario Sensi, "Angela nel contesto religioso folignate," 74.

56. A document dated 9 April 1268 mentions that a certain Giliola was a servant in the hospital of San Lazzaro. See Sensi, "Angela nel contesto religioso folignate," 74–75.

57. Eyewitnesses report a similar gesture in the life of St. Francis. The *Legend of Perugia* records that his brothers saw him, as an act of penance, eat from the same bowl as a leper ("my Christian brother"), whose fingers were so ulcerated that when he dipped them in the bowl to eat, blood dripped from them (*Omnibus of Sources,* 22, pp. 998–99); see also *The Mirror of Perfection* 58, ibid., pp. 1183–84; 1 Celano 17, ibid., p. 242; 2 Celano 9, ibid., pp. 369–70; Bonaventure, *Legenda major,* Book 1, chap. 1, 5–6, ibid., pp. 638–39; *Legenda minor,* chap. 1, ibid., pp. 797–98. Concerning his experience with the lepers, St. Francis wrote in

his Testament: "While I was in sin, it seemed very bitter to me to see lepers. And the Lord himself led me among them, and I had mercy upon them. And when I left them, that which seemed bitter to me was changed into sweetness of soul and body; and afterward I lingered a little and left the world" (Armstrong and Brady, *Francis and Clare,* 154). As Caroline Walker Bynum notes, beside St. Francis and Angela, "there were several other Italian saints who ate pus or lice from poor or sick bodies, thus incorporating into themselves the illness and misfortune of others" (e.g., St. Catherine of Siena, St. Catherine of Genoa) ("The Female Body and Religious Practice in the Later Middle Ages," in *Fragments for a History of the Human Body,* 163, and n. 12). The followers of the sect of the "Spirit of Freedom" were known to drink vermin-ridden water and eat rotten meat (see Guarnieri, "Il movimento del Libero Spirito," 368).

58. This form of prayer, very much in vogue during the thirteenth and fourteenth centuries, was recited much like the rosary. For instance, a certain number of Pater Nosters were said, preceded by or interspersed with invocations to the five wounds of the crucified Christ repeated in the form of a litany (see Mario Sensi, "Reclusione," *DIP,* vol. 7 [1985], col. 1241).

59. The text appears mutilated, leaving the nature of this example obscure.

60. The topic of the simultaneous presence of the body of Christ on every altar was hotly debated by medieval theologians. See David Burr, *Eucharistic Presence and Conversion in Late Thirteenth Century Franciscan Thought* (Philadelphia: Transactions of the American Philosophical Society, 1984), vol. 74, part 3.

61. See chapter 6, where Angela is told that she is only the guardian of the graces she receives and must render them back to God to whom they belong (p. 168). In chapter 7, this theme is discussed in relationship with the knowledge of God and self: "The soul must preserve what belongs to it, and render to God what belongs to God" (p. 194).

62. This step began 9 August 1292 and lasted until the end of the summer of 1293 (*Il Libro,* 257, n. 1).

63. This sentence comes from the second redaction, but is based on the first. It makes the mistake of presenting the three things ("seeing, speaking, hearing anything except what comes from God") here, as if already known, before mentioning them for the first time in the next paragraph (*Il Libro,* 259, n. 3).

64. Feast of the Assumption, August 15.

65. This passage begins with Angela's prayer to the Blessed Virgin requesting certitude concerning her mystical experiences. Her request is referred to again only at the end of this section (p. 170), after her experiences of God's power and humility, which remove all her doubts and provide the answer to her prayers (*Il Libro*, 259, n. 3).

66. The revelation of divine power and everything else up to this point takes place on the same day and is followed by three days in which Angela does nothing without God's permission. The end of the third day falls on the feast of St. Clare, August 12. The sequence of events, then, is as follows: August 9: manifestation of divine power; August 12: temptation by the devil; August 22: Angela finds peace in the lower basilica in Assisi (see Ferré, *Le livre de l'expérience*, 120, n. 3; 122, n. 2).

67. The confusion of the time period is due to the overlapping of redactions. The immediately preceding trial, while Angela lay sick, is from the second redaction. The period she is now referring to is the earlier one, from the first redaction, when she was tempted by the devil (*Il Libro*, 89, n. 11).

68. The three persons who receive the blessing seem to be Angela, her companion Masazuola, and Brother Arnaldo.

69. This section alludes three times to a certain brother, without identifying him: (a) "Brother So-and-so was named guardian . . ."; (b) ". . . if that brother is named guardian"; (c) "Tell that brother that he should strive to become little." Probably he is the scribe, Arnaldo (*Il Libro*, 268, n. 16).

70. The saint in question is St. Anthony of Padua, whose feast is celebrated on June 13 (see Ferré, "Les principales dates," 14).

71. This game that God plays with the soul (*judus amoris*) is a classic metaphor used in mystical literature to describe the alternation between the bitter struggles of purgation and the full entrance into the illuminative state. For example, God tells St. Catherine of Siena: "When souls reach perfection I relieve them of this lover's game of going and coming back. I call it a 'lover's' game because I go away for love and I come back for love—no, not really I, for I am your unchanging and unchangeable God: what goes and comes back is the feeling my charity creates in the soul" (*Catherine of Siena: The Dialogue*, trans. with intro. Suzanne Noffke, O.P. [New York: Paulist Press, 1980], chap. 78, 178); also, Henry Suso: "The servant: 'Lord, what is the game of love?' Response of Eternal Wisdom: 'As long as love is together with love, love does not know how dear love is. But when love departs from love, then truly love feels how dear love was" (*Little Book of Eternal Wisdom* in *Henry Suso:*

The Exemplar, with Two German Sermons, trans., ed., and intro. Frank Tobin [New York: Paulist Press, 1989], 236); Hadewijch: "The fruition of Love is a game / That no one can explain truly" (*Hadewijch*, trans. with intro. Mother Columba Hart, O.S.B. [New York: Paulist Press, 1980], 245). See G. Petitdemange, "Jeu," *DS*, vol. 8 (1973), cols. 1159–62.

72. This is the only time in the *Memorial* that Angela refers to Christ as the suffering God-man (*Deo homine passionato*). This expression becomes frequent in the instructions (e.g., instructions 9 and 32).

73. According to Ferré, this is the earliest dramatization of the passion of which we have any record. It took place in Foligno near the Piazza S. Domenica, the most important piazza in the city, in front of the Church of S. Maria Infraportas (see Ferré, *Le livre de l'expérience*, 140, n. 1).

74. Such questions about creation and redemption were controversial topics in the twelfth and thirteenth centuries. For a good summary see Bernard McGinn, "Christ as Savior in the West," in *Christian Spirituality: Origins to the Twelfth Century*, ed. Bernard McGinn and John Meyendorff in collaboration with Jean Leclercq (New York: Crossroad, 1986), 253–59.

75. This is the first time that Angela uses the word "darkness" to describe her mystical state. She is probably making use of Pseudo-Dionysian apophatic terminology so widespread among medieval and later mystics. This theme will be more fully developed in supplementary step 7 (chap. 9).

76. This sentence is an insertion of the second redaction. It is possibly an attempt by the scribe to bridge Angela's present experience of apophatic darkness and beyond to the expression of it in the seventh supplementary state (*Il Libro*, 285, n. 29).

77. This closing comment is probably an allusion to St. Paul: "I know a man in Christ, who, fourteen years ago, whether he was in or outside his body I cannot say, only God can say—a man who was snatched up to the third heaven" (2 Cor 12:3).

78. Probable date of this step: Lent of 1294 (see Ferré, "Les principales dates," 11).

79. See the scribe's assertion in chapter 2 (p. 138) that he had been impeded in his work by fellow friars. He makes it seem as if this situation had been a more or less constant one from supplementary step 2 (chap. 4, p. 154), where he mentions having had to write "in haste" (also, chap. 5, p. 165 and chap. 9, p. 217), to the end of this present step

where his standing with his brothers seems to have improved. His statement that he did not change what the young boy had written is a note from the second redaction. He seems to have forgotten that he had previously said that "he would do all that he could to improve his text," which in fact he did (*Il Libro*, 288, n. 2).

80. The theme of the poverty of Christ is developed extensively in instructions 3 and 28; the divine power hidden in humility in instruction 22—another indication of the strong nexus between the *Memorial* and some of the instructions.

81. Practically all this paragraph, as well as a subsequent one on the pain of Christ's soul, belong to the second redaction. "Unable to understand" what the young boy had written, the scribe probably had the opportunity later to speak with Angela. On the basis of what she told him of her visions of the passion of Christ, he decided that this was the proper place to insert it (in a condensed form), and develop this theme more extensively in instruction 3 (*Il Libro*, 292, n. 4).

82. "Elect" probably refers to the Jews.

83. The theme of the divine plan is basic to Angela's spirituality. It is developed especially in instruction 3 (also instruction 34). Appearing here for the first time, it answers at a deeper level the question raised by Angela in chapter 6 (p. 177) concerning the meaning and methods of the salvation wrought by Christ.

84. Holy Saturday of 1294 (see Ferré, "Les principales dates," 26).

85. What is happening in this section (as well as in the preceding and following ones) is Angela's existential participation in the Paschal Mystery then being liturgically celebrated. Also in the background of this vision of Christ in the sepulcher are such sentences from the *Song of Songs* as: "Let him kiss me with kisses of his mouth!" and "His left hand is under my head and his right arm embraces me" (1:2 and 2:6).

86. The sickle image is a peculiar one. It most likely refers to the pendulum motion of God's love, which, as it advances toward Angela, makes her initially experience its fullness, then, as it withdraws, her aridity without it and languor for its return. Possibly, she took it from her own experience of seeing farmers working in the fields. Or, cf. Rv 14:14–20: "Then, as I watched, a white cloud appeared, and on the cloud sat One like a Son of Man wearing a gold crown on his head and holding a sharp sickle in his hand."

87. This sentence is repeated in instruction 2 (p. 225), in which the theme of the imperfections of love is developed.

88. Angela speaks of three forms of God's love: The first is the one

described by the image of the sickle; the second (a "deathly love") is perhaps the one mentioned just after this in which she wants to die as a result of a vision of Christ and the Blessed Virgin in their glorified state; the third, an in-between one described here (*Il Libro*, 303, n. 13).

89. On the medieval understanding of the role of tears as expressive of different stages of mystical development, see Pierre Adnès, "Larmes: époque médiévale," *DS*, vol. 9 (1976), cols. 296–300.

90. The editors of the critical edition suggest that this section can be considered the liturgical-sacramental expression of the Paschal Mystery previously lived mystically by Angela (*Il Libro*, 309, n. 19).

91. Until the end of the thirteenth century, it was the custom to drink some water from a chalice after receiving communion in order to wash out the mouth (*Il Libro*, 310, n. 20).

92. According to the editors of the critical edition, in the scribe's very first redaction, the text that ends here is immediately followed by the one that treats of Angela's perceptions of the judgments of God in chapter 9. The remaining part of this step, whether from the first or the second redaction, was added later (*Il Libro*, 310, n. 21).

93. In this section, Angela, speaking from her own experience, mentions seven ways (of increasing intensity) in which God comes into the soul, the highest being when it grants hospitality to the Pilgrim, as distinct from an ordinary experience of his presence when he comes into the soul. Since this experience occurs during Easter week, probably the Emmaus event is in the background (see Lk 24:13–35). In the light of Angela's later teachings, the Pilgrim is Christ, "poor, suffering, and despised," and the one identifying with him, thus fully and definitively granting him hospitality, shares in the riches of his risen glorified state as Son of God, one and Trinitarian. I have been unable to find any traces of Angela's special understanding of the theme of *Christus Peregrinus* in patristic or medieval writers (*Il Libro*, 312, n. 22).

94. In many respects this section of the seven ways (all from the second redaction) in which God, as Pilgrim, comes into the soul is the *Memorial* in miniature. The ways correspond to different stages in Angela's mystical ascension with implicit references to her experience. This first way seems to correspond to what took place in her initial experiences of God in chapter 1, especially steps 17–20.

95. See chapter 3, the Assisi experience and what immediately follows it.

96. See chapter 4, where Angela experiences a sign of God's perpetual love for her, discovers that he is the "love of the soul" who requires

of the soul that it love him in return with the same love with which he loved it. See also instructions 5 and 6, wherein the first degree of love consists in loving and wanting what God loves and wants.

97. This way, like the preceding one, corresponds to chapter 4, in which Angela says she saw God in all his fullness and beauty as he is in heaven.

98. See chapter 6, especially the first section, in which Angela experiences the "game of love" that God plays with her soul, renewing it and elevating it to ineffable states he alone could produce.

99. See, again, chapter 6 and the effect being produced in Angela's soul when she is embraced by the crucified Christ and then enters inwardly into his side.

100. The abundance of joy that Angela experiences in this state finds parallels again in chapter 6, i.e., the surpassing joy that was hers after visions of Christ crucified, after witnessing a representation of the passion, or as effects of the "game" God was playing with her soul.

101. This experience of granting hospitality to the Pilgrim could possibly find its parallel in chapter 9, which describes the highest states of Angela's mystical development.

102. For examples of this type of medieval discourse between the body and the soul, see R. W. Ackermann, "The Debate of the Body and the Soul and Parochial Christianity," *Speculum* 37 (1962): 541–65.

103. According to the editors of the critical edition, this final section of this step is the last one of the scribe's first redaction. Analysis of the text (e.g., the use of term *truth*) indicates that it presupposes the experience found in the seventh and last supplementary step. Furthermore, it is not typical of the *Memorial* and more properly belongs with the instructions, especially instruction 2. Evidently, the scribe did not have enough time to properly situate this text and inserted it here as a first attempt to present a reflection on the *Memorial* and its application for others (*Il Libro*, 327, n. 32).

104. The text in mind is from the book of Numbers 20:10–13: "Moses and Aaron assembled the community in front of the rock, where he said to them, 'Listen to me, you rebels! Are we to bring water for you out of this rock?' Then, raising his hand, Moses struck the rock twice with his staff, and water gushed out in abundance for the community and the livestock to drink. But the Lord said to Moses and Aaron, 'Because you were not faithful to me in showing forth my sanctity before the Israelites, you shall not lead this community into the land I will give them.' These are the waters of Meribah, where the Israelites contended

against the Lord, and where he revealed his sanctity among them." The commentary Angela gives so promptly applies to the entire text, but especially to the presumptuousness of Moses in overstepping his boundaries and being unfaithful in carrying out the Lord's command.

105. The theme of knowledge of self and God is a central one in Angela's spirituality and is treated in numerous instructions (see especially instructions 3, 14, 29).

106. This section, which treats of poverty, is echoed in many places throughout the instructions (e.g., instructions 3, 28, 34). Again, this insertion serves as what we might call a proto-instruction.

107. Lk 1:38.

108. The scriptural background for Angela's discovery of the complete truth about herself and about God is probably John's gospel: the completion of Jesus' salvific work is to grant the Spirit, who "will guide [humanity] to complete truth" (Jn 16:13, 17).

109. This entire selection is the only one conceived as a step (*passus*), as it is called in the opening sentence. As also indicated, the scribe at first took down only a few notes, "writing rapidly," because of the strong opposition his meetings with Angela encountered from other friars (see comments to this effect at the end of the next step), and also because he apparently was not fully aware of or did not fully understand the full horror of the terrible state Angela was in the first time he heard her speak very briefly about it. As indicated in the text, another friar attested to its credibility. It seems that it is only toward the end of his redaction of the seventh step that he understood the full nature and import of this sixth step and decided then to complete his notes and add new material (*Il Libro*, 336, n. 2). Date of this step: Spring of 1294 to Spring of 1295 (Ferré, "Les principales dates," 11).

110. Teresa of Avila, in speaking of the trials that occur in the sixth dwelling place in *The Interior Castle*, uses language that could very well have been influenced by Angela: "As for now, the reasoning faculty is in such a condition that the soul is not the master of it, nor can the soul think of anything else than of why it is grieving, of how it is absent from its Good, and of why it should want to live. It feels a strange solitude because no creature in all the earth provides it company, nor do I believe would any heavenly creature, not being the One whom it loves; rather, everything torments it. But the soul sees that it is like a person hanging, who cannot support himself on any earthly thing; nor can it ascend to heaven" (*Collected Works of St. Teresa of Avila*, trans. Kieran Kavanaugh, O.C.D., and Otilio Rodriguez, O.C.D., vol. 2 [Washington, D.C.: Insti-

tute of Carmelite Studies, 1985], 423). Similarly, John of the Cross in his description of the dark night of the spirit (with references to Jonas, Jeremiah, and the psalms): "He [the one undergoing the dark night] resembles one who is imprisoned in a dark dungeon, bound hands and feet, and able neither to move, nor see, nor feel any favour on heaven or earth" ("The Dark Night," in *The Collected Works of St. John of the Cross*, trans. Kieran Kavanaugh, O.C.D., and Otilio Rodriguez, O.C.D. [Washington, D.C.: Institute of Carmelite Studies, 1979], Book 2, chap. 7, n. 3, p. 341).

111. Angela is making her own Christ's cry of abandonment on the cross (cf. Mt 27:46; Mk 15:34). In this, she seems to be an unnoticed forerunner of the Rhineland mystics. Von Balthasar summarizes a thesis by G. Jouassard on this theme as follows: "Since Origen, two interpretations of Jesus' abandonment on the cross predominate: Jesus' spiritual sadness because of sinners (not direct abandonment by the Father) and the suffering of the head in his ecclesial members. A relationship between the mystical experience of abandonment by God and the cry on the cross would only have been established by the Rhineland mystics" (Hans Urs Von Balthasar, *Pâques: le mystère*, trans. R. Givord [Paris: Edition du Cerf, 1981], 119, n. 70; referring to G. Jouassard, *L'abandon du Christ par son Père durant sa passion d'après la tradition patristique et les docteurs du XIII siècle* [unpublished thesis, Fac. Cath. de Lyon, 1923]. Besides Angela, Von Balthasar names the following as having experienced mystical abandonment: Bernard of Clairvaux, Mechthilde of Magdebourg, Suso, Tauler, Marguerite Ebner, Catherine of Siena, Hilton, Mary of the Valleys, Magdalene of Pazzi, Rose of Lima, Ignatius of Loyola, Francis of Sales, Luther, Surin, Teresa of Avila, John of the Cross, Theresa of the Little Flower (ibid., 76–77).

112. For a similar, if not so harsh, example of self-punishment during attacks by the devils, cf. Teresa of Avila: "Another time I was tormented for five hours with such terrible interior and exterior pain and disturbance that it didn't seem to me I could suffer any longer . . . ; without being able to resist, I was striking myself hard on the body, head and arms" (*The Life* in *The Collected Works of St. Teresa of Avila*, vol. 1, 204).

113. Cf. Jacopone da Todi: "Why do you wound me, cruel charity, / Bind me and tie me tight? / My heart all trembling, in fragments / Encircled by flames, / Like wax melts into death. / I ask for respite. None is granted. / My heart, cast into a blazing furnace, / Lives and dies in that fire" (from Laud 90[89], "The Lament of the Soul for the Intensity of Infused Charity," Hughes, *Jacopone da Todi*, 257), and "On the

third branch, love increasing / I asked God for hell" (from Laud 69[84], "The Tree of a Hierarchy Similar to That of the Angels Based on Faith, Hope, and Charity," ibid., 212).

114. Cf. Rom 8:35–39.

115. It is important to note that the scribe, as indicated, wrote the sixth step after the seventh one had already taken place. (It is possible that only at this point did he begin his division of the seven supplementary steps.) As indicated, the two steps occurred almost simultaneously. In the original redaction, for a brief period, the experiences of the seventh step are to the fore, then those of the sixth dominate and gradually fade away to allow for the resumption and the full description of what took place in the seventh step. The two steps form part of an immense tableau in which the most sublime visions are interlaced with experiences of the greatest despair and suffering. Most likely for the sake of clarity, the scribe in his redaction decided to place the two dimensions of an almost single process in two separate steps (*Il Libro*, 347, n. 8). According to Ferré, the events of the two steps may have begun in the spring of 1294, probably after Easter ("Les principales dates," 24).

116. Angela is not the only mystic to have experienced the feeling of damnation. Poulain names the following: Francis of Sales, Philip Benizi, Hildegard, Margaret Mary Alacoque, Suso (*The Graces of Interior Prayer*, trans. from the sixth edition by Leonara L. Yorke Smith [Westminister, Vt.: Celtic Cross Books, 1978], 417–18.

117. The "hermit" Pope Celestine V was enthroned in Perugia, 5 July 1294, and dethroned on 13 December of the same year (see Ferré, "Les principales dates," 24).

118. Angela's visions of God "in and with darkness" in this step clearly bear the stamp of the Pseudo-Dionysian apophatic discourse on the divine darkness (see Introduction, sec. III C 2). These visions found in the scribe's second redaction may well contain his own elaboration on Angela's experience. Date of this step: the first months of 1294 to the end of the summer of 1296 (Ferré, "Les principales dates," 11).

119. The text of Augustine that is alluded to may be the following: "Inasmuch as St. Stephen saw him [Christ], did he lie who said [in the Creed]: 'He sits at the right hand of the Father'? For, in what sense does Stephen say: 'Behold, I see the heavens opened, and the Son of Man standing at the right hand of God'? Because he [Stephen] saw him standing, did he, perhaps, lie who said: 'He sits at the right hand of the Father'? Therefore, it has been expressed: He sits; he remains; he dwells. How? In the same way as you do. In what position? Who shall

say?" (*St. Augustine: Sermons on the Liturgical Seasons,* trans. Mary Muldowney, R.S.M. [New York: Fathers of the Church, Inc., 1959], 124–25; P. L. 38, Sermon 213, part 2, 4). For Stephen's vision, see Acts 7:55.

120. Cf. Marguerite Porete: "God possesses this [Annihilated] Soul by divine grace, and whoever God possesses, he possesses all things. And so she possesses nothing, for all that this Soul possesses from God within her by the gift of divine grace, seems to be nothing to her. And thus it is [nothing] compared to what she loves, which is in Him, and which He will not give to anyone except her. And according to this perception this Soul possesses all and so possesses nothing, she knows all and so knows nothing" (*Le Mirouer,* ed. Guarnieri, chap. 13, 534; trans. Babinsky). My thanks to Ellen Babinsky for allowing me to consult and make use of her unpublished translation of *Le Mirouer,* each time it is cited.

121. After the word *hidden* (*incluso*), two manuscripts change the text as follows: "She saw with darkness because everything not glorified is darkness in respect to the glorified body of Christ. The glorified body of Christ is darkness in respect to the glorified soul of Christ; and the glorified soul of Christ is darkness in respect to the divinity with which it is united. No matter how far the soul or heart expands itself, all this expanse is less than . . ." (*Il Libro,* 357, n. 4).

122. In contrast to its previous apophatic meaning, darkness here is used in the sense of deprivation and obscurity.

123. Angela is referring to her previous experiences of God, especially those described toward the end of chapter six.

124. Clearly the Dionysian apophatic schema is in the background. See the series of negations of the attributes of affirmative theology as inadequate to express God in chapters four and five of Pseudo-Dionysius, *Mystical Theology* (*Pseudo-Dionysius,* trans. Colm Luibheid [New York: Paulist Press, 1987], 140–41; P.L. 1045D).

125. Angela's expression, "the soul sees nothing and everything," has again strong affinities with the paradoxical formulas of the apophatic tradition. Cf. also Marguerite Porete: "Now she [the Annihilated Soul] is All and so she is Nothing for her Lover makes her One" (*Le Mirouer,* ed. Guarnieri, chap. 118, 612–13; trans. Babinsky).

126. Angela's description of this state bears close resemblance to the state of *apatheia* or dispassion described by some Greek Fathers as the goal of spiritual transformation. *Apatheia* means a state of tranquility, a perfect control of the irrational parts of the soul, which have been reordered to receive the fullness of divine indwelling. It is likely that this

theme infiltrated the Franciscan Spirituals and the Free Spirit movement, at least in part, through the influence of Angelo Clareno and his Latin translation of John Climacus's *The Ladder of Divine Ascent*, as well as passages from Macarius and other Greek Fathers. For the influence of the Greek Fathers on the Spirituals and the Free Spirit movement, see Guarnieri, *Il movimento del Libero Spirito*, 374–76. For a description of the state of *apatheia*, see step 29 of Climacus's *The Ladder of Divine Ascent* (trans. Colm Luibheid and Norman Russell with an intro. by Kallistos Ware [New York: Paulist Press, 1982], 282–85). Bernard McGinn suggests (personal communication) that Angela's experience here may be what later mystics have called "ligature," a state in which the self is unconscious of any acts of mind or will and is totally absorbed in the divinity.

127. The following passage is an illustration of what the scribe meant in the sixth step when he wrote that "the sixth step concurs with the seventh."

128. Cf. Jn 12:32: "I—once I am lifted up from earth—will draw all men and women to myself."

129. Probably, the moment of mystical marriage. Poulain explains that spiritual marriage or transforming union contains three principal elements: "1. a union that is almost *permanent* persisting even amidst exterior occupations, and this is in such a manner that the different operations do not interfere with one another; 2. *transformation* of the higher faculties as to their manner of operation; 3. generally, a permanent *intellectual* vision of the Blessed Trinity or of some divine attribute" (*The Graces of Interior Prayer*, 283); see also, Pierre Adnès, "Marriage spirituel," *DS*, vol. 10 (1980), cols. 389–408.

130. Cf. Jn 1:17: "No one has ever seen God. It is God the only Son, ever at the Father's side, who has revealed him"; also, Jn 14:8: "Whoever has seen me has seen the Father."

131. Angela's vision of seeing God without "intermediary" (*nihil erat medium inter me et ipsum*) has close parallels with the experiences of some Beguine mystics (and later Eckhart and Ruusbroec), who also characterized their deep mystical union with God as union without intermediary or distinction. Hadewijch: "I saw him [the Beloved] completely come to nought and so fade and all at once dissolve that I could no longer recognize or perceive him outside me, and I could no longer distinguish him within me. Then it was to me as if we were one without difference" (Hart, *Hadewijch*, Vision 7, p. 281). Marguerite Porete: "This Soul has six wings like the Seraphim. She wants no longer any-

thing which comes by mediation, which is the proper being of the Seraphim; there is no mediation (*nul moyen*) between their love and the divine love" (*Le Mirouer*, ed. Guarnieri, chap. 5, 524; trans. Babinsky); the fifth stage of Marguerite's description of the soul's sevenfold ascent to God: "Now she is All, and so she is Nothing, for her Lover makes her One" (ibid., chap. 118, 613). For the major passages in Eckhart which speak of the soul's unity with God "without a medium," see the glossary under *medium* and *âne mittel* in *Meister Eckhart: Teacher and Preacher*, trans. and intro. Bernard McGinn in collaboration with Frank Tobin and Elvira Borgstadt (New York: Paulist Press, 1986), 395 and 400. Ruusbroec writes of three levels of union with God: union with an intermediary, union without an intermediary, and union without difference or distinction. For a summary of his understanding of these levels see "The Little Book of Clarification" in *John Ruusbroec: The Spiritual Espousals and Other Works*, trans. and intro. James Wiseman, O.S.B. (New York: Paulist Press, 1985), 251–269.

132. This song is a laud, a form of composition widespread in the popular piety of the time.

133. This is the first time in Angela's *Book* that the triad "poverty, suffering, and contempt," as the "company" of Christ, is mentioned. It is repeated later on in this step and is developed extensively in the instructions (e.g., 28 and 34). Cf. Clare of Assisi: "But as a poor virgin, embrace the poor Christ. Look upon Him Who became contemptible for you, and follow Him, making yourself contemptible in the world for Him. Your Spouse, though more beautiful than the children of men (Ps 44:3), became, for your salvation, the lowest of men, despised, struck, scourged untold times throughout His whole body, and then died amid the sufferings of the Cross" (Armstrong and Brady, *Francis and Clare*, 197); Ubertino of Casale: "Both [the Virgin Mary and Jesus Christ], for our sake, were crucified, poor, and despised in this world" (*Arbor Vitae*, 3); Hadewijch: "If you wish to be like me in my Humanity, as you desire to possess me wholly in my Divinity and Humanity, you shall desire to be poor, miserable, and despised by all men" (Hart, *Hadewijch*, 268); Marguerite Porete: "Jesus Christ was poor and despised and tormented for our sake" (*Le Mirouer*, ed. Guarnieri, chap. 127, 625; trans. Babinsky).

134. The Franciscan thesis of the primacy of Christ holds that before the beginning of time, independently of sin, Christ had been foreseen by the Father as king and center of the universe and the ultimate manifestation of his love. See Alan B. Wolter, O.F.M., "John Duns Scotus on the

Primacy and Personality of Christ," in *Franciscan Christology*, ed. Damian McElrath (St. Bonaventure, N.Y.: Franciscan Institute Publications, 1980), 130–82.

135. See the *Song of Songs:* "On my bed at night, I sought him whom my heart loves" (3:1). Commenting on this passage, Gregory of Nyssa writes: "Having reached, as she [the soul] thought, the summit of her hope, and already thinking that she is united to her beloved, the bride calls 'bed' the time of darkness. By 'night,' the bride shows us the contemplation of what is unseen, and like Moses, she is in the darkness of God's presence [Ex 20:21]" (*Commentary on the Song of Songs*, trans. Casimir McCambley, O.C.S.O. [Brookline, Mass.: Hellenic College Press, 1987], 130); William of St. Thierry: "Upon this bed takes place that wonderful union and mutual fruition—of sweetness, and of joy incomprehensible and inconceivable even to those in whom it takes place—between man and God, the created spirit and the Uncreated. They are named Bride and Bridegroom, while words are sought that may somehow express in human language the charm and sweetness of this union, which is nothing else than the unity of the Father and the Son of God, their Kiss, their Embrace, their Love, their Goodness and whatever in that supremely simple Unity is common to both. All this is the Holy Spirit—God, Charity, at once Giver and Gift. Upon this bed are exchanged that kiss and that embrace by which the Bride begins to know as she herself is known" (*The Works of William of St. Thierry*, vol. 2: *Exposition on the Song of Songs*, trans. Mother Columba Hart, O.S.B., Cistercian Fathers Series 6 [Shannon, Ireland: Irish University Press, 1970], 77–78); Jacopone da Todi: "Soul, since you have come to Me / Gladly will I answer you. Come, / See, this is My bed—the cross. / Here we will be one" (from Laud 42 [15], "The Soul Begs the Angels to Help Her Find Christ" (Hughes, *Jacopone da Todi*, 145); also, "Tell me now, the fruits of that vision! / A life well-ordered in every respect, / And a heart, once impure and lower than Hell, / Now, the abode of the Trinity, a bed made holy" (from Laud 79 [21], "On Divine Goodness and the Human Will" (ibid., 231). Angela herself might have seen a thirteenth-century painting of St. Francis now located in the museum of the Portiuncula in Assisi. In it, the saint is depicted with the cross in one hand and in the other an open book in which one can read: "This is the bed in which he [Christ] lived and died" (*Il Libro*, 363, n. 15).

136. Ferré suggests that Teresa of Avila was familiar with the writings of Angela, either through the writings of Francisco Ossuna, Bernardino of Laredo, and Alonso of Madrid, or through the Spanish trans-

lation that appeared in 1505 by order of Cardinal Ximenes. He even affirms: "It is morally certain that St. Angela was one of St. Teresa's teachers of divine love and that she is the one who inspired the poem with its well known verse: 'I die because I do not die' " (*La spiritualité de sainte Angèle de Foligno*, 61). St. Teresa's poem is entitled "Aspirations toward Eternal Life" and this verse is repeated in each stanza of the poem. See *The Collected Works of St. Teresa of Avila*, vol. 3, 377.

137. Cf. Marguerite Porete: "Such a [Annihilated] Soul swims in the sea of joy, that is in the sea of delights, flowing and running out of the Divinity" (*Le Mirouer*, ed. Guarnieri, chap. 28, 545; trans. Babinsky); Jacopone da Todi: "Fused ('*nnabissato*) with God, it ventures forth (*se va notando*) / Into a sea without a shore / And gazes on Beauty without color or hue" (from Laud 91 [92], "Self-annihilation and Charity Lead the Soul to what Lies beyond Knowledge and Language," Hughes, *Jacopone da Todi*, 266); "To float in that immensity and to rest therein (*et en quel ben notare, e 'n isso reposare*)" (ibid., 267).

138. In this dialogue, Angela and the scribe may well be alluding to a text from John: "It is not by measure that God gives the Spirit" (Jn 3:34). Angela's response seems to be based on Pauline texts: "Each [is given] according to the measure of faith which God has assigned him" (Rom 12:3); "Each of us has received God's favor in the measure in which Christ bestows it" (Eph 4:7). This theme also underwent a number of variations in the tradition, Cf. Pseudo-Dionysius, "Again, the title 'Righteousness' is given to God because he assigns what is appropriate to all things; he distributes their due proportion, beauty, rank, arrangement, their proper and fitting place and order [*mensuram*] according to a most just and righteous determination (*The Divine Names*, chap. 8, n. 1 [Luibheid, *Pseudo-Dionysius*, 113]; P. L. 896A); Bernard of Clairvaux: "The cause for loving God is God himself. The way to love him is without measure" (*Bernard of Clairvaux: Selected Works*, trans. and foreword G. R. Evans [New York: Paulist Press, 1987], 174); for Bonaventure's understanding of this theme, see Trophime Mouiren, "Mensura," in *Lexique St. Bonaventure*, ed. Jacques-Guy Bougerol, O.F.M. (Paris: Editions Franciscaines, 1969), 99; Jacopone da Todi: "O Love so far beyond imagining or telling! / Your very absence of a sense of measure / Makes Measure complain and lament; / Such love, he argues, is torment. / Measurelessness intervenes and restrains Measure, / Afraid that love might be smothered, / Stripped of its wildness, / And placed beyond the experience of man" (from Laud 87 [82], "On Divine Love Whose Measure We Cannot Know," Hughes, *Jacopone da Todi*,

244–45). Angela herself will say later in this chapter: "God makes everything according to measure"; and in instruction 32: "Love without measure is the only name that I can think of giving to God."

139. Possibly, the future of the world.

140. This passage rightly belongs at the end of the *Memorial*. It seems that the scribe placed it here thinking, as on other occasions, that he had terminated his work. Manuscripts differ on its location in the text. See *Il Libro*, 370, n. 23. Ferré dates this moment in the beginning of 1294 ("Les principales dates," 25).

141. Perhaps the scribe *is* the celebrant?

142. Although Eucharistic piety flourished in the thirteenth century, frequent communion was rare. Popular devotion was focused entirely on seeing the Mass, forgetting almost completely sacramental communion. See Joseph Duhr, "Communion fréquente," *DS*, vol. 2 (1953), cols. 1234–92.

143. For Angela's teachings concerning the Eucharist, see instructions 30, 32, 33.

144. A friar's name is specifically mentioned only twice in the *Memorial:* here, and in chapter 5 (Bro. Dominic of the Marches).

145. The term *Throne* in Scripture is encountered only once, Col 1:16. According to Pseudo-Dionysius, in the celestial hierarchy, the Thrones belong to the first order of celestial beings and never leave the presence of God. Along with the Seraphim and the Cherubim, they are continually united to God without any mediation. See Luibheid, *Pseudo-Dionysius*, 160-61; P.L. HC 6, 2 [200D]). Jacopone da Todi says that he who has reached the ninth and highest branch of mystical ascension "is among the Thrones, / For faith shows him the way / And he can live in the starry heaven /" (from Laud 69 [84], "The Tree of a Hierarchy Similar to That of the Angels Based on Faith, Hope, and Charity," Hughes, *Jacopone da Todi*, 211).

146. According to the calculations of the editors of the critical edition, about half a year separates the preceding part from this one (*Il Libro*, 379, n. 33). Ferré dates it in 1295 ("Les principales dates," 26).

147. This is the first time in the text of Angela's *Book* that the term *abyss* (*abyssum*) is used to describe her immersion in the inner recesses of God's life. Later, in this step and in the instructions, the terminology of abyss (*abyssum, abyssalis, inabyssatio, inabissari*) characterizes Angela's deepest experiences of God. See instructions 4, 5, 19, 35, 36, 37. Cf. Jacopone da Todi: "[In the state of soul when it attains the 'crystal-

line sphere'], The cycle of the seasons is no longer, / The heavens are immobile, they spin no more. / Their harmonies are stilled, and the profound silence / Makes me cry out, 'O unsoundable sea, / I am engulfed by your depths / And shall drown in the abyss'!" (from Laud 92 [90], "How Firm Faith and Hope Bring One to the Threefold State of Self-annihilation," Hughes, *Jacopone da Todi*, 276–77); Hadewijch: "He must march far who presses on to Love— / Through her broad width, her loftiest height, her deepest abyss. / In all storms he must explore the ways; / Then her wondrous wonder is known to him; / That is—to cross her desert plains, / To journey onward and not stand still; / To fly through and climb through the heights, / And swim through the abyss, / There from Love to receive love whole and entire" (Poems in Stanzas 21, Hart, *Hadewijch*, 183–84); "Where love is with Love in love, / The abyss is unfathomable; / There all those who let themselves sink in her / Must be drowned in her; / And to those who attend her in her nature / She gives an unquiet life" (Poems in Couplets 10, ibid., 337); abyss language is also used in Visions 11 and 12 (ibid., 289 and 296).

148. Cf. Marguerite Porete: "This [Annihilated] Soul takes no account of shame, nor of honor, nor of poverty, nor of wealth, not of ease or of anxiety, not of love nor of hate, not of hell nor of paradise. And with this it says that this Soul possesses all and possesses nothing, she knows all and knows nothing, she wills all and wills nothing" (*Le Mirouer*, ed. Guarnieri, chap. 13, 533; trans. Babinsky); Hadewijch: "Fire is a name of Love by which she burns to death / Good fortune, success, and adversity; / All manners of being are the same to fire. / Anyone whom this fire has thus touched / Finds nothing too wide, and nothing too narrow. / But once this Fire gains control, / It is all the same to him what it devours; / Someone we love or someone we hate, refusal or desire, / Winnings or forfeits, convenience or hindrance, / Gain or loss, honor or shame, / Consolation at being with God in heaven / Or in the torture of hell: / This Fire makes no distinction. / It burns to death everything it ever touches: / Damnation or blessing no longer matters, / This I can confess" (Poems in Couplets 16, Hart, *Hadewijch*, 355).

149. Cf. Marguerite Porete: "Certainly the one knows this, and no other, to whom God has given the intellect—for Scripture does not teach it, nor the human mind comprehend it, nor does the work of a creature deserve to grasp it. Thus this gift is given from the most High, in whom this creature is ravished by the fertility of understanding, and nothing remains in her own intellect. And this soul, who has become

nothing, thus possesses everything, and so possesses nothing; she wills everything and she wills nothing; she knows all and she knows nothing" (*Le Mirouer*, ed. Guarnieri, chap. 7, 525; trans. Babinsky).

150. Angela here reflects the experience of mystics of all ages, who have tried to find some term to describe the deepest and most inward part of the soul where God dwells. Gregory of Nyssa called it the "heart," the "conscience," the "mind's depths"; Bernard of Clairvaux, a "cubicle"; Bonaventure, "the summit of the mind" or "spark of conscience"; Catherine of Siena, the "interior home of the heart"; Eckhart, the "little castle"; Tauler, the "ground of the soul"; Francis de Sales, "the highest point of the soul"; Teresa of Avila, the "inner castle"; John of the Cross, the "substance" or "deepest center of the soul." For a thorough study of this theme see Léonce Reypens, "Ame (structure d'après les mystiques)," *DS*, vol. 1 (1937), cols. 433–67.

151. Cf. Jacopone da Todi: "Participating in the essence of all creatures / It [the soul] can now say, 'All things are mine.' / The doors open wide, and entering within / the soul becomes one with God, / Possesses what He possesses" (from Laud 91 [92], "Self-annihilation and Charity Lead the Soul to What Lies beyond Knowledge and Language," Hughes, *Jacopone da Todi*, 265).

152. Interpretation of God's revelation to Moses ("I am the One who is" [Ex 3:13–15]) was a central problem of medieval hermeneutics —and a long-standing one in the Christian tradition. Both the text and the explanation given to it by Pseudo-Dionysius elicited a variety of commentaries among scholastic theologians and mystical writers. At issue was whether to give this passage a metaphysical or a mystical meaning, and what was the relationship between the two. For this complex question, see the papers in *Dieu et l'être, Exégèse d'Exode 3, 14 et de Coran 20, 11–24* (Paris: Études Augustiniennes, 1978). Another topic of medieval controversy was whether the vision of the divine essence is possible in this life. Angela is one of a small number of mystics who claimed it as the culmination of their mystical ascent. Marguerite Porete states that in the fifth stage of the soul's ascent it "considers [*regarde*] that God is Who is, of whom everything is, and she does not exist if she is not of the One whom all things are" (*Le Mirouer*, ed. Guarnieri, chap. 118, 611; trans. Babinsky). Guigues DuPont (a spiritual writer in the Dionysian vein, d. 1297) writes that in the eleventh degree of perfection, the soul sees God "per essentiam," and in the twelfth, the final degree, it sees the beatific vision; see J. P. Grausen, "Le 'De contempla-

tione' de Guigues DuPont," *Revue d'ascétique et de mystique* 39 [1929]: 282. See also Léopold Malevez, "Essence de Dieu (vision de l')" *DS*, vol. 4 (1961), cols. 1333–45; and Léonce Reypens, "Dieu (connaissance mystique)" *DS*, vol. 3 (1957), cols. 823–929.

153. Ferré dates this to 2 February 1296 ("Les principales dates," 25). For a different experience on the same feast in a different year, see instruction 19.

154. The reference to the "most high words" that Angela did not want to be written seems an obvious reference to St. Paul's vision of the third heaven (cf. 2 Cor 12:4).

155. Angela's awareness that "nothing can separate her from God" again seems Pauline (cf. Rom 8:35–39).

156. Angela is one of the rare mystics who claim to have attained the beatific vision at the apex of their ascent. Butler, quoting this passage in his *Western Mysticism*, asserts that Angela's experience is "the most arresting one" of his acquaintance (London: Constable, 1967, 3d ed., lxvi). Other strikingly similar texts: Hadewijch: "And he [Christ] took me out of the spirit in that highest fruition of wonder beyond reason; there I had fruition of him as I shall eternally" (Vision 5, Hart, *Hadewijch*, 277); Marguerite Porete: "The sixth stage is glorious, for the aperture of the sweet movement from glory, which the gentle Farnearness gives, is nothing but a preliminary glimpse [*apparition*] which God wishes the Soul to have of her glory itself, which will be hers forever" (*Le Mirouer*, ed. Guarnieri, chap. 60, 568; trans. Babinsky). It is significant to note that the Council of Vienne (1311–1312) explicitly condemned the notion associated with the Beguines that the perfect soul attains in this life the same beatitude as that of the blessed in heaven (see *Enchiridion Symbolorum*, ed. Henricus Denzinger, 32d ed. [Fribourg, 1963], 282, n. 474).

157. The scribe's redaction of Angela's spiritual ascent ends here.

158. This appendix properly belongs with the five Eucharistic visions mentioned earlier in this step, and, in particular, it complements the second one on Christ's presence in the Eucharist and everywhere.

159. This epilogue is the conclusion of the scribe's first redaction, when, as he indicates, "almost" everything in the book had been written. The second redaction, at least a quarter of the text, had not yet been written (*Il Libro*, 398, n. 3).

160. This paragraph is an insertion of the second redaction. Note that the scribe affirms that he "hardly" wrote anything unless Angela

was present. In the first redaction (previous paragraph and ch. 2, p. 137) he had said that he had written everything in her presence (*Il Libro*, 399, n. 45).

161. These two friars are unknown. See the Approbation at the beginning of the *Memorial*.

Notes to the *Instructions*

1. The critical edition does not follow the chronological order in which the instructions were written. This instruction belongs toward the end of the series. It is placed here at the beginning because this is its location in manuscript M followed by the critical edition (see Introduction, sec. IV). Meant to extol Angela's humility and sanctity over that of other saints, it is typical of the emendations of medieval hagiography, and may not come from Angela herself. The style clashes with that of the *Memorial* (e.g., frequent use of the term *iniquity*). Furthermore, this instruction is not included in manuscript B (the first redaction). The editors of the critical edition suggest sometime after 1310 for the date of its composition (*Il Libro*, 403, n. 1). For similar (and perhaps more genuine) confessional statements by her, see the beginning of instruction 7 and the end of instruction 9.

2. Examples of similar extraordinary behavior abound in medieval hagiography. Angela's contemporary Margaret of Cortona (1247–1297), during the celebration of a parish Mass, genuflected with a rope tied around her neck and publicly asked for the forgiveness of her sins (see Fra. Giunta Bevegnati, *Leggenda della vita e dei miracoli di santa Margherita da Cortona,* new translation from the Latin with preface and notes by Eliodoro Mariani, O.F.M. [Vicenza: L.I.E.F., 1978], 47–48). Later, she overcomes a temptation of the devil to pride by crying out tearfully all her past sins (ibid., 51). On another occasion, if her confessor Brother Giunta Bevegnati had not prohibited her from doing so, she would have gone to Montepulciano, place of her preconversion dissolute behavior, and, with head shaved, wearing only undergarments, shamefully begged from door to door at the homes of her former acquaintances. She also would have liked to be blindfolded and, with a rope around her neck, led through the city by a woman who would cry out: "Behold, Margaret, a native of this city, the one who behaved so haught-

ily, and through her vanity and bad example has done so much harm to everyone here!" (ibid., 33); and, out of her desire "to conform herself in part to the suffering Christ she would have liked to be known by all as a fool" (ibid., 33). Jacopone da Todi (1236?–1306), another of Angela's contemporaries, likewise wanted to be considered a fool for Christ. One of the "lives" of Jacopone records that one day, during the celebration of a feast in Todi, he took off his clothes, put a packsaddle on his back, set a bit on his mouth, and went about on all fours like an ass. Saddled this way, he went among those who were at the feast (see *Le vite antiche di Jacopone da Todi*, ed. Enrico Menestò [Florence: "La Nuova Italia" Editrice, 1977], 27). On another occasion, during a family wedding reception, he took off all his clothes, covered himself completely with honey, then stuck on a coating of feathers of different colors, and thus feathered joined the party (ibid., 28). Francis of Assisi himself, as Celano, one of his early biographers, reports, "was not afraid to show himself in every way contemptible," and "not ashamed, when he had failed in something, to confess his failing in his preaching before all the people" (I *Celano* 19, n. 54, in *Omnibus of Sources*, 274). On the fool-for-Christ tradition, see François Vandenbroucke, "Fous pour le Christ," *DS*, vol. 5 (1964), cols. 763–66.

3. This instruction contains a synthesis of Angela's teachings on love and is probably intended for her spiritual progeny as a warning against the aberrations of the sect of the Spirit of Freedom. Probable date, 1306 (*Il Libro*, 410, n. 1).

4. Umberto Eco, in his best-selling novel *The Name of the Rose*, puts these warnings from Angela about the perils of spiritual love in the mouth of her disciple Ubertino of Casale (trans. William Weaver [San Diego, Calif.: Harcourt Brace Jovanovich, 1980], 230–31).

5. Angela had mentioned the illusions of love in the *Memorial* (chap. 7, pp. 193–94) but only in a general way. Here she is more specific. Marguerite Porete counsels that "one have fear of all kinds of love, whatever they might be, for the perils which can be there" (*Le Mirouer*, ed. Guarnieri, ch. 13, 533; trans. Babinsky).

6. Although the term occurs only once in the *Memorial* (chap. 6, p. 176), Angela, throughout the instructions, refers to Christ as the suffering God-man (instructions 4, 5, 13, 15, 17, 18, 21, 22, 23, 34). The Latin is *Deus homo passionatus*.

7. The three transformations of love are also mentioned in instruction 7, and the first transformation is further explained in instruction 6. See also instruction 34.

8. Here, as later on in her description of the third transformation of love, Angela is referring to the state of *apatheia* or dispassion as experienced by her in the final step of her journey. The notion is derived from the Eastern Greek Fathers. See chap. 9, n. 126.

9. In an exhortation to her spiritual sons on the necessity of never abandoning prayer (instruction 18), Angela describes similar effects or properties of love.

10. Chronologically, the first use of the expression "seat of truth" is found in instruction 7. It corresponds to the "complete truth" that Angela had experienced at the peak of her mystical ascent in chapter 9 of the *Memorial* (see also the end of chap. 7). The description of the third transformation of love found in this instruction likewise refers to this final step.

11. The ordering of love was a central topos of medieval mysticism and Angela makes it her own in this instruction as well as in later ones (see instructions 3, 25, 32). Bernard of Clairvaux (drawing from Augustine, *De Civi. Dei.*, 15, 22) treats of the ordering of love in his commentary *On the Song of Songs*, Sermon 49 (vol. 3, trans. Kilian Walsh, O.C.S.O., and Irene M. Edmonds, Cistercian Fathers Series, no. 31 [Kalamazoo, Mich.: Cistercian Publications, 1979], 21–29); Jacopone da Todi: "O you who love Me, put order into your love, / For without order there is no virtue!" (from Laud 90 [89], "The Lament of the Soul for the Intensity of Infused Charity," Hughes, *Jacopone da Todi*, 261).

12. A reference to Angela's vision of the divine essence, the One who is, in chap. 9, p. 214. See also chap. 9, n. 152.

13. Clare of Montefalco was asked by one of the followers of the sect of the Spirit of Freedom (whom she was later to denounce before church authorities) whether someone who has attained perfection can do what he pleases and whether the soul in this life can lose all capacity to desire. She responded as follows: "It is possible that God puts such order in the will of a person that his will is replaced by God's will, and the will of such a person becomes so ordered that it cannot will anything contrary to God's will. Such a person then can do as he pleases because he wants only what God wants. Those who say that they can do as they please do not say the truth unless they too are in the state just described. The soul can only lose its capacity to desire in the following way: not that it does not desire anything that exists in this life, but it is possible and it does happen that the soul in the fervor of contemplation is absorbed, immersed, and drawn into God through a rapture or some other form of spiritual elevation. As a result, the soul enters into a state of

wonderful union and quiet with God. During the time the soul is in this state, it desires nothing else but what it possesses in it" (Berangario di S. Africano, *Vita Sanctae Clarae de Cruce*, ed. A. Semenza [Rome: 1944], 41). In a similar vein, Ubertino of Casale describes the sixth and highest state of perfection as one in which the soul has attained such peace and quiet and is so immersed in Christ that "it does not desire, have a taste for, or want anything for itself other than what Christ wants" (*Arbor vitae*, Book 3, p. 154).

14. Angela's instructions on the proper behavior of the soul when the full vision of God is withdrawn are developed at length in instruction 18. See also instructions 7 and 28.

15. For more on the theme of the imitation of the suffering God-man as a sign of perfect love, see instruction 6.

16. One of the manuscripts (Ve) contains the following more detailed accusation against the sect of the Spirit of Freedom: "Likewise, beware of those who say they have acquired and possess the spirit of freedom and claim that they now have such an abundance of divine grace and love that they can live as they please. They think that they are so free and secure that they cannot sin. It seems to them that they are above every human law, and are not bound by the regulations of the church, or any other tradition—God alone is to be obeyed, and not men. Furthermore, they claim for themselves the statement of the apostle: 'Where there is the spirit of the Lord, there is freedom.' And, likewise: 'If you are guided by the Spirit, you are not under the law.' They make use of Paul's authority without subscribing to his intentions. All of them speak and act directly contrary to the life of Christ, who was free, and yet, for our sake, became a servant; who was above the law, its author and bestower, and yet, along with his mother, subject to it. It is about them that the apostle Peter said: 'They promised freedom of spirit to others while they themselves were slaves to sin'" (*Il Libro*, 424, n. 14). See also Angela's warnings against the false teachers of prayer in instruction 3, and my comments on the Free Spirit heresy in the introduction to this volume (sec. I, I; sec. V, H).

17. St. Francis, as mirror of holiness and perfection, is a common theme among his early biographers. One of them (an anonymous friar), in fact, entitled his biography the *Mirror of Perfection* (date of composition ca. 1318). See also I *Celano*, chap. 1, n. 9 (*Omnibus of Sources*, 305).

18. This quotation from St. Francis is found in I *Celano*, chap. 6, n. 103 (*Omnibus of Sources*, 318).

19. This same sentence is found in Angela's descriptions of the

workings of love in chapter 7 of the *Memorial* (p. 183). For a parallel description of imperfect and suspect love see instruction 3. For similar considerations on true and false love, see Jacopone da Todi, Lauds 33 [46] and 34 [47] (Hughes, *Jacopone da Todi*, 125–29).

20. Almost the same terminology has been used earlier in this instruction to describe the transformation wrought by divine love and is likewise found in instruction 6.

21. In the background of Angela's observations on illicit sexual behavior are the beliefs and practices attributed to the sect of the Spirit of Freedom, which, according to one contemporary observer, Arnaldo da Villanova (a Franciscan), maintained that "sexual intercourse and caresses were never sinful" (quoted by L. Oliger, *De secta spiritus libertatis in Umbria saec. XIV, Disquisitio et Documenta* [Rome: Edizioni di "Storia e Letteratura," 1943], 277).

22. This vision of the supreme Being, as a description of the highest state of perfection, is mentioned in chapter 9 of the *Memorial* and also in instruction 7.

23. It is the first time that the theme of "uncreated love" is treated extensively; it refers to the being or love we possess from all eternity in God. The expression is not found in the *Memorial*. Cf., however, instructions 14, 18, 22.

24. In the state of the third heaven, Jacopone da Todi writes: "Faith at this point ceases, for the soul sees; / hope ceases, for it clings to the One it once hoped in. / Gone is desire, the straining of the will, the fear of loss. / The soul has more than it knew how to yearn for . . . So the soul drawn to that light is resplendent, / Feels self melt away. / Its will and actions no longer its own. / So clear is the imprint of God / That the soul, conquered, is conqueror; / Annihilated, it lives in triumph / . . . The soul wills and yet does not will: / Its will belongs to Another" (from Laud 91 [92], "Self-Annihilation and Charity Lead the Soul to What Lies Beyond Knowledge and Language," Hughes, *Jacopone da Todi*, 270–71). For Marguerite Porete, in the fifth stage of grace, the "Annihilated Soul knows no longer how to work, and without fail she is thus excused and exonerated, without works, by believing that God is good and incomprehensible . . . [In this state] the Soul cannot do anything if it is not the will of God, and thus she cannot will some other thing; and so she leaves nothing to do for God. She allows nothing to enter into her thought which might be contrary to God, and for this reason she omits nothing to be done for God" (*Le Mirouer*, ed. Guarnieri, chap. 11, 529–30; trans. Babinsky).

25. The annihilation of the will in order for the soul to be reduced to nothingness and at the same time to be established in the uncreated dimension of God's life is a theme that finds many parallels in Jacopone da Todi, Hadewijch, and Marguerite Porete. Hadewijch: "To be reduced to nothingness in Love / is the most desirable thing I know" (Poems in Stanzas 38, Hart, *Hadewijch*, 239). Jacopone: "The soul wills and yet does not will: / Its will belongs to Another. / It has eyes only for this beauty; / It no longer seeks to possess, as was its wont— / It lacks the strength to possess such sweetness. / The base of this highest of peaks / is founded on *nichil*, / Shaped nothingness, made one with the Lord" (from Laud 91 [92], "Self-annihilation and Charity Lead the Soul to What Lies beyond Knowledge and Language," Hughes, *Jacopone da Todi*, 271). As the title of her work suggests (*Le Mirouer des simples âmes anéanties . . .*), the theme of annihilation of the will, in order to be aware of one's nothingness or wretchedness and God's goodness, is a major one in Marguerite Porete's writings. E.g., "Now such a[n Unencumbered] Soul is nothing, for she sees her nothingness by means of the abundance of divine understanding which makes her nothing and places her in nothingness. And so she is all things, for she sees by means of the depth of the understanding of her wretchedness, which is so deep and so great that she finds there neither beginning nor middle nor end, only an abyss without bottom" (*Le Mirouer*, ed. Guarnieri, chap. 118, 612; trans. Babinsky).

26. This phrase "causes neither laughter" is also found in the *Memorial* in the context of the visions of God in darkness (chap. 9, p. 203).

27. The expression "spirit of truth" in contrast to the false spirit of freedom of the sect of the Spirit of Freedom recalls Angela's observations on the deceptions of love in chapter 7 of the *Memorial* and on "complete truth" as the ultimate sign of God's presence in chapter 9.

28. During Angela's lifetime and for a short time afterward, this instruction, which contains many of her central teachings, was known as "Angela's book." It was probably composed in 1300 (*Il Libro*, 442, n. 1). The theme of the divine plan as the source of Angela's sufferings is found in rudimentary form in the fifth supplementary step of the *Memorial* (chap. 7, p. 181); the theme of suffering reappears in a condensed form in instructions 28 and 34.

29. Cf. "God dwells in unapproachable light" (1 Tm 6:16).

30. According to the editors of the critical edition, the abbreviation "M." in the manuscript most likely stands for *mater* (Angela); see *Il Libro*, 447, n. 4.

31. These considerations on the knives that wounded Christ seem to be an expansion of Angela's reflection on the sufferings of Christ's passion found at the beginning of chapter 7 of the *Memorial.* Instruction 34, which also speaks of "knives," is closely related to this one. Similar themes appear in the Bible, in such passages as "bitter enemies tear me to pieces" (Ps 69:9); "they did as they pleased with him" (Mt 17:12).

32. Mt 27:46.

33. Cf. Mt 10:38 and 16:24; Mk 8:34; Lk 9:23 and 14:26; Jn 19:17.

34. Cf. Mt 26:38; Mk 14:34.

35. The theme of Christ as the Book of Life was widespread in medieval and Franciscan literature. For a summary of Bonaventure's use of the term, see W. Rauch, "Liber," in *Lexique Saint Bonaventure,* 91–92. Ubertino of Casale used it in the title of his major work, *Arbor vitae crucifixae Jesus,* Jacopone da Todi: "I [Christ] am the book of life, sealed with the seven seals; / When I am opened you will find five signs, / The color of red, red blood. Ponder them" (from Laud 40 [27], "The Angels Ask the Reason for Christ's Pilgrimage to this World," Hughes, *Jacopone da Todi,* 141). Cf. Phil 4:3 and Rv 3:5; 21:19.

36. According to her biographer, Berengario da S. Affricano, Clare of Montefalco likewise warned against the wiles of the Free Spirit heretics: "She feared above all else that these false and hypocritical religious, under the appearance of virtue, would try to seduce some of the women in the monastery by speaking too familiarly with them" (quoted in Andreoli, *Angela, la poverella di Foligno,* 77).

37. On the sect of the Spirit of Freedom see instruction 2, and the introduction to this volume (sec. I, I; sec. V, H).

38. Latin: *ordinem.*

39. The concept of knowledge of God and self is further developed in instruction 14.

40. For these three kinds of prayer, see also instructions 28 and 34.

41. One of the manuscripts (Ve) contains an account of the bodily expression of Angela's prayer. Speaking of the ways in which she prayed, the author writes: "I recall hearing that Angela attached such significance to the sign of the cross and the tau that she made use of these even when she was praying with others, in choir or outside of it, during the canonical hours as well as during other devotions, and the more so as her soul attained stability, so that in one year her prayer was different than in the seven previous years.—Note the way she did this (as was related me privately): She observed certain places on her body where she signed herself: under her breasts on behalf of the feet, twice over each of

her breasts for the hands, the place in her side where one can reasonably imagine that our redeemer was pierced with the lance, and in the middle of the upper part of her chest for the crown. When reciting the psalms she would begin the first verse by signing the place of the left foot with the sign of tau or of the cross or by striking that place in some manner, then the place of the right foot, and so on to the places of the left and right hands, the heart, and crown, always with blows to better impress upon her heart what she said with her mouth. Thus she would continue to run through the series of wounds until the end of the psalm. And I was told that whereas at first she could not remain in a state of peace and quiet for the duration of a brief psalm, eventually, as this practice became habitual, her heart was rarely distracted from God or from his wounds even for the duration of a lengthy Matins with notes, that is, chanted" (*Il Libro*, 464–65, n. 17).

42. Mt 26:41.

43. Lk 22:43.

44. Mt 26:39.

45. Lk 22:42.

46. Though not found in the Scriptures, Mary's presentation in the temple to consecrate herself totally to God by a vow of virginity is the object of a special liturgical feast, the Presentation of Mary, celebrated on November 21. It is based on a tradition found in patristic and later church writers. See Richard Kieckhefer, "Main Currents in Late Medieval Devotion (Marian Devotion)," in *Christian Spirituality: High Middle Ages and Reformation*, 89.

47. This sentence demonstrates Angela's faith in the immaculate conception of Mary; the champion of this doctrine was Angela's contemporary John Duns Scotus (d. 1308). The statement is all the more striking because this doctrine was opposed by the dominant thought of the time, represented by Albert the Great, Thomas Aquinas, Bonaventure, and, before them, Bernard of Clairvaux. Jacopone da Todi likewise expressed belief in Mary's immaculate conception: "To conceive without corruption, untouched, intact! / Reason and experience know nothing of such a possibility; / Never was woman made pregnant without seed. You alone, / Mary Immaculate, you alone; in you the Word, *creans omnia*, / residing in majesty, becomes flesh, God incarnate" (from Laud 2 [32], "The Blessed Virgin Mary," Hughes, *Jacopone da Todi*, 70). For this doctrine and the controversy surrounding it, see *The Dogma of the Immaculate Conception: History and Significance*, ed. Edward D. O'Connor (Notre Dame, Ind.: University of Notre Dame Press, 1958).

48. Cf. Phil 2:6–8.

49. Lk 1:38.

50. Lk 23:40 *et seq.*

51. An obvious allusion to the stigmata of St. Francis.

52. On this theme of recollection in prayer, see the beginning of instruction 10.

53. This passage—as indeed this entire section—brings to mind the highest stages of Angela's spiritual development as described in chapter 9 of the *Memorial* (pp. 205–07), where among other things she mentions "swimming" in the ineffable goodness of God.

54. Chapter 9 of the *Memorial* (pp. 205–06) informs this reference to the cross as "the bed" of Christ.

55. The anonymous author of this instruction was certainly one of Angela's most fervent disciples; on the basis of his distinctive style, we can say that this is his only contribution to her *Book*. He probably belonged to the Spiritual party of the early Franciscan movement, and this could be the reason behind his being called away or sent into exile (see Ferré, *Le livre de l'expérience*, 288, n. 2).

56. This instruction and instruction 26 deal with the same events surrounding Angela's participation in the feast of the Portiuncula or Indulgence celebrated in 1300 at the church of St. Mary of the Angels. According to tradition, because of his special fondness for this church, the cradle of the Franciscan order, Francis had obtained from Pope Honorius III, in 1216, the granting of a plenary indulgence to pilgrims who visit it on the feast of its dedication, August 2 (which they did in great numbers). For the history and controversy surrounding the Portiuncula Indulgence, see Raphael M. Huber, O.F.M. Conv., *The Portiuncula Indulgence: From Honorius III to Pius XI* (New York: Joseph W. Wagner, Inc., 1938). The visions and locutions mentioned in this instruction and instruction 26 complete those found in the *Memorial* and are the only ones among the instructions that, according to the editors of the critical edition, are historically certain. Other visions and locutions are found in instructions 19, 20, 21, 23 (*Il Libro*, 484, n. 1).

57. "*Secretum meum mihi*" (Is 24:16). These are the words with which William of St. Thierry ends his *Letter to the Brethren of Mont-Dieu* (*The Golden Epistle*) and which each monk is to engrave on his soul, and at the entrance to his cell. See William of St. Thierry, *The Golden Epistle*, trans. Theodore Berkeley, O.C.S.O., vol. 4, The Cistercian Fathers Series, no. 12 (Kalamazoo, Mich.: Cistercian Publications, 1980), 105. St. Francis was likewise reticent to disclose the revelations

he had received from God and advised his brothers to behave in like fashion: "Blessed is that servant who stores up in heaven (Mt 6:20) the good things which the Lord has revealed to him and does not desire to reveal them to others in the hope of profiting thereby, for the Most High Himself will manifest His deeds to whomever He wishes. Blessed is the servant who keeps the secret of the Lord in his heart (cf. Lk 2:19, 51)" (Admonition 28 in Armstrong and Brady, *Francis and Clare*, 28); see also I Celano, Book 2, chap. 3, no. 96, in *Omnibus of Sources*, 310, and 2 Celano, chap. 98, no. 135, in ibid. 472.

58. The procession, which departed from the basilica of St. Francis and arrived at the church of St. Mary of the Angels, took place on Monday, 1 August 1300. According to Ferré, the chronological sequence of the events in question is as follows: Mass at the altar of the Virgin in the upper church of the basilica of St. Francis, Sunday, 31 July 1300; Mass at the altar of St. Michael in the upper church of the basilica of St. Francis, Monday, 1 August 1300; procession from Assisi to the Portiuncula, Monday afternoon, 1 August 1300; Mass and revelations at the Portiuncula, Tuesday morning, 2 August 1300. The Mass of the morning of August 1 is not indicated in this instruction; instruction 26 fills this lacuna (see Ferré, "Les principales dates," 29).

59. Jn 1:29.

60. Tuesday, 2 August 1300. Instruction 26 will complete the narrative of this part and include, among other things, a vision of the Portiuncula suddenly enlarged.

61. This admonition is a clear evidence of Angela's intervention in the struggle among the Franciscans between the Spirituals and the "community." See the introduction to this volume (sec. I, E).

62. Cf. 1 Cor 10:31; Col 3:17. Cf. instruction 11.

63. A possible allusion to John Climacus's *Ladder of Divine Ascent*.

64. Date proposed for the composition of this important instruction: 1305/1306 (*Il Libro*, 506, n. 1).

65. Mt 11:29.

66. Mt 4:2.

67. Lk 1:48.

68. The synthesis of Angela's teachings on humility found in this instruction has its antecedents in her experience of this virtue at various stages of the *Memorial*. In chapter 5, Angela understands God's love as a mystery of humble condescension, that is, how Christ "descended to such a level of indignity and vileness for her"; this makes her aware of her own unworthiness. In chapter 6, she understands the mystery of

divine power and humility, and becomes aware of her pride. In chapter 7, she sees how, in Christ's passion, God's power takes the form of powerlessness, and she suffers greatly from a more radical awareness of her own pride. She concludes that "pride can exist only in those who believe that they possess something, for only one has being, God. Humility can exist only in those who are poor enough to see that they possess nothing of their own." In the same chapter, she defines poverty as "the root and mother of humility, and every other virtue." In this instruction the order is reversed: "Humility is the foundation, the basis, and the guardian of all the other virtues." In Angela's understanding the two virtues are meant to complement one another. Concerning the theme of humility in medieval spirituality (e.g., Bernard of Clairvaux and Bonaventure), see Pierre Adnès, "Humilité," *DS,* vol. 7 (1969), 1164–66.

69. 2 Cor 11:29.

70. The word "predestined" evokes the Pauline doctrine concerning it (Rom 8:28 *et. seq.;* Eph 1–15).

71. Rom 8:35–39. Probably here referring to the quarrel among the Franciscans between the Spirituals and the "Community." Angela makes a similar exhortation to her sons to avoid contention and become humble peacemakers in instruction 28.

72. Cf. Eph 3:14–21.

73. This section is strongly inspired by the Scriptures. In the background is the image of Christ, the Lamb of God, who was led to sacrifice without opening his mouth (Acts 8:32; Is 53:7; Ps 38:14, 39:10). See also Rom 12, which describes the duties of a true member of the body of Christ. For parallel passages, see instructions 9 and 28.

74. For the point of departure of Angela's teachings in this section on prayer as a means to acquire humility, see instruction 3.

75. For similar guidance on how to read the Book of Life, see instructions 18 and 22.

76. Scriptural texts in the background: Mk 15:16–20; Mt 27:27–31; Jn 19:1–5; and Mt 26:67 *et seq.;* Mk 14:65 *et seq.;* Lk 22:63–65; Jn 18:22 *et seq.*

77. For the scriptural background for the sins of the ears, see 2 Tim 4:3 *et seq.* and for Christ's atonement for the sins of the ears, see Mt. 27:22–26, 29; Mk 15:12–15, 17; Lk 23:10 *et seq.,* 21–25; Jn 19.

78. Pontius Pilate.

79. Cf. Mt 27:34; Mk 15:23; Lk 23:36 *et seq.;* Jn 19:28 *et seq.;* Ps 69:22.

80. Cf. Mt 26:67.

81. Cf. Mt 27:31; Mk 15:20; Lk 23:26; Jn 19:17.

82. The entire passion of Christ on the cross is in the background. Cf. Mt 27:35–50; Mk 15:24–37; Lk 23:33–46; Jn 19:18–30. For another equally important but different meditation on Christ's passion, see instruction 22.

83. Cf. Mt 27:35; Mk 15:24; Lk 23:34; Jn 19:23 *et seq.*

84. Cf. Mt 27:26; Mk 15:15 (Lk 23:16, 22); Jn 19:1–3, 33–37.

85. For the sufferings of Christ's soul, see chapter 7 of the *Memorial* (p. 180) and instruction 3 (pp. 230–33).

86. "Circumcision of heart" is a theme developed in a number of passages in the letters of St. Paul (cf., e.g., Rom 2:29; Gal 5:6; Phil 3:3). Here the circumcision of Christ is presented as a model of our redemption. St. Bonaventure in *The Tree of Life* explains it as follows: "On the eighth day the boy was circumcised and named Jesus (Lk 2:21). Thus not delaying to pour out for you the price of his blood, he showed that he was your true Savior. . . . For this reason he received the mark of circumcision so that coming and appearing in the likeness of sinful flesh, he might condemn sin by sin (Rom 8:3) and become our salvation and eternal justice, taking his beginning from humility, which is the root and guardian of all virtues. Why are you proud, dust and ashes? The innocent Lamb who takes away the sins of the world does not shrink from the wound of circumcision. But you, who are a sinner, while you pretend to be just are fleeing from the remedy of eternal salvation, which you can never reach unless you are willing to follow the humble Savior" ("The Tree of Life," in Cousins, *Bonaventure*, 129–30; *Opera Omnia*, vol. 8, 72).

87. This instruction complements what is said about the transformations of love found in instruction 7. It develops more extensively the first transformation by indicating the three activities necessary for the transformation into the will of the Beloved. The proposed date of its composition is early 1300 (*Il Libro*, 530, n. 1).

88. In the order in which the instructions were written, this is the first one that deals concretely with the rapport established between Angela and the spiritual circle that formed around her. Possible date of composition, around 1298. See also instructions 18 and 22 (*Il Libro*, 533, n. 1).

89. None of the letters sent to Angela have been found.

90. Cf. Wis 11:16: "Man is punished by the very things through which he sins."

91. Angela is developing the notion of the purification of capital sins, the list of which varied in the Middle Ages. She mentions pride, avarice, luxury, vainglory, acedia, and gluttony, but does not speak of envy and anger. On the capital sins, see Aimé Solignac, "Péchés capitaux," *DS*, vol. 12 (1984), cols. 853–62.

92. In the order in which the instructions were written, this is the first time that the theme of the transformation of the soul into that of the Beloved is presented and treated systematically. The other developments of this theme depend on this one. See, according to the following order, instructions 22, 7, 6, 3, 2, 34. It is also the first time that "true obedience" is added to Angela's customary triad: "poverty, suffering, and contempt" (*Il Libro*, 539, n. 9).

93. This is the first appearance of the word *book* as referring to "Christ, the suffering God-man." It is quite likely also that the concept of "the Book of Life," a central one for Angela, originates here (*Il Libro*, 543, n. 12).

94. The use of books was a bone of contention between the Spirituals and the Community.

95. This letter seems to be addressed to Brother Arnaldo himself, who was very likely sick at this time, most likely 30 August 1300 (see instruction 26). After this instruction Angela's communications to her spiritual sons break off, and become rather rare. This evidence leads us to suppose that her confidante and beloved secretary was no longer (*Il Libro*, 544, n. 1).

96. In the background of this instruction is the dissension that at this time divided the Franciscan Order into two factions, the Community and the "zelanti" or Spirituals (see Introduction, sec. I, E). The reference to Angela's companion, Masazuola, at the beginning of the letter seems to be an indication that the common life between the two of them was not always easy. Possible date of composition for this instruction: end of 1298, beginning of 1299 (*Il Libro*, 547, n. 1). Cf. also 1 Cor 1:10 *et. seq.*

97. It is significant to note, in view of the existing discord among the Franciscans, that the two mentions here of the word *truth* in the first redaction were changed to *humility* in the second (*Il Libro*, 549, n. 2).

98. This instruction connects perfectly with what is said in instruction 14 (p. 267). The theme of knowledge of God and self is more detailed here. The second sentence, a sort of definition of prayer, is also noteworthy, for it is taken up again at the beginning of instruction 28.

This instruction also brings to mind what was said in instruction 7 concerning the capital sins. Proposed date of composition: 1299, perhaps in Lent (*Il Libro*, 551, n. 1).

99. The Latin is *curialitatem*. The term was used at this time for "chivalry" in the sense of beneficent magnanimity, but here a general meaning of anxious taking care of things seems appropriate. The term could also connote an office or position of ecclesial responsibility.

100. As the initial sentence indicates, this instruction was written without Angela's direct collaboration. It contains her words, which, at a certain moment, the scribe remembered and noted. It also springs from the historical context mentioned in instruction 4 (*Il Libro*, 552, n. 1).

101. This instruction is not found in the first redaction. It is part of a group of four letters the editors of the critical edition consider to be later imitations. These are instructions 12, 13, 15, and 17, three of which have "tribulations" as their theme. See chapter 5 of the *Memorial*, which treats of "the legitimate sons," and chapter 6, which treats of the tribulations Angela experienced as preparation for her transformation in chapter 7. Proposed date of composition: after 1310 (*Il Libro*, 556, n. 1).

102. Ferré advances the hypothesis that parts of this letter were supressed because they alluded to persecutions the redactor felt best unmentioned. This would explain why this sentence is incomplete. See *Le livre de l'expérience*, 358, n. 1.

103. Like the preceding, this instruction may not be authentic. It is not a letter strictly speaking, but a meditation on the role of tribulations in spiritual development. Probable date of composition: 1310 (*Il Libro*, 558, n. 1).

104. This instruction was written during Lent; the "cell" Angela refers to was a narrow room to which one would retire during this period in order to do penance. Another indication that this is the Lenten period is found in the sentence that speaks of Angela's greetings finding fulfillment in "the Resurrection of the Lord." Proposed date of composition, Lent of 1299. This is also the first instruction (in order of composition) in which Angela mentions the duty of the knowledge of self and God. The origin of this expression is found in the "protoinstruction" in the *Memorial*, which treats of "the knowledge of self and the knowledge of the goodness of God" (see the end of chap. 7). For further developments of this theme see instructions 10, 3, 29, and 34 (*Il Libro*, 562, n. 1).

105. The final three paragraphs of this instruction are additions of the second redaction. Their purpose is to clarify the meaning of the

"silence" phenomenon. It is possible that this is silence not only in the sense of not writing letters, but also the total silence about her inner life that Angela probably observed after the death of Arnaldo (see instruction 26) (*Il Libro*, 565, n. 4).

106. This instruction, not found in the first redaction, is the only one among the letters considered imitations (the others are instructions 12, 13, and 17) that does not treat of the theme of tribulations. It can be considered an attempt to systematize Angela's entire spirituality, which centers around the theme of the cross. For themes and expressions on which this piece depends, see instructions 3, 7, 18, 22. Proposed date of composition: around 1309 (*Il Libro*, 567, n. 1).

107. This brief instruction, not found in the first redaction, contains in itself a condensation of the entire *Memorial*. The parallels are as follows: the blessing refers to chapters 3 and 4; the communications of God's riches, chapter 5; the admonition, chapter 6; the correction, chapter 7; the guardianship and defense, chapter 8; the preservation, chapter 9. Proposed date of composition: after 1310 (*Il Libro*, 570, n. 1).

108. This instruction is not found in the first redaction and is the third letter treating of tribulations (the other two are 12 and 13). It is strongly influenced by instruction 14. Proposed date of composition: well after 1310 (*Il Libro*, 572, n. 1).

109. This instruction, in the form of a letter, is the initial one in the chronological sequence of the manuscripts of the first redaction (B). Another manuscript (Ve) gives a clue to the possible recipient of this letter: "Once, a certain devout young man, whom she called her son, sought from her how to attain love." The letter, whose tone is similar to instruction 8, was probably written around 1297/1298 (*Il Libro*, 577, n. 1).

110. Even though there is no closing salutation, it is possible, given the difference in style, that this instruction contains two letters, one of which ends here. The fact that they are sent to the same recipient might explain why they have been put together (*Il Libro*, 579, nn. 3 and 4).

111. This present instruction develops ideas initially found in chapter 7 of the *Memorial* (pp. 193–94) where Angela treats of the ways in which love can be deceived by the illusions of the world.

112. The minister general at that time was Giovanni Minio da Murrovalle. He was elected in 1296 in the presence of Pope Boniface VIII and remained in office until 1304. The "help" he provided was possibly an approbation of Angela's experience (*Il Libro*, 585, n. 10).

113. This instruction belongs with a group of instructions (20, 21,

23) that mention new visions Angela received. The editors of the critical edition doubt their authenticity. They date this one after 1310 (*Il Libro*, 587, n. 1).

114. A comparison with the narrative describing mystical events surrounding this same feast in chapter 9 of the *Memorial* (pp. 215–16) shows how this instruction has been worked over and rearranged by the redactor.

115. Angela has only one other vision of the Christ Child. It occurs during a Eucharistic celebration in chapter 3 of the *Memorial* (p. 147). For similar experiences among medieval mystics see Irenée Noye, "Enfance de Jésus (Dévotion), II. La piété mediévale" *DS*, vol. 4 (1961), cols. 656–65.

116. Instruction 4, which describes Angela's visions concerning her spiritual sons, seems to have served as a model for this section (*Il Libro*, 589, n. 5).

117. For this last section, cf. instructions 24, 25, and 26.

118. This instruction is one of four containing visions that the editors of the critical edition consider to be imitations (the others are instructions 19, 21, and 23). Date: after 1310 (*Il Libro*, 592, n. 1).

119. According to the hierarchy established by the Pseudo-Dionysius, the Seraphim rank first in the highest order of angels, those who enjoy perfect knowledge and love of God (see also Is 6:2). Their ministry is to arouse a desire in the lower levels of the hierarchy for a similar union with God. In Beguine circles, "seraphic" experiences were often characterized by the absence of any intermediary between God and the soul (see *Marguerite Porete: Le miroir des âmes simples et anéantis*, intro., trans., and notes by Max Huot de Longchamp [Paris: Albin Michel, 1984], 239, n. 5). There are abundant references to the Seraphim in Marguerite Porete's *Le mirouer*, e.g., "This [Annihilated] Soul has six wings like the Seraphim. She wants no longer anything which comes by mediation, which is the proper being of the Seraphim: there is no mediation between their love and the divine love" (ed. Guarnieri, chap. 5,524; trans. Babinsky). The reference in this instruction to the experience of the Seraphim may also be an allusion to the stigmata of St. Francis: Christ who appeared to him in the form of a Seraph. The vision occurred at the end of his forty-day fast in honor of St. Michael the Archangel. See "Life of St. Francis" (*Legenda major*) in *Bonaventure*, trans. and ed. Ewert Cousins (New York: Paulist Press, 1978), 303–14. Bonaventure also foresaw that a new religious order was to appear in the end

time. This "Seraphic" order, whose characteristic was to attend to God through ecstasy and rapture, had already been initiated by St. Francis and would blossom soon (*Collationes Hexaemeron* 22, no. 22–25 [*Opera omnia*, vol. 9, 440–41]). Jacopone da Todi: "Still higher I rose, to the ninth branch, / There where I praised the Omnipotent Himself. / He who comes to this point is filled with the Holy Spirit; / Seraphim-like, he contemplates the Trinity" (Laud 69 [84], "The Tree of a Hierarchy Similar to That of the Angels Based on Faith, Hope, and Charity," Hughes, *Jacopone da Todi*, 216).

120. This instruction is one of four that mention new visions Angela received and that are considered imitations by the editors of the critical edition (the others are instructions 19, 20, and 23). Date: after 1310 (*Il Libro*, 596, n. 1).

121. According to the original, chronological, order of the instructions (the first redaction), this one would be the first "circular letter" Angela addressed to her spiritual sons. Date: toward 1298 (*Il Libro*, 600, n. 1).

122. There is a close connection between this instruction and chapter 5 of the *Memorial*, which likewise treats of the legitimate sons of God.

123. Latin: *oboediens*.

124. This final exhortation, as does this entire instruction, develops the triad of "poverty, suffering, and contempt" that lies at the core of Angela's spirituality. It was formulated for the first time in chapter 9 of the *Memorial* (p. 211). It also appears in instructions 7, 18, and 23, among others. Here and in instruction 7, a fourth element is added, "true obedience." The background of this theme, which appears in chapter 7 of the *Memorial* (p. 196), is the obedience of the Son of God to the salvific plan of the Father.

125. There are textual dependencies between this instruction and chapters 4 and 5 of the *Memorial*, as well as with other instructions. It is one of four that mention new visions Angela received and that are considered imitations by the editors of the critical edition (the others are instructions 19, 20, and 21). Date: after 1310 (*Il Libro*, 613, n. 1).

126. The Latin word *truffa*, which I have translated here as "hoax," occurs in a number of places in the *Memorial*. "Amare per truffa" means to love without truth, intensity, or sincerity; to trifle with one's affections; to play games with someone.

127. The expression "deeper within your soul than your soul is to

itself" is reminiscent of St. Augustine's well-known phrase *interior intimo meo:* God is deeper within me than my own inmost being (*Confessions,* 3, 6).

128. Experiencing, seeing, and speaking with Christ is a theme developed in chapter 5 of the *Memorial,* which treats of the divine benefits bestowed on the true sons of God who dispose themselves to receive them (see pp. 158–62).

129. The "in the beginning" refers to chapters 4 and 5 of the *Memorial,* and instruction 22, where the triad "poverty, suffering, contempt" is mentioned (*Il Libro,* 617, n. 6).

130. Date: after 1310 (*Il Libro,* 618, n. 1).

131. This instruction further develops Angela's teachings concerning the sect of the Spirit of Freedom, treated in instructions 2 and 3. Date: after 1310 (*Il Libro,* 621, n. 1).

132. Latin: *Et haec est libertas usus exterioris.*

133. This instruction is to be understood in connection with the mystical events that occurred on the feast of the Portiuncula (between 31 July and 2 August 1300) and that are related in instruction 4. It seems that the scribe, Brother A. (Arnaldo), had received this fourth instruction composed by another friar, and saw the necessity of adding data either forgotten or unknown by this friar. One can also conjecture that Brother A. had spoken to Angela before or after receiving this fourth instruction (*Il Libro,* 624–25, n. 1).

134. "Brother So-and-so" is likely Brother A. Perhaps she thought he was very sick and therefore not likely to be in Assisi. This Mass in which Brother A. participated is not mentioned in instruction 4 (*Il Libro,* 625–27, n. 2).

135. It was generally believed that the indulgence could not be gained before the procession actually entered the chapel. See Huber, *The Portiuncula Indulgence,* 77.

136. The present basilica of St. Mary of the Angels built over the little chapel of the Portiuncula, erected in 1569, at the request of Pope Pius V, is indeed a very large one.

137. This final section of this instruction is not found in the first redaction and is situated in diverse places in other manuscripts. The writer who added it here as part of the second redaction is probably the friar who continued Brother A.'s work and who wished to insert a posthumous elegy to him at just the point his predecessor had ended his task. It is likely that he was present in Assisi when the events narrated took place (*Il Libro,* 628–29, n. 4).

138. Capuche: hood or cowl worn by Franciscans.

139. An addition from one of the manuscripts of the first redaction makes it quite clear that this was indeed the last Mass Brother A. celebrated: After "he took off his capuche, bowed his head, and wept," it continues, "but after the death of this friar when the Mass for the repose of his soul was being celebrated, after the elevation of the body of Christ I was lamenting his state before the Host, and I heard: 'He is already in the glorified state,' and I saw that he was indeed before the divine majesty, and he told me: 'I have attained this state through the grace of God and because of you.' I responded: 'I pray you, lead me now to this state.' Then the divine majesty told this Brother: 'Tell her that if she wishes to attain this state her life must be such as to be a light for all'" (*Il Libro*, 629, n. 5).

140. This instruction is unlike any other. It is an attempt by the author to systematize Angela's spiritual teachings into a rule of life divided into seven chapters and it is directed to those who wish to follow her example. See also instruction 28. Date of composition: 1305 (*Il Libro*, 632, n. 1).

141. The theme of loving God without the hope of a reward was an important one in medieval spirituality—e.g., Bernard of Clairvaux: "God is not loved without reward, even though he should be loved without thought of reward" ("On Loving God" in *Bernard of Clairvaux: Selected Works*, trans. G. R. Evans [New York: Paulist Press, 1987], 187).

142. The theme of the divinization of the soul, as central to Christ's work of redemption, was a prominent one in medieval spirituality. It was inherited from both the Latin and the Greek Fathers. For a brief summary see Bernard McGinn, "Christ as Savior in the West," *Christian Spirituality: Origins to the Twelfth Century*, 253–59. See also "Divinisation," *DS*, vol. 4, cols. 1389–1413.

143. For similar considerations on the role of consolations, see instruction 31.

144. This instruction is the first one written after the death of Brother A. Like the others that follow, it contains very little that is new (Angela seems to have preferred to maintain silence after the death of her confessor). Like the preceding one, it is an attempt to systematize Angela's teachings, in particular those on prayer and the ways to imitate Christ. Date of composition: 1302 (*Il Libro*, 638–39, n. 1).

145. See the beginning of instruction 10. See also instruction 3 for the three types of prayer.

146. The redactor's sources for his description of these three types of prayer are to be found in instructions 3, 7, and 18. See also instruction 34.

147. Apparently there was only one "noble" in Foligno, Guido da Montefeltro, who became a Friar Minor in 1296 (*Il Libro*, 643, n. 7).

148. The texts for this section on poverty in the life of Christ are taken from chapters 5 and 7 of the *Memorial* (pp. 133, 160). See also instructions 3 and 34.

149. On the sufferings in the life of Christ, see instructions 3 (pp. 230–329) and 34 (pp. 306–07).

150. Mt 26:38; Mk 14:34.

151. On contempt in the life of Christ, see instruction 34 (pp. 305–06).

152. On obedience in the life of Christ, see the end of instruction 22 (p. 124).

153. For the virtues mentioned in this last section, see instructions 3, 5, 7, and 9.

154. In this instruction, as in the two preceding ones—28 and 31 (according to the original, chronological order)—the author attempts to systematize Angela's teachings demonstrating here the interdependency between following the "poverty, suffering, and contempt" of Christ, knowledge of God and self, and the sign of true love. See chapter 7 of the *Memorial*, and instructions 10, 14, 28 (*Il Libro*, 650, n. 1).

155. Again, the author attempts to systematize Angela's teachings, this time those on the Eucharist. Date of composition: 1307. See also the Eucharistic visions in chapter 9 of the *Memorial* (*Il Libro*, 653, n. 1).

156. These are not exact quotations from Holy Scripture, but texts that come close to them can be found in the Latin vulgate; cf. Rom 11:33–36 and Lk 1:37.

157. A number of biblical texts (the resemblance is clearer in the Latin vulgate) serve as background for this instruction: "All this is the work of the kindness of our God; he, the Dayspring, shall visit us in his mercy" (Lk 1:78); "As a mother comforts her son, so will I comfort you (Is 66:13); "I will run the way of your commands when you give me a docile heart" (Ps 119:32); "Strengthened by that food [Elijah] walked . . . to the mountain of God" (1 Kgs 19:8). The way these biblical texts are used and closely woven together indicates that the language of this text is not Angela's. Like instruction 11, it can be considered a record or free interpretation of her thought. Date of composition: around 1303 (*Il Libro*, 660–61, n. 1).

158. This instruction is the longest of those (30, 32, 33) that treat of the Eucharist. Date of composition: 1307 (*Il Libro*, 662, n. 1).

159. A recourse to the customary medieval approach of explaining the Eucharist in the light of its foreshadowings in the Old Testament. E.g., the phrase in the *Tantum Ergo*, from Thomas Aquinas's hymn in honor of the Eucharist: "*et antiquum documentum novo cedat ritui.*"

160. The formulation here is of impeccable scholastic theology, as the definition of "transubstantiation" demonstrates.

161. As indicated in chapter 9, the last step of the *Memorial* (p. 209), Angela desired to receive the Eucharist daily, an unusual practice for the time. The text quoted is not from St. Augustine but from Gennadius of Marseilles, of around the fifth century: "To receive the Eucharist daily does not incur praise or blame" (*De Ecclesiasticis Dogmatibus Liber Gennadio tributus*, chap. 53, *P.L.* 53, 994). This text was well known in the Middle Ages. Date of composition of this instruction: some time after 1310 (*Il Libro*, 667–68, n. 1).

162. This instruction is the last and perhaps most important attempt to develop a synthesis of Angela's spirituality. At least three manuscripts transcribe it by itself, separate from the *Memorial* and the other instructions; this gives some indication of its wide diffusion. Except for the "testament" (instruction 35), and the narrative of Angela's last illness and death (instruction 36), it may be the last instruction written while Angela was still alive. Date of composition: 1308 (*Il Libro*, 682, n. 1).

163. For the theme of knowing God in truth, see end of chap. 7 of the *Memorial*.

164. For similar descriptions of the soul's progression in love, see for example, instructions 3, 7, 15, 28, 29, etc.

165. The metaphor of iron transformed into fire as an expression of divine union is a common one in medieval mysticism. Bernard of Clairvaux: "Red-hot iron becomes indistinguishable from the glow of fire and its own original form disappears . . . The substance remains, but in another form, with another glory, another power" ("On Loving God," in *Bernard of Clairvaux*, trans. G. R. Evans [New York, Paulist Press, 1987], 196 [*De diligendo Deo* 10.28]). Marguerite Porete: "All this [transformation of the soul into the Godhead] is like iron invested with fire which has lost its own semblance because the fire is the strongest and thus transforms the iron into itself. So also this Soul is completely invested with this greater part [divine love], and nourished and transformed into this greater part, on account of the Love from this greater part, taking no account of the lesser [the Soul]. So she remains and is

transformed into the greater part of the distant eternal peace without anyone finding her" (*Le Mirouer,* ed. Guarnieri, chap. 52, 562; trans. Babinsky). The most complete study of the history of the images of the iron in the fire, the drop of water in a vat of wine, and the air transformed into sunshine as metaphors for union with God is to be found in Jean Pepin, " 'Stilla aquae modica multo infusa vino, ferrum ignitum, luce perfusus aer.' L'origine des trois comparaisons familières à la théologie mystique médiévale," *Miscellanea André Combes (Divinitas* 11), vol. 1 [Rome, 1967], 331–75.

166. For a good introduction to the relationship between knowledge and love on the path to union with God in the Christian mystical tradition see Bernard McGinn, "Mystical Union in the Western Tradition," in *Mystical Union and Monotheistic Faith: An Ecumenical Dialogue,* 50–86.

167. "Transformation" is one of the most frequently used words in the instructions to designate the spiritual process that leads the soul to union with God. See instructions 2, 3, 4, 6, 7, 22.

168. Latin: *superlibro.*

169. For a similar discourse on prayer, see instruction 3.

170. Cf. instruction 3.

171. Formulated for the first time toward the end of the *Memorial* (chap. 9), the triad of poverty, suffering, and contempt constitutes what Angela calls the companions of Christ. It occurs repeatedly in the instructions and is central to her spirituality.

172. For the theme of the three poverties of Christ, see instruction 28.

173. Cf. instruction 28.

174. This third degree of poverty is the one that is developed the most in Angela's writings. Cf. instructions 3, 22, 28.

175. For a similar consideration on the poverty of Christ, see the end of chapter 7 of the *Memorial.*

176. For contempt in the life of Christ, see instruction 28.

177. The theme of suffering in the life of Christ is the one that Angela meditates on and treats the most extensively in her writings. See especially instruction 3.

178. For the knives that wounded Christ, see instruction 3.

179. For a similar synthesis of the sufferings of the passion of Christ, see instructions 5 and 28.

180. In many editions, this instruction carries the title "Angela's Testament." Date of composition: around the middle of 1308 (*Il Libro,*

712, n. 1). The incarnation is at the center of Angela's praises of the mysteries and the gifts of the Savior.

181. This last instruction describing Angela's final illness and death was probably written after her death in early 1309 (*Il Libro*, 725, n. 1).

182. The feast of the Holy Angels was celebrated on 29 September 1308.

183. Angela's testament is recorded and synthesized here: mutual love and the three companions of Christ: poverty, suffering, and contempt.

184. For the scriptural background, see Jesus' sacerdotal prayer to the Father in Jn 17:11 *et seq.*

185. This notice is included in all the existing manuscripts.

186. This epilogue is not found in all the manuscripts and some contain only part of it. It seems to indicate that Angela's book was used as a weapon in the struggle between the various tendencies in the Franciscan movement during the early fourteenth century. In his prologue to Mechthild of Magdeburg's *The Flowing Light of the Godhead*, Bro. Henry of Halle, O.P., makes a similar defense of women: "We read in the Book of Judges (4:5) that the holy woman, Deborah, wife of Lapidoth, filled with the spirit of prophecy, sat for a time under a palm tree in the mountains of Ephraim to devote herself to God in solitude. The people of Israel climbed up the mountain to hear the judgments of God from her. Likewise, in the fourth book of Kings (2 Kgs 22:14–20), it is said that the prophetess Huldah, in Jerusalem, revealed to King Josias the evils that were to come. . . . For almighty God often chooses the weak in the eyes of the world to put the strong to shame" (*Mechthild von Magdeburg: Das Fliessende Lich Der Gottheit*, ed. Margot Schmidt [Einsiedeln / Zurich / Koln: Benziger Verlag, 1955], 47). I am grateful to Sr. Jeremiah Johnson for the translation of this text. As Barbara Newman notes, the topos of God choosing weak women to shame powerful men (an argument used by Hildegard of Bingen) enjoys a long history in hagiographic writing, and significantly, this theme is "taken up not so much by women as by male writers eager to justify their female protégées or spiritual mothers": e.g., an anonymous male author for Juliana Cornillon, John Marienwerder for Dorothy of Mantau, Raymond of Capua for Catherine of Siena (*Sister of Wisdom: St. Hildegard's Theology of the Feminine* [Berkeley: University of California Press, 1987], 256).

187. For the more or less direct quotations from the book of Wisdom, see Wis 7:15, 21, 26–28. Contrary to the claims of the text, there are no direct references to Wisdom 8.

188. Fidelity to the rule of Francis was a central issue for the Franciscan Spirituals in their contention with the Community. See Introduction, sec. I, E.

189. The priest Hilkiah and others turned to the prophetess Huldah, keeper of the wardrobe in the temple of Solomon, and asked her to comment on the recently recovered book of the law (the Pentateuch), which the ministers of the temple were no longer able to interpret (see 2 Kgs 22:8–19; 2 Chr 34:22–28). On the significance of Huldah's commentary, William E. Phipps writes: "Huldah the prophetess—let us celebrate her—holds a unique place in history. It was she who, for the first time, designated a written document as Holy Scripture. She began a process that culminated more than half a millennium later in the canonization of the Bible" ("A Woman Was the First to Declare Scripture Holy," *Bible Review*, 6, n. 2 [April 1990]:94). For Jerome's commentary in which the prophetess Huldah's calling is described as "a secret reproof of the king, and priests, and all men," see his *Dialogus contra Pelagianos* II, 22 (*St. Jerome: Dogmatic and Polemical Works*, trans. John Hritzu [Washington, 1965]; *P.L.* 23, 660).

Select Bibliography

1. CRITICAL TEXT

Thier, Ludger, O.F.M., and Calufetti, Abele, O.F.M. *Il Libro della Beata Angela da Foligno*. Grottaferrata (Rome): Editiones Collegii S. Bonaventurae ad Claras Aquas, 1985.

2. STUDIES

Lachance, Paul, O.F.M. *The Spiritual Journey of the Blessed Angela of Foligno according to the Memorial of Frater A*. Rome: Pontificium Athenaeum Antonianum, 1984.

Santae e Beate Umbre tra il XIII e il XIV secolo. Mostra Iconografica. Foligno: Edizioni dell'Arquata, 1986.

Vita e spiritualità della Beata Angela da Foligno. Atti del Convegno di studi per il VII centenario della conversione della Beata Angela da Foligno (1285–1985). Edited by Clément Schmitt, O.F.M. Perugia: Serafica Provincia di San Francesco O.F.M. Conv., 1987.

3. BIBLIOGRAPHIES

Andreoli, Sergio. "Bibliografia sulla Beata Angela da Foligno (1248/49–1309)" and "Angela da Foligno: Bibliografia (1984–1987)." *L'Italia Francescana* 60 (1985): 75–92; 63 (1988): 185–200.

Thier and Calufetti also provide an extensive bibliography in their critical edition, pp. 10–22.

Index

INDEX

Bartolomeo da Pisa, 111, 113, 169

Bataille, George, 116

Beatrice of Nazareth, 39, 41, 105

Beauvoir, Simone de, 117

Beghards, 37, 45

Beguines, 35, 37, 38, 39, 40, 44, 105–06, 112; suppression of, 42

Bell, Rudolf, 117

Benedetta, Abbess, 103

Benedict XI, Pope, 24

Benedict XIV, Pope, 115

Bentivoglia of San Severino, 31

Béranger de Saint'Affrique, 41

Berardo of Attignano, Bishop, 43, 47

Bernadino de Laredo, 114

Bernanos, George, 116

Bernard of Clairvaux, St., 10, 26, 28, 37, 39

Bernard of Quintaville, 31

Bevegnati, Giunta, 41, 110

Bible. *See* Scriptures

Blasucci, Antonio, 116

Blessed Virgin, 58, 95, 99–100, 128, 130, 156, 157–58, 166–67; Angela's visions of, 87, 99–100, 273–74; as image of femininity, 27; as example of humility, 252; as example of poverty, 239–40; as example of prayer, 93, 99, 238–39

Bly, Robert, 117

Bollandus, Johannes, 115

Bonagratia of Bergamo, 33

Bonaventure, St., 10, 27–28, 30, 41

Boniface VIII, Pope, 24, 29, 32, 50, 111

Bonvoisin, Bérangère, 116

Book of Visions and Instructions (Angela of Foligno), 7, 15, 47–54; dedication, 1; *Instructions*, 9, 15, 16, 22, 66–67, 78–80, 81–84, 89, 93, 219–318; *Memorial*, 1, 7, 9, 15, 16, 20, 55–81, 88, 123–218; two-redaction theory, 53–54; *see also* specific headings, e.g.: Prayer; Trinity

Bossuet, Jacques, 115

Bridal mysticism, 38, 40–41; Beguines, 37; experienced by Angela, 142–44

Bridget, St., 115

Burr, David, 32

Bynum, Caroline Walker, 36–37, 87, 117

Caesar of Speyer, 31

Calufetti, Abele, 50, 53–54, 65, 118

Catharists, 26

Catherine of Genoa, St., 114, 116

Catherine of Siena, St., 7, 114, 115

Celano [Thomas of], 95

Celestine V, Pope, 24, 32

Celle qui ment (Clévenot), 116

Chenu, Marie-Dominic, 26

Christ: contempt in life of, 289, 305–06; mysteries, 308–12; obedience of, 289; as example of poverty, 179–80, 239, 287–88, 303–05; as example of prayer, 93, 101, 237–38

419

INDEX

INDEX

Other Volumes in this Series

John Climacus • THE LADDER OF DIVINE ASCENT
Francis and Clare • THE COMPLETE WORKS
Gregory Palamas • THE TRIADS
Pietists • SELECTED WRITINGS
The Shakers • TWO CENTURIES OF SPIRITUAL REFLECTION
Zohar • THE BOOK OF ENLIGHTENMENT
Luis de León • THE NAMES OF CHRIST
Quaker Spirituality • SELECTED WRITINGS
Emanuel Swedenborg • THE UNIVERSAL HUMAN AND SOUL-BODY
    INTERACTION
Augustine of Hippo • SELECTED WRITINGS
Safed Spirituality • RULES OF MYSTICAL PIETY, THE BEGINNING OF WISDOM
Maximus Confessor • SELECTED WRITINGS
John Cassian • CONFERENCES
Johannes Tauler • SERMONS
John Ruusbroec • THE SPIRITUAL ESPOUSALS AND OTHER WORKS
Ibn 'Abbād of Ronda • LETTERS ON THE SŪFĪ PATH
Angelus Silesius • THE CHERUBINIC WANDERER
The Early Kabbalah •
Meister Eckhart • TEACHER AND PREACHER
John of the Cross • SELECTED WRITINGS
Pseudo-Dionysius • THE COMPLETE WORKS
Bernard of Clairvaux • SELECTED WORKS
Devotio Moderna • BASIC WRITINGS
The Pursuit of Wisdom • AND OTHER WORKS BY THE AUTHOR OF THE
    CLOUD OF UNKNOWING
Richard Rolle • THE ENGLISH WRITINGS
Francis de Sales, Jane de Chantal • LETTERS OF SPIRITUAL DIRECTION
Albert and Thomas • SELECTED WRITINGS
Robert Bellarmine • SPIRITUAL WRITINGS
Nicodemos of the Holy Mountain • A HANDBOOK OF SPIRITUAL COUNSEL
Henry Suso • THE EXEMPLAR, WITH TWO GERMAN SERMONS
Bérulle and the French School • SELECTED WRITINGS
The Talmud • SELECTED WRITINGS
Ephrem the Syrian • HYMNS
Hildegard of Bingen • SCIVIAS
Birgitta of Sweden • LIFE AND SELECTED REVELATIONS
John Donne • SELECTIONS FROM *DIVINE POEMS,* SERMONS, *DEVOTIONS AND
    PRAYERS*
Jeremy Taylor • SELECTED WORKS
Walter Hilton • SCALE OF PERFECTION
Ignatius of Loyola • *SPIRITUAL EXERCISES* AND SELECTED WORKS
Anchoritic Spirituality • *ANCRENE WISSE* AND ASSOCIATED WORKS
Nizam ad-din Awliya • *MORALS FOR THE HEART*
Pseudo-Macarius • THE FIFTY SPIRITUAL HOMILIES AND THE *GREAT LETTER*
Gertrude of Helfta • *THE HERALD OF DIVINE LOVE*